# MISSIONS IMPOSSIBLE

# MISSIONS IMPOSSIBLE

## EXTRAORDINARY STORIES OF DARING AND COURAGE

HAZEL FLYNN

FIREFLY BOOKS

# A Firefly Book

Published by Firefly Books Ltd. 2014

First printing

Publisher Cataloging-in-Publication Data (U.S.)

A CIP record for this title is available from the Library of Congress

Library and Archives Canada Cataloguing in Publication

A CIP record for this title is available from Library and Archives Canada

Published in the United States by
Firefly Books (U.S.) Inc.
P.O. Box 1338, Ellicott Station
Buffalo, New York 14205

Published in Canada by
Firefly Books Ltd.
50 Staples Avenue, Unit 1
Richmond Hill, Ontario L4B 0A7

Printed in China by IBook Printing Limited

Developed by Global Book Publishing
201 Lakeside Corporate Centre
29–31 Solent Circuit
Baulkham Hills
NSW 2153, Australia

**PUBLISHER** James Mills-Hicks
**PROJECT EDITOR** Chrysoula Aiello
**AUTHOR** Hazel Flynn
**CONSULTANTS** Andrew and Ailsa Heritage, Heritage Editorial Services
**DESIGN CONCEPT** Paul Bezerkin
**PICTURE RESEARCH** Chrysoula Aiello
**MAPS AND DIAGRAMS** James Mills-Hicks
**LAYOUT** book design by saso; Kylie Mulquin
**INDEXER** Puddingburn Services

# CONTENTS

# CONTENTS

# CONTENTS

# THE AGE OF
# HEROISM
## *c.*1250 BCE–1588

The stories in the Age of Heroism cover a period of almost 3,000 years. The trappings—clothing, weapons, language—changed over the centuries, as did the triggers for conflict, but the essential experience of those who went to war remained the same. Achilles, Odysseus, Hector, and the other Bronze Age warriors from the Trojan War might have been baffled by the armor worn by Henry V at Agincourt or the cannon used by Sir Francis Drake, but they would instantly have understood the spirit of the men fighting under those leaders.

We do not know how much of the story of the siege of Troy, woven into an epic poem by Homer, is true. In fact, we do not even know exactly who Homer was or when he lived. As late as the 1800s, before archaeologists found the remains of the mighty city, his work *The Iliad* was presumed to be a work of fiction. But strip away the meddling gods and goddesses and it is clear the story captures something authentic about the experience of being in battle. So much so, military genius Alexander the Great took a copy of Homer's *Iliad* with him for inspiration as he conquered much of the known world. Alexander, in turn, inspired Hannibal, another brilliant martial strategist, who, in turn, inspired Napoleon.

Just as Odysseus and Hannibal had done, Charlemagne's men two millennia later in Spain, and the Turks in Malta eight hundred years after that, took up arms unsure if they would ever see their homes and loved ones again. Some could not wait to face the enemy; others were reluctant heroes. But all went into the unknown and fought for their lives and those of their comrades.

The world changed greatly during this period. The Great Wall of China had yet to be built when Hannibal crossed the Alps. The Vikings had not reached North America in the eighth century when Roland fought with Charlemagne's rearguard at Roncesvalles. And although the earliest known printed book was produced in China in 868 CE, European printing presses did not exist at the time of Agincourt (fortunately, by the end of the following century when Shakespeare was ready to render his immortal version of the battle, printers were abundant).

The passage of time does not just change technology; it also changes our understanding of historical events. Modern research suggests a very different picture of the iconic Jewish stand against the Romans at Masada. And while the conquistadors were valiant explorers to their own people in their own time, we now view their actions and the calamitous effect they had on the Aztec and Incan civilizations very differently. Today, it might be the warriors defending Tenochtitlán we see as heroic, rather than Cortés and his men.

So, perspectives shift and change; however, the fascinating human drama in these stories from our past ensures they will live on long into the future.

# THE TROJAN HORSE

DATE **c. 1260–1250** BCE
LOCATION **Troy (now Hisarlik, Anatolia, Turkey)**
OBJECTIVE **An ingenious end to a ten-year siege**

Much like the deeply layered archaeological site where Troy once stood, the story of the Trojan War is built from myth upon myth, retold and elaborated over centuries. We are unlikely to ever know the precise truth—our narrative derives from poetic accounts by Homer and Virgil—but the story's rich drama resonates through the ages.

### Trigger for War

A snub began it. Mortal Peleus was marrying sea-nymph Thetis, and troublesome Eris, goddess of discord, had not been invited. Enraged, she sent a golden apple inscribed "To the fairest," and goddesses Hera, Athena, and Aphrodite all claimed it. Paris, outcast prince of Troy, was asked to decide the winner; he chose Aphrodite after she promised him the world's most beautiful woman, Helen.

Undeterred that Helen was already married, Paris sailed to Sparta and was welcomed by her unwitting husband, King Menelaus. Paris fled to Troy with Helen and much of Menelaus's fortune; Menelaus and a force under the command of his brother, the king of Mycenae, Agamemnon, set off after them. When the Trojan king Priam refused to return what his son had taken, the Greeks laid siege.

### Heroes in Battle

Troy apparently withstood the siege for nine years, during which Greek war parties devastated the nearby countryside. Leading these attacks was the greatest Greek warrior, Achilles, made all but invulnerable when his mother Thetis (she of the wedding) had dipped him in the River Styx; only on the heel she gripped could he be mortally wounded.

After killing Briseis's husband in the war, Achilles made her his slave companion, and when Agamemnon demanded to have her, Achilles refused to fight on. Only after his cousin and boon companion Patroclus was killed by Paris's brother Hector did Achilles charge back into action, killing Hector and, insultingly, dragging his body behind a chariot. Paris then killed Achilles with an arrow to the heel, before being killed himself.

### Troy Falls

For ten years the Greeks remained outside the city walls. Then Odysseus had an idea: to build a hollow wooden horse huge enough for warriors to hide inside. The Greek fleet sailed away, seemingly in retreat (actually hiding nearby), leaving the horse outside the city's walls, seemingly a gift from the gods. Ignoring warnings by Priam's daughter Cassandra, the Trojans dragged it into their city. That night the warriors came out of hiding and opened the gates from the inside, letting in more Greeks, who destroyed Troy, killing or enslaving most of its people. One of the few survivors, Aeneas, is said to have founded Rome. The legend is related in Virgil's *Aeneid*.

ABOVE: Pithos found in Mykonos, Greece, depicting one of the earliest-known representations of the Trojan Horse (670 BCE).

ABOVE RIGHT: The Wooden Horse at the gates of Troy. Troy's mythic events delivered ever-popular concepts to our culture: "Achilles heel" (a fatal weakness); "Trojan horse" (something destructive that appears deceptively benign); "beware of Greeks bearing gifts"; and "the face that launched a thousand ships," (Christopher Marlowe's description of Helen in *Doctor Faustus* (1604)).

## TIMELINE

**c. 1250 BCE**

Most probable date of the end of the Trojan War, estimated from archaeological evidence of destruction and burning on Troy Level VIIa.

**c. 750 BCE**

Epic Greek poet Homer shapes the end of the Trojan War into the narrative *The Iliad* (from Troy's Latin name, Ilium), followed by *The Odyssey*.

## STEP-BY-STEP

**01** Paris elopes with (or abducts) Helen—daughter of Zeus and wife of Menelaus, king of Sparta—having also stolen part of Menelaus's fortune.

**02** Menelaus demands help from Helen's former suitors, sworn to protect her honor. Some, including Odysseus, are reluctant. A force led by Menelaus's brother, Agamemnon, sails after Paris and Helen to besiege Troy.

**03** Agamemnon, Menelaus, and Odysseus attempt to parley with Priam, King of Troy; when he rebuffs them, the war begins. Despite relentless Greek attacks, Troy withstands (legendarily) the siege year after year.

**04** Odysseus conceives a plan to end the stalemate by constructing an enormous wooden horse, concealing a contingent of Greek troops, which will be left on the shore outside the gates of Troy. Meanwhile, the Greek forces withdraw as if in defeat.

**05** The Trojans, falling for the Greek trick, regard the huge horse as a gift from the gods in celebration of their victory. They ignore the advice of both Cassandra (Priam's daughter, known for her doom-laden advice) and the Trojan priest Laocoön, who is promptly killed, along with his two sons, by enormous sea serpents sent by Poseidon, God of the Sea.

**06** The Trojans haul the wooden horse inside the city walls, amid great celebrations marking the apparent end of the long war.

**07** Overnight, with the Trojans in drunken slumber, the Greek militia exit the horse, overpower the guards, and open the gates of the city to Greek troops. The city is looted, devastated, and burned.

**08** During the final decisive action, upon finding Helen, Menelaus moves to kill her but, overcome by her beauty, relents. They return to Sparta and remain together for the rest of their days. At the same time Aeneas escapes the flames and goes on to found Rome, while the unfortunate Odysseus embarks on a dangerous decade-long voyage home.

| c. 19 BCE | 1822 | 1847 | 1864 | 1871 |
|---|---|---|---|---|
| Roman lyric poet Virgil completes the mythic legend with *The Aeneid*. | Scottish journalist Charles Maclaren suggests the mound in Turkey known as Hisarlik is the site of Troy, but is dismissed by historians who regard the Trojan War as simply myth. | British consul Frederick Calvert buys Turkish land, including the eastern half of the Hisarlik mound. | Frederick's brother Frank Calvert, an amateur archaeologist, begins excavations on the mound. In 1865, Frank Calvert announces his conviction that this is indeed the site of Troy. | German archaeologist Heinrich Schliemann excavates the mound, discovering treasure two years later, which he smuggles out of Turkey. He makes three more excavations. |

# THE BATTLE OF THERMOPYLAE

DATE **August 480 BCE**
LOCATION **Thermopylae, on the Gulf of Maliakós, Greece**
OBJECTIVE **To hold back the massive Persian invasion of Greece**

**In a fight to the death that has become a byword for bravery, camaraderie, sacrifice, and defiance, a tiny force of Greeks—though not quite as tiny as legend has it—held back a vast Persian army for days, until a traitor's actions brought them defeat.**

### The Persian Advance

The Persians, led by King Xerxes, crossed from Asia into Europe via a pontoon bridge on the Hellespont, then began to march south into Greece, their 200,000-strong army supported by a naval force of over 1,000 ships in the Aegean Sea. After some debate between the states of Sparta and Athens, the Greeks decided to use the narrow 4-mile-long (6-km) mountain pass at Thermopylae to stop the advance. Because both the Carneian and Olympic festivals were being held—and to not attend would insult the gods—a relatively small force was sent; the main army would follow later. Leading the 7,000 Greek allied fighters was Spartan king Leonidas.

### Holding the Pass

Pitching camp north of the pass, Xerxes sent a mounted scout who returned with the news that the apparently unconcerned Greeks were combing their hair and doing gymnastic exercises. Apparently, unable to believe such a small force would oppose him, Xerxes waited four days for his enemy to retreat. He sent an emissary demanding the Greeks lay down their arms. "*Molon labe,*" ("Come and take them"— pronounced *mo-lone lah-veh*) was Leonidas's laconic response.

Finally, the Persians attacked, but their short spears and light shields were no match for the long weapons and oversized bronze shields of the Greeks, who deployed in phalanxes, creating a wall of overlapping shields from behind which they could strike out without being injured. The Greeks killed 20 or more men for every one of their own who died. Xerxes then sent in the "Immortals," a handpicked elite corps, but they fared no better.

### Betrayed but Undaunted

For another day the battle raged; still the Persians failed to break the Greek line. But Xerxes had finally located a Greek who knew a way around, along the mountain flank. Following this path, on the third day the surviving Immortals rounded on Leonidas from the rear. Learning of their approach, he directed the majority of his army to board the waiting ships and sail for safety. He would stay, along with 300 fellow Spartans, 1,100 Boeotians (Thebans and Thespians), and 100 or so helots (slaves).

Despite certain death they fought ferociously. As Greek historian Herodotus wrote: "They defended themselves to the last, such as still had swords using them, and the others resisting with their hands and teeth." So furious was Xerxes at the huge losses he had suffered, including two of his brothers, he ordered Leonidas's body to be decapitated then crucified. But the Spartan king and his men live on in legend.

ABOVE: Leonidas became a hero throughout Greece. Forty years after the battle, Sparta retrieved what were believed to be his remains and built a shrine to him.

## TIMELINE

**490 BCE**
The Persian king Darius attempts to extend his vast empire by invading the Greek mainland. His army of 25,000 is easily beaten at Marathon.

**481 BCE**
The Greek city-states, so often at odds, form a league to protect themselves against invasion.

ABOVE LEFT: King Leonidas and his allies standing against the invaders following the betrayal by Ephialtes (whose name means "nightmare").
ABOVE RIGHT: Xerxes's men whipping the waters of the Hellespont, following his orders after a storm destroyed the bridge he built across it.

## STEP-BY-STEP

**01** Xerxes and an army drawn from throughout the Persian empire cross the Hellespont and march south toward Athens.

**02** Seeing the enemy's numbers, the Greek alliance abandons plans to stop them at Thessaly, switching to the much narrower pass at Thermopylae, whose name ("hot gates") refers to nearby sulfur springs.

**03** With much of the combined Greek army required to attend religious festivals, a holding force of 7,000 is dispatched to Thermopylae under the leadership of Leonidas.

**04** As the Persians near Thermopylae, a third of their fleet is destroyed in a storm.

**05** When some Greek soldiers quail at the sheer Persian numbers, saying when they loosed their arrows, "the sun would be darkened by their multitude," Spartan Dieneces makes a speech welcoming it, because "we shall have our fight in the shade."

**06** With superior weaponry and training, the Greeks withstand wave after wave of Persians, many of whom drown or are trampled to death while charging.

**07** Surrounded and down to about 1,500 men, led by the 300 Spartans, the Greeks finally succumb after a battle lasting three days.

| | | | | |
|---|---|---|---|---|
| **04.480** BCE | **08.480** BCE | **09.21.480** BCE | **09.29.480** BCE | **479** BCE |
| Darius's son Xerxes attempts another invasion of Greece, bringing 250,000 men and 1,050 vessels. | The Persian army reaches Thermopylae, where they are thwarted for three days before breaking through. | Persian forces burn Athens but casualties are low because almost the whole population (more than 100,000 people) has been evacuated by ship. | Xerxes is lured into an all-out naval battle in the narrow Straits of Salamis, losing 200 ships to the Greeks' 40. After this decisive loss he withdraws from Greece, though some of his army remains. | Following their defeat at the Battle of Plataea, the remaining Persian forces are driven out of Greece. |

# HANNIBAL CROSSES THE ALPS

DATE **May–October, 218** BCE
LOCATION **The Pyrenees, Gaul (now France), and the Alps**
OBJECTIVE **A surprise overland attack on the Roman Republic**

The name Hannibal is inextricably linked with elephants, and these behemoths must have been a spectacular sight as the North African general cut his swathe through Europe. But Hannibal's true claim to fame is as one of the greatest military geniuses who ever lived.

### An Audacious Plan

Hannibal was raised to see Rome as the enemy; by age 26, when he became Carthaginian commander in Spain, he had already spent years pondering Rome's downfall. Learning from the defeat of his father due to Roman naval superiority in the First Punic War, he developed an extraordinary plan: to invade Italy by land. This would mean taking his army—mostly mercenaries, from different cultures, speaking different languages—almost 1,500 miles (2,400 km) through unfamiliar, often hostile territory, and over two mountain ranges, the Pyrenees and the Alps.

He planned meticulously, using scouts to build a thorough knowledge of his intended route: the geography, vital supplies, the tribes (mostly Celtic) he would encounter, and how friendly or otherwise they were to Rome. He sent envoys to make alliances with tribal chieftains and, in May 218 BCE, Hannibal and his 50,000-strong army, including some 80 elephants, marched north from the Carthaginian stronghold of Cartagena in southeast Spain.

### Over the Alps

After besieging Saguntum, Hannibal's troops crossed the Pyrenees and continued into Gaul, encountering both hostile and friendly tribes along the way. He then crossed the Rhône River, and headed north, outwitting a Roman counterattack near Massilia (Marseille).

As Hannibal began his ascent of the Alps he learned hostile warriors were ahead, ready to attack. He outflanked them on the sheer, narrow track, but it took two days and cost him dearly, with many soldiers and pack animals plummeting to their deaths, along with much-needed supplies. Then other Celtic mountain tribes attacked, inflicting more losses. On the ninth day, Hannibal reached the summit and made camp. His soldiers were exhausted and demoralized when it began to snow. Hannibal gathered his men and showed them the panorama below: Italy, their goal.

### Into Italy

Two days later, somewhat revived, they began the descent. Hard as the climb had been, this was steeper and far worse. Sliding on ice, sinking in snow, their path blocked by rockslides, but undeterred, Hannibal eventually led his men and the now starving elephants through. Finally, 15 days after beginning the climb, five months since leaving Cartagena, they completed the crossing—a remarkable achievement. Within a few days, near the Po Valley, Hannibal defeated a Roman force on the Ticinus River—the first of a series of humiliating defeats that he would inflict on Rome over the next 15 years that he spent in Italy.

## TIMELINE

**238** BCE

Carthaginian general Hamilcar Barca's nine-year-old son, Hannibal, swears to become an enemy of the Romans. Seventeen years later, Hannibal takes command of the Carthaginian army.

**219** BCE

Hannibal besieges Saguntum, a Greek city in eastern Spain, allied to Rome. When the city falls after eight months, Rome declares war on Carthage, thus beginning the Second Punic War.

## STEP-BY-STEP

**01** Hannibal and his army depart Cartagena in Spain, bound for Italy. He aims to weaken Rome by breaking up the Roman republican confederation—although many of Rome's "allies" are merely vassal states.

**02** North of the Ebro River is hostile territory. Hannibal seizes cities and battles local tribes. In order to protect the huge area he now controls, he leaves 11,000 men in northern Spain.

**03** The Roman consul Publius Cornelius Scipio intended to confront Hannibal in Spain but has been delayed; his fleet of 60 warships lands near Massilia (now Marseilles). He dismisses the idea that Hannibal could cross the Alps.

**04** Welcoming assistance from Celts he has won over while continuing to battle those who oppose him, Hannibal's men build boats and rafts to cross the Rhône River, covering the rafts with soil in order to not spook the elephants. Then Hannibal heads north.

**05** Before beginning the ascent of the Alps, probably through the Mont Cenis Pass, Hannibal settles a kingship dispute between two brothers of the Allobroges. The tribe resupplies him in gratitude.

**06** Unfriendly Celts lie in wait on the ascent; Hannibal's army suffers significant losses in the two days it takes to fight them off.

**07** Fighting more tribes, freezing conditions, and a blocked descent, Hannibal finally leads his men into Italy, a feat previously believed improbable, if not impossible.

LEFT: Napoleon Bonaparte described Hannibal as, **"This most daring of all men, perhaps the most astonishing; so bold, so assured, so broad of vision in all things; who at the age of 26 conceives what is scarcely conceivable and carries out what is deemed impossible."**

---

**03.10.218 BCE**

Hannibal, leading an estimated 50,000 troops, including some 80 war elephants, crosses the Pyrenees, traverses Gaul, and approaches the Alps.

**10.218 BCE**

Hannibal leads his men into Italy, having done the "impossible" and crossed the Alps. With men garrisoned en route, others discharged, and casualties suffered, his army is only 26,000.

**12.218 BCE**

As tribal warriors abandon their allegiance to Rome and join Hannibal, his army grows to 38,000. Hannibal destroys a 40,000-strong Roman army in the Battle of the Trebia River.

**06.217 BCE**

Hannibal traps and encircles the Romans in battle at Lake Trasimene. He loses 2,000 men to the Romans' 15,000. Rome orders a "scorched-earth" policy wherever Hannibal is likely to pass.

**08.02.216 BCE**

In his final great triumph against Rome, Hannibal devastates its army at Cannae and remains in control of southern Italy until his recall to Carthage in 203 BCE.

# THE SIEGE OF MASADA

DATE        **70–73** CE
LOCATION  Masada, Judaea (now Israel)
OBJECTIVE To make a final stand against the Roman conquerors

The siege of Masada has long symbolized resolute Jewish independence, with the story's unforgettable setting and dramatic conclusion giving it resonance far beyond Israel. But some modern archaeologists think events unfolded quite differently from the cherished version, in which lengthy resistance culminates in a mass suicide in preference to surrender.

### Resisting the Romans

Four years before Jerusalem fell to the Romans in the First Jewish Revolt, members of Jewish splinter group the Zealots launched a lethal surprise attack on the small Roman garrison at Masada. Having gained control of the mountain fortress, they held it throughout the war. When Jerusalem fell, the Zealots in Masada refused to surrender—becoming the last bastion of Jewish resistance to Roman rule in Judaea.

### The Masada Legend

Its position atop a 1,420-foot (433-m) mesa rising steeply from the desert floor made Masada almost impregnable, and fewer than 1,000 Jewish defenders—including women and children—easily held out against a huge Roman army for over two-and-a-half years. When it became clear the Romans would break in, after constructing an enormous ramp in order to breach the fortress's walls, the Zealots, led by Eleazar ben Jair, decided to sacrifice themselves rather than be taken prisoner. Only two women and five children, who had hidden, survived. These women reported ben Jair's stirring words: "a glorious death is preferable to a life of infamy."

### Modern Findings

There are two main sources for the Masada legend: the historian Josephus, who joined the Roman forces after surviving a mass suicide when he was one of the leaders of the Jewish revolt; and archaeologist (and former military leader) Yigael Yadin, who excavated the entire site in the 1960s. More recent archaeological digs and historical analyses have cast doubt on the Josephus version, which was endorsed by Yadin and previously accepted as definitive.

Experts such as Professor Jodi Magness, codirector of a major 1995 archaeological dig at Masada, believe the siege lasted only two to three months. From the remains of the encampment encircling the mountain's base, Magness also estimates there were 8,000 Romans, rather than the oft-quoted 15,000. Further, she contends it is likely that while some rebels did choose to die, others were killed or surrendered and were then butchered. Israeli Professor of Sociology Nachman Ben-Yehuda points out that Josephus identified the Masada resisters as members of the Sicarii, a violent offshoot of the Zealots who assassinated fellow Jews they thought were insufficiently resisting Roman rule, and had massacred more than 700 women and children in one village alone. Ben-Yehuda claims Yadin was so intent on confirming the heroic legend that he bent his findings to fit. The debate continues.

ABOVE: The magnitude of the ramp constructed by the Romans in order to enter Masada.

ABOVE: By time of the siege of Masada, the highly organized Romans had a system of cleverly engineered siege machinery, including three-story siege towers (similar to that pictured) with a battering ram on the bottom level, a drawbridge allowing troops to pour over defensive walls, and an open-top platform for archers and other artillery.

## TIMELINE

| 35 BCE | 15 BCE |
| --- | --- |
| Judaean ruler Herod the Great begins building a refuge at Masada, an enormous mesa whose flat summit covers 18 acres (7 ha). | Having created a lavish palace complex over two decades, Herod surrounds the summit with a casemate wall. |

## STEP-BY-STEP

**01** As the First Jewish Revolt begins in 66 CE, Sicarii Zealots opposed to Roman rule seize the fortress at Masada.

**02** When Jerusalem falls to the Romans in 70 CE, Masada soon becomes Judaea's last point of resistance.

**03** Masada is besieged by the Romans for almost three years, but the natural defenses offered by its rainwater cisterns, steep sides, and single narrow, winding "Snake Path" to the summit means the Zealots can easily withstand the siege.

**04** The Romans build two large camps and six smaller camps. Between the camps a large dyke is built to prevent the exit of any of the defenders.

**05** The Romans begin construction of an enormous ramp, which will allow them to reach the summit. An armature of timber beams supports huge quantities of soil and stones.

**06** Built on an incline that will eventually allow wheeled siege towers to be taken up it, the siege ramp rises inexorably.

**07** As the ramp reaches the level of the fort, allowing the Romans to use a battering ram to breach the outer wall, the Sicarii heed the words of leader Eleazar ben Jair and choose death over capture—although it seems likely that many were killed by fellow Zealots, or so Josephus writes in his *Bellum Judaicum* (*History of the Jewish War*).

**ABOVE:** Photograph of the Masada plateau fortress site. Masada's World Heritage listing notes that the fortress had a particularly sophisticated and extensive water collection and storage system, "collecting run-off water from a single day's rain to sustain life for a thousand people over a period of two to three years," allowing "the transformation of a barren, isolated, arid hilltop into a lavish royal retreat," and later into a place to easily withstand a siege.

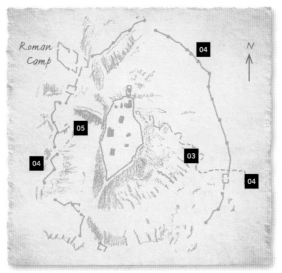

| 4 BCE | 66 CE | 70–73 CE | 1963–1965 | 12.13.2001 |
|---|---|---|---|---|
| Following Herod's death, the Romans capture Masada and establish a small garrison. | The First Jewish Revolt begins with the expulsion from Jerusalem of the Romans, who then besiege the city. Jewish Zealots seize the fortress at Masada. | Jewish Zealots at Masada resist a prolonged Roman siege | Aided by volunteers from around the world, Professor Yigael Yadin excavates the ruins at Masada, using his findings to confirm Josephus's account. | UNESCO adds Masada to its World Heritage List, citing, in part, its "emblematic value for the Jewish people." |

# THE BATTLE OF RONCESVALLES

**DATE** August 15, 778 CE
**LOCATION** Roncesvalles (Roncevaux in French), Navarre, Spain
**OBJECTIVE** A dramatic defensive retreat through a steep mountain pass

If it were not for the medieval love of romance, few, other than locals and the Catholic pilgrims following *El Camino de Santiago* (St. James's Way), would know the name Roncesvalles today. But it lives on, due to the epic ballad *La Chanson de Roland (The Song of Roland)*.

### Thwarted in Spain
By August 778, the Frankish king Charlemagne had spent three months campaigning in Spain, drawn there by rebel Muslim governors chafing under the authority of the Ummayad caliph Abd al-Rahman I. They promised Charlemagne control over much of northern Spain if he would help them overthrow al-Rahman.

The Spanish expedition did not end well. Despite their shared Christianity, Charlemagne had overwhelmed the Gascon Basques at Pamplona, but had found Muslim-held Saragossa (Zaragoza) not as welcoming as promised. Receiving news of a Saxon uprising in the north of his empire, and negotiating a ransom to depart, Charlemagne turned for home, destroying Pamplona on the way. Most of his army had already negotiated the narrow mountain pass through the Pyrenees at Roncesvalles when Basque and Muslim guerrillas launched an ambush.

### The Battle Unvarnished
Charlemagne's army was spread along a steep path winding through dense forest. The troops and baggage train making up the rear guard were under the leadership of Charlemagne's nephew Roland. The Basques, with some Muslim forces, hidden in the thick trees, attacked in a gorge, which allowed them to block the rear guard's passage. Frankish historian Einhard describes how they chased and slaughtered Charlemagne's men and then, as darkness fell, plundered the baggage and disappeared into the night. After a furious fight, Roland and many others were killed, although the bulk of Charlemagne's forces made it safely back into Gaul (France).

### Romanticizing Roland
It was probably more a skirmish than a battle, but the story became embellished. *La Chanson de Roland* entered the French ballad tradition as early as the ninth century; in 1066, a Norman minstrel Taillefer rode into the Battle of Hastings singing of Roland. The 4,000-line version we know today has Roland overly trusting and impetuous but heroic, proud, and honest. As Charlemagne withdraws, the traitor Ganelon arranges the Roncesvalles ambush, which pits an improbable 400,000 Saracens (Muslims) against 20,000 Franks. Roland refuses to blow his ivory horn to summon help until only 60 of his men remain alive. Charlemagne (described as an old man, in reality in his thirties) charges back and routs the enemy. In punishment, Ganelon is quartered. Roland's sacrifice is celebrated in stained glass in Notre Dame, Paris, and his legend further inflated by Ariosto in his epic poem *Orlando Furioso* (1516).

**FRANKISH EMPIRE**

Bay of Biscay

Bordeaux

Roncesvalles Pass

*Pyrenees*

Pamplona

Saragossa

Barcelona

**IBERIA**

*Mediterranean Sea*

## TIMELINE

**777 CE**

Three "Saracen" (Muslim) governors of northern Spain visit Charlemagne, seeking his intervention against the Umayyad Muslim caliph, Abd al-Rahman I.

**05.778 CE**

Charlemagne leads his army into Spain. Meeting little resistance on the way to Pamplona, they quickly capture the Basque city.

BELOW: A tableau of the battle from the *Chroniques de France ou de Saint Denis*, a fourteenth-century French manuscript. Each year on August 15, the anniversary of the battle, there is a reading of the entire *Chanson de Roland* in the Church of Santiago de Orreaga-Roncesvalles.

ABOVE: In this 1916 painting, which evokes the romantic vision of the battle, Roland is pictured blowing his horn as the "Saracen" arrows fall about his head and his men at the "eleventh hour."

## STEP-BY-STEP

**01** Failing to receive the welcome he has been led to expect by Muslim rebels at Saragossa, and with a Saxon uprising to suppress on the Rhine, Charlemagne abandons his Spanish expedition and heads home.

**02** Passing back the way they came, he orders his soldiers to tear down the walls of Pamplona, to ensure it can never be used by the Basques or the Muslims as a base to stand against him.

**03** The bulk of the army has passed safely through the narrow defile at Roncesvalles, leaving only the rear guard, including troops, baggage, gold, and prisoners, under the command of his nephew Roland.

**04** As the tail end of Charlemagne's army crosses the summit of the pass, Basques and armed Muslim supporters, hidden in the thickly forested slopes, attack, separating the rear guard from the forward column.

**05** Many Frankish soldiers and pack animals fall to their deaths in the steep valley; the others, Roland included, are killed in a short but fierce fight.

**06** The Basque guerrillas seize the gold and other valuables from the baggage and disappear into the forest.

**07** The legend of Roland is born. Charlemagne exacts his revenge 22 years later, by successfully invading northern Spain.

| 08.778 CE | 08.778 CE | 800–801 CE | 10.14.1066 | 1485 |
|---|---|---|---|---|
| Retracing its steps from an inconclusive engagement at Saragossa, the Frankish army tears down the walls of Pamplona, provoking Basque enmity. | On a Pyrenean mountain pass at Roncesvalles, the army's rear guard is attacked by Basques and Muslims. | Charlemagne returns to northern Spain, quelling the Basques, driving the Muslims south of the Ebro River, and successfully besieging Barcelona. | Minstrel Taillefer dies at the Battle of Hastings, having inspired William the Conqueror's army by singing of Roland's legendary deeds at Roncesvalles. | Caxton publishes *The English Charlemagne Romances, Parts III and IV*, recounting the adventures of Charlemagne, including *The Song of Roland*. |

# THE BATTLE OF AGINCOURT

DATE        October 25, 1415
LOCATION   Agincourt (now Azincourt), Pas-de-Calais, France
OBJECTIVE  The French army aimed to stop the English reaching Calais

**Never did a king have a better publicist than Henry V had in William Shakespeare. As impressive as Henry's triumph at Agincourt was at the time, after the playwright put his stirring words—"We few, we happy few, we band of brothers"—in the king's mouth, the victory truly became part of the English psyche.**

### Planning
Henry V prepared thoroughly before invading Normandy in August 1415, commandeering shipping, stockpiling armor-piercing arrows, and recruiting professional soldiers. With his formidable 10,500-strong army he aimed to reclaim English territories in France, and ultimately to claim the French crown.

Henry's initial target, the seaport of Harfleur, however, withstood siege for a month, surrendering mid-autumn. The "campaigning season" would soon be over; the strife-riven French were finally uniting against Henry; and disease (particularly dysentery), casualties, and manning his new Harfleur garrison had reduced his army to less than 6,000. It was time to make the 100-mile (160-km) march to English-controlled Calais.

### Against the Odds
The English were within 30 miles (48 km) of Calais when Henry's scouts reported huge numbers of French troops ahead, blocking the route. The exhausted, apprehensive English had a somber night listening to laughter and music from the French camp.

The following morning the two armies faced off. The French had a significant advantage, numbering at least 12,000 men, but this was negated by the place they chose to meet: a recently plowed field only 3,000 feet (914 m) wide, hemmed in by woods on either side. Frustrated by inaction, Henry led his 5,000 archers forward. They fixed sharpened stakes as best they could in the mud, then began to fire. Small groups of French cavalry charged, but their horses stumbled on the stakes and, panicking, trampled backward over the heavily armored French knights struggling on foot through the mud behind them.

Wave after wave of French attacked but, unlike the English, they were not centrally coordinated. Very quickly the crush was such that, wrote French eyewitness Jean de Wavrin, virtually none "could lift their arms to strike their enemies." Still the French at the rear forced forward. Many in front were trampled or suffocating or drowning in the sucking mud. Having done tremendous damage with their long-range bows, the English archers now picked up swords and axes. Only those likely to bring ransom were spared. Within two hours the surviving French began to retreat.

### A Final Attack
As the battle wound down, Henry got word of a French attack on the rear guard. He ordered the killing of all prisoners, reasoning he could not spare men to guard them. There was reluctance, since a dead prisoner brought no ransom, but he insisted, so, wrote de Wavrin, "the nobility of France was beheaded and inhumanely cut to pieces." Despite this, Henry arrived in Calais with over 1,000 hostages, having killed thousands of the French, at a cost of around 300 English dead. Agincourt was a resounding, if bloody, English victory.

ABOVE: There are several interesting near-contemporary manuscript illustrations of the Battle of Agincourt including this colorful work that depicts the hand-to-hand fighting typical of the battle.

## TIMELINE

**06.1415**
French–English negotiations running for more than two decades end after Henry V's demands to territory and to the French throne are refused.

**09.22.1415**
Taking advantage of French political divisions, Henry attacks Harfleur, which surrenders only after a month-long siege.

RIGHT: Henry V of England attacked by the Duke of Alençon at the Battle of Agincourt, 1415. Having led a French counterattack during the battle, the Duke of Alençon, some records say, succeeded in cutting an ornament from Henry's crown before being subdued and killed by the king's bodyguard.

## STEP-BY-STEP

**01** Alarming his advisers, who expect him to travel by sea, Henry V announces his intention to march his army, now reduced to less than 6,000 men, from Harfleur to Calais. He has less than eight days' supply of food.

**02** The battered, hungry, and exhausted English reach the village of Maisoncelles, where their path is blocked by a much larger French army.

**03** They make camp. Rain pours down, as it has for two weeks.

**04** Henry passes along his ranks, making "fine speeches everywhere," writes de Wavrin.

**05** There is an odd standoff the following morning as Henry waits in vain for the French to attack. Finally he moves forward with his archers. They plant sharpened stakes to fend off the cavalry.

**06** The well-trained English archers, who can fire six long-range arrows per minute using armor-piercing heads, which can wound at 400 yards (365 m) and kill at 200 yards (183 m), inflict enormous damage on French foot soldiers and armored cavalry alike.

**07** Charles d'Albret, Constable of France, and Marshal Boucicaut lead the French troops, but their authority is not recognized by many of the nobles present. Lack of central command leads to fatal crowding on the battlefield and chaotic disorganization as one wave of attackers meet or trample those in front of them, while French crossbowmen are not deployed.

**08** Having suffered heavy losses, and realizing they are beaten, the surviving French retreat. In a final act of steely rationalism, in order to preserve his troops, Henry orders the execution of French prisoners, a command not met without resistance from his senior knights.

| 10.24.1415 | 10.25.1415 | 05.21.1420 | 08.31.1422 | 10.21.1422 |
|---|---|---|---|---|
| After a draining march in which his men have crossed the Seine and Somme rivers, and been shadowed and harassed by French troops, Henry's path is blocked. | On St. Crispin's Day, then an English public holiday, the two armies meet at Agincourt. The English win, beating an army more than twice their size. | After Henry has successfully resumed his war against France in 1417, the French sign the Treaty of Troyes, recognizing Henry V as heir to the French throne on the death of Charles VI. | Henry V dies of dysentery at age 34. His infant son becomes King Henry VI of England. | Charles VI of France dies. Henry VI is now also nominal King of France. |

# THE SIEGE OF TENOCHTITLÁN

DATE        April 28–August 13, 1521
LOCATION    Tenochtitlán (now Mexico City), Mexico
OBJECTIVE  To seize control of the capital of the Aztec empire

**Hernán Cortés, the conquistador who opened the way for Spanish colonization of the Americas, was ruthlessly ambitious. His determination to make both his mark and his fortune changed the course of history for millions and led to the destruction of one of history's most intriguing civilizations, the Aztecs.**

## All or Nothing

In November 1519, Cortés sailed from Cuba for the Yucatán coast with 500 men, 10 cannon, and 17 horses. Receiving reports of floating castles bearing pale-faced creatures, Aztec emperor Montezuma II sent gold and other gifts in the hope that the strangers would move on. Instead, Cortés became focused on the empire's wealth.

After befriending the local Totonacs and founding the town of Vera Cruz, Cortés took the breathtaking step of sinking his own ships, impelling his expedition inland. As they progressed, his troops fought, then allied with, the Tlaxcalans who joined him on the march. Finally, he reached the Aztec capital of Tenochtitlán. The gigantic city, seemingly floating on Lake Texcoco, with a population of around 250,000, amazed the Spaniards; chronicler Bernal Díaz described it as "an enchanted vision." Within two years it was all gone.

## From Guests to Enemies

Despite his misgivings, Montezuma welcomed the Spaniards as honored guests. Eight days later, Cortés placed the emperor under house arrest, then spent five months trying to quell growing unrest about the Spaniards' incessant demands for gold.

In April 1520, Cortés rushed from Tenochtitlán to Vera Cruz with most of his men to stop a 900-strong force sent from Cuba to arrest him for insubordination. Cortés took their leader prisoner and co-opted the men. In his absence, the Spaniards and Tlaxcalans had shed Aztec blood, as Cortés learned on his return. Five days later a crisis point was reached. Montezuma died and his body was thrown into the street; the Spaniards denied killing him. That night, attempting to flee, they fought a pitched battle on a causeway—"The Night of Sorrows"—in which more than 600 conquistadors and several thousand Tlaxcalans died.

## Death Reigns Down

The Spaniards had left a deadly legacy: smallpox, which killed vast numbers including newly installed emperor Cuitláhuac, who was replaced by Cuauhtémoc. Meanwhile, Cortés developed a remarkable plan to beat the Aztec fleets of war canoes on Lake Texcoco. He had 13 prefabricated brigantines built and carried to within 3 miles (4.9 km) of the lake. It then took 8,000 of his native allies 50 days to build a canal to the lake.

Cortés then launched the brigantines, eradicating the Aztec canoes with cannon fire, and besieged Tenochtitlán, aiming to starve the Aztecs out. Realizing they would fight to the death, he entered the city. When the masonry buildings would not burn, Cortés's men flattened them systematically as they advanced, forcing the Aztecs to the northern edge, which they defended for 80 days. Finally, the Spaniards found Cuauhtémoc in a canoe, trying to either flee or surrender now there was nothing left to defend. Destruction was total.

ABOVE: The Aztec capital Tenochtitlán was a marvel of engineering and design. A planned city in the middle of a great lake, it grew from nothing to a population of 250,000 in less than 200 years. Much of it was built on reclaimed land that extended the islands in the great lake, with causeways connecting it at three points to the mainland.

## TIMELINE

**10.23.1518**

Cuba's Spanish governor, Diego de Velásquez, appoints Hernán Cortés, "captain-general" of an expedition to the Yucatán Peninsula. The order is rescinded, but Cortés leaves anyway.

**04.20.1519**

Cortés receives a messenger bearing gifts from Aztec emperor Montezuma II. He responds with a display of the destructive force of his cannon.

## STEP-BY-STEP

**01** After a costly fighting retreat from Tenochtitlán on June 30, 1520, his plans to coerce the Aztecs into submission by diplomacy and threats having failed, Cortés plots an elaborate campaign to gain control of the capital.

**02** Having by now assembled a force of around 1,000 Spanish troops, including 86 cavalry and over 100 archers and musketeers, augmented by allied native forces numbering up to 100,000, Cortés realizes that he is still vastly outnumbered by a potential Aztec army of over 200,000.

**03** Cortés commissions 13 prefabricated brigantines to be built at Vera Cruz—the key to taking command of Lake Texcoco. Powered by oars and single sails, the boats have a cannon mounted on the prow.

**04** The brigantines are transported to within 3 miles (4.9 km) of the shores of Lake Texcoco and are assembled while some 8,000 native allies dig a canal to Lake Texcoco.

**05** At the end of May 1521, Cortés launches his assault, devastating the fleet of Aztec war canoes patrolling the lake. One by one Cortés secures the causeways linking the city to the mainland.

**06** Tenochtitlán is now potentially isolated and at the Spaniards' mercy, but the Aztecs fight back tenaciously, the masonry buildings of the city providing robust defenses. Meanwhile, under the cover of darkness the Aztecs repeatedly breach the causeways in an attempt to in turn cut the Spaniards off from the mainland.

**07** Cortés orders the block-by-block demolition of the city as his forces advance. By July, most of the city is in ruins, and its population starving despite continuing to offer stout resistance.

**08** On the night of August 12–13, a final attack on the northern quarter of the city proves decisive. The remaining population is slaughtered, and the last Aztec emperor, Cuauhtémoc, is captured trying to escape by canoe.

ABOVE: This lithograph reproduction of a nineteenth-century painting by O. Graeff depicts *La Noche Triste*, when Aztec soldiers overwhelmed Cortés's forces. While the Spaniards had superior weaponry to the Aztecs (crossbows, muskets, cannon, steel armor, and horses against arrows and spears), and a tightly disciplined fighting style, there was also a crucial difference in combat aims. The Spaniards fought to kill; the Aztecs fought to disable then capture for the human sacrifice they believed necessary to repay their blood debt to the gods.

**11.08.1519**
The Spaniards and their native allies enter the city of Tenochtitlán. Cortés described it as "the most beautiful thing in the world." Within eight days Montezuma is under house arrest.

**06.25.1520**
Having dealt with a punitive Spanish expedition, Cortés arrives back in Tenochtitlán from Vera Cruz to find his men have opened hostilities with the Aztecs.

**06.30.1520**
Attempting to flee, the Spaniards and Tlaxcalans are set upon in a bloody battle known as *"La Noche Triste"* (The Night of Sorrows).

**09.08.1565**
As part of his far-reaching plan to take Tenochtitlán, Cortés launches his prefabricated brigantines on the canal he has had built and besieges the city.

**08.13.1521**
Tenochtitlán falls after an eleven-week struggle. The Aztec empire is no more.

# PIZARRO'S CONQUEST OF PERU

DATE    1533
LOCATION    Tawantinsuyu, the Inca empire (most of modern Peru, Ecuador, and northern Chile)
OBJECTIVE    To subjugate the Inca empire and seize its wealth

The Spanish adventurer Francisco Pizarro had already made a small fortune in the new Spanish colony of Panama but he was not satisfied. After two exploratory expeditions down the Pacific coast of South America, in 1532 he led an expedition of less than 200 men to seize control of the largest empire in the world—that of the Incas.

### A Fatal Misjudgment

Atahualpa, fighting to become the Inca emperor, knew the Spaniards had landed at Tumbes, but they were so few in number he dismissed them as posing no threat. As Don Felipe Guamán Poma de Ayala wrote 70 years later, Atahualpa sent the Spaniards gifts of "male servants and sacred virgins. Some of the virgins were also offered to the Spaniards' horses, because, seeing them eating maize, the Peruvians took them for a kind of human being … and it seemed advisable to treat them with respect."

### Trapping an Emperor

By November, Atahualpa had secured the Inca throne and Francisco Pizarro requested a meeting. The emperor arrived at Cajamarca in great ceremony, with up to 4,000 of his soldiers and huge numbers of civilians crowding the city square. Spanish priest Vicente Valverde approached Atahualpa saying the Incas must renounce their gods. Asked by what authority, Valverde handed Atahualpa a Bible, saying it explained all. Failing to hear anything when he held the book to his ear, the emperor threw it down, at which point the Spaniards, waiting with their guns out of sight, fired on the unarmed crowd. Fleeing from guns and horses' hooves, hundreds were crushed to death.

Pizarro imprisoned the shocked emperor. Atahualpa proposed a ransom: enough gold and silver to fill the large room he was in thrice, in exchange for his freedom. Pizarro agreed and gained so much treasure that it took the Spaniards a month to melt it down. Then Pizarro had Atahualpa executed—threatened with being burned alive and thus denied an afterlife, he agreed to be baptized in exchange for a more "merciful" garroting.

With their ruler gone, the Inca armies surrounding Cajamarca retreated, allowing Pizarro to march through the Andes to the royal capital Cuzco, seize it without resistance, and appoint Atahualpa's half-brother, Manco Capac, as emperor.

### Pizarro's Short-lived Victory

Manco served as Pizarro's puppet for two years before leading an uprising against "these cruel enemies." He crossed the Andes with several thousand troops and some captured Spanish weapons and horses, but he was soon driven into hiding. Having largely conquered the Incas, Pizarro found himself fighting Diego de Almagro, once his right-hand man, but now alienated by Pizarro's fierce self-interest. Two years after Manco revolted, Pizarro's followers killed Almagro and, two short years later, Pizarro himself was murdered in revenge in 1541. Inca resistance to Spanish rule would continue until 1572.

RIGHT: Atahualpa was threatened, by the conquistadors, with being burned alive, but he eventually chose to be garroted. In 1527, on Pizarro's second voyage of adventure, his crew smuggled out a message asking to be rescued from their crazed "butcher" commander. Six years later, the Incas saw the full force of his single-mindedness.

BELOW: In this engraving by Theodore de Bry, the Incas provide the gold demanded by Pizarro.

## TIMELINE

**1526–28**

On Pizarro's second Pacific voyage he lands in the Inca territory Tawantinsuyu, which he names Peru. He finds evidence of immense wealth.

**1527**

Smallpox, carried by the Spaniards, reaches Peru, killing 200,000 people including the emperor Huayna Capac. Civil war breaks out as two of his sons fight for the throne.

## STEP-BY-STEP

**01** Seeing the Inca empire as an immense treasure to be seized and plundered, Pizarro and four of his brothers and their henchman Almagro set out in a very small force of less than 200 men for Peru.

**02** After three decades of stability and security under emperor Huayna Capac, the Incas reel under the effects of smallpox and a civil war in which two of Capac's sons claim to rule.

**03** At a crucial meeting at Cajamarca, Pizarro springs a trap on the triumphant new emperor Atahualpa and takes him prisoner.

**04** Atahualpa arranges for gold and silver to be brought from all parts of the empire in exchange for his freedom.

**05** Pizarro reneges on their deal and has Atahualpa executed for treason.

**06** Pizarro's small force takes the capital, Cuzco, unhindered, and he installs an emperor, Manco, who agrees to Peru becoming a "client state" of Spain.

**07** Furious at the Incas' treatment by their supposed allies, Manco leads an uprising. He has an initial battle victory over the Spaniards, but the Inca empire is in its death throes.

---

**07.26.1529**
Spain's Queen Isabella names Pizarro governor of an area stretching 600 miles (965 km) south of Panama and instructs him to "discover and conquer Peru."

**05.1532**
Pizarro lands at Tumbes and begins his march inland to Cajamarca.

**11.16.1532**
Pizarro's men slaughter unarmed Incas and seize the emperor, Atahualpa. Nine months later, despite having delivered an immense ransom, Atahualpa is murdered on Pizarro's orders.

**03.1534**
Pizarro installs Manco Capac in the Inca capital, Cuzco as his puppet emperor. Two years later, Manco leads an unsuccessful Inca revolt, setting up the rebel capital Vilcabamba.

**1572**
After decades of guerrilla warfare, the Spaniards finally take Vilcabamba and behead emperor Tupac Amaru, ending the Inca empire.

# THE GREAT SIEGE OF MALTA

DATE      May 18–September 8, 1565
LOCATION  The island of Malta
OBJECTIVE Two opposing cultures aiming to control a strategic island stronghold

In the eighteenth century, French writer and historian Voltaire could declare, "Nothing is so well known as the Siege of Malta." Three hundred years on, this conflict between the Ottoman Empire and a small Christian outpost is largely forgotten, though rarely has war been more ferocious or gruesome.

### "So Small a Son"

Rivalry between the Ottoman Turks and the Christian nations of Western Europe frequently focused on control of the central Mediterranean. Following several clashes, a massive Turkish fleet under Mustafa Pasha bearing some 40,000 men arrived at Malta on May 18, 1565. After a skirmish in the southeast, Pasha focused his attack on the lesser, but more modern, of the island's forts, St. Elmo, expecting to capture it within 72 hours. Despite almost nonstop cannon bombardment, and wave after wave of infantry attack, the small force of Knights of St. John, regular soldiers, and civilian militia in the fort, held out for 36 days.

At sunrise on June 23, eve of the feast day of Knights' patron saint John the Baptist, the Turks broke through. Fewer than 40 of the 1,500 inside survived the siege, but the Turkish losses were truly catastrophic: 8,000 dead, including siege commander Dragut (Turgut) Reis. And there was still the much larger Fort St. Angelo to take, prompting Mustafa Pasha to cry, "If so small a son has cost so dear, what price shall we have to pay for so large a father?"

### Macabre Tactics

That night Mustafa had the bodies of the Knights from St. Elmo beheaded. The corpses were nailed to wooden crosses and sent on the harbor current across to St. Angelo. The Knights' Grand Master, Jean Parisot de La Valette, retaliated by ordering all his Turkish prisoners decapitated. Their bodies were cast into the harbor and their heads fired back at the Turks as grotesque cannonballs.

Demoralized by their huge losses and suffering in the summer heat as disease and dysentery spread throughout their camp and the corpse-strewn surrounds of St. Elmo, the Turks turned their attack on St. Angelo, bombarding the walls, tunneling beneath to try to blow it up, and constructing siege engines designed to reach the battlements (the defenders created holes at the walls' base, poking through cannon with which they blew up the engines). When the walls were breached, the Knights improvised ambushes, slaughtering those who broke through. La Valette, aged 70, took up his sword and joined the fray, vowing never to surrender.

### Turning the Tide

Finally 8,000 Spanish reinforcement troops arrived from Sicily. It was not the hoped-for 25,000, but it proved enough and the Turks fled, thousands more being killed in retreat. Only 10,000 of the 40,000 who had landed 112 days earlier survived. The defenders had suffered badly too—with only 250 surviving Fort St. Angelo, all of them wounded—but throughout Europe theirs was seen as a great victory.

ABOVE: The Knights' Grand Master, Jean Parisot de La Valette was 70 at the time of the siege; educated and cultured, he was a veteran knight-soldier and had survived four years as a slave on a Turkish galley. Siege historian Ernle Bradford described him as "that rarest of human beings, a completely single-minded man."

RIGHT: The defending Knights of St. John during the assault on the Post of Castille.

## TIMELINE

| 01.01.1523 | 1530 |
| --- | --- |
| After 200 years of ruling Rhodes, and a six-month siege by Ottoman Emperor Suleiman the Magnificent, the Hospitallers (Knights of St. John) are allowed to sail away. | Holy Roman Emperor Charles V gives the Knights the Maltese archipelago. |

## STEP-BY-STEP

**01** Certain that the Turks will return after their attack on Gozo in 1551, the Knights systematically reinforce Malta's defenses, including the construction of the modern star-shaped fort of St. Elmo; they also stockpile food and weapons, and train the civilian population for war.

**02** La Valette requests reinforcements from leaders throughout Europe. Most are too busy dealing with internal conflict to help, or unwilling to damage trade relations with the Turks.

**03** The usual Fort St. Elmo garrison of six Knights and 600 soldiers is boosted by 46 Knights and 200 Spanish infantry, all that arrive of the thousands promised by the Spanish Viceroy of Sicily.

**04** Turkish bombardment of St. Elmo during daylight hours is relentless, but at night La Valette is able to send reinforcements from St. Angelo.

**05** The defenders of St. Elmo hold off the Turks for over a month. One of their weapons is the fire-hoop—dropped alight from the fort walls, it can burn three men alive at a time. They also deploy grenade-like pots of an incendiary mixture called "wildfire," which is also compressed into tubes called "trumps,"

then squirted at the enemy, a primitive flamethrower. In all, 1,500 Maltese soldiers and 89 Knights, and 8,000 Turkish troops die in the struggle.

**06** The St. Elmo siege has allowed La Valette to further strengthen Fort St. Angelo before the Turks turn their attention to it. It also fails to yield to the increasingly demoralized Ottoman forces, although the defenses are regularly but unsuccessfully breached.

**07** After more than three months, the defenders are almost at the end of their strength when reinforcements arrive from Sicily and the Turks finally flee.

---

**1550**
The Knights defeat an Ottoman fleet led by Dragut Reis at Mahdia.

**1551**
Dragut Reis attacks Malta. Unable to seize the large island itself, he storms the smaller island of Gozo, carrying off most of its population.

**05.18.1565**
Wanting to be rid of the troublesome Knights and use the island as a springboard into the western Mediterranean, the Turks sail to Malta in huge numbers.

**09.08.1565**
After a brief but costly battle with the reinforcements arriving from Sicily, the Turks flee.

**1565**
La Valette announces he intends to found a city in celebration; funding comes from Spain, France, Portugal, and the Pope. In 1570 Valletta becomes Malta's capital.

# DRAKE'S RAID ON CÁDIZ

**DATE** April 19, 1587
**LOCATION** Cádiz, Andalusia, Southwest Spain
**OBJECTIVE** The disruption of Spain's preparations to invade England

Francis Drake was boldness personified. A decade before Queen Elizabeth I dispatched him to safeguard England from Spain's invasion plans he had circumnavigated the globe, sailing uncharted waters, while bringing back information and Spanish treasure plundered from the New World. Now the knighted former slave-trader was to strike at Spain itself.

### Distressing the Enemy

Francis Drake's target was the Armada King Philip II was preparing to invade England—Drake was to "distress" the enemy fleet in harbor. Half the booty captured along the way would go to Elizabeth, with the rest split between Drake and the speculators who helped fund his expedition.

At the last minute Elizabeth, characteristically, changed her mind, deciding against provoking the Spanish king. But it was too late, Drake had sailed, and the messenger ship sent after him was forced back by bad weather.

### Like a Huge Volcano

Drake targeted Cádiz after learning of a large fleet at anchor there. His long-range guns easily got past the few Spanish galleys trying to keep him out, and on April 19 he entered the outer harbor. Here resistance was stiffer, notably from a galleon from Biscay and a merchantman from Genoa armed with up to 40 guns, but they, too, were soon beaten.

In the early hours of the following morning, Drake navigated the dangerous path to the inner harbor. He set about reprovisioning his fleet and plundering then burning the ships he found there, among them a warship belonging to the Armada's leader, Marqués de Santa Cruz. One Spaniard described smoke and flames "like a huge volcano, or something out of Hell."

### Invasion Delayed

Cádiz's batteries, in the castle and in the town, did little damage to Drake's fleet, but the call had gone out for help and, while the English were wreaking havoc, 6,000 Spaniards were pouring in. They set up a battery in a more effective location, firing down upon the outer harbor and hitting the ship of Vice Admiral William Borough, Drake's second-in-command. Failing to persuade his leader of the need to withdraw the fleet, Borough took his own ship out, anchoring 2 miles (3.2 km) from the fray.

Later, as Drake himself started to leave, the wind dropped, becalming him until the early hours of April 21. According to Drake, during the 30-hour raid he had captured four ships and destroyed 35 others, although the Spaniards claimed it was fewer than this. What is certain is that with this raid and the others he conducted in the following weeks along the coast between Lisbon and Sagres, Drake weakened the Armada in crucial areas and pushed King Philip's invasion plans back by a year.

## TIMELINE

**02.25.1570**

Pope Pius V excommunicates Protestant Elizabeth I of England.

**8.10.1585**

The Treaty of Nonsuch between England and the Protestant Netherlands begins the Anglo-Spanish War.

ABOVE: Hand-colored halftone reproduction of a portrait of Francis Drake.

LEFT: English and Dutch ships in the bombardment of Fort Puntal; detail from a painting by Francisco de Zurbarán, 1634.

## STEP-BY-STEP

**01** Francis Drake's mission is to gather intelligence on Armada preparations and destroy or capture Spanish or Portuguese ships.

**02** Capturing a small boat off Lisbon, Drake learns of a large fleet in Cádiz.

**03** Drake's ships easily outmatch ships attempting to protect Cádiz.

**04** In the outer harbor Drake battles an armed 1,000-ton (907-tonne) Genoese merchant ship. When it refuses to surrender he sinks it together with all of its merchandise.

**05** That night, he navigates the many treacherous channels through to the inner waters of the harbor.

**06** Here he sets to seizing provisions and booty, and burning ships.

**07** William Borough reacts to his ship *The Golden Lion* being fired upon in the outer harbor by departing.

**08** Drake follows the successful raid with more coastal attacks, during which he destroys many staves destined to be used in the manufacture of wooden barrels.

**09** The barrels would have held up to 30,000 tons (27,000 tonnes) of food and water. Their loss will cause significant problems for the Armada when it sails the following year.

---

**4.19.1587**
Francis Drake leads the raid on Cádiz.

**07.1587**
With the English fleet not ready to battle the Armada, Elizabeth I apologizes to Spain over the raid, claiming she was "greatly offended" by Drake's actions.

**05.1588**
As the Armada again readies for invasion, Drake is informed Lord Howard will command England's fleet; he will be second-in-command.

**1629**
In *Considerations touching a warre with Spaine*, Francis Bacon recalls Drake describing the Cádiz raid as "singeing the King of Spain's beard."

# THE DEFEAT OF THE SPANISH ARMADA

DATE      July 31–August 9, 1588
LOCATION  The English Channel
OBJECTIVE To prevent a large Spanish force invading England

After the setback caused by Sir Francis Drake's raid on the Spanish fleet at Cádiz in 1587, Spain's Philip II was more determined than ever to invade England. Against advice, he rebuilt his invasion Armada. What happened next changed the course of history and marked the start of a new kind of naval warfare.

### Opposing Tactics

The Armada's plan was to sail to the Netherlands, meet the Duke of Parma's 30,000 troops and escort them across the Channel to England where they would seize the throne. The absence of a Spanish-controlled deepwater port where the forces could safely unite was a major problem.

Commanding the English was Queen Elizabeth I's cousin and adviser, Lord Howard of Effingham. Like Spain's commander, the Duke of Medina Sidonia, Howard lacked much sea experience. He was, however, an excellent leader. Spain's ships were slower but carried more men; their aim was close battle, allowing infantry to board and overwhelm the enemy vessels. But the English ships were not just faster, they carried longer-range guns and could fire broadsides. Howard planned to keep his distance while doing plenty of damage.

### A Deadly Delay

On July 29, the Spanish reached English waters. From the flagship *Ark Royal*, Howard shadowed the Armada, which sailed up the English Channel in a defensive crescent formation. Despite three engagements over the next five days, neither side suffered significant damage.

On August 7, Medina Sidonia learned Parma needed more time. Strong prevailing westerly winds were forcing the Armada east or north: east lay the shipwrecking Flemish shoals; north meant abandoning the plan. The only alternative was to wait at anchor, exposed, off Calais.

At midnight, the English deployed eight unmanned fireships. Ready, Medina Sidonia dispatched patrol boats. They stopped two of the fireships but the primed cannon and gunpowder on others started to explode. Hours earlier, Medina Sidonia had ordered that buoys be tied to his ships' anchors in case crews were forced to cut them loose in an emergency; now they did just this.

### More Perils after Battle

Although their flight was remarkably orderly in the circumstances, the Spanish were unable to regroup effectively and suffered badly from broadsides in the attack the English launched at dawn off the French port of Gravelines. The fighting eased only when the English, already low on basic supplies, ran short of ammunition. Limping in retreat, the Spanish were forced—by the wind and the English—to continue north and aim for home by sailing north around the British Isles and into the fierce North Atlantic. Less than half the Armada made it back. England's victory prevented its invasion and, as the first major battle featuring guns under sail, laid a blueprint for naval warfare for the next 250 years.

ABOVE: This map of the British Isles shows the route of the Armada.

RIGHT: The use of fireships dates back to the Ancient Greeks. The eight old merchantmen used against the Armada were volunteered by their owners, including Drake. It was not a selfless gesture. On the open market these worn-out ships would have fetched a fraction of the compensation paid later by the Queen: £1,000 to Drake, for *Thomas of Plymouth*.

## TIMELINE

**1587**

Following Drake's Cádiz raid, Spain's King Philip II spares no expense preparing his Armada; two-thirds of the Crown's income from the entire Spanish empire goes to the cause.

**1587**

Shortly after Walter Raleigh's galleon Ark Raleigh is launched, Queen Elizabeth I seizes it in lieu of debt. Renamed the Ark Royal, it becomes Lord Howard's flagship.

## STEP-BY-STEP

**01** In March 1588, the Armada sets sail from Lisbon. Gales force it into the Spanish port of La Coruña for repairs. Two months later it sets off again.

**02** The Armada is spotted off Cornwall on July 29. England's beacon system, established under Henry VIII, is used to send the alert across the nation. Disadvantaged by the strong westerly winds, the English fleet is trapped at Plymouth.

**03** According to legend, Lord Howard's Vice Admiral, Sir Francis Drake, was bowling at Plymouth Hoe when told the Armada was approaching; he insisted on finishing the game. His lack of urgency may have had more to do with the need to wait for a favorable tide, and for the Armada to pass by so that the English could get upwind of them, than mere sangfroid.

**04** Lord Howard divides his fleet into four squadrons, commanded by himself, Drake, Drake's fellow former slave-trader and pirate John Hawkins, and Martin Frobisher.

**05** Avoiding close combat, the nimble British fleet fires long-range cannon at the Armada in the English Channel in encounters on July 31, then off Portland Bill and the Isle of Wight two days later. While many personnel are killed and injured, just two Spanish ships are knocked out of action, and no English vessels.

**06** After nearly a week there has still been no decisive engagement, and the Armada is now precariously anchored off Calais awaiting the Duke of Parma's troops. Then, at midnight on August 7, the English deploy eight fireships to disturb the Armada. This is sometimes presented as a panicky disaster for the Spanish; however, with 132 ships moving out of formation in the dark, only one vessel is damaged, losing its rudder. The fireships burn themselves out on the shore.

**07** The real devastation comes the next day. Unable to effectively regroup into a defensive formation, the Armada is easy pickings for the English when Drake attacks the fleet off Gravelines. Delivering devastating broadsides, the English ships only withdraw when low on ammunition. With some 1,800 cannon to supply with shot, this is a fundamental logistics problem.

**08** Prevented from going back the way they came, and continually harried by English ships, the Spanish must sail northwest around Scotland and Ireland (a route for which they have no charts) facing autumn gales in the North Atlantic. Casualties are enormous: 70 ships and up to 20,000 men are lost. Only 60 ships reach Spain, many beyond repair.

**09** England lose far fewer men in battle, but up to 7,000 die from dysentery and typhus during and after the brief campaign.

---

**02.1588**
When Spain's most senior admiral dies the Duke of Medina Sidonia is made head of the Armada—despite his own strenuous protests.

**05.1588**
The Armada leaves Cádiz but is soon beset by gales, failing to reach its rendezvous with the Duke of Parma's forces in Flanders until August 6.

**08.06.1588**
Medina Sidonia reaches the Strait of Dover as planned but the army of the Duke of Parma is still preparing, so the Armada sets anchor off Calais and waits.

**08.08.1588**
After a decisive engagement led by Howard's second-in-charge, Sir Francis Drake, off the French port of Gravelines, the Armada flees north.

**1588**
Philip II abandons further plans for an English invasion, focusing instead on the burgeoning rebellion in the Low Countries.

# THE AGE OF
# **SUBTERFUGE**
## 1605–1815

If you lacked a talent for subterfuge, you were not going to get far in seventeenth-century Europe. If, on the other hand, you had a gift for plotting, secrecy, and undermining rivals, your star was likely to burn bright—at least for a while.

The most famous plot of the time was that to blow up the British king. These days we remember only one of the 13 Gunpowder Plotters: Guy Fawkes. But the whole story of Fawkes and his accomplices is dramatic and lurid, featuring desperate horseback rides, accidental self-sabotage and the hideous "traitor's death": hung, drawn, and quartered.

This was a time when monarchs were locked in power-struggles with their parliaments. Palace corridors were full of whispered secrets, blackmail, and bribery, and so, it seemed, was the rest of the country. As England descended into Civil War, Parliamentary Army Commander Sir William Brereton was said to have "spies under every hedge."

Where there is subterfuge, there will be disguise. Charles II, on the run for his life, dressed up as a woodsman and a servant. Bonnie Prince Charlie, the "Young Pretender" to the throne, surely had his great-uncle's experiences in mind a century later when he made his own escape disguised as a servant girl.

Thomas Blood had dark deeds, not escape, in mind when he went in disguise to befriend the Keeper of the Crown Jewels. He was caught red-handed stealing the treasure, yet far from punishing Blood, Charles II, restored to the throne, rewarded him, fueling rumors of suspicious deeds and royal secrets.

There was plenty of intrigue in the New World, too. The feared Captain Henry Morgan assembled a huge group of pirates to sack Panama, only to see his victory go up in smoke. And eighteenth-century British military leader Edward Braddock scandalized the American colonists he had been sent to protect as he made no secret of his disdainful, superior attitude toward them; an attitude that saw him lead his troops to slaughter.

In time, America seized independence, but even then the British were not prepared to stay away. In 1814 they marched into Washington and burned much of it—President James Madison fled in such a hurry, he left behind a White House banquet for the Redcoats to enjoy. That certainly kept the gossips busy.

Undoubtedly, though, the man who sparked the most speculation, admiration, condemnation, and gossip in the Age of Subterfuge was Napoleon Bonaparte. This brilliant, egotistical, unpredictable character influenced much of Europe before meeting his match at Waterloo.

Napoleon's lifespan roughly coincided with the Industrial Revolution: a time of immense change that saw the rise of cities and the development of manufacturing and mass transport. One thing that did not change, and still has not, was the love of a good secret. Then, as now, everyone wanted to know not just the official version but the real story that lay behind it.

# THE GUNPOWDER PLOT

DATE      November 5, 1605
LOCATION   London, England
OBJECTIVE To assassinate King James I and return England to Catholicism

**Devout Robert Catesby was of the second generation to suffer for his religion. Unlike many other English Catholics, he was not optimistic things would change when James I became king. After two stints in prison, Catesby's bitterness had turned murderous. He patiently recruited a group of coconspirators then set the stage for regicide.**

### Ready to Act

Just two months into James's reign, Catesby was scheming to eliminate both parliament and the monarch. Twelve months later, he began to assemble his team: fellow disenfranchised, angry Catholics.

His first recruits were Thomas Winter, John (Jack) and Christopher (Kit) Wright, Thomas Percy, and Guido (Guy) Fawkes. Percy came from an influential family; Fawkes, who had been fighting for the Spanish army, was sought for his explosives expertise.

### The Conspiracy Builds

The aim was to set off a massive explosion during the State Opening of Parliament, killing the king, his queen, their two sons, the entire government, and many prominent observers. Princess Elizabeth, nine years old, would be taken from her Midlands convent and installed as a puppet ruler, and the country would be converted back to Catholicism.

Percy rented a house close to Westminster in London, allowing the plotters to tunnel under the Houses of Parliament, and Fawkes moved in as caretaker "John Johnson." Over the coming months, the group expanded to 13, which included well-connected Francis Tresham. But fears about plague delayed the opening of Parliament. The plotters revised their plans, leasing a cellar that lay under the House of Lords and, over a period of months, secreted 36 barrels of gunpowder there.

### A Spectacular Unraveling

After so long, they were just days away from the rescheduled November 5 opening when, on October 26, Catholic sympathizer Lord Monteagle received an anonymous letter warning him off the ceremony. Monteagle alerted officials, who decided to wait before pouncing. One of Monteagle's servants warned the plotters, but they decided to proceed regardless.

On the eve of the opening, Catesby and two others set off for the Midlands, leaving Fawkes in the cellar (he was to light the fuse, then escape via the Thames River) where, around midnight, he was arrested. The remaining plotters fled London. Fawkes withstood three days of interrogation and torture before admitting the plot. In the meantime, seven conspirators, including Catesby, raided Warwick Castle, stole horses, and holed up in Holbeche House, Staffordshire. Here, after a brief standoff, Catesby, Percy, and the Wrights were killed, and four others captured. The remaining plotters were soon arrested. Tresham died before the trials could begin in late January. The others were found guilty of high treason and received the hideous "traitor's death": half-hanged, drawn (disemboweled), and then quartered.

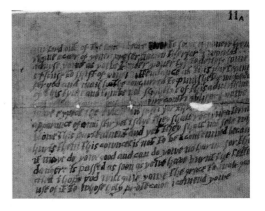

ABOVE: The anonymous letter written to Lord Monteagle, warning him to stay away from Parliament, which "shall receive a terrible blow."

ABOVE RIGHT: The arrest of Guy Fawkes in cellars of Parliament, depicted in a nineteenth-century wood engraving. The British still mark the events of the Gunpowder Plot with Guy Fawkes Day—each November 5 there is a ceremonial search of the Parliament building and, throughout Britain, fireworks and bonfires on which effigies are burned. The traditional accompanying children's rhyme is: Remember, remember, the fifth of November / Gunpowder treason and plot / We see no reason / Why gunpowder treason / Should ever be forgot …

## TIMELINE

| 02.25.1570 | 03.24.1603 |
|---|---|
| Pope Pius V declares England's Queen Elizabeth "the servant of crime" and promises excommunication for Catholics who obey her. | With Elizabeth's death, James VI of Scotland I becomes King James I of England, giving hope to English Catholics—after all their new queen, Anne, is Catholic. |

## STEP-BY-STEP

**01** After 18 months of planning, just days from completion, the Gunpowder Plot is exposed in an anonymous letter sent to Francis Tresham's brother-in-law, Lord Monteagle, warning of "a terrible blow" to Parliament.

**02** One of Monteagle's servants sends warning to the plotters, but they put out their own feelers and decide their secret is still safe.

**03** Having deliberately waited until the night before the ceremony, officials raid the cellars and arrest caretaker "John Johnson" (Guy Fawkes). Bonfires of thanksgiving for the king's salvation are lit across London. They continue to be lit on November 5 across Britain to this day.

**04** The other plotters head to the Midlands where they hope to start an uprising. With their names now known, the hunt for them is on, and they are soon tracked down.

**05** Barricading themselves in Holbeche House, they decide to dry their wet gunpowder by laying it out in front of the fire. The resulting explosion blinds conspirator John Grant.

**06** The Sherriff's 200 men make short work of seizing the plotters.

**07** Less than 12 weeks after Fawkes's arrest, all 13 plotters are dead, the heads of eight displayed, and a harsh two-century crackdown on England's Catholics begins. Catholics would not receive the vote again until 1829.

---

**05.1603**
Catholic Robert Catesby, who has been jailed for religion-driven actions and has forfeited a university degree because he would not swear the Protestant Oath of Supremacy, begins to plot the king's overthrow.

**02.1604**
James I declares his "utter detestation" of Catholicism. Three months later, at London's Duck and Drake Inn, the conspirators meet and begin to plan the assassination in detail.

**11.05.1606**
In a search, the gunpowder set for use at the next day's parliamentary opening is discovered in the cellars of the House of Lords, and Fawkes is arrested at the scene.

**11.08.1606**
All but five of the 13 plotters are killed or captured. In December, Robert Winter, the last of the fugitives, is caught.

**1621**
Having served 16 years of the life sentence imposed because of his cousin Thomas's actions, Henry Percy is released from the Tower of London.

# THE ASSASSINATION OF THE DUKE OF BUCKINGHAM

DATE · August 23, 1628
LOCATION · Portsmouth, Hampshire, England
OBJECTIVE · To kill a prominent royal adviser detested by his countrymen

His good looks and charm quickly made George Villiers a firm favorite of both King James I and his son King Charles I, with the wealth, titles, and power to prove it. But so naked was his self-interest, and so numerous his political and military missteps, that his violent murder was celebrated throughout England.

## A Meteoric Rise

George Villiers worked hard pleasing the king and, almost from the start, James I rewarded him lavishly. By 1617, he had been named Earl of Buckingham and appointed to the powerful Privy Council.

Exercising his power, Buckingham (as he was known) made enemies of senior courtiers. The year 1623 seemed to put him beyond their reach, as he was named Duke of Buckingham; in reality it was the beginning of his downfall.

## Hostility Grows

Early in his reign, James had made peace with England's old enemy Spain, and now he hoped to bind the nations together via the marriage of his son Charles to the Spanish *infanta* (princess) Maria Anna. The English Parliament—already resistant to high royal taxes and angered by corruption—opposed the plan, so James dissolved Parliament.

Buckingham and Charles then unexpectedly went to Spain, but instead of negotiating successfully they alienated the Spanish and returned advocating war (despite the wishes of the ailing James). Buckingham then arranged for Charles to marry French princess Henrietta Maria, which he did two months after he had succeeded to the throne in March 1625. To the fury of Buckingham's rivals, Charles proved just as dependent on him as his father.

## One Enemy Too Many

The new parliament initially supported Buckingham's plans for war on Spain, but grew concerned about the money he demanded. Their growing hostility was cemented by a disastrous, expensive, and shambolic attack Buckingham and Charles oversaw on Cádiz, Spain. Under new leader Sir John Eliot, the House of Commons moved to impeach Buckingham. Charles sent Eliot to the Tower of London for this but was forced by Parliament to release him. Stubbornly sticking to his course, and with Charles's support, Buckingham led an English army against the French at La Rochelle—another debacle, with huge casualties.

Parliament petitioned Charles about their many concerns, but he took no action—and for this they blamed Buckingham: on June 5, 1628, Sir Edward Coke described him as "the cause of all our miseries." Still undeterred, Buckingham went to Portsmouth to prepare another military expedition to La Rochelle in France. John Felton had served in the navy during the Cádiz attack and felt Buckingham had much to answer for. Convinced it was his patriotic duty to kill him, he sought Buckingham out at Portsmouth's Greyhound Inn and stabbed him to death.

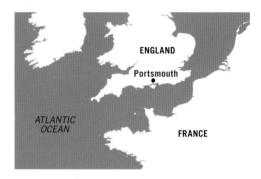

ENGLAND

Portsmouth

ATLANTIC
OCEAN

FRANCE

ABOVE: Charles I ordered Buckingham be buried in a chapel in Westminster Abbey that had previously been reserved for royalty, but kept ceremony to a minimum to avoid backlash.

RIGHT: George Villiers, Duke of Buckingham, meeting his end at the Greyhound Inn.

## TIMELINE

**08.1614**
Almost 22, George Villiers is introduced to King James I, 48.

**08.1616**
Having already been knighted, given an estate, and made Earl of Buckingham, Villiers now gains the title Viscount and lands worth £30,000 (more than £100 million today).

## STEP-BY-STEP

**01** As a son of a twice-married knight, George Villiers is raised with courtly manners but very little money. Considered exceptionally handsome, he catches the eye of King James I.

**02** Enemies of previous royal favorite Robert Carr arrange for James's wife, Queen Anne, to recommend Villiers as Gentleman of the Bedchamber. He is soon indispensable to the king and they seemingly become intimates in every sense.

**03** Increasingly powerful, Villiers is made Duke of Buckingham. But parliamentary mistrust of him is growing, adding to the animosity of senior royal advisers.

**04** Seeing off the internal threats, Buckingham and Charles I push England into costly failed wars with Spain and then France.

**05** The English parliament presents the Petition of Rights to King Charles, expressing concern at decisions made by Charles and Buckingham.

**06** By now Buckingham is widely loathed throughout England.

**07** Deciding he must kill Buckingham, John Felton writes a declaration of intent, which he sews into his hat. Seeing no alternative but murder, Felton seeks out his target in Portsmouth and fatally stabs him.

**08** Felton is executed for the murder on November 29, but his crime has sparked celebration throughout England and crowds gather at his prison asking God to bless him.

**05.1623**

Despite appalling economic conditions in England, James makes Villiers a duke (the highest British noble title), the first time in a century the honor goes to a commoner.

**03.27.1625**

On James I's death, his son takes the throne as Charles I. In November, Charles and Buckingham spend £250,000 of public money on a disastrous raid on Cádiz, Spain.

**10.30.1627**

In another military disaster, Buckingham brings back fewer than half the 6,800 soldiers he led to France to free besieged Protestants at La Rochelle.

**06.05.1628**

Charles continues to protect Buckingham, while barrister and parliamentarian Sir Edward Coke writes of him, "all our disasters … reflect upon him."

**08.23.1628**

Disgruntled naval lieutenant John Felton attacks and kills Buckingham in an inn in Portsmouth.

# THE CAPTURE OF BEESTON CASTLE

DATE   1643–1645
LOCATION   Beeston, Cheshire, England
OBJECTIVE   To seize control of a strategically located stronghold

**With its 6-feet (2-m) thick outer bailey (or wall) punctuated by D-shaped towers, its deep defensive ditch, solid inner bailey, imposing gatehouses, and bird's-eye view of up to eight counties on a clear day, Beeston Castle must have promoted feelings of invulnerability. But ultimately it proved susceptible to siege during the English Civil War.**

### The Castle on the Rock

During the war, the opposing sides took over and refortified a number of abandoned castles, including neglected Beeston, known as the Castle on the Rock. In February 1643, when the Parliamentarians established a garrison of 200–300 men there, under Cheshire commander Sir William Brereton, the first job was to mend gaps in the walls and clean the wells. Brereton was famed for his intelligence network; it was said he had "spies under every hedge and friends in every village" and the garrison was untroubled for ten months until, with Brereton occupied elsewhere and Captain Thomas Steele in command, it fell to a mere handful of Royalist soldiers.

### A Daring Raid

Captain Thomas Sandford was part of the Royalist Irish army, which had arrived in Cheshire in late 1643. Leading a company of just eight men, with a small number left at the castle gate, he launched a daring commando-style raid on the castle on the night of December 13, first scaling the sheer rock face then climbing the castle walls. When Sandford and his men made their presence known, Steele thought they were part of a far larger force and ordered his men to surrender (he was subsequently executed for cowardice). From their new base, the Royalists gained more ground, seizing nearby Parliamentary garrisons.

### Fighting Back

By November 1644, the Parliamentarians had renewed their efforts in Cheshire, besieging the capital, Chester. They also besieged Beeston Castle. The Royalists put up a spirited defense, killing more than two dozen of their opponents in a single raid, but the Parliamentarian forces constructed siege works to prevent such attacks. The struggle continued throughout the following year, with the Royalists destroying the Parliamentary fortifications and the Parliamentarians rebuilding them. Twice Royalist field armies managed to break through in an attempt to relieve the siege, but both times the blockade was reestablished.

Seven weeks after their king's defeat at Rowton Heath, the starving Royalists surrendered. Toward the end, they had been forced to eat the castle's cats, and the Parliamentarian soldiers who took the castle reported that the only supplies left were one piece of turkey pie, two biscuits, and a live peacock and peahen.

## TIMELINE

**08.22.1642**
Decades of tension between the Parliament and Charles I erupt into the first English Civil War.

**02.20.1643**
Parliamentary forces seize Beeston Castle and establish a small garrison.

ABOVE: A contemporary photograph of Beeston Castle in Cheshire.
ABOVE RIGHT: Portrait of Sir William Brereton.
BELOW: Engraving of Beeston Castle by Buck Brothers, 1727.

## STEP-BY-STEP

**01** Led by Sir William Brereton, Parliamentarian forces repair Beeston Castle defenses and establish a garrison.

**02** With Brereton campaigning elsewhere in Cheshire, the garrison is under the command of Captain Thomas Steele.

**03** A small raiding party from an Irish "Firelock" company, named for the new style of flintlock muskets they carry, makes a bold surprise attack on the castle.

**04** Mistakenly believing he is outnumbered, Steele surrenders; he and his men are allowed to leave the following day. He is later tried and executed for his actions.

**05** The Royalists hold the castle for almost a year, until the Parliamentarians launch a concerted effort to recapture it.

**06** Initially the besieged Royalists are able to fight back, destroying siege machinery, launching raids, and welcoming reinforcements, but gradually they are starved into submission.

**07** The castle is "slighted," that is, its defenses are demolished, on order of Parliament, to prevent it being used against them in the future.

| 12.13.1643 | 11.1644 | 12.7.1644 | 09.24.1645 | 11.15.1645 |
|---|---|---|---|---|
| Royalist Captain Thomas Sandford and eight men break into the castle, secure its surrender, and establish their own garrison. | Parliamentarians begin a blockade of the castle. | Royalists from the castle attack a nearby Parliamentarian billet, killing 26 soldiers. | Charles I is defeated in battle at nearby Rowton Heath. | Having held out for a year, the starving Royalists surrender. |

# THE ESCAPE OF CHARLES II

DATE        September 3–October 16, 1651
LOCATION    Worcester, Worcestershire, to Shoreham, West Sussex, England
OBJECTIVE   To keep the king safe from the Parliamentarians hunting him

The six weeks that 21-year-old Charles II spent on the run with a price on his head is sometimes treated as little more than a footnote in his story. But the experiences he had moving for the first time among common people changed him as a man and subsequently as a king.

### Sudden Flight

Charles's escape sounds like a boys' own adventure, but at stake was his freedom and most likely his life. From the top of Worcester Cathedral, he had watched the defeat of his forces by the Parliamentarians' New Model Army led by Oliver Cromwell. With their opponents in hot pursuit, the king and his retinue raced into the city itself. He had his first narrow escape fleeing out of their lodgings' back door as Cromwell's men burst in at the front.

On horseback, Charles and his supporters headed north, where Royalist support was stronger, as was Catholicism. The Catholics might have seemed odd allies given that Charles was Protestant and had accepted the Scottish anti-Catholic, anti-Protestant Presbyterian Covenant in order to be crowned king of Scotland (and putatively Ireland, England, and France), but they shared a common enemy in Cromwell and the Parliamentarians.

### Traveling Incognito

Early the next morning, the fugitives arrived at the Boscobel Estate in Shropshire. Here Charles met the five Catholic Penderel brothers, who vowed to help him. His long hair was cut and he was given old clothes to disguise himself as a woodsman. At 6 feet (1.8 m), he stood 6 inches (15 cm) above most men of the day, and no shoes could be found to fit him, but a pair was cut in such a way he could jam them on.

In the following days, Charles encountered a miller aroused to suspicion by the king's smooth hands and spent a day hiding in an oak tree with a supporter while Parliamentarian soldiers scoured the woods below.

### Close Shaves

Over the coming weeks, Charles slept in barns and priestholes, as well as inns and the houses of sympathizers. He witnessed villagers celebrating news of his death. He traveled in a group pretending to be an eloping wedding party. His identity was nearly revealed more than once.

At Broadwindsor, his party was hidden in the loft by a Royalist innkeeper when a constable and 40 Parliamentary soldiers arrived seeking billet. Only the distraction caused when a woman traveling with the troops went into labor allowed Charles to slip away.

Finally, after a number of frustrated attempts, the "precious cargo" made it aboard the ship *Surprise* at Shoreham in Sussex on October 15 and the next morning the king landed in France, and was reunited with his mother, entering almost nine years of exile.

ABOVE: Engraving of Charles II in disguise with Jane Lane, whose resourcefulness and cool head helped him travel from the Midlands to Dorset.

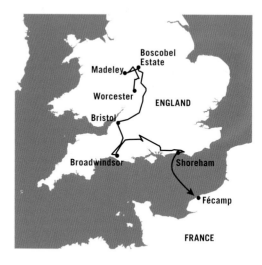

## TIMELINE

| 08.22.1642 | 01.30.1649 |
| --- | --- |
| The English Civil War breaks out, dividing the country between Royalist supporters and the Parliamentarian faction. | Declared a traitor by the English parliament, King Charles I is executed. |

## STEP-BY-STEP

**01** The defeat of Charles II and his largely Scottish army by the Parliamentarians' New Model Army at Worcester effectively ends the Third English Civil War.

**02** Charles flees for his life as the victors declare him an enemy of the people and put a £1,000 price on his head.

**03** Taking help where he can find it—among Catholic families and Royalists—Charles disguises himself as a commoner.

**04** Charles and supporter Colonel Carlis spend all day hiding in an oak tree near Boscobel.

**05** With New Model Army soldiers searching for him all over England, Charles is in constant danger. He needs to travel to the south coast to get to France.

**06** Catholics may travel no more than 5 miles (8 km) from home without a special permit. Sympathizer Jane Lane has such a permit for herself and a manservant to travel from Bentley, West Midlands, to Bristol. Charles poses as her servant.

**07** After several failed attempts to get Charles aboard a ship, he finally reaches Shoreham in Sussex, and gets to France on the *Surprise*.

RIGHT: *King Charles II at Whiteladies (King Charles II; Richard Penderel)*, by Isaac Fuller, depicts Richard Penderel assisting Charles II to transform into a woodsman.

---

**01.01.1651**
After being offered its throne, Charles I's namesake son travels to Scotland and is crowned Charles II, King of Scotland, England, Ireland, and France.

**09.03.1651**
England's Parliament has declared Charles II their enemy and put Oliver Cromwell in charge of their New Model Army, which routs the Scottish army in the Battle of Worcester.

**10.16.1651**
Having spent six weeks as a fugitive with a £1,000 bounty on his head (70 years' wages for a musketeer), Charles II finally sails safely to France.

**05.23.1660**
With English public opinion again favoring monarchy, Charles returns from his French exile on his 30th birthday.

**02.06.1685**
Having overseen "the Restoration" of the monarchy, Charles II dies after receiving the Last Rites from Catholic priest Father John Huddleston, who had helped shelter him when he was on the run.

# CAPTAIN MORGAN'S RAID ON PANAMA

DATE        January 28, 1671
LOCATION    The city of Panama, Panama
OBJECTIVE   To loot and pillage the city's enormous wealth

The Welsh privateer Henry Morgan was the leading buccaneer of his day, already feared throughout the Caribbean—and wealthy from previous raids on Spanish bases at Portobello, Panama, and Maracaibo, Venezuela—when he set out on his most audacious expedition, leading a huge group of pirates to raid the Spanish riches in the city of Panama.

### A Tempting Target

The city of Panama as a target had two major drawbacks—it was on the other side of the isthmus that separated the Caribbean from the Pacific, and it was unfamiliar territory for the pirates. Outweighing this was its status as one of the wealthiest cities on the Spanish Main, used as a central point to move gold and silver around Spain's global empire.

### Pitched Battle and Shipwreck

Morgan sent three ships with 470 men to establish a beachhead at Chagres. The town, at the mouth of the river of the same name, was protected by the elevated fort of San Lorenzo, meaning attack by water would have been suicidal. Instead, the pirates canoed and then hiked through the jungle to the fort's rear.

The battle was fierce and unrelenting. The Spanish garrison fought to the death for two days, only being overcome when the pirates managed to send fire bombs inside the huge stone wall that set alight the fort's wooden buildings. But pirate celebrations turned to shock when, as Morgan and the rest of the fleet sailed in, his flagship *Satisfaction* and four others were wrecked on Lajas Reef, where the water is as shallow as 12 inches (0.3 m).

### Seizing the City

Undaunted, Morgan left 300 men to guard the ships. The rest, in a flotilla of 36 canoes and seven boats, headed up the Chagres River, which bisects the isthmus. The Spaniards had set up a series of planned ambushes, but their men were so afraid of Morgan—"*el Diablo*" (the Devil)—that they fled rather than fight him. After ten days, the last part on foot, 1,300 pirates reached the plains outside the city of Panama. Here they were met by nearly 4,000 defenders. Although outnumbered, the pirates won easily in just a few hours. A Spanish plan to stampede 2,000 cattle and oxen toward the enemy proved a dismal failure.

The city was Morgan's, but the Spaniards had planted gunpowder in several strategic buildings; as the pirates entered the fuses were lit. The explosion was audible miles away and pirates fought in vain to stop the city going up in flames. Once the ruins could be searched, the haul of booty (mainly silver and gold) proved disappointing—although it still required 175 mules to finally cart it all out.

S.ʳ HEN: MORGAN

## TIMELINE

**1654**

Henry Morgan arrives in the Caribbean. Within 15 years, based in Jamaica, he has become England's most successful privateer on the Spanish Main.

**12.02.1670**

With a huge international fleet of 36 ships gathered at Isla Vaca off Haiti, Morgan and the most senior captains meet to decide their target.

The Battel Between the Spaniards and the pyrats or Buccaniers before the city of PANAMA.

ABOVE: Henry Morgan and pirates sacking Panama. Legend long held that the ornate altar of the Church of San José in Panama was one of the few treasures to have survived the sacking of the city, after a priest disguised its gold with tar, however historians now date the altar to after Morgan's time.

LEFT: An engraving of Sir Henry Morgan from *The Buccaneers of America*, 1684. While he was officially reprimanded for the raid on Panama by England at a time when the nation was trying to accommodate Spain, two years later Morgan was knighted and returned to the Caribbean as Governor of Jamaica.

## STEP-BY-STEP

**01** Newly commissioned by England to recruit privateers, seize enemy ships, and attack Spanish-controlled cities, Captain Morgan sends out a call for pirates.

**02** He waits patiently at Isla Vaca (now Île à Vache) off Haiti as the world's largest buccaneer fleet gathers.

**03** Morgan and senior captains consider, but reject, attacking Santiago de Cuba and Cartagena before agreeing on the city of Panama.

**04** Having captured San Lorenzo, the pirates' river flotilla sets off up the Chagres River, but after seven days must struggle the rest of the way through the jungle on foot.

**05** On marching into Panama, the pirates find themselves trying to stop the conflagration started by departing defenders.

**06** After nearly a month, the pirates leave, taking 600 prisoners back to San Lorenzo where they are ransomed.

**07** Early sources claimed Morgan deserted his men, taking most of the booty, but there is no evidence of this. Rather, he disbands the fleet once the pirates reach San Lorenzo.

---

**12.08.1670**
A raiding party sails to Old Providence Island off the Mosquito Coast to seize Spanish guides for the unfamiliar territory of Panama.

**12.28.1670**
The fort of San Lorenzo, on the Chagres River, falls. Although the battle costs the pirates dozens of men, the Spaniards lose almost 300.

**01.18.1671**
Morgan and his men begin the arduous trip up the Chagres River.

**01.28.1671**
Morgan takes Panama after defeating its defenders; however, the routed army sets fire to the city, having removed much of the booty to safety in Ecuador.

**02.24.1671**
After a month spent sifting through ashes, hunting for secreted treasure, and torturing Panamanians to reveal where it is hidden, Morgan's men depart the razed city.

# THE THEFT OF THE CROWN JEWELS

DATE      May 9, 1671
LOCATION  The Tower of London, London, England
OBJECTIVE To steal the precious royal regalia

The Anglo-Irish Thomas Blood was an extraordinary character, time and again leading criminal conspiracies for which he escaped the consequences while his accomplices were punished—in some cases paying with their lives. His decision to steal England's Crown Jewels should have led to execution if he were caught. Intriguingly, it did not.

### The Setup

What we call the Crown Jewels, British royalty knows as the Regalia: scepters, orbs, swords, crowns, and other ceremonial trappings. In 1671, they were all new. Only a twelfth-century anointing spoon and three coronation swords survived the destruction ordered by Oliver Cromwell after King Charles I was executed. The rest was melted down and the gems sold. When the monarchy was restored in 1660, Charles II ordered new Regalia. Colonel Thomas Blood decided to make it his.

Blood was bold but not impulsive—his theft was carefully planned. Disguising himself as a parson, he and a female accomplice began visiting Martin Tower within the Tower of London, where the Crown Jewels were watched over by Talbot Edwards, Keeper of the Jewels. He won Edwards's trust to such a degree that they began discussing a marriage between the Keeper's daughter and Blood's (fictitious) nephew.

### The Heist

On the day of the robbery, Blood brought his son Holcroft and friend Robert Perot with him and asked Edwards to show them the Crown Jewels. After the Keeper let them in, they knocked him out with a mallet and bound him. Blood used the mallet to bash the St. Edward's Crown flat so that he could hide it in his clothes. The other two busied themselves sawing the royal Scepter in half and hiding the Sovereign's Orb. When Edwards stirred, they stabbed him. They were making their escape when Edwards managed to call out "Treason! Treason!" to alert guards who then captured the thieves.

### A Strange Aftermath

Blood was imprisoned in the Tower of London, but far from showing repentance for an act punishable by death, he refused to speak to anyone other than the king. To some surprise, Charles II not only agreed to see Blood, but he pardoned him, restored the valuable Irish estates Blood had been granted by Cromwell but lost at the Restoration, and gave him an annual £500 pension. Charles II had forgiven various rogues (notably, repeatedly, the volatile 2nd Duke of Buckingham), but still this seemed odd. However, the evidence suggests that Blood was never the Republican he seemed, but was instead a double agent, meaning he knew both figuratively and literally where the bodies were buried, in which case Charles made a wise investment.

ABOVE: Engraved portrait of Thomas Blood, 1813. George Villiers, the 2nd Duke of Buckingham, was believed to have been Blood's secret paymaster, at least in some of his enterprises, but near the end of Blood's life they fell out spectacularly enough for Buckingham to take legal action against the Irishman. However, Blood died of natural causes before the case could be settled.

## TIMELINE

**1648**

Thomas Blood, after fighting for the Royalists, marries Mary Holcroft in England and soon afterward goes home to Ireland as an officer in Cromwell's New Model Army.

**1660**

When the monarchy is restored in England, Blood loses the considerable landholdings he was given for his services to the Parliamentarians.

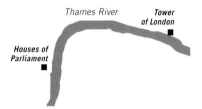

**LONDON**

*Thames River*

**Tower of London**

**Houses of Parliament**

## STEP-BY-STEP

**01** With virtually all the royal Regalia, known as the Crown Jewels, destroyed, Charles II commissions recreations and new pieces at the cost of £13,000.

**02** Thomas Blood concocts a plan to steal the Crown Jewels and recruits accomplices.

**03** Disguised as a parson and accompanied by a woman, Blood begins visiting Talbot Edwards, Keeper of the Jewels, winning his friendship and trust.

**04** Blood takes his son, and a friend— more accomplices to his crime—to see Edwards under pretext of showing them the Jewels.

**05** The three attack and subdue Edwards, then flatten and cut the Jewels to fit inside their clothes.

**06** They begin to make their escape, but Edwards's cries alert guards who catch and arrest them.

**07** Charles II agrees to an audience with Blood, pardons his treasonable capital crime, and grants him land and wealth. His accomplices also thrive, with his son, Holcroft Blood, rising to Brigadier General in the army.

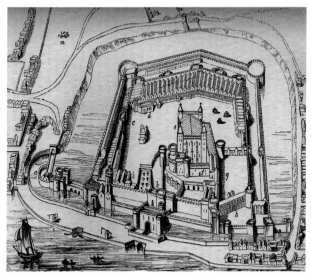

ABOVE: An illustration from *The Illustrated London News* depicting Blood's attempt of "royal" larceny.

LEFT: A plan of the heavily fortified Tower of London depicted after a survey in 1597.

| 1663 | 1667 | 1670 | 05.09.1671 | 1680 |
|---|---|---|---|---|
| Deeply bitter at his loss, Blood leads a kidnapping attempt on the Lord Lieutenant of Ireland, the Duke of Ormonde. His accomplices are arrested but Blood, a wanted man, escapes to the Netherlands. | Back in England, Blood attempts to rescue a friend who is under government guard, killing several troopers. Again, a price is on his head: £500. | Blood again attempts to abduct— and hang—the Duke of Ormonde. Ormonde's son publicly accuses Charles II's on-off confidant the 2nd Duke of Buckingham of being behind the attack. | Blood leads a failed attempt to steal the Crown Jewels from the Tower of London. Blood is pardoned and walks away a free man. | Blood dies peacefully at home but, such is his reputation for cunning tricks, his body is exhumed to make sure it is really his. |

# THE ESCAPE OF BONNIE PRINCE CHARLIE

DATE        April 16–September 20, 1746
LOCATION    The Western Highlands and Outer Hebrides, Scotland
OBJECTIVE   To avoid capture by the British army

In 1745, Charles Edward Stuart—the Catholic "Young Pretender" to Great Britain's rulers; "Bonnie Prince Charlie" to his supporters—landed in Scotland determined to lead a Jacobite rebellion and restore his family to the throne and to depose the Hanoverian ruler George II. It began well, but after losing decisively at the Battle of Culloden he was a wanted man, on the run for his life.

### The Odyssey Begins

By April 25, Charles and four supporters, including Irish officers Felix O'Neil and John O'Sullivan, had made it safely across to the southwestern shore of the mainland. From here, they performed the Herculean task of rowing 70 miles (113 km) through a raging storm to the tiny Outer Hebridean island of Benbecula—this was land controlled by the Macdonalds of Clanranald, a clan that had been among Charles's earliest Scottish rebels. Waiting for them here was Neil MacEachan Macdonald, a man with vital local knowledge that the fugitives lacked.

### Flora Macdonald and "Betty Burke"

The Macdonalds had hatched a plan to spirit Charles to safety from under the nose of the Redcoats who were scouring the country for him; the plan centered on Neil's 24-year-old cousin Flora Macdonald. They waited until sunset, then hiked to her cottage where they told her the plan: her stepfather had arranged a travel permit for Flora and her servant to go to the mainland, with six men to row them. Prince Charles was to be disguised as the servant. Flora, wrote Neil Macdonald, "joyfully accepted" and provided the prince with the clothes that transformed him into Irish serving girl "Betty Burke."

The following evening they rowed to the Isle of Skye (the trip is commemorated in the "Skye Boat Song"). Local militia were searching for the prince, but despite the locals' disgust at "Betty's" unladylike demeanor, he was undetected. As arranged, Flora said good-bye here.

### Midges, Mountains, and Caves

An arduous hike across Skye, one night of which was spent in a cave, set the tone for the following months, during which the prince and his companions made it back to the mainland and kept moving through the harsh highland landscape. In one five-night period alone they crossed 50 miles (80 km) of valleys and mountains, taking in 20,000 feet (6,096 m) of climbing. They were hungry and tormented by midges, they often slept rough or in caves, and frequently had the British Redcoats within sight. At last Charles received word that two French frigates awaited him near the village of Arisaig: his ordeal was over.

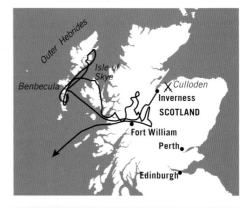

ABOVE: A contemporary painting of Flora Macdonald.

ABOVE RIGHT: Colored engraving of Charles in his "Betty Burke" garb, 1885.

RIGHT: Prince Charles meeting with Flora Macdonald on the island of Benbecula. The memorial to Flora Macdonald at Kilmuir says, in part, hers is "a name that will be mentioned in history, and if courage and fidelity be virtues, mentioned with honour." Charles died an alcoholic, in the room in Rome in which he was born.

## TIMELINE

| 07.05.1745 | 09.17.1745 |
| --- | --- |
| Intent on leading a Jacobite rebellion, Charles Stuart and seven supporters leave France in two ships, landing on the Isle of Eriskay on July 23. | Having raised an army—though smaller than hoped—Charles seizes Edinburgh (though not the castle) and declares his father, James Edward Stuart, King. |

## STEP-BY-STEP

**01** Great Britain's Hanoverian King George II put a £30,000 reward on "the Bonnie Prince" shortly after his arrival in Scotland. But then he was protected by an army; after the defeat at Culloden, he is on the run with just a few loyal supporters.

**02** Charles and his companions make it to Benbecula, where he is aided by the Jacobite Macdonalds.

**03** Flora Macdonald readily agrees to dress Charles in women's clothes and travel with him disguised as her servant "Betty Burke."

**04** They are rowed to the Isle of Skye where locals who see "Betty" on the road comment on the unladylike way "she" walks and hitches her skirts.

**05** Before they part, Charles gives Flora a locket containing his portrait and promises they will meet again—they do not.

**06** Two weeks later, Flora Macdonald is arrested and spends a year in prison for helping the fugitive.

**07** Charles spends the following months amid Scotland's harsh western highlands, narrowly evading British troops.

**08** Finally, the French succeed in getting rescue vessels through. Charles makes it to the rendezvous and is taken back to France.

**11.15.1745**
Despite dissent among his war council about the wisdom of going south, Charles does, and Carlisle surrenders to him.

**12.04.1745**
Charles and his troops reach Derby, just 130 miles (209 km) from London. Triumph turns to ashes when his generals decide, lacking reinforcements, that they must retreat.

**01.17.1746**
Back in Scotland, the Jacobites have their last victory in battle at Falkirk.

**04.16.1746**
Charles agrees to fight the Hanoverians on the exposed moor at Culloden. The Jacobites are severely routed in the last land battle fought on British soil.

**09.20.1746**
After five months as a fugitive in the wilderness, Charles leaves Scotland forever. He lives in exile in France, then joins his family in Rome.

# THE BATTLE OF MONONGAHELA RIVER

DATE      July 9, 1755
LOCATION  Near Fort Duquesne, Province of Pennsylvania, English North America
OBJECTIVE British colonial forces aim to seize Fort Duquesne from the French

**Amid escalating conflict between Great Britain and France over their American holdings, Major General Edward Braddock was sent to the British colonies to seize the strategically placed Fort Duquesne from the French. With his greater numbers and "superior" military conventions, Braddock, almost as disdainful of the colonists as he was the Natives, thought he could not lose.**

### A Dangerous Hubris

From the start, Braddock was dismissive of the Natives and their fighting methods despite their effectiveness in attacking (with French encouragement) British colonists, whom he disdained. He ignored advice from junior officers including George Washington and colonial leaders such as Benjamin Franklin. The colonists became reluctant to join his campaign and, while Native knowledge and intelligence was vital, the few Natives who served him did so reluctantly.

### The Agonizing March

Braddock's goal was just 110 miles (177 km) away. But the route was a mountainous, heavily forested wilderness with no roads (river flow direction ruled out traveling by water). Accompanying the 2,150 troops were 2,500 riding horses, 600 pack horses, 300 wagons, and 12 field guns. After an advance party of 600 troops took two days to travel 5 miles (8 km), road-building as they went, Braddock returned some equipment to Fort Cumberland. Even so, just 25 more miles (40 km) were covered in the following nine days. Even after Braddock split his troops into a "flying" column and the slower supply column, the lead "flying" column still averaged only 3 miles (5 km) a day, battling dysentery, fevers, exhaustion, and the landscape.

### Battle Slaughter

By noon on July 9, after six long weeks, the 1,450-strong first column crossed the Monongahela River and came within sight of Fort Duquesne, 10 miles (16 km) away with flags flying and drums beating. The French sent out a party under Captain Daniel-Hyacinthe Liénard de Beaujeu, who had briefed his men to target mounted officers. On a narrow hill path the battle began. The British vanguard fired a volley that scattered the French and their Native allies, and killed Beaujeu. But, fatally for them, they did not secure the hill.

French captain Jean-Daniel Dumas took command and, with the Natives using the shelter of the woods, cut the British down from three sides. The vanguard fell back to the main column amid blinding musket smoke. Braddock, riding through the chaos waving his sword and threatening his own men if they did not regroup, was hit, along with the majority of British officers. (Braddock would die four days later). The British fought a desperate rearguard action back to the river, with many more dying at the hands of the enemy or their panicked comrades in what had become an unmitigated disaster.

ABOVE: Plan of field of battle for attack at Monongahela River. Following this battle there was a sharp increase in Native attacks on British colonists, reducing their faith in Britain's capacity to protect them. The defeat also sparked significant changes to Britain's military organization, with the formation of light infantry units and the introduction of specialist sharpshooter training.

RIGHT: Major General Braddock facing his defeat. He had 45 years' military experience, covering various European conflicts, but had never participated in actual fighting before the Battle of Monongahela River.

## TIMELINE

**10.1753**

Virginia Colonial Army Major George Washington begins a four-month, 900-mile (1,448-km) trip to reconnoiter French intentions in the colonies.

**1754**

Vastly outnumbered by the British in North America (80,000 to 1.16 million), French colonists consolidate their links with various Native tribes. They build Fort Duquesne.

CANADA

*Lake Ontario*

AMERICA

*Lake Erie*

●Fort Le Boeuf

●Fort Machault

●Fort Dusquesne
●Fort Necessity

Philadelphia●

## STEP-BY-STEP

**01** Major General Edward Braddock is chosen to travel to America and lead a force to seize Fort Duquesne.

**02** Braddock retains his unshakable belief in the superiority of symmetrical attack formations, regardless of the terrain.

**03** Braddock does allow some local adaptions, giving his men lighter-weight uniforms and water-filled leather bladders inside their hats, to prevent sunstroke.

**04** Three days after Braddock splits the troops into two columns, 50 miles (80 km) separate them.

**05** As the British near Fort Duquesne they are shadowed by French and Native raiding parties, who pick off stragglers.

**06** Rather than wait for the second column to catch up, Braddock decides to press ahead.

**07** Hindered by rigid formations, unforgiving terrain, and lack of leadership, the British crumble under French and Native attack. Many die by "friendly fire" in the chaos.

**08** With Braddock wounded, his aide-de-camp George Washington capably organizes a rearguard action, but many British are trampled at the river by fleeing comrades.

**09** The British suffer 914 casualties; the French and Natives less than 30. In 1763, Great Britain, France, and Spain sign the Treaty of Paris, ending the Seven Years' War.

| 07.03.1754 | 07.09.1755 | 05.18.1756 | 11.25.1758 | 02.10.1763 |
|---|---|---|---|---|
| French and Native troops attack and defeat Washington and his men at Fort Necessity, Pennsylvania. | The British force led by Major General Braddock is destroyed in the Battle of Monongahela River. | Two years after the commencement of hostilities in their American colonies, Great Britain declares war on France. | The British rout the French at Fort Duquesne at great expense, but the French burn the fort as they retreat. | Great Britain, France, and Spain sign the Treaty of Paris, ending the "Seven Years' War," which ran for nine years and encompassed the French and Indian War. |

# THE CAPTURE OF HMS *SERAPIS*

DATE        September 23, 1779
LOCATION  North Sea, off Flamborough Head, Yorkshire, England
OBJECTIVE  Victory in a naval battle between American and English ships

Russia's Empress Catherine described him as a rogue; Rudyard Kipling called him a pirate; the US Navy honors him as its spiritual father—Scottish-born John Paul Jones was full of contradictions, but above all he was a maritime genius. His victory, against enormous odds, over the British frigate HMS *Serapis*, in British home waters, was the apogee of his career.

### The Conquering Hero

In 1778, John Paul Jones became famous in America and France (where he was a hero), and Great Britain (where he was reviled), following a triumphant cruise in the Irish Sea in which, over a 28-day period, he seized a British man-of-war and two merchantmen, destroyed several other merchant ships, took 200 prisoners, and made a land raid on England at Whitehaven. As a consequence, the French government gave Jones, a merchantman, the *Bonhomme Richard,* to make his own in America's operations against the British.

All of Jones's many facets were on display during the battle that led to the sinking of *Bonhomme Richard* and the capture of HMS *Serapis*: courage, quick thinking, pride, resolve, leadership, and red-hot anger.

### Engaging the Enemy

In 1779, Jones was in command of a squadron of five American and allied ships in the North Sea when a lookout on *Bonhomme Richard* spotted vessels to the north: a 41–ship merchant convoy from the Baltic that Jones had been watching for, guarded by the British frigate HMS *Serapis* and a requisitioned sloop *Countess of Scarborough*.

At 18:30, after a shouted exchange between Jones and *Serapis*'s Captain Richard Pearson, establishing identity and intent, Jones opened fire with his starboard broadside guns. *Serapis*, which had more guns and was more maneuverable, returned fire. Then, on their second volley, two of *Bonhomme Richard*'s 18-pound (8-kg) guns exploded, killing or wounding many "of the best of the crew" and terrifying others, Jones wrote later.

### A Bold Victory

Instantly changing tactics, Jones maneuvered closer and intentionally collided with Serapis, whose anchor fouled his ship's hull, binding them together. With grappling hooks and lines, Jones tightened the grip. *Serapis* continued to fire, damaging *Bonhomme Richard* so badly she began to sink. Both ships were aflame. Jones's senior warrant officer and carpenter called for surrender, at which the enraged Jones attempted to shoot them. Pearson shouted: "Have you struck? Do you call for quarter?"; Jones made the, now famous, reply: "I have not yet begun to fight!" Inspired, his remaining crew fought "with double fury." After they, by chance, set off a deadly flash-fire on *Serapis*'s gun-deck, it was Pearson who finally surrendered. Jones transferred his men to his newly won prize and, despite efforts to save her, his own ship went down 36 hours later. Jones sailed *Serapis* to safe waters in the Netherlands.

ABOVE: John Paul Jones. Throughout his life, Jones won admiration and generated friction in almost equal measure. In June 1780 Benjamin Franklin wrote to Jones warning, "Criticizing and censuring almost every one you have to do with, will diminish friends, increase enemies, and thereby hurt your affairs."

FAR RIGHT: *Bonhomme Richard* and HMS *Serapis* engaged in the fight that will see the latter's crew defeated.

## TIMELINE

| 1761 | 1768 |
| --- | --- |
| On his first voyage as apprentice mariner, John Paul, 13, visits his brother in Fredericksburg, Virginia, in the 13 Colonies, America. | When the captain and first mate of the brig taking him from Jamaica to Scotland die, Paul assumes command and gets ship and crew back safely. |

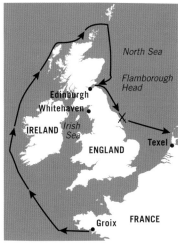

## STEP-BY-STEP

**01** On September 23, there are five ships in the squadron John Paul Jones commands in the North Sea in 1779—the *Alliance*, the *Pallas*, the *Cerf*, the *Vengeance*, and his own *Bonhomme Richard*—when his lookout spots the British-guarded convoy Jones has learned about from captured pilots.

**02** The wind is so light it takes Jones more than three hours to get within striking distance of convoy guard HMS *Serapis* off Flamborough Head.

**03** *Bonhomme Richard* has only 40 guns to *Serapis*'s 50, but Jones does not hesitate to attack.

**04** A deadly exploding gun on Jones's ship seems to spell disaster, but he simply changes tactics, attaching the *Bonhomme Richard* to the *Serapis* and fights on.

**05** *Serapis*'s cannon-fire tears apart *Bonhomme Richard*, which begins to sink. One hundred British prisoners are released and told to pump for their lives.

**06** With half their crewmates dead or injured, two of Jones's men call for surrender. The infuriated Jones tries to shoot them, but his pistols are empty, so he throws the guns, knocking the ship's carpenter out.

**07** One of Jones's men hits spare cartridges piled on *Serapis*'s crowded gun deck, setting of a lethal flash fire that kills 20, and badly injures 30. Serapis surrenders.

**08** In the 210-minute battle, more than 130 men on *Serapis* have been killed or wounded, and more than 150 on *Bonhomme Richard*. Jones and his remaining crew board the *Serapis*, and head for the safety of the Netherlands.

---

**1772**
Now a captain, 24-year-old Paul takes command of his first ship, *Betsy*. The next year Paul kills a mutineer on *Betsy*'s crew. Claiming self-defense, he flees to America and changes his surname to Jones.

**04.19.1775**
The American Revolutionary War against Great Britain begins. Jones, already appalled by conditions on slave ships, changes allegiance.

**08.1776**
As captain of the American Continental Navy ship *Providence*, Jones begins a run of spectacular successes against British shipping, culminating in the Irish Sea raid in 1778.

**10.03.1779**
After the Battle of Flamborough Head, Jones sails HMS *Serapis* into Texel in the Netherlands. Acclaimed as a hero, he fans the flames of his own publicity and neglects his squadron.

**1788**
Jones accepts the post of Rear Admiral in the Imperial Russian Navy. It proves a deflating experience. Four years later, 45-year-old Jones dies of illness, neglected, in Paris.

# THE BURNING OF THE WHITE HOUSE

DATE      August 24, 1814
LOCATION   Washington, District of Columbia, United States
OBJECTIVE To cause maximum public destruction in the US capital

For two years, the "War of 1812" (between the United States and Great Britain) was fought as a series of skirmishes and relatively small battles—devastating to the residents of places such as Buffalo, which were razed, and to the Natives, who lost their great leader Tecumseh, but not decisive. However, with Napoleon defeated, Great Britain could now focus on quelling its troublesome ex-colony.

### Redcoat Reinforcements

The 4,500 British Redcoats who disembarked near Chesapeake Bay in sweltering summer heat had already defeated the French in the Peninsular War. With victory theirs and Napoleon exiled to Elba, they had hoped to be sent home to Great Britain. Instead, they were sweating through their woolen tunics on the other side of the world, sent to give the Americans "a good drubbing."

Their commander, Major General Robert Ross, met with Rear Admiral George Cockburn, who had spent 15 months raiding and torching American settlements around the bay and, following his recommendation, they began to march on the US capital, Washington.

### A Brief Defense

US President James Madison was not well served by those charged with the nation's security. His Secretary of War, John Armstrong, was so sure Baltimore would be the British target that he refused to strengthen Washington's defenses. And Madison had repaid a political debt by appointing the Governor of Maryland's inexperienced nephew, William Winder, as his military commander. Winder could call on 500 barely trained regulars, having appealed in vain to the 18 states in the Union for men. This small force was supplemented by haphazard militia: many strong on spirit but poorly organized.

On August 24, the British reached Bladensburg, Maryland, 5 miles (8 km) from Washington. Here they were met in battle with a motley group of regulars, sailors, marines, and militia, arrayed in three lines spaced too far apart to be effective. Madison was there to witness it. The British won easily (albeit with 250 casualties) and most of the Americans fled with such haste their opponents scornfully nicknamed it the "Bladensburg races."

### The Capital Blazes

The Redcoats marched into Washington, a city of 8,000. Those residents who had not already piled their belongings on carts and fled now did so, while Ross's British troops set fire to public buildings including the Capitol, the Treasury, and the Navy dockyard. A detachment sent to destroy the Executive Mansion (now known as the White House), found it abandoned. Dolley and James Madison and their staff had gone, taking a portrait of George Washington, some cabinet records, and a few other valuables. Madison had been so sure of victory he had arranged a banquet for 40 and the British helped themselves to the fine wine and food before setting fire to the building.

ABOVE: Rear Admiral George Cockburn, who urged Major General Robert Ross to torch Washington, had become so hated during the period in which his troops terrorized American settlements that in August 1813 a Baltimore newspaper reported one Virginia resident had posted an offer of $1,000 for the head of "the notorious incendiary and infamous scoundrel" or $500 "for each of his ears."

BELOW: A print showing the Potomac River and Washington, D.C. under attack by British forces under Major General Ross, August 24, 1814.

## TIMELINE

**1806**

US Secretary of State James Madison reports that thousands of Americans are being wrongly pressed into service on British ships. His opponents claim he is exaggerating.

**11.21.1806**

France introduces trade restrictions on third parties (including America) dealing with its enemy, Great Britain. The British follow suit.

## STEP-BY-STEP

**01** Having defeated the "Chesapeake Bay flotilla" led by Joshua Barney, the Royal Navy sails up the Patuxent River and disembarks 4,500 men near Benedict, Maryland.

**02** Rear Admiral George Cockburn, who has been fighting the Americans for more than a year, urges Major General Robert Ross to burn Washington.

**03** The British reach the eastern shore of the Potomac River. Seven thousand American defenders are on the opposite shore.

**04** A detachment of 2,600 British seize control of the bridge at Bladensburg, an unbeatable strategic advantage.

**05** Although some Americans, including Joshua Barney, continue to fight, most flee in disarray.

**06** US President James Madison and his wife, Dolley, flee the Executive Residence (now the White House) with whatever they can fit on a cart, leaving behind a "celebratory" banquet.

**07** Under a flag of truce, Ross enters Washington to negotiate terms but his party is fired upon and his horse killed.

**08** At this attack, "All thoughts of accommodation were instantly laid aside," recalled one British soldier, and the troops "proceeded, without a moment's delay, to burn and destroy everything in the most distant degree connected with the government."

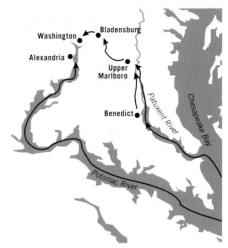

BELOW: Drawing of the White House ruins, which includes the missing face and roof of the rotunda, by George Munger, 1814. Three weeks after the burning of Washington, Ross was killed in the unsuccessful British attack on Baltimore. The American defense of the city's Fort McHenry inspired Francis Scott Key's poem "The Star-Spangled Banner" (originally titled "Defence of Fort M'Henry"). Put to music soon afterward, it became the American national anthem in 1931.

| 06.21.1806 | 12.1807 | 06.16.1812 | 04.27.1813 | 02.17.1815 |
|---|---|---|---|---|
| HMS *Leopard* fires upon the American ship *Chesapeake* in a dispute over suspected deserters. | US President Thomas Jefferson forbids all US export shipping and most British imports—a highly unpopular move. In 1809, Jefferson's rival James Madison is sworn in as US President. | A new British government eases trade with America; the news will take months to arrive. Despite opposition, Madison declares war on Great Britain. | After months of cross-border incursions from both sides, American troops capture and burn the British-held York (now Toronto). Sixteen months later, in retaliation, the British burn Washington. | With the US Senate's ratification of the Treaty of Ghent (signed December 24, 1814) the "War of 1812" ends. |

# THE DEFENSE OF HOUGOUMONT

DATE        June 18, 1815
LOCATION    South of Waterloo, in present-day Belgium
OBJECTIVE   To hold an isolated farm adjacent to the main Waterloo battlefield

With Napoleon Bonaparte unexpectedly back from exile, Great Britain, Russia, Austria, and Prussia mobilized their armies against him. The "Little Corporal" was fighting for his political survival at Waterloo—a battle that for both him and his opponent the Duke of Wellington, pivoted around the fight to take the walled farm at Hougoumont.

### Outmatched in Experience
When the battle began at Waterloo, the opposing forces were reasonably even in number: 72,000 French troops against 68,000 British, Dutch, Belgian, and German. But unlike the French, the coalition force led by the Duke of Wellington was very inexperienced—only half of the 24,000 Britons, for instance, had fought before. Many of the best men who had served under Wellington previously had been dispatched to America to fight there. Furthermore, some of the Dutch and Belgian troops had previously fought *for* Napoleon.

### Farmyard Stronghold
It was critical for the allies that their flanks hold. Wellington was relying on support from the 48,000 Prussians led by Field Marshal Gebhard von Blücher, but their arrival was uncertain. Expecting Blücher to approach from the east, Wellington deployed his strongest, most tested troops at the western end of his line. The walled farm at Hougoumont lay at the foot of a slope in front of them. If Hougoumont fell to the French, the line would surely break.

The farm complex consisted of a small château, other residences and farm buildings, two gardens, and an orchard. A sunken lane, or the "Hollow Way," ran in front. Wellington initially sent 400 Coldstream and Scots Guards under Lieutenant Colonel James Macdonell to hold the farm. When the duke's Spanish liaison officer, Miguel de Alava, expressed concern about the small number he responded: "I've put Macdonell into it. You don't know Macdonell."

### Wave after Wave of Attacks
Wellington's faith was well placed. In all, from mid-morning to evening, the French mounted eight separate waves of attack. Napoleon's brother Prince Jérôme led the assaults that were intended to force Wellington to redeploy troops and so weaken the opposition Napoleon would meet on the Brussels road.

The French had a small initial success, driving Nassau infantry and Hanoverian sharpshooters out of the wood, but were driven back. The second attack came closest to succeeding. A bear of a man, Sous-Lieutenant Legros, forced his way through the north gate with 30 comrades behind him. Macdonell fought back, succeeding with the help of Sergeant James Graham to close the gate and bar it, then kill the interlopers.

Wellington would later write: "The outcome of the Battle of Waterloo turned on the closing of the gates at Hougoumont."

ABOVE: Field Marshal Arthur Wellesley, Duke of Wellington KG, GCB, wearing the cloak he used at the Battle of Waterloo.

RIGHT: British Army officer Major Macready described the battle scene as "grand beyond description. Hougoumont and its wood sent up a broad flame through the dark masses of smoke that overhung the field; beneath this cloud the French were indistinctly visible … 400 cannon were belching forth fire and death on every side."

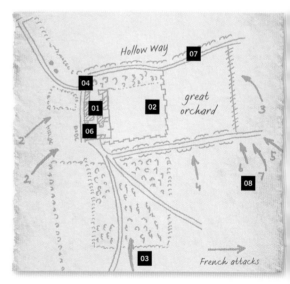

## TIMELINE

**03.10.1814**
Napoleon rejects a peace treaty from Austria, Prussia, Russia, and Great Britain; they vow to continue fighting until he is overthrown.

**04.06.1814**
Napoleon finally agrees to abdicate and is granted the Mediterranean island of Elba as a sovereign principality.

## STEP-BY-STEP

**01** Four Coldstream Guards light companies occupy the walled farm at Hougoumont, only just beating French cavalry to the strategic location. The only link between Wellington's troops and the Hougoumont outpost is a depressed track, the "Hollow Way."

**02** The Guards spend the night before the battle loopholing walls and building a fire step from which to shoot over the wall.

**03** The Battle of Waterloo commences with what Wellington calls "a furious attack upon our post at Hougoumont."

**04** The farm's North Gate has been left unlocked, allowing for the arrival of troops and ammunition from the "Hollow Way." During the course of the battle, Wellington will use 12,000 troops to keep control of this road.

**05** Thirty French troops force their way through the gate, damaging it. Coldstream Guards officers Macdonell and Graham secure it, preventing the farm from being overrun.

**06** The French use incendiary shells to set fire to the farm's buildings; urgent attempts are made to remove the injured British men.

**07** With troops in Hougoumont running short of ammunition, Private Joseph Brewer courageously drives a cart full of ammunition down the "Hollow Way."

**08** As the Prussians close in, Napoleon dispatches troops from the center of his line in a last ditch effort to take Hougoumont and break through the allied center. They are destroyed by artillery before even reaching the farm.

---

**02.26.1815**

Eight months after arriving, Napoleon leaves Elba bound for France with a detachment of his official guard.

**03.13.1815**

As he makes his way from Cannes to Paris, gathering support, the Congress of Vienna declares Napoleon an outlaw. However, in June, he leads his army to victory over Blücher's Prussians at Ligny.

**06.18.1815**

After a tactical error in delaying the battle, Napoleon loses to allied forces led by Wellington and Blücher at Waterloo. Wellington calls it "the nearest-run thing you ever saw in your life."

**06.22.1815**

Napoleon is forced to abdicate for a second time.

**05.05.1821**

After five-and-a-half years there, Napoleon dies in exile on the remote Atlantic island of St. Helena.

# THE AGE OF
# DERRING-DO
## 1836–1916

In 1819, Sir Walter Scott's hugely popular adventure novel *Ivanhoe* popularized the term "derring-do" to describe what he called a desperate courage. The 14 stories in the Age of Derring-Do include some remarkable real-life examples of the dashing heroism with which we associate the term now, along with some gritty desperate last stands, which produced national icons.

Jim Bowie and his comrades in arms are prime among the latter; they are remembered to this day for their fight-to-the-death determination against huge odds at the Alamo. For the British, a similar spirit of self-sacrifice was exhibited by the doomed men of the Light Brigade as they charged into battle: "theirs not to reason why, theirs but to do or die." The French, meanwhile, lionized Foreign Legionnaires who refused to give up despite being outnumbered 20 to 1 in Camarón, Mexico. They are still commemorated in an annual ceremony centering on the recovered wooden hand of one of the doomed officers. Other heroes of the time, like General Gordon of Khartoum and the British soldiers fighting the Zulus at Rorke's Drift, have been mythologized in contemporary accounts. The unvarnished versions of their stories are more complicated and less glorious—in other words, altogether more human.

The nineteenth century brought sweeping changes to the world. The first telegraph message was not sent in the United States until the decade after the last stand at the Alamo; the Pony Express did not start until two decades after that; and the transcontinental railroad was yet another decade away. In 1837, the year following the Alamo defense, 18-year-old Victoria ascended to the British throne. She was still queen six decades later when young foreign correspondent Winston Churchill was filing reports from South Africa, where the Boers' guerrilla tactics were confounding the British. She did not, however, live to see the end of the Boxer Rebellion, in which the Eight-Nation Alliance invaded China after it had turned against the thousands of foreigners within its borders.

Two of the most extraordinary tales in the Age of Derring-Do involve a very British spirit and stoicism. The first is the Lynmouth–Porlock lifeboat rescue. This incident is little known now, except by locals and maritime historians, but it shows the remarkable feats of which ordinary people are capable; it is a stirring story that once heard is never forgotten. The second is the tale of Ernest Shackleton's expedition to the South Pole. Along with the explorers' incredible courage, determination, and endurance, what strikes modern readers is their stiff-upper-lip attitude. Imminent rescue after months lost at the end of the world was, wrote one, almost enough to make him cry.

Shackleton's departure two years before this had coincided with the outbreak of World War I. This deadly conflict involved acts of courage large and small every single day on both sides from people such as Robert Quigg, "the Irish Saint," as he became known, who put themselves in danger time and time again, simply because someone had to do so. Sir Walter Scott would have understood.

# THE ALAMO

DATE       February 23–March 6, 1836
LOCATION   San Antonio de Béxar, Texas
OBJECTIVE  To prevent the Mexican army taking the fortified Alamo Mission

By early 1836, the disputed territory of Texas was at flash point. Centralist supporters of the Mexican government, which controlled the vast area, had repeatedly fought with Tejanos (Hispanic Texans) who wanted more autonomy—the Federalist cause—and Texians (American Texans), who were seeking independence.

### The Lines are Drawn

Eleven days after a rebel force drove Mexican soldiers out of San Antonio, the town's tiny mission fort, the Alamo, became garrison for 100 US Army troops under the control of Colonel James Neill. Small numbers of supporters began to arrive, including Texas Ranger Colonel James (Jim) Bowie on January 19. On February 2, another 30 men came, under Lieutenant Colonel William B. Travis, who also brought his slave, known only as Joe. Bowie and Neill declared, "We will rather die in these ditches than give it up to the enemy."

Having missed out on a fourth term in Congress, and declaring, "You may all go to Hell and I will go to Texas," West Tennessean David ("Davy") Crockett arrived with 12 men on February 8. With Neill given leave of absence to go to his sick family, 26-year-old Travis shared command with Bowie.

### A Mexican Standoff

Determined to crush the growing Texan rebellion, Mexican President General Santa Anna marched at the head of 1,800 men, arriving at San Antonio on February 23 and laid siege to the Alamo. From the first, Travis sent messages pleading for aid from the provisional Texan government. But even after it declared independence on March 2, the faction-ridden body sent no help. On March 3, Travis wrote, "I am determined to perish in defense of this place, and my bones shall reproach my country for her neglect." Seven days into the siege, 32 further volunteers made it through Mexican lines, bringing the total inside the Mission (which had a number of buildings within its three acres) to 189 men, some accompanied by women and children.

### Massacre at the Mission

On March 6, Santa Anna launched a predawn raid, the first of three. Cannon and small arms fire held his men off, but not for long. Planting ladders against the Alamo's walls, as survivor Susanna Dickinson recalled, the Mexicans "jumped down within, many of them to immediate death. As fast as the front ranks were slain, they were filled up again by fresh troops." Although shot and bayoneted, Joe was the only adult male in the fort to survive the slaughter. Six hundred Mexican soldiers died. Six weeks later the new Texan army routed Santa Anna's troops at San Jacinto, voicing their commander General Sam Houston's rallying cry: "Remember the Alamo!"

## TIMELINE

**1830**

Mexican-controlled Texas has only 4,000 Tejanos to its 30,000 American colonists, who increasingly flaunt Mexican law.

**1834**

Having defeated a Spanish army at Tampico, Santa Anna becomes Mexican president and severely limits Texan autonomy. Rebellion builds.

disputed territory

UNITED STATES

TEXAS

San Antonio

Rio Grande

Nueces River

MEXICO

**LEFT:** *The Battle of the Alamo* by Percy Moran (1912). The painting focuses on Davy Crockett's final stand, the Mexicans having breached the walls of the Mission.

**FAR LEFT:** Despite his inexperience and his youth, 26-year-old William Travis became default commander of the enlisted men after the departure of Colonel James Neill, while Jim Bowie led the volunteers.

## STEP-BY-STEP

**01** Santa Anna's army arrives at San Antonio and begins siege preparations on February 23. Santa Anna orders that the enemy fighters are to be killed, even if they surrender. The following day, with Bowie falling ill, Travis assumes command.

**02** A two-hour skirmish on February 25 sees Santa Anna's troops repulsed when they attempt to occupy peasant huts near the Mission compound. Later the huts are destroyed by the defenders.

**03** Artillery bombardment of the Alamo begins on February 28.

**04** Santa Anna completes the encirclement of the fort on February 29. Some evidence indicates that an informal truce permits some civilians to leave the Alamo.

**05** Thirty-two members of the Gonzales Ranging Company enter the Alamo, marginally increasing its strength.

**06** On March 3, Travis receives assurance of support if he can hold out a little longer. Meanwhile, a further 1,100 Mexican troops arrive to reinforce Santa Anna's army.

**07** The following day, Mexican artillery batteries are moved closer to the fort and a prolonged bombardment ensues.

**08** According to tradition, on March 5 Travis draws a line in the sand with his saber, inviting any who want to leave to do so. A single man crosses the line.

**09** Santa Anna launches a full assault just before dawn on Mar. 6. Travis is shot on the walls of the Mission early in the attack. Two subsequent attacks, during a 90-minute battle, sees the Alamo finally fall. Santa Anna orders the cremation of the slain defenders. In all, 600 Mexicans die as do all but one of the defenders.

| 12.10.1835 | 02.23.1836 | 03.02.1836 | 04.21.1836 | 03.1.1845 |
|---|---|---|---|---|
| Texian and Tejano rebels defeat the Mexican troops occupying San Antonio. | Santa Anna's 1,800 soldiers march on the town. The rebels retreat into the Alamo Mission. Outnumbered almost ten to one, they hold the Mexicans off for 13 days. | Led by a newly formed coalition, Texas declares independence from Mexico. | The Texan army defeats Santa Anna's forces and captures him at San Jacinto. The following month Santa Anna signs the Treaty of Velasco. Mexican troops withdraw south of the Rio Grande. | Texas is formally annexed to the United States. Open warfare breaks out between Mexico and the United States in March 1846. |

# THE CHARGE OF THE LIGHT BRIGADE

DATE        October 25, 1854
LOCATION    Balaclava, Crimean Peninsula, Russian Empire
OBJECTIVE   The interdiction of Russian forces removing captured Turkish guns

Many noteworthy events happened during the one-day Battle of Balaclava in the Crimean War (including the confrontation that gave us the expression "the thin red line"), but none is more famed, or controversial, than the Charge of the Light Brigade. To this day, military enthusiasts argue fiercely about who was to blame.

### The Ingredients of Disaster

Did arrogance, confusion, topography, or animosity cause the death of 113 men and the wounding of 247 in an unwinnable action? Each played a part, but nothing detracts from the courage and sacrifice of the Light Brigade.

Personalities mattered. Commander of the British cavalry and the Light and Heavy Brigades was Lieutenant General the Earl of Lucan. Under him, commanding the Light Brigade, was Major General the Earl of Cardigan. Cardigan was married to, but separated from, Lucan's sister; there was intense dislike between the men. Lucan was not well-liked by his men, either. A previous failure to engage in battle earned him the nickname "Lord Look-On," despite the decision being that of the Commander in Chief Lord Raglan.

The layout of the battleground, two valleys separated by a ridge called Causeway Heights, was significant. From his elevated position, Raglan could see everything; Lucan could see little of the Russians.

### The Order is Given

Observing Russian troops preparing to remove Turkish guns after taking their redoubts, Raglan gave an order that his Quartermaster General, Lord Airey, wrote down. Airey chose his aide-de-camp, Captain Lewis Nolan, to deliver the note, which read: "Lord Raglan wishes the Cavalry to advance rapidly to the front and try to prevent the enemy carrying away the guns. Troop of Horse Artillery may accompany. French Cavalry is on your left. R. Airey. Immediate."

Nolan was a talented but mercurial career officer who had written two books on cavalry and showed little respect for Lucan. Accounts differ, but credible sources say Lucan expressed surprise, asking Nolan what Raglan meant: "Attack, sir! Attack what? What guns, sir?" Nolan replied, with a sweep of his arm toward the far end of the North Valley rather than the Causeway, saying, "There, my Lord, is your enemy! There are your guns!"

### Into the Fray

Cardigan expressed disquiet, but led the charge of 673 men, including Nolan. As they set off along the valley floor between elevated rows of Russian artillery, Nolan dashed in front of Cardigan, waving his sword. Many believe he had realized the error, but this remains speculation because almost immediately Nolan was fatally shot. The Brigade continued for one-and-a-quarter miles (2 km) under unrelenting fire. More than half were killed or wounded, and 475 horses were lost. Only a counterattack by French cavalry—the 4th Chasseurs d'Afrique—prevented their total annihilation.

ABOVE: Lord Cardigan leading the charge in which 113 men died. Disease, including dysentery, killed more than 16,000 soldiers during the course of the Crimean War.

RIGHT: This print shows the Enniskillen Dragoons and the 5th Dragoon Guards engaging the Russian cavalry in the midst of battle.

## TIMELINE

**07.21.1774**
Following the Russo-Turkish War begun in 1768, the Treaty of Küçük Kaynarca gives Russia key Crimean Peninsula territories.

**07.13.1841**
Russia, Great Britain, France, Austria, Prussia, and Turkey sign the London Straits Convention, aimed at propping up the ailing Ottoman Empire.

## STEP-BY-STEP

**01** Turkish troops begin building redoubts along Causeway Heights, positioning nine heavy naval guns there.

**02** Russians bombard the Number One redoubt; the Turkish force of 500 suffers 400 casualties. Under attack, Turks from the other redoubts retreat.

**03** Though greatly outnumbered, the British cavalry's Heavy Brigade charges and decisively drives back advancing Russian cavalry.

**04** The Russians withdraw to a defended position, where they have eight artillery guns, at the far end of the North Valley from the British.

**05** Raglan's staff see Russians preparing to remove the Turkish guns from the captured Causeway Heights redoubts. With infantry still en route, the cavalry must stop them.

**06** Quartermaster General Airey pencils Raglan's orders. Aide-de-camp Captain Nolan delivers the note to cavalry commander Lord Lucan.

**07** Lucan passes the orders to Lord Cardigan, commander of the Light Brigade. Lucan expresses concern; Nolan gestures toward the far end of the valley.

**08** Cardigan leads the charge. Nolan races ahead of him and is fatally shot. The Light Brigade is mown down by cannon and rifle fire. No strategic advantage is gained by the Light Brigade's sacrifice.

| 07.02.1853 | 10.05.1853 | 11.4.1853 | 03.28.1854 | 09.13.1854 |
|---|---|---|---|---|
| Eighty thousand Russian troops cross the Pruth River into Ottoman-controlled Moldavia. | Turkey declares war on Russia. | The Russians attack the Turkish fleet at Sinope on the Black Sea, sinking seven frigates. Two months later French and British ships enter the Black Sea to protect Turkish vessels. | France and Great Britain declare war on Russia, in support of Ottoman Turkey. | Allied forces land in the Crimea to besiege the Russian naval base of Sevastopol. Within a month major battles occur at Alma and Balaclava. |

# THE DEFENSE OF CAMARÓN

DATE     April 29–30, 1863
LOCATION Camarón, Veracruz, Mexico
OBJECTIVE To ensure the safety of a valuable French convoy

With Mexico defaulting on its foreign debts, French, Spanish, and British forces landed in December 1861 to recover what they were owed. Meeting unexpectedly stiff resistance, Spain and Great Britain withdrew just a few months later. Among the remaining French forces was a Foreign Legion company assigned to protect a convoy laden with bullion and other important supplies.

### On Guard

While the French army laid siege to the inland city of Puebla, a vital stop en route from coastal Veracruz to Mexico City, its Legionnaires were dispersed along the road, fighting off incursions and maintaining lines of communication. Diseases, including malaria, had taken a heavy toll on the 3rd Company when, on April 29, it received orders to march back down the track to meet and protect a convoy of 60 carts and 150 mules carrying vital French supplies, including three million francs' worth of gold bullion for army pay.

Only 62 of the 112 men, and one of its three officers, Sublieutenant Jean Vilain, were fit for duty. Two regimental staff officers, Sublieutenant Clément Maudet and Captain Jean Danjou, a battle veteran with a distinctive prosthetic wooden left hand, volunteered to join them.

### Taken by Surprise

They set out before dawn on April 30, passing the ruined Hacienda Camarón around 07:00. A mile down the road Danjou called for a rest; water for coffee had just boiled when hundreds of enemy cavalry were spotted. The Legionnaires grabbed their 70-caliber smallbore muskets, but in the confusion their mules—bearing water and extra ammunition—bolted. Danjou formed his men into a rectangle and, firing occasionally to keep the Mexicans at bay, they inched back to Camarón. Sixteeen were captured but the other 49 took up positions behind the remaining walls of a farmhouse. The heat was searing, but Mexican fire prevented the parched Legionnaires reaching a nearby well.

### To the Death

Under a flag of truce, Mexican commander Colonel Milán demanded their surrender, pointing out that some 1,200 infantry had joined the cavalry. Danjou refused and, before he was shot and killed, made his men also promise not to surrender. Vilain took over, vowing they would fight to the death. He, too, was shot. By late afternoon, only five men survived, including Maudet. They fired their last shots at point-blank range then charged with fixed bayonets. The enraged Mexicans, who had lost 300 men, shot two and began to club the other three; only the intervention of an officer prevented their death. Meanwhile the convoy, which had been alerted to Milán's planned ambush, had halted in safety and reached its destination five days later.

ABOVE: As the Legion's official history notes, "This battle, whose name adorns every Legion flag, remains the symbol of a mission carried out to the bitter end." It was Emperor Napoleon III who directed the name be added to the flag.

RIGHT: Jean Basin's depiction of the battle. The site is still known as "Camerone" to the Legion, thanks to a misspelled contemporary report.

## TIMELINE

## STEP-BY-STEP

**01** Led by Captain Jean Danjou, who had lost a hand to an exploding musket a decade before, 65 Legionnaires set out to protect a French bullion convoy en route from Veracruz to Puebla, some 150 miles (240 km) away.

**02** On their way to meet the convoy, the Legionnaires spot a large contingent of enemy cavalry.

**03** Realizing he is outnumbered, although not knowing by how much, Danjou gets his Company to the relative safety of La Trinidad farmhouse at the Hacienda Camarón.

**04** Mexico's Colonel Francisco de Paula Milán has positioned sharpshooters around the farmhouse, but the Legionnaires take shelter and settle in for the fight.

**05** Despite having no water in the extreme heat, no food, and little ammunition, the Legionnaires refuse to surrender, though one officer after another is killed.

**06** Out of ammunition, the five surviving Legionnaires, led by Sublieutenant Maudet, undertake a defiant bayonet charge.

**07** Legionnaire Victor Catteau throws himself in front of Maudet in a vain effort to protect his officer—both are shot.

**08** Impressed by their courage, Milán gives a special order that the two survivors be treated well. They are allowed to escort Danjou's body back to Veracruz.

---

**10.31.1861**
France, Great Britain, and Spain sign the Treaty of London, allying in their efforts to recover the money they are owed by Mexico.

**04.09.1861**
Two of the three allies withdraw: Great Britain after just four months, and Spain after five.

**04.30.1863**
The defense of Camarón gives rise to the Foreign Legion's holiest of days; its name is added to the Legion's flag.

**05.03.1863**
French reinforcements bury the Legion's dead, including Danjou, but find no trace of his wooden hand. It is found two years later, in a rancher's possession.

**04.30.1931**
The Legion institutes an annual "Camerone Day" commemoration, the centerpiece of which is Danjou's wooden hand.

# THE BATTLE OF GETTYSBURG

DATE July 1–July 3, 1863
LOCATION Gettysburg, Pennsylvania, United States
OBJECTIVE To turn an unexpected confrontation into a critical battle

Two years into the vicious American Civil War (1861–65), which divided the nation into a Union North and a "rebel" South, and nine months after his first unsuccessful attempt to invade the North, Confederate General Robert E. Lee tried again. He threw the full weight of his heavily outnumbered army against the Union in an opportunist battle at the small town of Gettysburg, Pennsylvania. The battle, marked by tremendous valor and enormous loss, changed the course of the war.

### An Accidental Encounter

Although the Confederacy had amassed armaments impressively quickly, it could not compete with the industrial North on basic supplies. In July 1863, the need for shoes drew Confederate infantry into Gettysburg where they unexpectedly encountered Union cavalry. What followed was the deadliest single battle in US military history.

Both sides sent urgently for reinforcements. Lee's army was nearby, ready for his planned push north; by mid-afternoon, Confederates had driven the Union army back through the town, home to 2,400 people. Led by Major General George Meade, Union soldiers took up a fishhook-shaped defensive line, occupying the hills known as Big and Little Round Tops at one end and, at the other, Culp's Hill and Cemetery Hill. Head of the Confederate forces, General Robert E. Lee, arrived mid-afternoon and ordered his men to seize the high ground before nightfall if General Richard Ewell deemed it "practicable." Ewell decided to rest his men until daybreak.

### Massed Forces

Reinforcements poured in on both sides. By morning, 85,000 Union soldiers faced 65,000 Confederates. As the Confederates maneuvered into attack position, Union General Daniel Sickles disobeyed orders and moved his men from Cemetery Ridge, leaving the Round Tops undefended. The fierce fight for the high ground began in earnest, using cannon, rifles, muskets, pistols, bayonets, and swords. It was, one survivor said, "a perfect hell on earth." As night fell the Union line held.

The next day Lee insisted on charging, despite the concerns of corps commander General James Longstreet. Lee chose General George Pickett to lead the attack. Around 15:00, 13,000 Confederate soldiers obeyed orders and marched quickly and silently toward the long stone wall behind which the Union army sheltered. "Pickett's Charge" was a slaughter; 6,500 Confederates died or were captured. Told to rally his men, Pickett said, "General Lee, I have no division now."

### Aftermath

Gettysburg was the war's bloodiest encounter: 51,000 soldiers were killed, wounded, or captured—an estimated 23,000 Union and 28,000 Confederates. Also killed were 15,000 artillery horses and one Gettysburg resident. War dragged on for two years but, in conjunction with its loss of the stronghold at Vicksburg on the Mississippi (which occurred even as Lee was retreating from Gettysburg), this was a blow from which the South never recovered.

## TIMELINE

| 11.06.1860 | 02.04.1861 |
|---|---|
| Having campaigned on a platform including opposition to the expansion of slavery, Abraham Lincoln is elected US President. Inaugurated Nov. 3, 1861, as 16th president of the United States. | South Carolina, Mississippi, Florida, Alabama, Georgia, Louisiana, and Texas, southern states that seceded from the United States in protest to Lincoln, sign a Confederate Constitution. |

**ABOVE:** The conflict that resulted in mass casualties on both sides was sparked after Confederate soldiers entered Gettysburg searching for desperately needed shoes; Confederate survivors pulled shoes off the Union dead as they retreated.

**LEFT:** Map of the Battle of Gettysburg.

## STEP-BY-STEP

**01** Hearing rumors of a supply of shoes in Gettysburg, Confederate infantry approach.

**02** Three miles (5 km) from town they run into Union cavalry. Both sides send for reinforcements.

**03** Tens of thousands begin to converge but the Confederates get there first, pushing back Union forces onto defensive positions on high ground.

**04** Confederate Army commander Robert E. Lee arrives and orders General Richard Ewell to attack. Ewell elects to wait.

**05** Lee's trusted corps commander General James Longstreet argues against the engagement. Lee overrules him.

**06** By the morning of July 2, 65,000 Confederates and 85,000 Union troops stand ready.

**07** In less than 90 minutes, 40,000 rounds are fired. The earth is literally blood-soaked. Ferocious fighting continues throughout the day.

**08** On July 3, again ignoring Longstreet's advice, Lee orders 13,000 men, led by General George Pickett, to charge directly on the Union line. Half are killed or captured. The Union line holds.

**09** The next day, July 4, Lee begins the long retreat to Virginia.

**04.12.1861**
Confederate forces fire on Union troops at Fort Sumter, South Carolina, beginning the American Civil War.

**11.19.1863**
Four months after the battle of Gettysburg, a new Union cemetery is dedicated. Lincoln delivers what becomes known as "the Gettysburg address."

**04.09.1865**
The Confederates are routed and at the town of Appomattox Court House, Virginia, Lee agrees to surrender.

**04.14.1865**
Confederate sympathizer and slavery supporter John Wilkes Booth shoots Lincoln at Ford's Theater in Washington, D.C. The President dies the following morning.

**05.13.1865**
In a skirmish in Texas, Union soldier Private John J. Williams becomes the last man killed in the war. More than three million men fought, and 620,000, two percent of the population, died.

# MAPPING THE ROOF OF THE WORLD

DATE  1863–1881
LOCATION  Tibet and the Himalayas
OBJECTIVE  A covert survey of the closed country of Tibet

Throughout British rule in India, accurate surveying was a high military and mercantile priority. Over six decades, the subcontinent was mapped with remarkable accuracy under the auspices of the Great Trigonometrical Survey. But to the consternation of the British, already engaged in "the Great Game"— the struggle with Russia for control in Central Asia—India's northern neighbor Tibet remained a geographical unknown.

### A Cunning Plan

In 1862, Tibet was literally a blank on British survey maps. Its borders were closed and unauthorized travelers were executed. But Royal Engineers' Captain Thomas George Montgomerie noticed that locals passed easily back and forth. In a letter to his superiors he wrote, "If a sharp enough [Indian] man could be found, he would have no difficulty in carrying a few small instruments amongst his merchandise, and with their aid good service might be rendered to geography."

Montgomerie tested the idea by recruiting Mohamed-i-Hameed, a young Muslim who knew surveying fundamentals. In mid-1863, Hameed left the British outpost of Ladakh equipped with tiny hidden instruments, heading for Chinese-controlled Yarkand. His mission: to note altitude, distance, and topographical features. He performed well and, although he died on the return journey, his notes made it back to Montgomerie.

### Travelers on the Roof of the World

Next Montgomerie recruited Nain Singh, a 33-year-old headmaster, and his cousin Mani. The Hindu men knew the Himalayas well, spoke Tibetan, and were brave and resourceful. Over the next two years, they undertook intense training, learning, among other things, to take a precisely measured step no matter what the terrain. Finally, in 1865, they set off, heading to Tibet through Nepal's mountain passes. Secrecy was paramount: a British spy faced instant death. Mani's route brought him back to India but Nain Singh, known as the "Pundit" or "Pandit," (Sanskrit for "learned man") pressed on, covering 1,200 miles (1,930 km) posing as a Buddhist pilgrim and using ingenious equipment to make his measurements: his specially adapted "prayer beads" kept track of mileage, 2,000 paces per mile. His "prayer wheel" had a secret compartment where he kept his notes. He had concealed binoculars, and a thermometer that he used in boiling water to estimate altitude.

### Aftermath

In 1873, Montgomerie departed India, but the remarkable Nain Singh persisted for two more years, completing his third epic journey through the region. In 1876, his identity and achievements were revealed in the *Geographical Magazine* and he was granted a village of his own, a life pension, and the Gold Medal of the Royal Geographical Society. Singh was succeeded by Krishna Singh and the Bengali Sarat Chandra Das, who between them effectively completed the survey.

ABOVE: The hostile terrain of the Himalaya ranges photographed in 1865 by Samuel Bourne.

RIGHT: A map from the survey, produced in 1870. It was decades until Europeans were able to retrace some of the pundits' journeys. In 1922, a British expedition to Tibet noted that the information they were relying on was still mostly that gathered by the Singhs.

FAR RIGHT: A stamp commemorating Nain Singh. From his home in England, Captain Montgomerie was among those who campaigned to see Nain Singh's achievements recognized.

## TIMELINE

| 1830 | 1858 |
| --- | --- |
| Nain Singh is born in the Johar Valley in the Himalayas. | The British East India Company's control of India is transferred to the British Crown. |

## STEP-BY-STEP

**01** In 1863, Captain Montgomerie recruits Mohamed-i-Hameed, who sets out through the Karakoram Pass toward Yarkand.

**02** After six months collecting data in the city, Hameed attracts the suspicions of Chinese authorities. He sets out for home but becomes ill and dies en route.

**03** During two years' training, Montgomerie's new recruit Nain Singh perfects his 33-inch (84-cm) stride; he will use "prayer beads" to count off the thousands of miles he walks.

**04** Measuring the temperature of boiling water, Singh calculates the altitude of the Tibetan capital, Lhasa, as 10,629 feet (3,240 m); he was out by only 1,345 feet (410 m).

**05** His eyesight damaged by years of detailed high altitude observations and his general health affected by the rigors of his journeys, Singh nevertheless continues to train younger "pundits" such as Krishna Singh and Sarat Chandra Das.

**06** In 1882, Krishna Singh completes a four-year journey through Tibet and Western China.

**07** Between 1879 and 1881 Sarat Chandra Das completes two extensive journeys into Tibet.

**08** While it now goes by its Tibetan name, the remote mountain range Aling Kangri was, for a time, known as the Nain Singh range in honor of "the pundit of pundits."

| 1863 | 1866 | 1875 | 1878–81 | 1901 |
|---|---|---|---|---|
| Captain Montgomerie receives permission to train undercover Indian surveyors. | Nain Singh returns to India with valuable information gathered on his first lengthy and dangerous journey. | Singh concludes his final journey and retires. He dies in 1895, visiting the village awarded to him for his explorations. | Covert survey of Tibet and Western China is continued by Krishna Singh and Sarat Chandra Das. | Rudyard Kipling publishes his spy novel *Kim*, with characters based on Montgomerie and his "pundits." In 1904, India issues a postage stamp commemorating Nain Singh. |

# THE DEFENSE OF RORKE'S DRIFT

DATE    January 22–23, 1879
LOCATION    Rorke's Drift mission station, colony of Natal, southern Africa
OBJECTIVE    The defense of an unfortified British hospital station against a Zulu army

The defense of Rorke's Drift during the Anglo-Zulu War of 1879 has long been a symbol of British courage and indomitability against seemingly overwhelming odds. It resulted in the unparalleled award of 11 Victoria Crosses (VCs), and the 1964 film *Zulu* brought the event into the popular imagination. But the reality is darker than the legend.

### Bad News
Mid-afternoon on January 22, survivors of the nearby Isandlwana massacre of a British force by a huge Zulu army reached Rorke's Drift, a former trading station, where a small number of the column led by the British commander Lieutenant General Lord Chelmsford had established a hospital and depot. They brought warning: the Zulus were coming.

The senior officers, Lieutenant Gonville Bromhead and Lieutenant John Chard, met with Assistant Commissary James Dalton to decide whether to defend or retreat. They accepted Dalton's view that, slowed by patients and without cover in the open countryside, they would stand no chance. Stay and fight they must.

Improvising, and working quickly, they built makeshift barricades from the supplies at hand: "mealie" or maize bags, crates of tinned meat, and biscuit boxes.

### Under Attack
The attack began around 16:30, at which point most of the Natal Native troops fled, leaving only 140 or so British soldiers and a few Natal Native volunteers.

Around 4,000 Zulus, led by the Zulu king Cetshwayo's half-brother Dabulamanzi kaMpande, had some rifles and outmoded muskets, but their main weapons were their assegais, or spears, either thin for throwing or broader for stabbing. The British barriers might have been improvised but they were effective, with the assegais unable to make contact. Wave after wave of Zulu warriors were shot at point-blank range or bayoneted as they tried to break through.

The battle raged. The Zulus set fire to the hospital and began to spear patients until they were fought off. In darkness, the British withdrew to their last resort, a defended position at the station's center. As day dawned, after 12 ferocious hours' battle, the Zulu warriors saw approaching British reinforcements and retreated.

### The Untold Story
Just 17 of the defenders had died, although virtually all the survivors were wounded. The Zulus lost at least ten percent of their men, with 400 or more dead. The courage and nobility of the British was immediately lauded by the government—in the hope, as the British National Army Museum puts it, "of diverting public attention away from the disaster at Isandlwana."

The conduct of Her Majesty's soldiers toward their enemy was hidden for many years. As testimony from those who fought reveals, wounded Zulus were bayoneted, hanged, and even buried alive. Most of this was done by the relief force that had seen the carnage at Isandlwana as they marched to Rorke's Drift.

## TIMELINE

**04.1877**

Britain's colonial secretary, the Earl of Carnarvon, aims to federate Boer and British territories in southern Africa under British dominion.

**12.11.1878**

Sir Henry Bartle Frere, High Commissioner for southern Africa, delivers an ultimatum to Zulu king, Cetshwayo, with demands including that he disband his 40,000–60,000-strong army.

ABOVE: Lieutenant Gonville Bromhead. The 1964 film *Zulu*, in which Michael Caine plays Lieutenant Bromhead, depicts the Zulus saluting the British at the end of the battle, supposedly moved to do so by their courage. It is an invention of the movie makers; the Zulus who were able to retreated when Chelmsford's column became visible in the distance. Those too wounded to retreat were dealt with mercilessly.

LEFT: *The Defence of Rorke's Drift* by Alphonse-Marie-Adolphe de Neuville (1882) is a remarkably accurate rendition of the battle including a number of portraits of the leading protagonists.

## STEP-BY-STEP

**01** A huge Zulu army all but wipes out the British troops at Isandlwana.

**02** Survivors of the massacre flee across the Buffalo (Mzinyathi) River to Rorke's Drift, in British territory.

**03** The Rorke's Drift troops spring into action, improvising barricades and fortifying buildings as best they can.

**04** At 16:30, the Zulus attack from the west and northwest, the first of six full-scale attacks over the next 14 hours. Although outnumbered almost 30 to one, the British hold them off. Those too injured to shoot reload and pass ammunition.

**05** Evening: the Zulus break through and set the hospital alight. Some patients are rescued by troopers using their rifles to smash holes through the walls and drag them into the yard; others die in the flames.

**06** As ammunition runs low there is hand-to-hand, assegai-to-bayonet fighting throughout the station.

**07** Overnight, the British withdraw to a last barricaded area and bitterly defend it by the light of the burning hospital.

**08** As dawn approaches, the attack lessens then ceases; seeing Chelmsford's relief column nearing, the Zulus retreat.

**01.11.1879**
Cetshwayo refuses. The British army invades the Zulu kingdom, beginning the Anglo-Zulu War.

**01.20.1879**
British commander Lord Chelmsford splits his force into three columns, then further splits the 5,000-strong column he is leading, leaving 1,700 men in camp at Isandlwana.

**01.22.1879**
A Zulu force of up to 20,000 massacres 1,350 British forces at Isandlwana, disemboweling many.

**01.22.1879**
Isandlwana survivors cover the 10 miles (16 km) to Rorke's Drift, pursued by around 4,000 Zulus, who proceed to besiege the stronghold.

**07.04.1879**
The British capture and burn Cetshwayo's royal capital, Ulundi, effectively ending the war.

# THE BATTLE OF MAIWAND

DATE  July 27, 1880
LOCATION  Maiwand, Kandahar Province, Afghanistan
OBJECTIVE  To prevent the advance of the Afghan warlord Ayub Khan

**The need to determine who held power in Afghanistan was a natural extension of British rule over India; it was part of "the Great Game"—Britain's rivalry with Russia to control Central Asia. In 1878, amid power struggles between Afghan leaders, the Second Anglo-Afghan War began. Maiwand proved to be its bloodiest battle.**

### Into Afghanistan

Brigadier General George Burrows took his troops from Kandahar intending to support 6,000 Afghan tribesmen armed by the British at Girishk, 75 miles (120 km) away. The idea was to block the path of Ayub Khan's rebel forces. But the Afghans mutinied, joining the man they were supposed to fight.

This defection badly hindered the British: it emboldened local villagers to attack them, while encumbering them with masses of equipment that could not be stored for fear it would be plundered.

Burrows had not seen active service for 25 years. He led a force consisting of 500 British and 2,000 Indian soldiers, including the 30th Regiment of the Bombay Native Infantry (Jacob's Rifles), who had seen no active service, and included many recruits still in training. The expedition included a further 3,000 support personnel.

### The Battle Begins

Burrows's men began their advance tired, after a night spent striking camp, and mostly unfed. The heat was searing and the landscape deceptive.

Passing beyond a wide ravine onto open ground, the infantry took up position with the cavalry behind them. At 10:50, an artillery bombardment began. The Afghans had 36 guns to the British force's 12 and soon ran out of ammunition. Burrows ordered an infantry attack but canceled it once underway, concerned about casualties. This proved a fatal mistake. Using a ravine connected to the one the British had crossed, the Afghans came within 1,500 feet (458 m) of the British advance and cut off their passage to water and supplies. After three hours of holding position under devastating artillery fire, the cavalry were brought into the attack, but it was too little, too late.

### An Ignominious Retreat

By 15:00, outnumbered, outgunned, and all but overrun, Burrows began the retreat to Kandahar. It was hellish: as Captain John Slade said, "helpless wounded suffering the tortures of the damned" with "hordes" of Afghan horsemen "relentlessly cutting our men down and looting." In all, 962 of the British-Indian troops died in battle or during the retreat. While Maiwand is generally seen as one of the worst defeats in Britain's colonial history, the Afghans also suffered—it took Ayub a week to clear up to 5,500 of his dead from the battlefield—critically weakening their military strength.

ABOVE: Canine bravery in the battle was also rewarded. Bobbie was a mixed breed dog belonging to Lance Sergeant Peter Kelly, who went into battle with the 66th Regiment and despite being wounded and lost in the confusion, found his way back to the 66th as they retreated. Queen Victoria presented Bobbie with the Afghan Medal during the medal presentation for the human survivors of the battle.

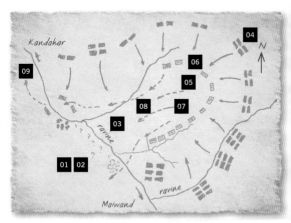

## TIMELINE

**11.21.1878**

Three columns of British-Indian troops, around 40,000 men, under the command of Sir Frederick Roberts, march on Afghanistan, beginning the Second Anglo-Afghan War.

**02.21.1879**

Having fled Kabul, leaving his son Yaqub Khan to rule, Afghan Emir Sher Ali dies. Khan and Britain's representative Sir Louis Cavagnari sign the Treaty of Gandamak. Cavagnari becomes an envoy in Kabul.

ABOVE: Cavalry charge at the Battle of Maiwand. HM 66th Foot Regiment lost 286 men or almost two-thirds of their number in the battle. The bravery of the group known as The Last Eleven, who died while trying to keep their Colors aloft, spurred this tribute from one Afghan artilleryman, "before [they] died with their faces to the foe, fighting to the death … The conduct of these men was the admiration of all that witnessed it." Maiwand marked the last time a British military unit ever carried Colors into battle.

## STEP-BY-STEP

**01** Near Maiwand on July 24, Brigadier General Burrows receives word Ayub Khan's forces are close.

**02** Burrows waits two days for confirmation, then at 22:30 gives the order to attack the following morning.

**03** At 05:30, tired and hungry, British and Indian soldiers begin their advance. The temperature rises to 120°F (48°C).

**04** What, in the heat haze, officers mistake for masses of distant trees, prove to be Afghan warriors—not 10,000 as expected, but 25,000.

**05** The British halt on an exposed plain beyond a ravine, failing to realize it connects to a ravine near the Afghan position; the Afghans use it to outflank the British as the battle progresses.

**06** During three hours of artillery bombardment, British cavalry hold position on the open plain, suffering enormous casualties.

**07** British guns are withdrawn to restock ammunition, unsettling the infantry.

**08** Cut off from water and other supplies by the Afghans, the defeated British begin to withdraw.

**09** Parched, injured, and under attack from villages they pass, British forces limp back to Kandahar. The last of the rear guard stagger in 36 hours after their advance began.

RUSSIAN EMPIRE

Kabul  Jalalabad

AFGHANISTAN  Ghazni

Maiwand  Kandahar

BRITISH INDIA

| **09.03.1879** | **05.31.1880** | **07.04.1880** | **07.27.1880** | **04.22.1881** |
|---|---|---|---|---|
| Cavagnari and all in the British compound in Kabul are massacred by mutinous Afghan soldiers in an eight-hour siege; Yaqub Khan refuses to help. | Yaqub Khan has abdicated; the British briefly support his brother Ayub Khan before installing the Khans' pro-British cousin Abdur Rahman Khan as Emir. | A 2,500-strong British-Indian force under Brigadier General Burrows heads north from Kandahar to stop Ayub Khan's march south from Herat. | They meet in the battle of Maiwand near Girishk. Bloodily defeated, the British retreat to Kandahar. | The British evacuate Kandahar, effectively ending the Second Anglo-Afghan War. |

# THE SIEGE OF KHARTOUM

DATE        March 13, 1884–January 26, 1885
LOCATION    Khartoum, Sudan
OBJECTIVE   To hold a remote fortified city against an Islamic uprising

**More than 11,000 people died in this confrontation, which caused uproar among the British public and helped to topple a prime minister. At its heart it was a struggle to the death between two men: each a hero to his people; each driven by religious fervor; and each unshakably convinced that right was on his side.**

### The Stage is Set

As Ottoman power in the Near East waned, imperial Britain sought to increase its influence. Egypt and the Sudan, and control of Suez and the Red Sea, proved critical. Neither empire was popular among local communities.

Outside the walls of Khartoum was Muhammad Ahmad, better known by his adopted title, al-Mahdi (Arabic for "right-guided one"), a messianic redeemer, supported by a 30,000-strong coalition of "Mahdists": disaffected taxpayers, fanatics, dirt-poor peasants, slave-traders, and tribesmen.

Opposing him was General Charles "Chinese" Gordon, a hero at home in Great Britain for his actions in the Second Opium War and his subsequent anti-slavery campaigning and philanthropy. Gordon adhered to an unorthodox, mystical form of Christianity and believed he was an agent of God's purpose. In 1884, as an expert imperial troubleshooter, Great Britain sent him back to Sudan, where he had previously been Governor-General. His mission was to evacuate Egyptian forces from Khartoum in the face of Mahdist threats, then withdraw.

### The Confrontation Begins

On his arrival, Gordon evacuated 2,000 women, children, and the infirm, plus 600 Egyptian soldiers, leaving the remainder of a garrison of some 7,000–8,000 and a civilian population of almost 40,000. Against the wishes of the British prime minister William Gladstone, he then began to administer the city, laying in supplies and increasing the fortifications.

On March 13, the Mahdists laid siege. Gordon was undaunted, despite unrelenting attacks. On April 19, he telegraphed Cairo to say he had five months' provisions, and with 2,000–3,000 further Turkish troops could soon triumph. As with subsequent requests for troop support, he was refused. Over the next few months, Gordon sent out several attack forces, which were defeated. Food ran low and he knew the upcoming seasonal fall in the Nile's waters would render the city vulnerable. He sent messages to al-Mahdi seeking to negotiate, but was rebuffed.

### Forty-eight Hours Too Late

After much public agitation, in August, the British government finally agreed to send a relief force. Taking three months to prepare, it set out into Sudan in October. Progress was slow, with engagements with Mahdist forces along the way. On the night of January 25, knowing reinforcements were nearing, al-Mahdi's men made a twofold push, one flank wading across the low White Nile while another attacked the city gate. They overran the weakened defenders and, against al-Mahdi's orders, Gordon was killed. Two days later the relief force arrived. News of Gordon's death caused uproar in Great Britain. In his name, the British returned in force in 1898, led by General Kitchener, and took Sudan, in effect controlling it for the next half-century.

## TIMELINE

**03.1881**
Muhammad Ahmad tells his followers he has been sent by Allah to overthrow the Sudan's infidel leaders and restore righteousness: he is al-Mahdi. Mahdist forces begin to control Sudan.

**02.18.1884**
Gordon reaches Khartoum. Within a week he telegrams to Cairo, "if Egypt is to be quiet the Mahdi must be smashed up."

## STEP-BY-STEP

**01** British Prime Minister William Gladstone directs Gordon to evacuate Khartoum then leave.

**02** Gordon reaches Khartoun in February 1884. He evacuates a small number and asks Great Britain to install his previous foe Al-Zubayr Rahma as Sudan's ruler. The response is appalled refusal, given Rahma's slave-trader history.

**03** Khartoum is besieged by Mahdist forces on March 13.

**04** Under siege, Gordon disarms 250 "mutinous" Bashi-Bazouks (Ottoman mercenaries).

**05** Queen Victoria and the public press the British government to act to help Gordon. Gladstone relents to the mounting pressure, but the relief force will take five months to reach Khartoum.

**06** Gordon's assistant, Colonel Stewart, sails north on September 10 in a convoy of five steamers hoping to meet the relief force. Eight days later he is ambushed and killed.

**07** Gordon makes his final diary entry on December 14: "Now, mark this, if the Expeditionary Force—and I ask for no more than 200 men—does not come in ten days the town may fall, and I have done my best for the honour of our country. Good-bye."

**08** The city is overrun and Gordon is killed against al-Mahdi's orders; his head is carried on a pike through the streets.

LEFT: The Battle of Abu Klea, January 17 1885. The British forces despatched to relieve Gordon faced resistance from the Mahdists and arrived two days after Khartoum fell.

ABOVE: Classic Victorian mythmaking such as George William Joy's heroic painting *General Gordon's Last Stand* (1885) cemented his place as a patriotic martyr in British consciousness.

---

**04.16.1884**
Gordon sends a message to the British Consul General of Egypt, Sir Evelyn Baring: "I shall hold on here as long as I can" but if beaten "the indelible disgrace" of abandoning Sudan will be Great Britain's.

**05.10.1884**
The relief force led by Gordon's friend General Wolseley reaches Wadi Haifa in northern Sudan.

**01.26.1885**
The Mahdists storm Khartoum, killing all the soldiers, around 4,000 civilians, and Gordon.

**06.22.1885**
Al-Mahdi dies suddenly, probably of typhus. Mocked as the "murderer of Gordon," Gladstone has resigned (although he will be Prime Minister twice more).

**09.02.1898**
At the battle of Omdurman, Major General Kitchener defeats the Mahdists and reestablishes British control of Sudan.

# THE JAMESON RAID

DATE        December 29, 1895–January 2, 1896
LOCATION    South African Republic (Transvaal)
OBJECTIVE   The overthrow of Transvaal's Boer government

The Dutch began colonizing what we now call South Africa in 1652. The Dutch word "boer" (meaning farmer) and later the name "Afrikaners" became the catch-all term for these settlers. In 1806, the British took Cape Colony from the Dutch, and over the next century there was increasing tension between the British and the Boers. In 1895 it reached flash point.

### Cecil Rhodes's Ambition
The only thing bigger than the fortune Cecil Rhodes built from diamonds and gold was his plan to extend British control from the Cape of Good Hope to Egypt. Expatriate Scot Dr. Leander Starr Jameson shared his dream. Rhodes and Jameson saw Boer-controlled Transvaal as the major hurdle to their expansionist plans.

### Taking Action
By 1890, "Uitlanders" (foreigners), drawn by gold finds, outnumbered Afrikaners two-to-one in Transvaal. The Boer President Paul Kruger restricted their influence by passing a law preventing anyone who had lived there for less than 14 years from voting. Prominent Uitlanders chafed against this. Rhodes encouraged their discontent, and hatched a plan to launch an armed raid on the Transvaal capital, Johannesburg, sure that the initial incursion would spur the Uitlanders to revolt and overthrow Kruger's government. The plan was encouraged by the anti-Boer British Colonial Secretary Joseph Chamberlain.

Meanwhile, Jameson assembled a private army at Mafeking and waited near the Transvaal border for word from Rhodes. But, in the United Kingdom, Chamberlain had changed his mind, and sent urgent word to Rhodes, who was also facing factional indecision among the Uitlanders. Rhodes decided to call off the raid. But Jameson was impatient for action and, on December 29, 1895, he led an armed column of 511 men, plus a large support column, into the Transvaal.

### An Unfolding Fiasco
Jameson planned a three-day ride to Johannesburg, thinking he had the advantage of surprise and support from the disaffected Uitlanders. But Boer Commandos (civil militia) tracked him from the start, engaging in frequent skirmishes that cost Jameson many men and horses. By daybreak on January 2, the exhausted raiders stopped at a farm two hours' ride from Johannesburg where they were surrounded by the Boer militia. After 30 more of his men were killed, Jameson surrendered. There was no uprising; his plan had failed. Jameson was sentenced in England to 15 months' jail (but released early because of illness); Rhodes was forced to resign as prime minister of Cape Colony; and his British South Africa Company paid almost £1 million compensation to Transvaal. The Jameson Raid polarized Anglo-Boer supporters, becoming one of the triggers for the Second Anglo-Boer War, which broke out in 1899. Remarkably, Jameson returned to Africa, served as prime minister of the Cape Colony from 1904–08 and was awarded a British baronetcy in 1911. Rudyard Kipling cited him as the inspiration for his poem "If."

RIGHT: The Battle of Doornkop, where Jameson was defeated on January 2, 1896. The Raiders' field guns included six Maxim self-powered machine guns.

ABOVE: Jameson taken prisoner after the raid's failure (as featured in *Le Petit Journal*, January 2, 1986). While Rhodes's reputation only fully recovered after his death, Jameson was briefly disgraced, then lauded and honored with a peerage. After death his body was taken to the Matopo Hills (in what is now Zimbabwe), where he was buried near Rhodes.

## TIMELINE

| 1871 | 1883 |
| --- | --- |
| British adventurer Cecil Rhodes is drawn to the diamond fields of Kimberley, where he will meet Dr. Leander Starr Jameson. | Paul Kruger is elected president of the Boer-controlled South African Republic, known as Transvaal. |

## STEP-BY-STEP

**01** In 1895, Cecil Rhodes plots to incite the overthrow of the Transvaal government; in the United kingdom, Colonial Secretary Joseph Chamberlain lends his support.

**02** Dr. Leander Starr Jameson amasses a small private army at Mafeking, near the Transvaal border, in readiness.

**03** Chamberlain becomes fearful, saying, "If this succeeds it will ruin me," and sends urgent word to Rhodes to call it off.

**04** Rhodes finds the Uitlanders—on whose uprising the plan depends—cannot agree. The plan must be abandoned.

**05** December 29, 1895: Claiming not to have received the message from Rhodes to stand down, Jameson takes the decision into his own hands and crosses the border.

**06** Transvaal Boer Commandos track the raiders' movements and engage them in rearguard skirmishes, slowing them and inflicting casualties.

**07** Having ridden for two days continuously, Jameson's men stop at daybreak on January 2, 1896, at a farm called Doornkop, two hours' ride from Johannesburg.

**08** Jameson soon learns that there is no Uitlander citizen uprising and that he and his forces are surrounded and outnumbered. They fight on through the day, finally surrendering around 20:00. After burying their dead, the survivors are taken to prison in nearby Pretoria.

| 1886 | 1889 | 07.17.1890 | 01.12.1896 | 03.26.1902 |
|---|---|---|---|---|
| Discovery of huge gold reserves in Transvaal draws fortune-seekers from around the world, dubbed "Uitlanders" (foreigners). | Dr. Leander Starr Jameson begins undertaking trade and diplomatic missions on Rhodes's behalf. | Cecil Rhodes is elected prime minister. He connives with Jameson to mount a raid on Johannesburg, the Boer capital of Transvaal. The raid turns into a disaster. | Disgraced by the failed raid, Rhodes is forced to step down as prime minister but refuses to denounce Jameson. Under a deal with Transvaal, Jameson is tried and sentenced by the British government. | Cecil Rhodes dies at age 48, endowing the Rhodes Scholarships for the University of Oxford in his will. In 1904, Jameson becomes prime minister of Cape Colony. |

# THE LYNMOUTH–PORLOCK OVERLAND LIFEBOAT RESCUE

DATE        January 12–13, 1899
LOCATION    Lynmouth, Devon, and Porlock, Somerset, England
OBJECTIVE   The rescue of the crew of the imperiled sailing ship *Forrest Hall*

A fearsome storm was smashing the coastline of the notorious Bristol Channel when a distress signal alerted lifeboat volunteers to the imminent destruction of the ship *Forrest Hall*. The northwesterly gale prevented the launch of the lifeboat in Lynmouth; the only hope was a desperate plan to drag the lifeboat overland to Porlock, 15 rugged, hilly miles (24 km) away across Exmoor.

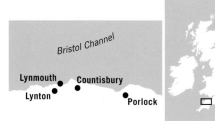

*Exmoor*

### Planning

At 19:52 on January 12, Jack Crocombe, a ship's captain and coxswain of the lifeboat *Louisa*, based in the north Devon village of Lynmouth, received a telegram. The fully rigged three-masted ship *Forrest Hall* was being pushed on to the Porlock shore; the 13 crew and five apprentices aboard were powerless to stop her. The gale prevented *Louisa*'s crew launching in Lynmouth and rowing around the headlands as usual. Crocombe realized the ship's only chance was if the *Louisa* could be dragged up and down the huge hill separating the two villages.

Overcoming some initial reluctance among his fellow villagers to this seemingly unachievable plan, he sent six men ahead with shovels and pickaxes to widen the road as best they could. Then he sent a messenger to the local coach supplier in neighboring Lynton, who provided 20 shire horses. These were harnessed to the *Louisa*'s wheeled carriage—a total weight of 10 tons (9 tonnes). With around 100 men, women, and even children to help, the crew set off up the steep 1:4.5 Countisbury Hill that rises out of Lynmouth.

### Implementation

In freezing cold, and driving rain, the villagers eventually got their load to the top of Countisbury Hill, a steep 1,423 feet (434 m) above sea level. Here a wheel came off the carriage and progress stopped while it was repaired. At this point, many returned to the shelter of their homes, leaving 20 men to travel a further 13 miles (21 km) across bleak, storm-swept Exmoor, and then to control the horses and their load on the even steeper (1:4) descent down Porlock Hill. Despite obstacles, including a garden wall and numerous hedges that had to be demolished to allow the boat to pass, they made it safely to Porlock Weir at 06:30.

### Outcome

Cold, hungry, and exhausted as they were, the crew, the youngest just 15, immediately launched the *Louisa*. They rowed for an hour to the *Forrest Hall,* then stood by until daybreak when the tug that had been towing her the previous day arrived. *Louisa*'s crew helped get a line from the tug to the ship and also went aboard to hoist the ship's anchors because her own crew was too exhausted to do it. They then rowed in the wild seas by the ship's side as she was towed to safety in Barry, Wales.

## TIMELINE

| 03.04.1824 | 1854 |
| --- | --- |
| The National Institution for the Preservation of Life from Shipwreck is founded by Sir William Hillary. | The name is changed to the Royal National Lifeboat Institution, and lifejackets (made of cork) are first issued to rescuers. |

## STEP-BY-STEP

**01** The 1,900-ton (1,724-tonne) cargo ship *Forrest Hall* sets out from Bristol to Liverpool.

**02** What will become a Force 8 gale builds. The *Forrest Hall*, unable to make headway, is put under tow.

**03** The towing cable snaps and the ship's rudder is lost. Despite lowering two anchors, she begins to drift ashore in the tempest.

**04** In Lynmouth, Jack Crocombe and his lifeboat crew get an urgent telegram: they are the ship's only hope.

**05** The smashing northwesterly prevents the launch of lifeboat *Louisa* from Lynmouth. Crocombe declares: "We'll launch from Porlock."

**06** Fighting the elements and the harsh landscape, *Louisa*'s crew, Lynmouth villagers, and 20 horses drag the lifeboat 15 miles (24 km) to Porlock. It takes ten hours and four horses die as a result of the strain.

**07** Thanks to the *Louisa*, the *Forrest Hall* and all aboard are saved.

**08** On the centenary of the rescue, the heroes are honored with a reenactment—using tractor-power.

ABOVE: A crowd gathers as the lifeboat sets out to sea on its heroic mission.

OPPOSITE PAGE, TOP: A view of Countisbury Hill. The 1:4 hill climbs out of Lynmouth and over Exmoor—the route of the *Louisa* lifeboat in 1899.

OPPOSITE PAGE, BELOW: 1960s painting *The Overland Launch* by George Hooker, depicting the *Louisa*, as the obstructed route at the base of Porlock Hill was being negotiated, which involved the part demolition of a cottage to allow its passage.

ABOVE: Heroic Jack Crocombe, the local ferry boat captain.

---

**01.12.1899**
The *Forrest Hall* faces destruction; Captain Jack Crocombe and his *Louisa* lifeboat crew set out on an audacious rescue, dragging a lifeboat across Exmoor.

**01.13.1899**
Eleven hours after they received the urgent telegram, they reach the ship and help her to safety.

**1899**
Each heroic crew member receives £5 and a silver watch; Crocombe and his deputy, George Richards, also receive gold watch chains.

**12.11.1901**
Built in response to the events of 1899, a new lifeboat station opens at Minehead, one headland east of Porlock.

**08.18.1906**
The sturdy lifeboat *Louisa* is retired from service. Captain Crocombe dies at age 79 in 1933; he spent 40 years as a volunteer lifeboat rescuer.

# THE SIEGE OF LADYSMITH

DATE        November 2, 1899–February 28, 1900
LOCATION    Ladysmith, colony of Natal, southern Africa
OBJECTIVE   The isolation of the British force inside the city

In 1899, tensions between the Boers and British in southern Africa flared into war for the second time in a decade. The Boers immediately moved to attack the British townships of Mafeking, Ladysmith, and Kimberley. Great Britain sent 70,000 extra troops under General Sir Redvers Buller but, before they arrived, Field Marshal Sir George White led his contingent north of the Tugela River, where they became besieged at Ladysmith.

### A New Kind of War

With its far greater numbers and well-drilled soldiers, fighting a loosely organized civilian militia, imperial Britain expected to win the Second Anglo-Boer War easily. The early months proved a rude shock.

White, in charge of British troops in Natal, was of the old school. Twenty years after he had won a VC, at age 44, in Afghanistan, he was pulled into service again. But he had little knowledge of South Africa, and was unprepared for the guerrilla tactics of the Boers, who traveled light, were well armed, and made clever use of the topography.

Against the advice of Buller, who was in transit with reinforcements, White marched into northern Natal. After several costly engagements, White decided to make a stand at Ladysmith, a British depot and garrison town. Here, his force was surrounded and cut off by Boers who pinned them down for 118 days. Estimates of the number of besieged troops varies widely, from 5,500 to more than 20,000, but in his book *London to Ladysmith via Pretoria*, the future UK prime minister Winston Churchill, on the scene as a newspaper correspondent, put the number at 10,000. In addition, there were at least 8,000 civilians. The Boers aimed to starve them into surrendering.

### Life under Siege

Life inside Ladysmith was an odd mix of deadly threat and mundanity. Boer shellfire disrupted life at the officers' club, the local hotel, and on the cricket pitch. Military communication was maintained with forces south of the Tugela River by runners, heliograph, and searchlight. The Boers fired an average of two tons' worth of artillery a day—except on Sundays—and mockingbirds learned to mimic the whistle that preceded a heavy "Long Tom" shell. Viewing the siege became a pastime for local Boer families. But things then became grim. Under truce, a temporary relief camp was established for ailing civilians. The artillery caused some casualties, but disease was a far greater problem due to unclean water, killing 60 percent of those who died. By January, food was so scarce that the remaining horses were shot for meat. Morale sank. But rescue was a month away.

### Relief, At Last

Having been beaten back at battles at Colenso and Spion Kop, Buller and his men finally crossed the Tugela River by pontoon on February 25, and two days later captured Boer positions outside Ladysmith. The following day, the Boers, suffering from lack of forage for horses and dwindling numbers, withdrew. The siege was finally over, but with an estimated total of 3,200 dead.

ABOVE: A bird's-eye view of the siege. The crossroads town of Ladysmith, founded in 1849, was named for the wife of Cape Colony governor Sir Harry Smith. Note the surveillance balloon used to observe the besiegers.

RIGHT: The intense hand-to-hand fighting of the siege during the battle of Spion Kop.

## TIMELINE

**10.02.1899**

Amid rising British–Boer tensions, Boer conscription begins: men aged 16–60 must join a Commando and equip themselves with a horse, rifle, ammunition, and eight days' provisions.

**10.09.1899**

Kruger delivers an ultimatum: the British withdraw troops from Boer colony borders and send back reinforcements in transit, or there will be war.

## STEP-BY-STEP

**01** Spotting the Boers in the hills east of Ladysmith, British troops march out from the garrison. The outnumbered Boers are easy victors in the battle that follows, losing 200 men to Britain's 1,200.

**02** The British retreat to the town, which the Boers cut off and then lay siege.

**03** Sir Redvers Buller arrives in South Africa to command the Natal Field Force; he splits the force in three and sets out to relieve the besieged towns of Ladysmith and Mafeking.

**04** The Ladysmith relief force loses to the Boers in the first of its battles, at Willow Grange.

**05** In the battle of Colenso, British troops are again heavily beaten by a much smaller Boer force. The British public is shocked at this and even more so by news of the message General Buller sends later to Field Marshal White suggesting that, if he cannot break through, he should consider surrendering.

**06** Buller, suffering a crisis of confidence, asks to be relieved of his post; Lord Roberts has already been installed above him.

**07** On January 23, 1900, British forces attempt to secure Ladysmith from the west but withdraw after suffering heavily in the battle of Spion Kop, despite their far greater numbers.

**08** Finally, after four months, Buller's force crosses the Tugela River; the Boers withdraw, and he relieves Ladysmith.

**10.11.1899**
The Boer premier Kruger's deadline passes without response; the Second Boer War, known in South Africa as the Second War of Independence, begins.

**10.11.1899**
A Boer force of up to 35,000, led by General Piet Joubert, crosses into the British colony of Natal.

**10.29.1899**
Following their defeat at the battle of Ladysmith, the British retreat to the town of that name.

**11.02.1899**
The Boers surround Ladysmith and cut telegraph and railway access. The siege begins.

**02.28.1900**
Buller's force crosses the Tugela River, the Boers withdraw, and the Ladysmith siege ends after 288 days. Mafeking is relieved three months later.

# 55 DAYS IN PEKING

**DATE**      December 1899–September 7, 1901
**LOCATION**  Peking (Beijing), Zhili Province, China
**OBJECTIVE** The defense of foreign ministers against a Chinese populist rebellion

Social unrest and economic disadvantage lay behind the violent chapter known outside China as the "Boxer Rebellion" and inside as the "Foreign Intervention," during which up to 100,000 civilians—both Chinese and foreign—were killed. The events of this brief period (between December 1899 and September 1901) contributed greatly to the overthrow of imperial rule in China in 1912.

### The Pressure Builds

In the 60 years leading to the Boxer Rebellion, China had lost the First and Second Opium Wars against Great Britain and France, and the First Sino-Japanese War, with humiliating, disadvantageous settlements following each conflict. Great Britain, France, Germany, Japan, Russia, and the United States—the so-called "Great Powers"—took trade control over areas of the country, attracting expatriate merchants and missionaries. For the foreigners, this had the benign name "spheres of influence," but to concerned Chinese it was *guafen* (carving the melon). Flooding, then drought, in the north added to the unrest, created the conditions for the rise of the zealously anti-foreign populist group the *Yihequan* (Right and Harmonious Fists).

### The Crisis Develops

Dowager Empress Cixi's effective seizing of the throne allowed the *Yihequan* to flourish. The governor of Shandong put the *Yihequan* on his payroll, renaming them *Yihetuan* (Righteous and Harmonious Militia), but to the foreigners they opposed they were called "Boxers," because of the physical training rituals that supposedly made them invulnerable.

In early 1900, Boxer attacks became more blatant, violent, and widespread in the north. By June, thousands had converged on the national capital Peking (Beijing) in Zhili province. The "Great Powers" had grown more and more concerned, and by the end of May, Great Britain, the United States, and Italy had warships off the coast, with armed contingents from France, Germany, Austria-Hungary, Russia, and Japan, who formed the "Eight-Nation Alliance," in transit.

On June 10, British Vice Admiral Edward Seymour attempted to lead an international force of 2,088 from Tianjin to Peking. While outwardly reassuring foreign governments, the Empress had in fact ordered imperial forces to support the Boxers in stopping Seymour.

With Boxer violence in the capital unchecked, foreign diplomats, missionaries, and Chinese Christian converts took refuge in the compound that housed international legations and diplomatic missions; here, they were besieged by Boxers, and by the Imperial Army.

### The Relief Expedition

Significantly boosting troop numbers, the Eight-Nation Alliance took Tianjin on July 14 after almost a month of fighting, then marched on Peking, occupying it on August 14 and breaking the siege after 55 days of torment. "At last our ears have heard the sweet music for which we have been listening for two months—the cannonading of the relief army," wrote besieged American teacher Luella Miner. As the imperial court fled, some among the international relief force proceeded to terrorize the city, raping, pillaging, and looting.

## TIMELINE

**09.21.1898**

Under enormous pressure from Japan, Russia, Germany, and France, Empress Dowager Cixi places her reformist adopted son, the Guanxu emperor, under house arrest and takes control of China.

**12.31.1899**

In one of the first Boxer attacks, a Catholic chapel in a converted temple in Li Lien Yuan, Shandong, is burned and two Chinese converts brutally killed. Magistrates support the Boxers.

ABOVE: One notice posted by the Boxers declared the group would "expel the foreign bandits and kill Christian converts, in order to save our people from miserable suffering" and warned, "Everyone who intends to spare someone, or to disobey our order by concealing Christian converts … will be burned to death to prevent his impeding our program." In this image, published in *La Domenica del Corriere* in 1900, Catholic-converted peasants are executed by firing squad.

LEFT: Clashes on the streets of Peking, August 15, during the rebellion.

## STEP-BY-STEP

**01** Angry about the influence of foreigners in China, members of the *Yihequan*, dubbed "Boxers" by non-Chinese, foment revolt.

**02** Initially targeting Christian missionaries and churches, Boxers are soon attacking any foreigner or foreign-owned property.

**03** Foreign governments with powerful trade holdings in China become increasingly concerned.

**04** The Dowager Empress Cixi reassures them, while at the same time condoning Boxer violence.

**05** The Great Powers attempt to send a force to Peking on trains commandeered at Tianjin, but are fought back by Boxers and Imperial Army troops.

**06** Foreigners and those seen as foreign sympathizers flee for their lives into the legation compound in Peking; they are besieged by Boxers and Imperial Army troops for 55 days.

**07** Increasing their force to more than 50,000, the Great Powers fight their way to Peking and occupy the city, ending the siege. The Dowager Empress flees. Many reports of cruelty and looting follow.

**08** The Empress, returned to her throne, paints the events as a mere "rebellion" rather than an uprising that had official support.

---

**05.22.1900**
Boxer attacks are now prevalent. Cavalry belonging to the Viceroy of Shandong's neighboring province Zhili are ambushed and killed.

**06.10.1900**
In response to alarm shared by Western and Japanese governments, an international force sets out from Tianjin but is forced back before reaching Peking (Beijing).

**06.17.1900**
The Empress orders the killing of all foreigners. Diplomats, missionaries, and Chinese Christian converts take shelter in the legation compound in Peking, where they are besieged.

**08.14.1900**
The force of the Eight-Nation Alliance captures Peking, breaking the siege, then loots and pillages the city.

**09.07.1901**
Declaring the activities of the Boxers a "rebellion" in order to minimize Western repercussions, the Empress signs the "Boxer Protocol," ending the conflict. She orders the execution of thousands of "Boxers."

# SHACKLETON'S THIRD ANTARCTIC EXPEDITION

DATE       August 8, 1914–August 30, 1916
LOCATION   Weddell Sea, Antarctica
OBJECTIVE  The first land crossing of Antarctica

**Officially, the "Imperial Trans-Antarctic Expedition" soon became known as "the *Endurance* expedition" for the ship on which Sir Ernest Shackleton traveled to Antarctica. Never has a name been more appropriate. For more than a year-and-a-half, the ill-fated expedition endured unimaginable conditions, always maintaining faith in the resourceful Shackleton to get them safely home.**

### Preparation for Antarctica

Shackleton's plans for a third trip to Antarctica changed when Roald Amundsen became the first person to reach the South Pole, in 1911. With that goal conquered, he decided to attempt the first land-crossing of the frozen continent.

There would be two ships. One, carrying Shackleton and his crew, would sail through the Weddell Sea and make landfall, then six men would travel the 1,800 miles (2,897 km) overland. Meanwhile, Captain Aeneas Mackintosh would sail to McMurdo Sound on the other side of Antarctica in the *Aurora* to place supply depots as far inland as possible.

Shackleton bought an oil- and coal-powered, 390-ton (398-tonne) barquentine, made for polar conditions, and named it *Endurance*, from his family motto. From nearly 5,000 applications, he chose 56 men, to be split between the two ships.

### The Adventure Begins

After three months' sailing south from Buenos Aires in Argentina on December 7, the expedition encountered pack ice in the South Atlantic; on January 19, the ice closed around the ship, less than 100 miles (160 km) from its intended landfall, Vahsel Bay.

Normal routine was abandoned. The ship withstood constant pressure from the creaking ice and, from May, permanent winter darkness fell for three months. Carpenter Harry McNish built two-man winter quarters between decks and the men gathered by the warmth of the stove in the snug fo'c'sle, which they named "The Ritz." Here they ate, wrote letters and journals, read, played music and games, and enjoyed magic-lantern lectures. They built "dogloo" shelters on the ice floe and exercised themselves and the dogs.

In late October, the pressure twisted the hull and water flowed in. Shackleton ordered his crew to remove supplies and lifeboats and to abandon the *Endurance*. It was -16°F (-27°C), and they were alone at the world's end.

### Attempting Rescues

After two months in Ocean Camp, and another three in the replacement Patience Camp, the splitting floe forced the men into lifeboats. They reached Elephant Island, from where Shackleton and five others set out for South Georgia, 800 miles (1,288 km) across the Southern Ocean. After crossing mountainous terrain, they walked in to the island's whaling posts. Three times between May and August, Shackleton tried to get back to Elephant Island but was thwarted by hostile weather. Finally, on August 30, Shackleton made it, rescuing the remainder of his crew, who had spent almost four months with two upturned rowboats as their only shelter. Astonishingly, all survived.

## TIMELINE

**02.04.1903**

Ernest Shackleton, snow-blind and suffering from scurvy, leaves Robert Falcon Scott's first Antarctic expedition on medical advice.

**01.09.1909**

Shackleton, Frank Wild, and two others come within 112 miles (180 km) of the South Pole before being forced to turn back. Shackleton is knighted on his return.

## STEP-BY-STEP

**01** After three months at sea, just one day's sail from its landing site, the *Endurance* is trapped in pack ice.

**02** Having drifted in an icy cage for nine months, the ship begins to break up. The ship is abandoned on October 27. On November 21, 1915, the last of the ship disappears beneath the ice. Frank Hurley captures it on film.

ABOVE: *The Endurance's* stern keeling over as captured by Frank Hurley in one of his extraordinary glass-plate photographs.
LEFT: Shackleton (right) with one of his team at the Antarctic base "Ocean Camp," where they waited following their aborted mission.

**03** Three days after abandoning ship, the crew begins a planned march to safety, forming Ocean Camp, but first the weakest animals, including the dogs and the company's cat, Mrs. Chippy, must be shot.

**04** After almost two months in Ocean Camp, scavenging from the remains of *Endurance*, they attempt another march, dragging lifeboats on sledges, but cover just 7.5 miles (12 km) in seven days. Patience Camp will be their home until the ice begins to break up.

**05** With the spring thaw, using lifeboats, they reach Elephant Island; then Shackleton and

five others strike out in the 22.5-foot (6.85 m) lifeboat *James Caird* for the island of South Georgia.

**06** Reaching South Georgia after battling mountainous seas for 16 days, Shackleton and two others hike over 22 miles (35 km) of glaciers and mountains in 36 hours, without a map, to reach Husvik Harbor on May 21.

**07** On August 30, despite being forced back three times by storms and ice, and once within sight of Elephant Island, Shackleton will not give up. On his fourth attempt, on the *Yelcho*, his rescue succeeds.

---

**08.08.1914**
On his third Antarctic expedition, after Shackleton first offers her up for the war effort, the *Endurance* sets sail from Plymouth.

**10.26.1914**
Shackleton and the final crew join the *Endurance* in Buenos Aires. It sets sail for Antarctica. Three months later, the *Endurance* is trapped by pack ice.

**02.22.1915**
The trapped ship is pushed to the 77th parallel, the furthest south it will go. Nine months later the crew abandon ship, but Shackleton will not be deterred.

**04.24.1915**
He sets out for South Georgia and, almost miraculously, returns to save the entire company.

**01.05.1922**
Shackleton dies from heart failure while preparing a further Antarctic quest. He is buried, at his widow's request, on South Georgia.

# THE IRISH HERO OF THE SOMME

DATE        July 1, 1916
LOCATION   The Somme Valley, France
OBJECTIVE  The location and rescue of his platoon commander

Northern Ireland's Robert Quigg, in his teens, went to work on local farms and estates, including the grand Macnaghten Estate at Dundarave. As World War I approached, Macnaghten heir Sir Harry enlisted as an officer and Private Quigg became his batman. The first hours of the Somme offensive on July 1, 1916 would prove fateful for both of them.

### Eager to Fight

As a prewar local Ulster Volunteer Force commander, Robert Quigg knew how to lead. But he also knew how to obey and went to France in 1916 as batman to platoon commander Lieutenant Harry Macnaghten, 11 years his junior. They had met when Quigg worked on the Macnaghten Estate and became close as they prepared to fight. Family legend has it that Sir Harry's mother, Lady Macnaghten, told Quigg not to come home without her son.

David Laverty, who served with Quigg, recalled him as remarkably eager to fight. As the clock ticked down to zero hour, 07:30, July 1, on the hot, sunny first day of fighting on the Somme, the tense men were given a tot of rum and reassurance by Macnaghten, who said, "Calm down, boys, we've plenty of time." Just minutes later, as the platoon went over the top near Beaumont-Hamel, Sir Harry was shot.

### Quick to Help

British forces made three advances, and each time the Germans forced them back. The battalion lost hundreds of men in those first few hours, cut down by shells and raking machine-gun enfilades, many lying in No Man's Land between the opposing trenches and suffering grievously. Quigg put himself into the line of fire, making trip after trip, crawling between the trench and shell-holes to pull his wounded comrades back for medical aid. In the early hours, word reached him that Sir Harry had been hit and was believed to be lying in open ground. Again, Quigg set forth. In all he made seven separate trips, during which he was subject to sniper and machine-gun fire, and mortar shelling. He carried or dragged back a fallen comrade each time. After seven hours, and seven rescues, he was too exhausted to continue. He had not located his commander; indeed Sir Harry's body was never found (on his death, the baronetcy passed to his only brother, Sir Douglas, who was killed in action just ten weeks later).

### Aftermath

Private Quigg became one of nine British soldiers to receive the ultimate accolade, the Victoria Cross, for his actions on the first day of the Somme offensive. The bereaved Lady Macnaghten also presented him with a gold watch for his valiant efforts to find her son.

TOP: Robert Quigg, a keen soldier, and one of the first Victoria Cross winners during the Somme Offensive.

ABOVE: The officers of the 12th Battalion Royal Irish Rifles. Lieutenant Harry Macnaghten is seen on the top row fifth from left.

RIGHT: An artist's impression of one the feats of bravery undertaken by Robert Quigg on July 1, 1916.

## TIMELINE

**01.1913**
Quigg, aged 28, joins the newly formed Ulster Volunteer Force and becomes commander of the Bushmills Volunteers.

**12.31.14**
On his father's death, at age 18, Edward "Harry" Macnaghten becomes a baronet.

## STEP-BY-STEP

**01** British forces, including Private Robert Quigg and Lieutenant Harry Macnaghten's Royal Irish Rifles platoon, begin fighting in what will become the four-and-a-half-month battle of the Somme.

**02** The platoon makes its first charge at the German trenches in the opening minutes of the battle on July 1, 1916; Macnaghten is shot.

**03** The English are forced back by the Germans.

**04** Twice more the platoon tries to charge the enemy; twice more they are forced back, with huge losses.

**05** Quigg puts himself into the line of fire repeatedly to rescue wounded comrades who are lying in No Man's Land, while trying to find his commander.

**06** Getting word that his lieutenant is still lying in No Man's Land, Quigg makes yet more trips. He does not find Macnaghten, but rescues other fallen soldiers hour after hour.

**07** On his seventh foray, Quigg goes within meters of German barbed wire to rescue a man he drags on a piece of waterproof cloth all the way to safety while under fire.

---

**09.14**
Quigg enlists as a Private in the 12th Royal Irish Rifles, a battalion of the British Army's Ulster Division.

**09.14**
Macnaghten is made Second Lieutenant in the Royal Highlanders (The Black Watch), attached to the 12th Battalion. Quigg becomes his batman.

**07.01.1916**
On the first day of the Somme offensive, Sir Harry, Quigg's platoon commander, is reported missing, believed killed or wounded in No Man's Land.

**07.02.1916**
After making seven rescue forays under fire, Quigg is finally forced to abandon efforts to find Sir Harry.

**01.08.1917**
King George V presents Quigg with the Victoria Cross. Quigg retires as sergeant in the Royal Ulster Rifles in 1934. He dies in 1955, aged 70, and receives a full military funeral.

# THE AGE OF
# **DIRTY TRICKS**
# **1914–1941**

The Age of Dirty Tricks includes some stories that deserve to be better known, such as the 1914 escape of German warships *Goeben* and *Breslau*. Barely a shot was fired, yet the ramifications were enormous; by some estimates the event extended World War I by two years.

In the case of the Czechoslovak Legion, it's the sheer drama and scale that warrants attention. In 1919, the Legion fought its way out of the Soviet Union by capturing the entire Trans-Siberian Railway from Moscow to Vladivostok: thousands of miles across two continents.

This was a time when people with huge personalities could make their mark—T.E. Lawrence, galloping across the Arabian desert on a camel; Mexican folk hero Pancho Villa provoking America with cross-border raids; and Paul Dukes, agent ST-25, defying death in Russia to become the only spy ever knighted for his actions in the field.

This Age does not quite span a full generation, yet that was enough time for the globe to plunge into two world wars. Even as World War I—"the War to End all Wars"—raged, US President Woodrow Wilson warned that its eventual resolution must be "a peace without victory" because a punitive postwar settlement would leave resentments and bitterness which would sow the seeds for more conflict. Unfortunately, with 1919's Treaty of Versailles, Wilson became party to precisely the thing he had warned against. Over the next decade and a half, Adolf Hitler and other German nationalists used the terms of the treaty as justification for their own extremism.

In 1939, Hitler manufactured an excuse for the war he had been building toward with a faked raid by "Polish insurgents" on a German radio station. The SS team who conducted the dirty operation even brought with them the victim they would leave as "evidence." Weeks later Hitler had the luckiest escape of his life when a meticulously planned bombing attack missed him by just eight minutes—we can only imagine how things might have changed if it had succeeded.

Airplane technology came into its own in this period. In 1916, thirteen years after the Wright Brothers' breakthrough powered flight, airdrops were used for the first time to try to resupply besieged troops—the British soldiers at Kut-al-Amara (in what is now Iraq). That same year, the US deployed aircraft for the first time in conflict, as aerial surveillance aided the force sent to hunt Villa.

By the early years of World War II, aerial attack and defense were vital. In 1940, when Hitler realized Britain would not concede despite its troops having been forced off mainland Europe, he began planning an invasion. But he had not accounted for the incredible effort and sacrifice of the Royal Air Force, which put paid to his "Operation Sealion." In the Pacific, it was the deadly aerial attack on Pearl Harbor that brought the United States into World War II, changing the course of not just the war but also the twentieth century.

# ESCAPE OF THE *GOEBEN* AND THE *BRESLAU*

DATE  August 2–10, 1914
LOCATION  Mediterranean Sea, Aegean Sea, and the Dardanelles
OBJECTIVE  To evade pursuing British forces

This seemingly trivial naval incident, where barely a shot was fired, changed the entire course of World War I and, in the words of Winston Churchill, brought "for the peoples of the East and Middle East more slaughter, more misery and more ruin than has ever before been borne within the compass of a ship."

### Under Orders

With Europe edging to war, the German Imperial Navy's Mediterranean Division consisted of the battle cruiser *Goeben* and the light cruiser *Breslau*, commanded by Rear Admiral Wilhelm Souchon. In the likely event of war with France, Souchon's orders were to prevent the French transporting troops from Algeria. On July 28, when Austria-Hungary declared war on Serbia, Souchon was in the Austro-Hungarian Adriatic port of Pola (now Pula, Croatia) refitting *Goeben*'s boilers. He sailed for the Mediterranean.

On July 30, First Lord of the Admiralty Winston Churchill telegraphed his Mediterranean commander, Admiral Sir Berkeley Milne, using imprecise wording that would cause confusion. In part the orders read: "aid the French in the transportation of their African army by covering and if possible bringing to action fast German ships, particularly *Goeben* … do not at this time be brought to action against superior forces." Milne relayed the instructions to his second-in-command, Rear Admiral Ernest Troubridge.

### Giving Chase

Souchon briefly bombarded Algeria on August 3 then made for Messina, Sicily, seeking coal, but, as he wrote, "ran straight into the British lion's jaws." Pushing ship and crew to their limits, he outran the British fleet. Milne gave his men orders not to engage.

With Italy still neutral, Milne stayed outside its territorial waters, focusing his resources on the northern passage of the Straits of Messina. Given existing treaties with Turkey, the British simply did not believe the Germans would seek port there. What they did not know was that Turkey had secretly been negotiating with Germany. Only the light cruiser *Gloucester* was waiting when Souchon's ships emerged from the Straits heading south.

### "Superior Forces"

Troubridge, sure Souchon was making for the Adriatic, signaled his intent to attack after dawn on August 7, but then changed his mind, deciding the enemy ships were "superior forces." *Gloucester* was still gamely shadowing the Germans and, when *Breslau* came within reach, fired at it. A brief duel ensued with no damage done. Under orders, *Gloucester* turned back.

On August 10, Souchon reached the Dardanelles and, following a declaration that the ships now belonged to Turkey, was welcomed. As a result, Turkey entered the war, with devastating consequences. Troubridge and Milne were officially exonerated, but their careers were irreparably damaged.

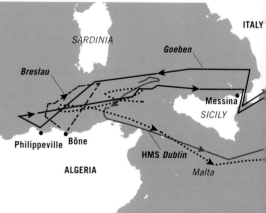

## TIMELINE

| 07.28.1914 | 08.02.1914 |
| --- | --- |
| Austria-Hungary declares war on Serbia. Austrio-Hungarian ally Germany declares war on Russia on August 1, and two days later on France. | Turkey's grand vizier signs a secret treaty promising to side with Germany against Russia. |

RIGHT: The German cruiser *Breslau* moves into the Dardanelles on August 6, 1914.

LEFT: Rear Admiral Wilhelm Souchon.

BELOW: The cruiser *Goeben*.

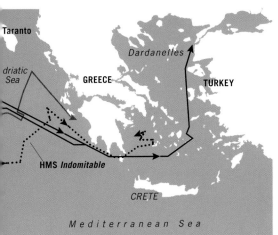

## STEP-BY-STEP

**01** Milne sends Troubridge with *Indomitable*, *Indefatigable*, five cruisers, and eight destroyers to cover the Adriatic.

**02** With *Goeben* near Taranto, Italy, *Indomitable* and *Indefatigable* are ordered to sail west, assuming the German ships will head for Gibraltar.

**03** Recoaling is a significant problem for Souchon; even with damaged boilers preventing *Goeben* reaching its top speed of 28 knots, it uses much coal.

**04** Having bombarded the ports of Bône and Philippeville in Algeria, Souchon feints northeast and is rejoined by *Breslau*. They turn east, passing *Indomitable* and *Indefatigable* going west. The British ships, now joined by the light cruiser *Dublin*, turn and shadow the Germans.

**05** The British battle cruisers are outrun but *Dublin* keeps up. With *Breslau* within reach, *Dublin* signals, asking if it should engage. Milne answers, "No." *Dublin*, too, is outrun.

**06** Souchon's ships refuel at Messina. *Indomitable*'s captain wants to position battle cruisers at either end of the Straits, but Milne orders the large ships north, with only *Gloucester* going to the Straits' south. Troubridge patrols the Adriatic.

**07** As Souchon's ships speed south from the Straits, *Gloucester* gives chase. *Dublin* races after them.

**08** Troubridge steams after them, signaling his intent to engage, but soon after decides conditions are not favorable and turns away from the chase.

**09** *Gloucester* exchanges fire with *Breslau* before being called back.

**10** The Germans reach the safety of the Dardanelles.

| 08.03.1914 | 08.04.1914 | 08.10.1914 | 10.29.1914 | 11.09.1914 |
|---|---|---|---|---|
| *Goeben* and *Breslau* bombard French ports in Algeria. Churchill requisitions two warships that have been built in Great Britain for Turkey, paid for by the people of Turkey. | After Germany declares war on, and invades, Belgium, Great Britain declares war on Germany. | *Goeben* and *Breslau* reach the Dardanelles and seek permission to enter. Turkish leaders and the German ambassador announce that Turkey has bought the ships, which reach Constantinople on August 16. | Led by Souchon, the ships bombard Odessa and other Black Sea Russian ports. He writes, "I have thrown the Turks into the powder keg and kindled war between Russia and Turkey." | After a court-martial, Troubridge is cleared of "forbear[ing] to pursue the chase" of *Goeben*. Later Milne publishes his own version of events after never receiving another command. |

# CAPTAIN POLLARD: "FIRE-EATER"

DATE        September 30, 1915
LOCATION    Sanctuary Wood, near Ypres, Belgium
OBJECTIVE   To recover lost ground and divert German forces from the Battle of Loos

The courageous actions of Alfred Pollard at Ypres during World War I justly won him military acclaim, but they were only a small part of the service record of this remarkable Englishman who enlisted at the start of the war and three years later was awarded the Victoria Cross.

### Keen for Battle
If ever anyone was born to serve his country in wartime, it was Alfred Pollard. He was an insurance clerk when the war started, 21, and "utterly irresponsible" as he wrote in his memoir. Handling his first rifle thrilled Private Pollard to the core: "I wanted to kill—not because I hated the enemy but because the primitive instinct was strong in me to fight."

### Undaunted in Action
Unlike many young men who gloried in the idea of war but were horrified by its reality, being in battle only made Pollard keener. In April 1915, at the Second Battle of Ypres, he witnessed the agonizing deaths of thousands when the Germans used chlorine gas. But all the suffering he saw only strengthened his resolve.

His abilities and enthusiasm saw Pollard rise quickly through the ranks. Promoted first to corporal, he was a sergeant at the time he earned a Distinguished Conduct Medal (DCM) for his courage in September 1915. As the British mounted their largest offensive of the year, the Battle of Loos, Pollard was among the troops sent to Sanctuary Wood, just east of Ypres, with a twofold purpose: to try to regain some of the ground lost months earlier and to draw German forces from Loos.

### Conspicuous Gallantry
Pollard led an eight-man bombing party—two riflemen with fixed bayonets in front, a bomb thrower and a bomb carrier following, with the same again behind them, then the leader of the party and a "spare" man, also carrying bombs—fighting for every step through trenches and wire entanglements. They were deep into No Man's Land when, he recalled, "A Hun bomb exploded right in front of me hurling me back … I sat up and shook myself like a dog. All over my body were little prickles where splinters of the bomb had pierced my flesh."

Despite his injuries, the captain continued to, as his DCM citation put it:

> throw bombs, at the same time issuing orders to and encouraging his men. By his example and gallant conduct he renewed confidence among the bombers at a time when they were shaken, owing to the enemy being in superior numbers and throwing many more bombs than were available on our side. He did not give up until he fell, severely wounded for the second time.

Pollard lived to fight another day.

ABOVE: Gun emplacements at the devastated Sanctuary Wood.

ABOVE RIGHT: Shell craters at Sanctuary Wood.

RIGHT: Portrait of Captain Alfred Pollard. Pollard's only brother, Frank, died at the Somme just before Alfred was wounded at Sanctuary Wood, although news took time to filter through. After Frank's death, Pollard wrote, "I felt that never again would I pity the enemy. Rather I would do my utmost to kill as many as possible."

## TIMELINE

| 08.18.1914 | 09.30.1915 |
| --- | --- |
| Alfred Pollard enlists in the Honourable Artillery Company (Infantry); his only brother, 25-year-old (James) Frank, has been with the regiment for seven years. | Sergeant Pollard leads a bombing party, counterattacking in Sanctuary Wood's No Man's Land. For his outstanding courage despite injury, he is awarded the DCM. |

## STEP-BY-STEP

**01** A year earlier, a forested area near Ypres was peaceful enough to earn the name Sanctuary Wood, now it is on the front line in the Ypres Salient.

**02** Fighting is so fierce and deadly that Captain Noel Chavasse, who will become one of only three people awarded a Victoria Cross twice, describes Sanctuary Wood as "the dearest and most dreadful spot in the whole of that desolation of abomination called the firing line."

**03** With the British and French making a major push in Artois, especially at Loos 25 miles (40 km) to the south, HAC infantry are deployed at Sanctuary Wood.

**04** Their goal is to regain ground lost over the summer to the Germans and to draw German forces from Loos. Sergeant Pollard's job is to lead a bombing party into No Man's Land.

**05** Despite receiving severe injuries from a German bomb, Pollard continues throwing bombs, giving orders, and encouraging his men, who are outnumbered and have a limited supply of bombs.

**06** Only another bad wounding is enough to stop Pollard.

---

**05.1916**
After extensive rehabilitation, Pollard returns to France as a second lieutenant. With his wounded right arm hindering him, he has taught himself to shoot left-handed.

**04.29.1917**
Having been awarded a Military Cross and added a bar, for two actions earlier in the year, Pollard's "most conspicuous bravery and determination" at Gavrelle bring him the Victoria Cross.

**06.1924**
Pollard begins a two-and-a-half-year stint as an RAF pilot.

**1932**
He publishes *Fire-Eater: the Memoirs of a VC.*

**12.04.1960**
Having written more than 50 books, mostly thrillers and adventure stories, and been a longtime newspaper columnist, Pollard dies, aged 67.

# THE SIEGE OF KUT-AL-AMARA

**DATE** December 7, 1915–April 29, 1916
**LOCATION** Kut-al-Amara, Ottoman Empire province of Mesopotamia
**OBJECTIVE** To vanquish British Army troops invading Mesopotamia

For many years, the surrender to the besieging Turks at Kut-al-Amara in April 1916 was considered Britain's greatest military defeat, despite the fact that, as Secretary of State for War Lord Kitchener told the House of Lords, the troops "did all that was humanly possible to resist to the last." Vengeance would occur a mere ten months later.

### A Harrowing Retreat

Considering that the all-important Anglo-Persian oil pipeline bases at Basra and Abadan in Mesopotamia's southwest had already been secured by a small force in November 1914, many modern historians view the 1915 British push to capture Baghdad as an ill-advised War Office attempt to save face after a year of disasters, including Gallipoli.

Easy victories in Mesopotamia achieved so far had made the British complacent; the heavy toll inflicted by the Turks at Ctesiphon came as a shock. A harrowing 12-day retreat to a defensive position at Kut-al-Amara, in a loop of the Tigris River, culminated in a 36-hour forced march covering 44 miles (70 km); lacking transport, supplies, and medical personnel, the 4,500 wounded among them suffered greatly.

### "Until Help Reaches You"

After General Charles Townshend's exhausted force reached Kut, he evacuated the wounded and Turkish prisoners to Basra and also sent the Cavalry Brigade south. With the Turks closing in there was no chance to rest. Kut was mud-walled—no use against artillery. Men worked around the clock digging trenches, setting up a hospital, and making other siege preparations. They expected a relief force any day.

Two months later the troops had withstood freezing cold, sandstorms, frequent shelling, fleas, lice, sniper-fire, bombing by enemy planes, dysentery, beriberi, scurvy, malaria, digging duty every night, and dwindling rations, when a message from Lord Hardinge, Viceroy of India, was passed to them. It said, in part, "I am confident resistance will be maintained until help reaches you in the near future."

### Worse to Come

Help did not arrive, and Kut was racked by more disease and starvation, then rain and flooding, and freezing temperatures. Supplies were dropped by plane, but not enough. The British troops resorted to eating horses, mules ("We all prefer Mule," wrote one soldier-diarist, "it is more tender though mule soup is pretty strong"), hedgehogs, and starlings. For religious and cultural reasons, the Indian soldiers refused meat, subsisting on leaves and grain instead.

After three failed relief attempts—at a cost of 23,000 casualties—and 147 days into the siege, Townshend surrendered, receiving promises his men would be treated humanely. In fact, as dreadful as the siege had been, what happened next was worse. Officers were comfortably detained (Townshend on an island near Constantinople), but the other ranks received horrendous treatment, with 4,250 (36 percent) dying on the march to Anatolia or in the prisoner-of-war camps there.

ABOVE: By March 17—with, as it turned out, six weeks still to go—rations were reduced to just "8 oz. bread and 1.25 lbs of horse flesh" (226 and 566 grams, respectively) a day. Many of the Indian troops refused the meat; photos of them post-siege are an eerie foreshadowing of WWII concentration camp victims.

RIGHT: Turkish prisoners during the progress of the British relief force.

## TIMELINE

**11.23.1914**
Having secured the oil pipeline at Abadan, an advance force of British troops in the Ottoman province of Mesopotamia easily takes Basra and Kurna.

**09.28.1915**
The 6th (Anglo-Indian) Division occupies Kut-al-Amara, then continues along the Tigris toward Baghdad, 120 miles (193 km) north.

## STEP-BY-STEP

**01** Following some easy Mesopotamian conquests, the 6th Division British and Expeditionary Force is ordered to push north and take Baghdad.

**02** General Townshend requests six months' worth of supplies but the Army's commander, General Sir John Nixon, authorizes six weeks' worth, directing him to find supplies in Baghdad.

**03** Having reached Ctesiphon, just 20 miles (32 km) from Baghdad, the British suffer heavy casualties in battle.

**04** Falling back to the garrison town of Kut-al-Amara, the Anglo-Indian forces bolster the town's defenses before they are besieged. Inside are 13,500 personnel, including some 3,500 Indian non-combatants, 2,000 sick or wounded, and 6,000 local Arab inhabitants. Townshend calculates he has enough supplies for one month.

**05** A British relief force fails to break the Turkish line at Hanna, with 2,600 killed or wounded.

**06** A further relief attempt is driven back at Dujaila, just 2 miles (3 km) from Kut.

**07** Conditions are hellish. On April 2, one soldier-diarist writes, "120th day of the siege—cold and wet—many of the men are dying from want and pneumonia." The siege would last for another four weeks.

**08** The relief boat *Julna,* with 270 tons (245 tonnes) of provisions, gets within half a mile (800 m) of Kut before being captured.

**09** Before surrendering, Townshend orders his men to burn and destroy guns, ammunition, saddlery, tents, and equipment.

| 11.26.1915 | 12.03.1915 | 01.21.–04.25.1916 | 04.29.1916 | 02.25.1917 |
|---|---|---|---|---|
| The British suffer heavily in the Battle of Ctesiphon, with more than half their 8,500-strong force killed or wounded. The British retreat to Kut. | Exhausted, the British forces reach Kut, where they prepare defenses. Four days later the Turks lay siege to the town. Townshend resists for 147 days. | Three British relief forces fail to break the Turkish lines. Townshend recommends a ransom of £2m—the Turks reject the offer . | Townshend receives permission to surrender. | After a daring nighttime desert encirclement, British forces regain control of Kut, going on to conquer Baghdad on March 11. |

# PANCHO VILLA'S RAID ON THE UNITED STATES

DATE     March 9, 1916
LOCATION     Columbus, New Mexico, United States
OBJECTIVE     Retaliation, restitution, and resupplying the Villistas

Two years earlier, Francisco "Pancho" Villa had been a Mexican revolutionary hero, but by 1916 he was locked in an increasingly precarious guerrilla resistance, fighting the government of his former ally Venustiano Carranza. With a single, foolhardy cross-border raid, he also brought the might of the US government after him.

### Mysterious Motives

Why did General Francisco "Pancho" Villa attack the tiny, primitive, border town of Columbus, New Mexico? Theories abound. Was it in retaliation for the assistance provided by US President Woodrow Wilson to Villa's revolutionary ally-turned-enemy Venustiano Carranza? Was it in response to a business deception?—according to some biographers, Villa paid for guns and ammunition from the Columbus-based Ravel brothers but never received his goods. Perhaps it was a supply raid, aimed at seizing weapons, food, horses, and other supplies for his forces. Most likely it was a combination of all of these. Villa certainly was not deterred by the US Army's Fort Furlong on the outskirts of town, but Villa's decision-making was also becoming increasingly irrational.

### "Viva Villa! Viva Mexico!"

Leading a heavily armed force of over 450 men, many with kerosene tins tied to their saddles, Villa crossed into the US just before 01:00. A mile (1.6 km) from town, they split into two columns in order to simultaneously approach from east and west, taking advantage of a large arroyo (ditch) running right through Columbus. Silently halting, they waited while three Villistas crept up to an army outpost and knifed its two soldiers to death. Then they split again into smaller raiding parties.

Just after 04:00, some of the Villistas entered the army camp. They were attempting to stampede the horses when a sleepless sergeant disturbed them, shooting one and sounding the alarm. Meanwhile, the attack began in town, with shouts of "Viva Villa!" and "Viva Mexico!" Villa's men targeted the commercial buildings, shooting, looting, and setting fires as they went.

### Defending Columbus

The troops ran to join the fight. Having had to break open the gun safes, the garrison's machine-gun platoon raced to set up their Benet-Mercier guns in two positions and fired a total of 20,000 rounds before dawn. The flames illuminated a chaotic scene, as school principal Dr. Roy Stivinson recalled: "In the lurid light we could distinguish men dashing hither and thither and riderless horses running about in all directions."

Almost unbelievably, only 18 Americans died in the raid: eight soldiers and ten civilians. With the coming of daybreak around 07:00, the gunfire tailed off and Villa's bugler sounded "recall." Major Frank Tompkins and 32 soldiers galloped after them, engaging the Mexicans in further fighting and causing them to lose much of the loot and horses they had grabbed. An estimated 100 or more Villistas, many young teenagers, died in the town or on the flight south. The ill-advised raid had turned into a shambles.

ABOVE: 1916 cartoon, "I've Had About Enough of This." Uncle Sam leaps across the border fence with Mexico to chase Pancho Villa.

ABOVE RIGHT: Columbus, largely burned to the ground, following Villa's attack.

## TIMELINE

**10.19.1915**
US President Woodrow Wilson gives de facto diplomatic recognition to the provisional Mexican government of Venustiano Carranza.

**01.19.1916**
Villista renegades slaughter 17 US mining personnel at Santa Ysabel. Pancho Villa denies responsibility.

COLUMBUS, N.M, AFTER VILLA'S RAID                    3784-6

## STEP-BY-STEP

**01** On February 27, Pancho Villa leaves San Geronimo, Chihuahua, with a force of around 450 heading toward the US border. Mexico-dwelling American Maud Hawkes Wright is taken along as a hostage after Villistas kill her husband.

**02** On March 7, Villistas encounter then hang three US cowboys who work for the Palomas cattle company. Another employee, Juan Favela, races to Fort Furlong. He tells Colonel Slocum an attack is imminent. Slocum dismisses the idea.

**03** A reconnaissance patrol dispatched to Columbus mistakenly advises Villa there are only 30 soldiers at Fort Furlong. In fact, there are over 300 members of the 13th Cavalry Division.

**04** At 04:00 on March 9, Villa begins his attack on the town, initially targeting Fort Furlong.

**05** Searching unsuccessfully for merchants Sam and Louis Ravel, who were out of town, two Villistas take 12-year-old Arthur Ravel hostage; when they are shot by US troops he flees into the desert. Meanwhile, drums of petrol near the Commercial Hotel are hit by stray bullets, adding to the confusion.

**06** Mr W.T. Ritchie offers the $50 he has on him in exchange for his life. The Villistas take the money, shoot him, and hurl his body into the fire consuming his eponymous hotel.

**07** After an hour or so, the battle begins to turn in the Americans' favor, thanks in large part to the US Army machine guns.

**08** More civilians are killed while trying to flee to the safety of the Hoover Hotel.

**09** At daylight, Villa frees Wright and his depleted men ride south, pursued for several hours by US troops.

**03.09.1916**
Villa and his men attack Columbus, New Mexico, leaving much of it in smoldering ruins.

**03.10.1916**
Wilson's cabinet agrees Villa should be pursued into Mexico. Additional US troops begin to pour into Columbus.

**03.15.1916**
Brigadier General John "Black Jack" Pershing leads 4,500 men across the border in a "punitive expedition."

**02.07.1917**
Despite the eventual involvement of around 10,000 US troops, and dozens of skirmishes with Villistas, Pershing's expedition ends without Villa's capture.

**07.20.1923**
Having "retired" in 1920, Villa is assassinated by disgruntled fellow countrymen. In 1959, in a gesture of US–Mexican goodwill, Pancho Villa State Park is established in Columbus.

# BLACK TOM SABOTAGE OPERATION

DATE    July 30, 1916
LOCATION    Black Tom Island, New York Harbor, New Jersey, US
OBJECTIVE    To destroy shipping facilities and munitions bound for the Allies

**The first large-scale terrorist attack on US soil was an act of sabotage from a foreign power with whom the US was then not at war. It terrified millions of citizens and caused a fortune in damages but, perhaps because of its miraculously small death toll, is little known today.**

### Diplomacy and Sabotage

In 1916, America was still officially neutral, its merchants theoretically free to trade with anyone. In practice, the British naval blockade prevented them selling goods to Germany or the other Central Powers. Instead, munitions and other exports flowed to Great Britain and its Allies. The German government maintained friendly diplomatic relations with the United States while secretly supporting and funding sabotage aimed at damaging this trade.

### A Juicy Target

For 18 months a propaganda and espionage team overseen by the German ambassador Johann Heinrich Count von Bernstorff attempted or carried out various illegal activities, including bomb-making and industrial sabotage. Then they targeted Black Tom.

Three-quarters of all the US munitions and armaments sold to the Allies moved through the New Jersey/New York docks, and the vast majority of these moved via Black Tom Island, nicknamed "the arsenal of democracy." For such an important site it was astonishingly poorly guarded.

### Terror Strikes

Nothing seemed amiss on the hot, humid evening of Saturday, July 29: the longshoremen had finished their six-day week and the dimly lit maze of rail sidings and warehouses was guarded by the usual eight men—six railroad detectives and two agency detectives. There was no guardhouse or gate preventing access to the railcars, which contained more than two million pounds (907,000 kg) of TNT, black powder, shrapnel, and dynamite. Contravening regulations, there was also a barge secured to one of the piers. It held 100,000 pounds (45,000 kg) of TNT.

At 00:12, guard Barton Scott noticed fire on the barge and ran to call the Jersey City Fire Department. Shells began to explode. At 00:40 three fire engines arrived, but their hoses could do nothing to stop the growing inferno, although they fought the blaze for 90 minutes. At 2:08 it all went up. The New York Times reported, "A million people, maybe five million, were awakened" by the explosion, which shattered windows in a 25-mile (40-km) radius, toppled tombstones, set fire to barges on the harbor, knocked out the phone system, and sprayed shrapnel into the Statue of Liberty. Shockwaves and smaller explosions continued for hours. A guard, a policeman, a barge captain, a baby, and possibly three others died. The property damage bill was $20 million ($375 million today). The truth about the German sabotage did not emerge for 23 years.

TOP: The fires raging on Black Tom island. Authorities initially blamed the explosion on Black Tom's guards, who had a history of lighting smudge lamps (against strict orders) to try to keep warm and get some relief from plagues of mosquitoes.

ABOVE: Dazed inhabitants surveying damage to telegraph poles and buildings in Jersey City.

## TIMELINE

**1914**
As World War I begins, the German ambassador to the US builds a secret propaganda, espionage, and sabotage network.

**01.01.1915**
The Roebling Steel Foundry in New Jersey, making war supplies for the Allies, burns, probably a result of German sabotage. The US Department of Justice exposes a German scheme to falsify passports.

ABOVE: The Jersey City pier after the explosion. Black Tom Island was just a few hundred feet across the water from the Statue of Liberty, which received $100,000 worth of shrapnel damage in the explosion. One study rates the blast force as equivalent to an earthquake over 5.0 on the Richter scale.

Hudson River

East River

Jersey City   Manhattan

Black Tom Island   Liberty Island

## STEP-BY-STEP

**01** While the truth may never be fully known, experts believe the following: Lothar Witzke and Kurt Jahnke approach Black Tom Island in a dinghy full of explosives on timed fuses.

**02** Their accomplice Michael Kristoff allegedly walks on to the pier from the shore. The three plant bombs and set fires in various places, then leave before the big explosion.

**03** Seeing a fire on a TNT-laden barge, the depot's guards call the Fire Department then flee.

**04** The explosion is so huge it is felt as far away as Connecticut and Philadelphia. "Bombs soared into the air and burst a thousand feet above the harbor," says a witness. Windows were shattered across Jersey City and Manhattan.

**05** Ten-week-old baby Arthur Tosson is fatally injured when the blast throws him from his crib. A guard, a policeman, and barge captain also die and hundreds are injured, many by flying glass.

**06** After his behavior arouses suspicion, police arrest Czech immigrant Michael Kristoff but, despite supposedly confessing his involvement in the Black Tom sabotage to a private detective, he is never charged.

---

**07.30.1916**
A massive explosion and fire destroys the munitions depot on Black Tom Island (although landfill and piers had by then joined it to the Jersey shore).

**07.30.1916**
Anna Rushnak and her daughter Lulu Chapman contact police about boarder Michael Kristoff's behavior. He is arrested but released due to lack of evidence.

**01.11.1917**
The Canadian Car and Foundry Company munitions plant in New Jersey is razed. Again, sabotage is suspected.

**08.10.1922**
The Mixed Claims Commission is established to deal with the US's war-related pecuniary claims against Germany. In 1939, the Commission finds the German government authorized the sabotage.

**1953**
Restitution of $95 million from the German government is finally agreed upon for sabotage claims, including Black Tom; the last payment is made in 1979.

# THE CAPTURE OF AQABA: LAWRENCE OF ARABIA

DATE       July 6, 1917
LOCATION   Aqaba, Jordan, then part of the Ottoman Empire
OBJECTIVE  To force the Turks out of the Arab homelands

The brief, adventure-filled life of T.E. Lawrence, archaeologist, British intelligence officer turned guerrilla warrior, was extraordinary by any standard. His keen eye for his own place in history, and skill as an autobiographer, ensured his role in the Arab Revolt became widely known; the 1962 film *Lawrence of Arabia* only added luster to the legend.

### Securing Arab Allies

The opening of hostilities between Great Britain and the Ottoman Empire (Turkey) in November 1914 focused attention on Egypt, where both exerted control. Securing the support of Arab tribes was key to controlling the region, and Thomas Edward Lawrence proved to be the man to do it.

Even before the war, Great Britain worked to win over the Arab leader Sherif Hussein Ibn Ali of Mecca and Medina. Securing agreement that an Allied victory would mean independence for the Arabs, Hussein agreed to fight the Turks, starting the "Great" Arab Revolt. Concerned that early victories were not followed up, British Oriental Secretary Ronald Storrs met Hussein, taking young intelligence officer Lawrence with him. After Storrs left, Lawrence stayed on as liaison officer with Hussein's third son, Faisal, whose forces advanced north.

### The Goal: Aqaba

Their ambitious goal was Aqaba (known to Lawrence as Akaba), held by the Turks. As (then) the only port on the Red Sea's Gulf of Aqaba, it was strategically valuable: holding it would enable the British to supply the Arabs and lessen the Turks' ability to threaten Suez access. "For months Akaba had been the horizon of our minds," Lawrence wrote. British and French navies had bombarded it, but its defenses prevented it being taken from the water. The Turks did not bother protecting the desert side, so harsh was the steep valley terrain—Lawrence and Faisal could only adopt this route with help from Bedouin chief Auda Abu Tayi.

Faisal, Lawrence, and a small group of men rode northwest from Al Wajh to meet up with Auda and his warriors. Lawrence, on a camel, wore Arab robes and brought 22,000 gold sovereigns. Over the next eight weeks they mounted guerrilla attacks on Turkish railroads and supplies, gathering fighters as they went.

### A Tactical Insult

Five-hundred-strong, the group attacked the outpost of Aba el Lissan. Despite surrounding and outnumbering the Turks, the Arabs were making no headway when Lawrence provoked Auda (whom he greatly respected), saying his men "shoot a lot but hit very little." The furious chief led his men in a charge that routed the Turks.

Now with 1,000 men, the Arabs advanced on Aqaba, greatly outnumbering the Turkish garrisons: those Turkish posts that had not been abandoned now surrendered. The city followed suit: Aqaba was theirs, and the Arabs had lost only two men.

TOP: Portrait of T. E. Lawrence in Arab dress.

ABOVE: Surviving embankment from the Hijaz Railway, built by the Ottoman Turks from Damascus to Medina to transport Muslim pilgrims.

RIGHT: Auda's flag bearer leads the Arab entry into Aqaba.

## TIMELINE

**1911**
Young archaeologist T.E. Lawrence begins a three-year stint on the Euphrates. He travels the region and learns Arabic.

**08.1914**
Lawrence becomes a civilian employee of the British War Office's Geographical Section. Four months later he is posted to Cairo as an intelligence officer.

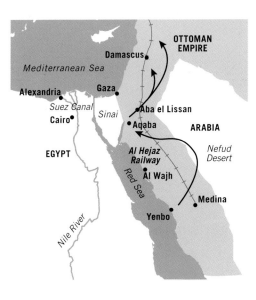

## STEP-BY-STEP

**01** T.E. Lawrence travels with Prince Faisal, encouraging his ambitions to overthrow Turkish rule. They secure the Red Sea port of Yenbo, then turn north.

**02** They set their sights on the Turkish-held port of Aqaba. Lawrence does not wait for approval: "I decided to go my own way, with or without orders."

**03** Lawrence and Faisal's warriors set out from Al Wajh, taking a circuitous route north and west into the harsh desert.

**04** They gather and lose fighters along the way as they move through the various tribes' territories: Bedouins fight within their own territories but drift away as the

action moves to a neighboring tribe's land. In this way thousands of Bedouins join the cause, but not all at the same time. At no time do they command more than around 1,000 fighters.

**05** Faisal and Lawrence's guerrilla attacks include destroying sections of the Hejaz railway and other Turkish supply lines.

**06** In el-Jefer they join forces with Bedouin chief Auda Abu Tayi, and approach Aqaba from the undefended, inland side.

**07** Faisal and Lawrence overrun the Turks at Aba el Lissan then seize Aqaba.

---

**06.10.1916**
Sherif Hussein fires the first symbolic shot in the Arab Revolt against Turkish rule. British Oriental Secretary Ronald Storrs meets with Hussein, taking Lawrence, who remains as British Liaison Officer.

**11.1916**
Deciding Hussein's third son, Prince Faisal, "will bring the Arab Revolt to full glory," Lawrence urges the British to supply arms and gold. Their anti-Ottoman campaign begins at Yenbo port.

**07.02.1917**
Faisal, Lawrence, Bedouin chief Auda Abu Tayi, and their warriors overrun the Turks at Aba el Lissan, clearing their path to Aqaba. The city falls four days later.

**10.31.1917**
The delayed British Expeditionary invasion of Palestine begins with the capture of Beersheba. Jerusalem falls on December 9.

**10.1.1918**
After flanking the British Expeditionary force through Palestine, the Arabs enter Damascus. The promise of Arab nationalism is soon dashed by the Great Powers.

# THE RAIDS ON ZEEBRUGGE AND OSTEND

DATE          April 22–23, 1918; May 10, 1918
LOCATION   Zeebrugge and Ostend, Belgium
OBJECTIVE To neutralize the threat posed by German U-boats

**These raids were among World War I's most paradoxical actions. They provided a national morale boost, the man who led them was knighted as a British hero, and the action garnered more decorations for valor than had ever been awarded for a single operation—all despite the failure of the raids to achieve their objectives.**

### The Nearby Menace

German U-boats berthed in the inland Belgian port at Bruges were out of range of British battleship bombardment, yet able to reach the North Sea at Zeebrugge via an 8-mile (13-km) canal. A connected 11-mile (18-km) system of smaller canals also provided sea access at Ostend. How to deprive the Germans of access to the North Sea via Zeebrugge and Ostend was a problem that had preoccupied Royal Navy strategists for years.

### A Multi-pronged Attack

Deciding the ports were too well defended to be taken from the sea, the British aimed to render them inoperable by scuttling three "blockships"—concrete-filled cruisers *Thetis*, *Intrepid*, and *Iphigenia*—in strategic locations.

Zeebrugge's canal entrance was shielded by a long curving mole, or breakwater. First the mole was to be stormed, using HMS *Vindictive* and modified Mersey ferries *Daffodil* and *Iris II*. The raiding party was to land on the mole and destroy the German battery. Two submarines were to be exploded under the viaduct in order to destroy it and prevent German reinforcements reaching the mole battery. The blockships could then reach the canal. All the crews were to be rescued and taken to destroyers offshore. Things did not, however, go to plan.

### Great Valor, but No Victory

Patrol boats zoomed in and laid smoke screens in front of the mole, but a sudden wind change revealed *Vindictive*. The Germans opened fire, causing many casualties and inflicting great damage to the ship, which included destroying its forward howitzer and 10 of the 12 landing ramps. Still under attack, *Vindictive* overshot its intended position, only reaching the mole with *Daffodil*'s help. Many of those in the raiding parties who did reach shore were cut down immediately. The rest found themselves, under constant fire, having to push through barbed-wire defenses, cross a parapet wall, and drop over iron railings to reach the German guns, which they were unable to destroy.

Only one submarine reached the harbor in time. It did successfully detonate, knocking out the viaduct railway and German reinforcements overhead (though the walkway remained). With the mole battery still operative, the blockships came under heavy fire. *Thetis* became entangled in the submarine net at the canal entrance and ran aground off-course. *Iphigenia* crashed into *Intrepid* before they sank, less than optimally placed, in the canal. The Ostend raid also failed to achieve its aims.

## TIMELINE

| | |
|---|---|
| **1897** | **1906** |
| The cruiser *Vindictive* is built, with a reinforced "battering ram" bow. | The introduction of the heavy gun-equipped, steam turbine–powered HMS *Dreadnought* renders *Vindictive* and its peers obsolete. |

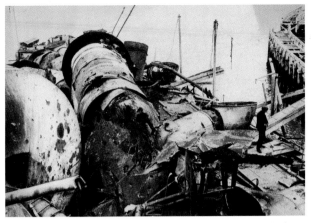

ABOVE: The remains of HMS *Vindictive* following the attack at Ostend. In 1920 *Vindictive* was raised from Ostend harbor for scrap. Its prow was presented to Belgium and still stands in a memorial park in the city.

LEFT: HMS *Intrepid* and HMS *Iphigenia* sunk as blockships at the entrance to the canal.

## STEP-BY-STEP

**01** HMS *Vindictive* is prepared for the raid on Zeebrugge with the removal of extraneous equipment, and the remodeling of the superstructure for more troops. *Iris II* and *Daffodil*, Mersey ferry steamers, are chosen for the raid after a long search.

**02** After two previous attempts are abandoned due to adverse weather, the attack force sets out again for Zeebrugge and Ostend.

**03** A wind-shift reveals the British vessels at Zeebrugge; they come under heavy German attack.

**04** *Vindictive* is pushed to the mole by *Daffodil*. A number of assault parties cannot reach the mole; those that can are under heavy attack.

**05** One of the two planned British submarine explosions destroys most of the viaduct.

**06** The blockships, also under heavy attack, sink, but only two are in the canal. Survivors of the 70-minute raid show enormous courage attempting to rescue the injured (412) and recover the dead (176). *Vindictive* withdraws.

**07** Meanwhile, at Ostend, British blockship cruisers *Brilliant* and *Sirius* come under German attack, miss the harbor entrance due to the Germans repositioning approach buoys, and run ashore.

**08** A second attack on Ostend on May 10 sees *Vindictive* successfully scuttled, but only partially blocking the harbor entrance. A third attempt is abandoned due to the lack of available resources.

LEFT: The crew of HMS *Vindictive* celebrating the Zeebrugge raid on April 23, 1918. In his official May 9 report, Admiral Keyes claimed "our operations were completely successful in attaining their first and most important object. The entrance to the Bruges ship-canal was blocked." In fact, German submarines were only stymied for two days.

| **08.04.1914** | **04.1918** | **04.22.1918** | **04.25.1918** | **05.09.1918** |
|---|---|---|---|---|
| Germany invades Belgium, gaining access to the inland port of Bruges, and its outports at Ostend and Zeebrugge, just 110 nautical miles (204 km) from England. | Throughout the war, Great Britain suffers what a naval dispatch calls "a continual menace": U-boats attack cross-Channel troop ships, and merchant shipping bringing food and other supplies. | An attacking British fleet sets sail for Zeebrugge and Ostend. Both raids ultimately fail. | Just two days after the Zeebrugge raid, the Germans have dredged a channel around the blockships and U-boats are getting through. Two sunken cruisers at Ostend fail to block the Germans' passage. | The badly damaged *Vindictive* becomes a blockship in a second raid on Ostend, which also proves unsuccessful. |

# THE STRANGE JOURNEY OF ALVIN C. YORK

DATE        October 8, 1918
LOCATION    Châtel-Chéhéry, Ardennes, France
OBJECTIVE   To secure the Deauville railroad

**Alvin York remains one of America's best-known war heroes, despite his own wish to be remembered only for his life in peacetime. A former hell-raiser who became a devoted Christian, York was a humble man who found himself at the center of a legendary action on France's Western Front during World War I.**

### The Reluctant Soldier

Being drafted in 1917 caused a crisis of conscience for 29-year-old Alvin York; the Church of Christ in Christian Union, to which he belonged, opposed war. York initially attempted to register his conscientious objections, but in November reported for military duty.

York was assigned to the 328th Infantry Regiment of the new US 82nd Infantry Division (the geographic spread of its members saw it nicknamed the "All-American Division"). His company commander convinced him that this was a just war and his faith would protect him. He reached the front line in France in June 1918.

### A Startling Appearance

Four months later, on October 8, the Americans were advancing through a narrowing valley in the rugged Argonne Forest, trying to capture the supply road and adjacent Deauville Railroad. German machine-gun fire rained down from three sides. Corporal Bernard Early led Corporal York and 15 others in an attempt to neutralize the German positions. Under cover of American artillery fire, they made it to a natural cutting that gave them the access they needed to outflank the German position.

Their appearance so far behind the line startled two German soldiers who took off through the trees toward their command post, with the Americans in hot pursuit. Mistakenly believing a large US force was coming at them, the men at the post surrendered. Seventeen men had captured 70.

### No Time to Miss

Seeing what was happening, German gunners higher up shouted to the captives to lie down, then opened fire. Six Americans were killed outright and three more, including Early, were wounded. York then assumed command and using the exceptional sharpshooting skills he had honed in the backwoods of Tennessee, he "exchanged shots" with the machine-gunners, killing 25. "I don't think I missed a shot," he recalled. "It was no time to miss."

The German commanding officer, thinking they were surrounded, gave the order to surrender. Collecting more surrendered men as they went, York and his seven companions marched 132 prisoners back to the American lines. Near the aid station at Châtel-Chéhéry they encountered brigade commander General Julian R. Lindsey who said, "Well, York, I hear you have captured the whole damned German army."

ABOVE: Aged 54, Sergeant York tried unsuccessfully to re-enlist when the US entered World War II. Instead, he promoted war bonds and provided other patriotic support. A stroke in 1954 incapacitated him for his last decade.

## TIMELINE

| 06.07.1917 | 10.7.1918 |
|---|---|
| Two months after the United States joins World War I, the first contingent of US troops arrives in France. | The 82nd Infantry Division begins offensive maneuvers on the Meuse-Argonne front. |

RIGHT: American soldiers and tanks in the Argonne Forest.

BELOW: York posing at the scene of his success.

## STEP-BY-STEP

**01** As US infantry advances in the Meuse-Argonne Offensive, Alvin York is among a 17-man detachment, led by Corporal Early, sent to try to silence German machine guns.

**02** An American artillery barrage causes the German gunners to take cover, allowing Early's men to run up the hill and reach shelter in a natural defile in the hillside.

**03** From here they pass into the shelter of the forest, turning west to outflank the German position. For an hour they move forward slowly so as not to alert the Germans.

**04** They startle two Germans filling water canteens in a stream. The pair race back to their command post yelling, "*Die Amerikaner kommen!*"

**05** Seeing the Americans charging across the field, and assuming they are part of a much larger group, the Germans at the post surrender.

**06** German machine gunners higher up fire upon the Americans, killing six and wounding three, including Early. York charges up the hill toward them, gets in position, and picks off one after another with his rifle.

**07** He repeatedly calls to them to surrender, and finally they do.

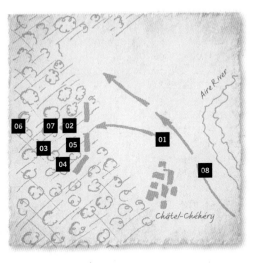

**10.8.1918**
Corporal York and seven other "doughboys" (US conscripts) bring 132 German prisoners back to US lines.

**10.12.1918**
82nd US Infantry Division crosses the German Hindenburg Line in the Meuse-Argonne sector, largely unopposed.

**04.18.1919**
York, now a sergeant, receives the Medal of Honor for his actions. His other awards include France's Croix de Guerre and Légion d'Honneur.

**1922**
The Nashville Rotary Club presents York with a farm and house bought and built using public donations.

**1941**
Having long resisted commercial and promotional requests, York agrees to allow a film of his exploits. Gary Cooper stars.

# AGENT ST-25

DATE 1919
LOCATION Petrograd (now St. Petersburg), Russia
OBJECTIVE To gather intelligence on the Bolsheviks

ST-25 was the code name for Paul Dukes, an extraordinarily bold and resourceful British undercover agent who risked his life many times in Russia after the revolution and during the Russian Civil War. Awarding him a knighthood—the only one ever given to an MI6 agent for his work in the field—King George V called Dukes "the greatest of all soldiers."

## An Old Russia Hand

In 1915, Dukes, who had lived in Russia for six years as a respected musician, joined the British Foreign Office and was assigned to "press" (propaganda) at the Moscow embassy. In 1917, he supported the tsar's overthrow but strongly opposed the Bolsheviks, who seized power eight months later. His experience of Russia and knowledge of languages saw him recalled to London where he was recruited into the Secret Intelligence Service (SIS, later MI6).

## Master of Disguises

In November 1918, given the code name ST-25, Dukes reentered Russia by way of the Finnish border. His mission: "disguise myself and seize whatever opportunities I could" to gather intelligence. Over the next ten months, he used more than a dozen false identities to infiltrate Bolshevik operations—which included the dreaded Bolshevik Cheka secret police—earning him the nicknames "The New Scarlet Pimpernel" and "The Man with a Hundred Faces" from admiring fellow spies. A removable false tooth aided his disguises.

In May 1919, Dukes enlisted as a volunteer in a Red Army regiment run by a secret anti-Bolshevist who contrived to send him, often, to Moscow and Petrograd on missions to buy supplies. The travel was useful cover for the hundreds of White Russian escapes he organized and, as a trusted Red Army soldier, he was invited to political and military planning meetings. He recorded his findings, he said, "in minute handwriting on tracing-paper," smuggling them out of Russia by various means.

## Nerves of Steel

Being discovered would have meant death; there were many narrow escapes. One of Dukes's tactics was learned from a doctor friend: "In an emergency I sometimes produced a 'fit'. I perfected 'fits' and became quite expert." Otherwise he just toughed it out. "A brazen show of self-confidence was the best security at such moments … In many a tight corner I was really shaking in my boots, [although I managed to] maintain an attitude of self-possession."

With his situation getting hotter, it was time to escape. Lieutenant Augustus "Gus" Agar continued to make rendezvous attempts after the Kronstadt raid, but Russian propaganda led Dukes to believe that Agar had been killed; he had to find his own way out. In the end, accompanied by two Red Army comrades who did not know his identity but also wanted to escape, he reached the Russian border shared with Estonia/Latvia, and eventually made his way safely to London. Too well known by now to serve in Russia again, Dukes undertook various covert missions for SIS in Europe.

ABOVE: The "Man with a Hundred Faces" in some of his disguises. Dukes was awarded a knighthood by King George V because as a civilian he was ineligible for the highest military honor, the Victoria Cross. He was, says former MI6 officer and historian Harry Ferguson, "The sort of spy we all wanted to be."

## TIMELINE

**1909**
Paul Dukes finishes school. His father vetoes his plans to become a concert pianist.

**1909**
Dukes absconds to mainland Europe. Starting in Rotterdam, he works his way east, through Germany, Poland, and eventually to Russia, learning languages as he goes.

## STEP-BY-STEP

**01** After ten months operating undercover in various guises in Russia, Dukes's position is becoming very precarious.

**02** He narrowly escapes arrest when a house where he is staying is raided on suspicion of harboring Allied spies. Only faking a fit saves him.

**03** Dukes flees Petrograd, spending days hiding in a crypt. He manages to get word to SIS.

**04** SIS orders Lt. "Gus" Agar to attempt a seaborne rescue from his base in Finland.

**05** Despite sustained effort, the men do not rendezvous; on one attempt Dukes secures a fishing boat, but a squall sinks it in the Gulf of Finland. He narrowly escapes drowning, then a patrol's gunfire.

In the meantime, Agar mounts attacks on Bolshevik shipping in the Gulf of Finland. The Bolshevik press reports that he has been killed.

**06** Dukes decides he has to make his own way out of Russia. Accompanied by two Russian escapees, with the complicity of his sympathetic Red Army commander, Dukes develops his own escape plans.

**07** Narrowly escaping train-guard searches, they reach the marshes and lakes on the Russian/Estonian/Latvian borders.

**08** Evading a guard who chases them into a swamp, they eventually find a decrepit boat; making oars from branches, they row to independent and neutral Latvia and to freedom.

BELOW LEFT: Dukes was only 30 when he returned from Russia. After receiving his knighthood, and delivering a US lecture tour about his exploits, he became an author, a professional acrobatic dancer, and a world-class yoga expert, living to age 78.

BELOW: The Detroit Hotel in Petrograd, a popular meeting place frequented by Dukes.

| 1913 | 1915 | 1918 | 08.1919 | 09.1919 |
|---|---|---|---|---|
| After four years' studying at the St. Petersburg Conservatoire, Dukes becomes assistant conductor at the Imperial Russian Opera. | He volunteers for British military service but is assigned to the Foreign Office. | With MI6 convinced Russia will soon close its borders, Dukes is recruited to spy on the Bolsheviks. In November, code-named ST-25, he reenters Russia from Finland. | In disguise, he joins the Red Army. After a British rescue attempt fails and Dukes learns his unit is to be posted to the Civil War front, he plans his own escape. | Dukes and two companions escape via Latvia. |

# THE EVACUATION OF THE CZECHOSLOVAK LEGION

DATE  May 1919
LOCATION  Vladivostok, Primorskaya Oblast, Russia
OBJECTIVE  To safely remove the Czechoslovak Legionnaires from Russia

**The Czechoslovak Legion and its role in the history of Russia is well known in Central and Eastern Europe, but elsewhere the story of these nationalists and army deserters-turned-heroes who rebelled against the Austro-Hungarian empire and made an epic, transcontinental fight for freedom is too often forgotten.**

### Shifting Alliances

Czech-Slovak independence campaigner Tomáš Masaryk long believed an army would be needed to achieve national independence. In 1917, after Russia's tsar abdicated, he secured the new provisional government's agreement to create a Czechoslovak Legion. Four émigré regiments formed and immediately proved their worth, fighting fiercely throughout the summer and recruiting compatriots who had been captured as Austro-Hungarian POWs by the Russians and now changed allegiance.

But Russia's political system was collapsing. The Bolsheviks seized power and signed the Treaty of Brest-Litovsk in March 1918. Suddenly Russia and Germany were no longer at war, stranding the Legion—an "army without a country," still loyal to the Allies. The Czechs wanted to reach the Western Front, but German armies blocked the west and north. Going east on commandeered armored trains was the only viable option.

### An Epic Journey Under Arms

The Czechs were avowedly neutral in Russian politics but when a minor scuffle turned into full-blown conflict between Legionnaires and Bolsheviks at Chelyabinsk, they began to fight alongside the anti-communist White Army, and they achieved significant successes. However, targeted now by both Bolsheviks and Germans, the Legionnaires needed a route out. So, unit by unit, they fought for, and won control over, the 5,772-mile (9,289-km) Trans-Siberian Railway from Moscow to Vladivostok.

The 70,000 Legionnaires were strung the length of the track but kept in close telegraphic communication, maintaining unity and fighting off countless attacks as they headed toward the Pacific Ocean. The forward units seized Vladivostok, where Allied troops were being sent to assist the evacuation.

### A Glittering Prize?

Legend has it that the Legionnaires captured eight carriages of tsarist gold, using seven to negotiate safe passage with the Bolsheviks and keeping one, with which they set up a bank in Prague. Czech historian Ivan Šedivý says that while this is a good story, the truth is uncertain, because the Legion had significant commercial dealings in Russia, and the gold they took out may (less romantically) have been business earnings.

By July 1918, around 14,000 Legionnaires had reached Vladivostok. Despite being desperately needed on the Western Front, Allied alarm at the Bolshevik threat left them cooling their heels, while those still en route were ordered to hold their positions. Almost a year later, in May 1919, the evacuations finally began; more than 12 months after that, the last of the Czechs departed for Europe.

## STEP-BY-STEP

**01** In the years before WWI, 100,000 Czechs and Slovaks emigrate to Russia.

**02** With their homelands subsumed by Austria-Hungary, remaining Czechs and Slovaks must fight for the Central Powers.

**03** Feeling more aligned with the "enemy" than the empire ruling them, these soldiers begin switching allegiances, voluntarily surrendering to the Russians.

**04** Lenin and other coup leaders mistrust the Czechs, who come under Bolshevik attack, then side for a time with the White Army.

**05** The Legion seizes the Trans-Siberian Railway, creating a power vacuum; harsh internal Russian crackdowns follow.

## TIMELINE

**03.15.1917**
Russia's Tsar Nicholas II abdicates. Aleksandr Kerensky's provisional Russian government sanctions the formation of the Czechoslovak Legion in July.

**11.07.1917**
The Bolsheviks, led by Vladimir Lenin, seize power in Russia.

ABOVE: *Orcik*, one of the Czech armored trains used by the Legion to control the Trans-Siberian Railway.

ABOVE LEFT: A group of Czech volunteer soldiers arriving at Vladivostok. Excellently organized while in Russia and on the Trans-Siberian Railway, the Czechoslovak Legion published its own newspaper and set up baking and hospital facilities. Some of the men traveled with wives and children.

**06** Czech-Slovak leader Tomáš Masaryk secures agreement from Allied leaders for the right to independence.

**07** The Allies launch an intervention in Russia; the Legion's evacuation is stalled as they continue to support the White Russian, anti-Bolshevik forces in eastern Russia—ultimately a doomed enterprise.

**08** Finally evacuated before Bolshevik forces reach the Pacific, the Czechs travel to the United States, then back to Europe via the Atlantic, or the Indian Ocean, then the Suez Canal.

**09** The First Czechoslovak Republic is proclaimed in Prague on October 28, 1918.

**03.03.1918**
Russia and Germany sign the Treaty of Brest-Litovsk. Commissar for Nationalities, Joseph Stalin, agrees to unhindered evacuation of the Czechs.

**05.14.1918**
An altercation between Hungarian and Czech soldiers at Chelyabinsk grows into a pitched battle between Legionnaires and Bolsheviks, dubbed the Revolt of the Legion

**05.29.1918**
War Commissar, Leon Trotsky, orders the Czechs to disarm; they refuse. Two months later, Czech soldiers seize Vladivostok, making it an Allied protectorate.

**07.17.1918**
As Czech troops near Yekaterinburg, the Bolsheviks holding Nicholas II and his family, fearing a rescue attempt, assassinate their prisoners.

**08.27.1920**
The final US ship carrying Czech Legionnaire evacuees leaves Vladivostok.

# THE RAID ON KRONSTADT

DATE **August 18, 1919**
LOCATION **Kronstadt, in what is now Leningrad Oblast, Russia**
OBJECTIVE **A hastily organized British attack on a Bolshevik naval fortress**

**If it were fiction, the story of the raid triggered by fearless Gus Agar against the might of Russia's Bolshevik-controlled navy would strain all credibility. But this daring attack during the height of the Russian Civil War was a very real British triumph, the epitome of what Agar's commanding officer described as "cool, disciplined, daredevil gallantry."**

### A Fearsome Fortress

In early 1919, British Rear Admiral Sir Walter Cowan was sent with a squadron to the Baltic to minimize the threat posed by the Russian fleet at Kronstadt. This naval base on Kotlin Island in the Gulf of Finland, 18 miles (30 km) west of Petrograd (now St. Petersburg) was so heavily defended it was regarded by many as Europe's strongest fortress.

By mid-year, Cowan was also overseeing the attempted rescue of British secret agent Paul Dukes from Petrograd. The man chosen to undertake this seeming suicide mission was Lieutenant Augustus "Gus" Agar, a 29-year-old intelligence officer and experienced skipper of Coastal Motor Boats (CMBs) who posed as a commercial traveler and based himself at the yacht club in the Finnish coastal village of Terrjoki, near the Russian border.

### A New Mission

In June, Agar, unable to contact Dukes, instead daringly attacked and sank the Russian cruiser *Oleg*, which had been bombarding a White Army-held garrison. Cowan and Agar, who won a Victoria Cross for this action, subsequently agreed a CMB attack on Kronstadt harbor was viable. CMBs had a three-man crew and were armed with two Lewis machine guns and torpedoes—built light, they could reach 34 knots.

First, the small team in their eight CMBs would have to evade mines, gunboat patrols, and submarines in the Gulf of Finland; once at Kronstadt they would have to pass through a chain of forts and navigate a hidden breakwater that lay as little as three feet (0.9 m) below the surface, all under the nose of the Russian batteries. Their only support would be an air raid from the eight planes aboard the newly built HMS *Vindictive*, a cruiser modified as an aircraft carrier.

### Speed and Daring

With two Finnish fishermen as pilots they set off at 12:30, losing one CMB to engine failure before reaching the harbor. The tremendous noise made by the boats was masked by the air raid, so a torpedo hit on the submarine depot ship *Pamiat Azova* was the Russians' first alert to the harbor attack.

Under intense fire, the CMBs torpedoed the battleships *Andrei Pervozvanny* and *Petropavlovsk* before the surviving four boats made their escape. The cost to the British was high relative to the number involved, with eight killed and nine captured, but the half-hour raid became the stuff of legend.

ABOVE: The damaged *Petropavlovsk* moored at Kronstadt.
ABOVE RIGHT: The Coastal Motor Boat (CMB), was used as a fighting boat and to smuggle agents into enemy territory.
BELOW RIGHT: The resourceful Captain Augustus "Gus" Willington Shelton Agar.

FINLAND
RUSSIA
*Kotlin Island*
Terrjoki
Petrograd
*Gulf of Finland*
Kronstadt
*Baltic Sea*
ESTONIA
RUSSIA
LATVIA

## TIMELINE

**1918**
Russia descends into civil war; the Bolsheviks fight against the White Army.

**1919**
Newly independent, Estonia, Latvia, and Lithuania fend off threats from Russia and Germany. The British Special Intelligence Service (SIS) forms a base in Finland to support spies in Russia.

## STEP-BY-STEP

**01** Agar and the flotilla of slightly larger CMBs led by Commander Claude Dobson rendezvous on a moonless night of unusually high tide.

**02** Approaching Kotlin Island, the boats' wash is seen and there is some machine-gun fire but the fort spotlights are not activated.

**03** CMB No. 86 breaks down. The others proceed into the harbor as the planned air raid from HMS *Vindictive* begins. After piloting them in, Agar patrols the harbor mouth under heavy fire.

**04** Three CMBs mount the first wave of attacks, torpedoing the depot ship *Pamiat Azova*.

**05** Alerted by the explosion, the Russians begin heavy machine-gun and artillery fire on the now spotlit boats.

**06** Despite suffering casualties and taking evasive action, the boats also successfully torpedo the battleships *Andrei Pervosvanni* and *Petropavlovsk*.

**07** The second wave goes in for attack, but one boat is lost when two CMBs collide, and another when it is shelled.

**08** Picking up the disabled No. 86, the surviving boats make it to safety in neutral Finland with the assistance of HMS *Vindictive*'s planes.

| **05.1919** | **06.17.1919** | **08.02.1919** | **08.18.1919** | **08.22.1919** |
|---|---|---|---|---|
| The head of SIS (later MI6), Sir Mansfield Cumming ("C"), gives Gus Agar a seemingly impossible task: to rescue British spy Paul Dukes from Russia. | Unable to contact Dukes, Agar decides to attack the Russian cruiser *Oleg*, sinking it in a risky mission, which is only retrospectively approved. | Towed from England, seven large CMBs reach Finland, ready for the Kronstadt raid. | The tiny British force successfully conducts the daring raid, temporarily knocking out the threat of the Bolshevik navy in the Baltic. | Agar is awarded a VC for the *Oleg* attack. In November, Commander Dobson and Lieutenant Steele are awarded VCs and Agar a DSO for the Kronstadt raid. |

# STARTING A WORLD WAR: THE RAID ON GLEIWITZ RADIO STATION

DATE **August 31, 1939**
LOCATION **Gleiwitz (Gliwice), Germany (now Poland)**
OBJECTIVE **To fake a border incursion as an excuse for war**

**In 1939, Europe was bound for war: Hitler was determined it would be so. He sent a "dirty tricks" SS team to launch this fake attack on a German radio station close to the Polish border and used it as the pretext to begin the conflict in which more than 60 million people would die.**

### "Practical Proof"

It began when Alfred Naujocks, an SS-Sturmbannführer (the Nazi security force's equivalent of major) was summoned to the Berlin office of Reinhard Heydrich, head of the General Reich Security Office. Within days, Heydrich told him, Germany would be at war with Poland. But Adolf Hitler wanted it to appear as though Germany had been provoked, and it was up to Heydrich and Naujocks to provide "practical proof" of Polish aggression. Given that there was no such aggression, the "proof" would have to be faked.

Naujocks, who had run a similar covert operation in the Czech Sudetenland in 1935, was ordered to take a team and seize control of a radio station outside Gleiwitz, Germany, four miles (6.4 km) from the Polish border, presenting the "raid" as the work of Polish insurgents.

### A Chilling Plan

After two weeks in Gleiwitz waiting for the go-ahead, Naujocks was summoned to the nearby headquarters of Heinrich Müller, notorious chief of the Gestapo. Müller told him that in addition to broadcasting a "Polish call to arms," Naujocks was to leave physical evidence: a civilian who would be murdered and presented as a Pole. Some 20 other planned faked border incidents would also require disguised corpses. Müller referred to them as *konserve* ("canned goods").

### War, as Planned

At 20:00 on August 31, Naujocks's team made its way to the radio station. They were met by Gestapo, who delivered their victim, a dying civilian first injected with a deadly poison that took five hours to act, then drugged unconscious, then shot in the head. (Years later he was identified as Franciszek Honiok, a German agricultural machinery salesman of Polish-Silesian origin, arrested on a spurious charge the previous day).

Laying Honiok's body on the steps outside, Naujocks's men burst into the station and ordered the crew away from the controls. Polish speaker Karl Hornack barked into the microphone, in Polish, "Attention! This is Gliwice. The broadcasting station is in Polish hands." Twenty minutes after their arrival, the Nazis drove off. News of the "raid" was broadcast throughout Germany. By the next day, when these reports were picked up by the BBC, *The New York Times*, and news outlets around the world, the war had already begun, with Hitler claiming that to put an end to "border violations … no other means is left to me now than to meet force with force."

The only evidence of the raid's orchestration is based on Naujocks's confession to US forces after he surrendered in 1944. Naujocks evaded prosecution, escaped from custody, and worked as a businessman in Hamburg until his death in 1966.

ABOVE RIGHT: The Gleiwitz radio station in 1940. Near the Polish border between Germany and Poland, Gleiwitz was a convenient location for the nefarious mission.

RIGHT: Former SS officer Alfred Naujocks was living under his own name in Hamburg when British author Comer Clarke located him in 1958. Naujocks confirmed the details of the Gleiwitz raid, saying, "Yes, I started it all. I don't think anyone will bother about me now."

## TIMELINE

**08.30.1939**
The Gestapo arrest agricultural equipment salesman Franciszek Honiok, a German of Polish heritage.

**08.31.1939**
Naujocks and a team of SS officers in plain clothes fake a Polish raid on a radio relay station at Gleiwitz. Honiok is implicated as the raid's mastermind and is killed.

## STEP-BY-STEP

**01** Naujocks is briefed by Heydrich, who gives him the code that will be the go-signal: *Grossmutter gestorben* (Grandmother died).

**02** Franciszek Honiok is seized by the Gestapo. Although not recognized as such at the time, he becomes, in effect, the first known fatality of World War II.

**03** Wearing civilian clothes, the SS briefly seize control of the Gleiwitz airwaves. This is only a local relay station, reaching just the immediate area. Honiok's body is left at Gleiwitz as evidence.

**04** In broadcasts across the nation, the German News Agency reports the "Polish attack," along with the "fact" that the Poles were overpowered by German police who opened fire, killing several.

**05** Following the Gleiwitz "raid," the Nazis stage a similar fake attack on a German border customs office among other falsified "infringements" of German sovereignty by the Poles. Here, the "newly killed rebels" are already suffering rigor mortis.

**06** The following morning, with the war declared, Hitler addresses the crowd at the Reichstag, saying the incursion on Germany by "Polish Army hooligans had finally exhausted our patience."

| 09.01.1939 | 12.1943 | 10.19.1944 | 09.11.1945 | 04.04.1966 |
|---|---|---|---|---|
| World War II commences in the early hours when a German battleship opens fire on Polish positions in Danzig (now Gdansk). | Naujocks commands the Petergruppe in Denmark, massacring captured partisans. | Naujocks surrenders to American forces. | Giving testimony in the lead-up to the Nuremberg Trials, he reveals the Gleiwitz operation. | Naujocks dies in Hamburg, having escaped from his POW camp and never faced trial. |

# SPECIAL OPERATION P: SINKING OF THE *ROYAL OAK*

DATE        October 14, 1939
LOCATION    Scapa Flow, Orkney Islands, Scotland
OBJECTIVE   To cause maximum disruption to the British Home Fleet

**Less than two months into World War II, a stealth action by a single U-boat caused a huge number of Royal Navy casualties in what had previously been considered a safe, well-defended anchorage off Scotland. A few horrific minutes resulted in Great Britain's loss of her second significant ship in less than a month and an appalling expense in lives.**

### Special Operation P

With the outbreak of war, the British Home Fleet assembled in the Orkney Islands' huge land-encircled bay, Scapa Flow. From there it could protect Arctic convoys and patrol the North Atlantic. The German *Kriegsmarine* knew Scapa Flow well, having scuttled their interned High Seas Fleet there in 1919.

Germany's commander of *Unterseeboots*, or U-boats, was Commodore Karl Dönitz (a World War I veteran, who would go on to briefly succeed Hitler as Führer in 1945). After unsuccessful prewar lobbying for a sixfold increase in his 56-boat submarine squadron, Dönitz sought an operation achieving maximum impact with minimum resources—an attack at Scapa Flow, code-named "Special Operation P."

### Best-laid Plans

First Lord of the Admiralty Winston Churchill had been warned the World War I defenses protecting Scapa Flow from submarines, notably steel nets, had considerably deteriorated. He urgently ordered new nets, blockships, and booms, but they were yet to be fully installed when U-47 entered the anchorage undetected on the night of October 13, 1939.

Dönitz's planning was meticulous. Another U-boat reconnoitered before the mission, reported the poor defenses, and observed that a stealthy boat might weave between the blockships (*Thames*, *Soriano*, and *Minich*) at the northeastern Kirk Sound inlet, despite the 10-knot current. The night of October 13–14 was chosen because of its unusually high tide and being moonless (though, as it happened, the Northern Lights blazed).

However, Dönitz did not know that days earlier a German squadron had sailed into the North Sea to draw the British Home Fleet out for a Luftwaffe attack. After the Germans retreated, the British regrouped at Loch Ewe on the Scottish mainland rather than Scapa Flow. If not for this, the Royal Navy might have suffered a Pearl Harbor–scale disaster.

### Young Lives Cut Short

The aging battleship HMS *Royal Oak* was anchored a mile (1.6 km) offshore when, at 00:58, a torpedo hit the bow and severed the starboard anchor chain. Many of those aboard, woken by the dull noise, thought it a harmless workshop explosion and went back to sleep. Minutes later, three torpedoes tore into the starboard side.

Within five minutes, *Royal Oak* keeled over and sank. Those who were able to escape—many burned and suffering other terrible injuries—struggled through thick choking oil covering the icy water. Only the quick actions of the captain and crew of *Royal Oak*'s tender, *Daisy II*, saved the 386 survivors. Of the 833 sailors lost, 120 were boys aged between 14 and 18.

BELOW: A German propaganda poster depicting the HMS *Royal Oak* being torpedoed.

## TIMELINE

**11.27.1918**

The last of the 74 vessels in Germany's High Seas Fleet arrives at Scapa Flow for internment during peace treaty negotiations.

**06.21.1919**

Wrongly believing the British are about to seize the ships, Rear Admiral Ludwig von Reuter orders them to be scuttled.

**LEFT:** U-47 commanded by Kapt. Günther Prien returns after the successful attack at Scapa Flow.

## STEP-BY-STEP

**01** As the Home Fleet sails, HMS *Royal Oak* remains to provide antiaircraft cover for Netherbutton Radar Station in the Orkneys.

**02** U-47 arrives at the Orkneys, having navigated from Kiel by dead reckoning and sounding.

**03** German captain Günther Prien works through intelligence information on the defenses and currents, "like a mathematical problem."

**04** At 19:00, U-47 enters the large Holm Sound, then over the next four hours steers through the much narrower Kirk Sound, fighting the current.

**05** Expecting an entire fleet in the bay, it takes Prien almost an hour to find a target. Of the six torpedoes fired, two fail.

**06** Despite armor plating 13 inches (33 cm) thick, *Royal Oak* can not withstand 2,204 pounds (1 tonne) of TNT.

**07** As the ship goes down its mast smashes though its large "liberty launch" lifeboat.

**08** John Gatt, skipper of *Daisy II*, and his crew save hundreds of lives, but 833 are lost.

**09** Announcing the disaster, the British government wrongly claims the U-boat was also sunk.

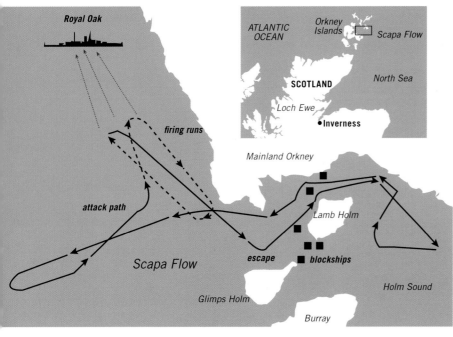

| 09.06.1939 | 09.17.1939 | 10.15.1939 | 10.18.1939 | 1940 |
|---|---|---|---|---|
| German aerial photos of Scapa Flow are taken as part of "Special Operation P" preparation. | Britain's cruiser HMS *Courageous*, converted to an aircraft carrier, is sunk by a U-29 in the Western Approaches. Three days later a submarine attack on the *Ark Royal* proves unsuccessful. | U-47 sinks *Royal Oak* at anchor on Scapa Flow, in what Churchill, grieving the nation's loss, nonetheless recognizes as "a wonderful feat of arms." | In Berlin, Hitler awards U-47 captain Günther Prien the prestigious *Ritterkreuz des Eisernen Kreuzes* (Knight's Cross of the Iron Cross) and agrees to commission more U-boats. | A year before his death in action, Prien publishes *Mein Weg nach Scapa Flow*, released in 1969 in English as *U-Boat Commander*. |

# A BOMB ATTEMPT ON HITLER'S LIFE

DATE    November 8, 1939
LOCATION    Munich, Bavaria, Germany
OBJECTIVE    The assassination of Adolf Hitler

**Between 1934 and 1945, there were up to 40 attempts on Adolf Hitler's life. The best known is the 1944 bomb set up by Claus von Stauffenberg inside the Nazis' East Prussian headquarters, which injured Hitler. But the one Hitler was luckiest to walk away from happened five years earlier.**

### A Concerned Citizen

Johann Georg Elser was a carpenter from Königsbronn who resented the privileges granted to Nazi party members and the deterioration in working conditions that were the hidden cost of Germany's "economic miracle." Elser believed that only eliminating Hitler could improve the situation.

Each November, the German leader commemorated his failed 1923 coup, the Beer Hall Putsch, by addressing up to 3,000 people at the Munich bar in question—originally the Bürgerbräukeller, renamed the Löwenbräukeller. Attending in 1938 to assess his options, Elser decided that a hefty explosive device inside a stone pillar behind the podium would bring an internal balcony crashing down on Hitler. A patient man, he set about readying everything for the next anniversary.

### Painstaking Preparation

Having also trained in a watch factory, Elser then got a munitions factory job and, bit by bit, smuggled out 110 pounds (50 kg) of explosives. Then he secured a quarry job, stealing detonators. In his free time he developed a blueprint for a timebomb.

With six months to go, Elser traveled to the German–Swiss border to identify an overland hiking escape route. In August, he moved to Munich, becoming a regular at the Löwenbräukeller beer hall, and was known to stay until closing time. He would hide until everyone left, then creep downstairs and work preparing the pillar. Before morning he would clear all debris, disguise his work with a false panel, and slip out.

### Eight Vital Minutes

Elser seemed to have thought of everything: the bomb timer could be preset 144 hours beforehand. There was a backup clock. The column cavity was cork-lined so ticking could not be heard. The false panel was even tin-lined in case someone nailed up decorations. He set the bomb for 21:20, 50 minutes into Hitler's customary 90-minute speech.

But on November 8, 1939, Munich airport was shrouded in fog; Hitler had to return to Berlin by train. So he started and finished early, leaving the venue eight minutes before the massive explosion. Once again, what Hitler called "the luck of the devil" had saved him. Meanwhile, the bomber should have been safely in Switzerland. But with Germany now at war, the borders were closed; he was arrested at 20:45 as he tried to cross. In Elser's pockets were a postcard of the Löwenbräukeller, bomb parts, and communist party–related documents, perhaps intended to establish his anti-Nazi stance with the Swiss. He was arrested, tortured, imprisoned, and finally executed at Dachau concentration camp six years later; Hitler had held him captive for a show trial after the war ended.

TOP: Georg Elser, under Gestapo torture after his arrest, said he decided to assassinate Hitler because of the decline in conditions for working-class Germans, the Nazis' opposition to Christianity, and the increasing likelihood of war as 1938 progressed.

ABOVE: The scene in the Munich Beer Hall after Elser's bomb went off.

## TIMELINE

| 1938 | 09.01.1939 |
|---|---|
| Johann Georg Elser decides to kill Hitler. He tells no one of his plans. | With Germany at war, its borders are closed. |

**ABOVE:** Hitler speaking to the old guard in the Löwenbräukeller.

**ABOVE RIGHT:** Destruction at the Löwenbräukeller following the bombing incident.

## STEP-BY-STEP

**01** Johann Georg Elser decides he must "eliminate the current leadership" in order to improve life for ordinary working Germans.

**02** Displaying his characteristic attention to detail and quality work, he embarks on year-long preparations, including training at a watch factory to learn about timers, working in a munitions factory, then at a quarry to secure detonators.

**03** Having secured bomb material, he begins a 35-night stint secretly preparing a column in the Löwenbräukeller. He waits to make each chisel blow when there is other noise to disguise it.

**04** Knowing Hitler begins his annual 90-minute address at 20:30, Elser sets the bomb timer for activation at 21:20.

**05** Two days after setting the bomb, a day before it will explode, Elser checks to make sure it is undisturbed. Despite all his planning, Hitler escapes the blast because of a change of schedule due to fog conditions.

**06** Elser is arrested at the Swiss border. With Elser their prisoner, and despite interrogation and torture, the Nazis initially refuse to believe that he worked alone.

**07** Undeterred by the truth, Hitler decides to keep Elser alive until after the war, when a show trial will "prove" British involvement.

**08** As Allied forces close in on Dachau, Elser is executed on Gestapo orders.

---

**11.08.1939**
Eight minutes after Hitler departs, Elser's bomb explodes, killing eight and injuring 63.

**11.08.1939**
Elser is arrested, then sent to Munich, where he is beaten, tortured, and even hypnotized to get him to tell "the truth" about co-conspirators.

**early 1940**
Elser is sent to Sachsenhausen concentration camp. Hitler plans to hold a postwar show trial "proving" British involvement.

**02.1945**
The "special prisoner" is transferred to Dachau concentration camp.

**04.09.1945**
Elser is shot to death on Gestapo chief Heinrich Müller's orders. In 2003, Germany issues a commemorative stamp featuring Elser.

# THE BOARDING OF THE *ALTMARK*

**DATE** February 16, 1940
**LOCATION** Jøssingfjord, Sokndal, Norway
**OBJECTIVE** To locate and free British POWs on a German "merchant" ship

**In just three months, German "pocket battleship" *Admiral Graf Spee* captured nine Allied merchantmen in the South Atlantic, imprisoning hundreds of crew then sinking the ships. By 1940, after the Battle of the River Plate, *Graf Spee* was no more, but its supply ship, the tanker *Altmark*, was still on the loose with, the British believed, hundreds of POWs aboard.**

### Neutral Waters

On February 14, a RAF patrol spotted *Altmark* in Norwegian territorial waters. With Norway still neutral, non-combatant ships could travel unhindered. The revelation of *Altmark*'s true purpose would prove German infringement of Norwegian rights, but the Allies had no evidence.

Over the next two days, Norwegian naval officers boarded the *Altmark* three times as the ship hugged the coastline, traveling south toward Germany. But Captain Heinrich Dau insisted his was a simple merchant vessel. The Norwegians, already concerned about German intentions and unwilling to force the issue, did not search the ship.

### A Delicate Cabinet Decision

With *Altmark* getting away, the British Admiralty, headed by Winston Churchill, ordered warship flotilla commander Captain Philip Vian to force the ship into international waters, board it, and search for prisoners. But although HMS *Intrepid* fired a shot across its bows, *Altmark* did not yield. The Norwegian gunboats trailing the German ship hampered *Intrepid*'s maneuvers, giving Dau the opportunity to slip into the narrow, icy Jøssingfjord.

Vian arrived at the fjord on HMS *Cossack* and consulted the Norwegian officers. The British War Cabinet discussed the delicate situation—by boarding *Altmark*, Great Britain, too, would violate Norwegian rights. But Churchill could not allow British POWs to be taken to Germany. He ordered Vian to escort *Altmark* to Bergen for a thorough search. If Dau resisted, all necessary force was to be used to liberate the prisoners.

### "The Navy's Here"

As *Cossack* entered the fjord, *Altmark* steamed, stern first, toward the destroyer. Only deft work from the British prevented the ramming. As the ships brushed, *Cossack*'s first lieutenant leapt onto *Altmark*'s deck and roped them together. The rest of the armed British boarding party followed, before *Altmark*'s momentum carried it stern first onto the opposite shore. Four Germans were killed and five injured in the taking of the ship.

Merchant sailor Thomas Foley was one of the 299 prisoners freed. He recalls a voice through the locked door of the hold: "Any Englishmen down here?" Hearing cries of "Yes!" the voice replied, "Well, the Navy's here. HMS *Cossack* has come to rescue you." In that moment, Foley says, "We cheered like ten thousand madmen."

TOP: The battleship *Admiral Graf Spee*.

ABOVE: HMS *Cossack* returns to Leith on February 17, following its rescue of British prisoners who had been held aboard *Altmark*.

RIGHT: Altmark in Jøssingfjord, Norway, in February 1940.

## TIMELINE

**01.06.1936**
*Admiral Graf Spee* is commissioned. Technically it is a cruiser that meets peace-treaty terms but its military capabilities make it a "pocket battleship."

**12.1939**
In Berlin, Norwegian fascist leader Vidkun Quisling and Adolf Hitler discuss a possible German-backed coup in Norway.

## STEP-BY-STEP

**01** Norwegian patrol torpedo boat *Trygg* stops *Altmark* as it travels down the coastline. An officer from *Trygg* boards, intending to search the ship.

**02** Reassured by *Altmark*'s captain, Heinrich Dau, that it is an unarmed tanker, the Norwegian officer departs, leaving a *Trygg* seaman as a guide to Alesund.

**03** At the port of Alesund, the seaman is replaced by two local pilots. A Norwegian port officer boards briefly, but does not search.

**04** Patrol boat *Snoegg* stops the *Altmark*. An officer boards, questions Dau, and leaves.

**05** Once more *Altmark* is stopped, this time by Norwegian destroyer *Garm*. Dau refuses to allow a search.

**06** Vian is ordered to find *Altmark* and force it into international waters. *Ivanhoe*, *Intrepid*, and *Arethusa* set out to intercept the German ship, as Vian on *Cossack* comes to meet them.

**07** Rather than be forced to sea, *Altmark* slips into Jøssingfjord. When *Cossack* follows, Dau attempts to ram it.

**08** *Cossack*'s boarding party seizes control of *Altmark* and frees its 299 prisoners.

---

**12.13.1939**
*Admiral Graf Spee*'s captain, Hans Langsdorff, makes tactical errors fighting the British in the Battle of the River Plate off the Argentine/Uruguay shore.

**12.17.1939**
Trapped in Montevideo, Uruguay, mistakenly believing a large British force is coming, Langsdorff scuttles his ship and then commits suicide.

**02.14.1940**
Carrying two of *Admiral Graf Spee*'s antiaircraft guns and 299 merchant marine prisoners, supply ship *Altmark* is spotted in Norwegian waters.

**02.17.1940**
With the freed British prisoners aboard and the German crew left on the run-aground *Altmark*, HMS *Cossack* docks at Leith, Scotland.

**04.09.1940**
Germany attacks Norway and Denmark, ending the "Phoney War."

# THE CAPTURE OF FORT EBEN-EMAEL

DATE        May 10–11, 1940
LOCATION    Eben-Emael, Wallonia, Belgium
OBJECTIVE   To seize a seemingly impregnable fort

Adolf Hitler wanted to spread Nazism across Europe. His *Fall Gelb* (Plan Yellow) called for a major push into France. But rather than advance on a single front, he aimed to isolate Allied forces in Belgium from those in France, which meant overrunning the Low Countries (Belgium, the Netherlands, and Luxembourg).

### Built to Withstand

Belgium's Fort Eben-Emael was designed to guard the vital bridges over the adjacent Albert Canal and to fend off any incursions across the border between Liège, Belgium, and Maastricht in the Netherlands.

With its thick concrete and retractable casemates, antiaircraft and anti-tank batteries, machine-gun emplacements, extensive views over surrounding countryside, 3 miles (4.9 km) of underground tunnels and bunkers, a water ditch to one side, an anti-tank ditch to another, and 195-feet (60-m) canal walls on a third, the fort seemed impregnable. Hitler thought otherwise.

### A New Aerial Approach

Given the impressive ground defenses, the initial attack had to be airborne. The Luftwaffe's JU-52 transport planes could carry just a dozen paratroopers, scattering them over a 900-feet (274-m) area with only light weapons and equipment (the rest had to be dropped separately). But DFS-230 meteorology gliders adapted for military use could silently deliver up to ten men and 4,400 pounds (2,000 kg) of equipment with 60-foot (18-meter) accuracy.

Eleven gliders carrying a total of 86 men led by Oberleutnant Rudolf Witzig would attack the fort, while 30 gliders carrying another 270 men would hit three bridges—Vroenhoven, Veldwezelt, and Canne—on the nearby Albert Canal. They had to neutralize the fort quickly: in case of invasion its guns would blow up the bridges.

### A Desperate, Doomed Defense

At 01:30, Eben-Emael commander Major Jean Jottrand received warning of German troop movements near the border. Although it was believed to be another training drill, he put the fort on alert, and also fired blanks from the artillery guns to warn the bridge troops. Hearing gunfire from Maastricht and realizing it was war, Jottrand followed plans to destroy the barracks and administrative building—this required gun crews leaving some positions unmanned. He then ordered the Canne bridge destroyed.

At 05:25 the four glider platoons landed. Eight G*ranit* gliders reached the fort (one went off course in Germany and Witzig's was delayed by a towing mishap). Within 30 minutes, using new "hollow charge" explosives, machine guns, grenades, and flamethrowers, the 62 Germans had destroyed or neutralized all the antiaircraft guns, surface-mounted machine guns, and the heavy artillery guns. Despite repeated attempts to counterattack, the Belgians were completely trapped. They held out for 36 hours, but at 12:27 on May 11 surrendered to the German 151st Infantry Regiment, which had relieved Witzig four hours earlier.

ABOVE: The Albert Canal running alonside Eben-Emael fort.
RIGHT: A captured Belgian bunker and Canne bridge in ruins.

## TIMELINE

**04.1932**

Construction begins of Fort Eben-Emael, located just inside the Belgian–Dutch border, east of the 16-mile (26-km) strip of the Netherlands separating Belgium from Germany.

**01.10.1940**

Engine failure forces a German plane down in Belgium. Aboard are detailed plans for an invasion of Belgium and the Netherlands.

## STEP-BY-STEP

**01** The fort has an official strength of 1,322 men; about 700 are on duty.

**02** At 05:00 lookouts report unidentifiable, silent aircraft.

**03** Following invasion protocol, fort commander Jottrand orders buildings demolished, to clear the field of fire, and the Canne bridge destroyed.

**04** The other two targeted bridges, not controlled by him, are not destroyed.

**05** On landing, Witzig's platoon quickly neutralizes gun batteries and seals the fort's entrances.

**06** Destroying the northernmost machine-gun bunker with a second 110-pound (50-kg) hollow charge, Helmut Wenzel hears a phone ringing in the crater. He answers it in English, "Here are the Germans." The caller responds, "*Mon Dieu!*"

**07** At 10:30, Jottrand, trapped in the fort, launches two more counterattacks. Both fail.

**08** At 13:45, a 233-strong reserve force attempts to reach the fort but German aerial attacks hold them back for hours.

**09** No help comes, and around midday on May 11, Jottrand surrenders. He has lost 26 men, the Germans six. The Belgian POWs will be isolated until July to keep the hollow charges and gliders secret.

guns
landing sites
barbed wire
Albert canal

| 09.27.1939 | 02.24.1940 | 05.10.1940 | 05.15.1940 | 05.28.1940 |
|---|---|---|---|---|
| Having defeated Poland, Hitler tells his General Staff he intends to invade France. | The fifth (and final) iteration of the *Fall Gelb* (Plan Yellow) for invading Western Europe is issued. | Germany invades and occupies Luxembourg, and invades Belgium and the Netherlands. | The Netherlands surrenders to the Germans. | Belgium's King Leopold surrenders. |

# OPERATION SEALION AND THE BATTLE OF BRITAIN

**DATE**    July 10–October 31, 1940
**LOCATION**    The southeastern corner of Great Britain
**OBJECTIVE**    The invasion of Great Britain by German forces

Following the retreat of the British Expeditionary Force from Dunkirk in 1940, Hitler saw Great Britain confronting "a hopeless military situation." The German leader expected the small island nation to withdraw from the war, or to seek terms. When newly appointed Prime Minister Winston Churchill instead vowed Britons would fight on for freedom, Hitler ordered his forces to draw up plans for invasion.

### Invading Britain
In the summer of 1940, Adolf Hitler was triumphant. Poland, Norway, Denmark, Luxembourg, the Netherlands, Belgium, and France had fallen. In all of Western Europe, only Great Britain stood against the Nazis.

Hitler had what Fritz Hesse, adviser to German Foreign Minister Joachim von Ribbentrop, described as "a strange love-hatred" of the British: he was convinced they would one day become allies. But Great Britain continued to oppose what Churchill called "the menace of tyranny," even after its huge Dunkirk evacuation. Hitler's response was Directive Number 16: a plan, code-named *Seelöwe* (Sealion), to invade Britain.

### The Battle of Britain
A motley armada, including 2,000 barges, was assembled in Germany, Belgium, and France. Plans were drawn, amended, and amended again as Germany's army generals rejected the navy's landing plans, fearing a slaughter. The planned date for the invasion was pushed back and back. Hitler agreed that a necessary condition before proceeding was the destruction of Great Britain's Royal Air Force and command of the skies over the English Channel. He approved a Luftwaffe bombing campaign—*Adlerangriff* ("Eagle Attack")—against military targets on British soil, particularly airfields, radar stations, and aircraft factories.

The RAF's Fighter Command responded fiercely in what became known as the Battle of Britain—the first purely aerial conflict. Although outnumbered, the British had some key advantages. Their early-warning radar system was the world's most sophisticated, and the German fighters and bombers had only limited time in which to wreak destruction before getting back over the English Channel to safety.

### Sealion is Scrapped, the Blitz Begins
As the end of August neared, the Luftwaffe had lost more than twice as many planes as the RAF. Both sides were, however, suffering badly from the loss of highly trained personnel. Churchill famously acknowledged the RAF crews' valor, saying, "Never in the field of human conflict was so much owed by so many to so few."

For 12 weeks the battle toll grew. On September 15, the RAF lost 26 planes and the Luftwaffe 60. Hitler recognized the futility: the British fighter planes were shooting down his bombers faster than they could be replaced. Two days later he indefinitely postponed the invasion. The Luftwaffe now changed tactics to night bombing on cities, industrial, and civilian targets—the Blitz—and Hitler turned east, to the Soviet Union.

ABOVE: British fighter pilots scrambling to their Spitfires during the Battle of Britain.

RIGHT: Heinkel He III flying over the Isle of Dogs, London.

BELOW (map): Opposing airfields either side of the English Channel.

## TIMELINE

**05.31.1940**
The German Naval Staff present plans for an invasion of Great Britain, which Hitler rejects.

**07.16.1940**
With Great Britain continuing to oppose him, Hitler issues Directive 16—Operation Sealion.

## STEP-BY-STEP

**01** After France's surrender and the evacuation of the British Expeditionary Force from Dunkirk, Hitler expects Great Britain to make peace with Germany.

**02** Instead, PM Winston Churchill declares, "the Battle of France is over. The Battle of Britain is about to begin … Hitler knows that he will have to break us in this island or lose the war."

**03** Hitler orders his army, navy, and air force to prepare to invade Great Britain.

**04** As German plans are amended and delayed, the Luftwaffe begins a campaign designed to eliminate the RAF.

**05** Some historians believe the plan was only intended as a bluff, but a makeshift armada is assembled, and other preparations proceed, awaiting the Luftwaffe's success.

**06** The RAF's Fighter Command suffers huge losses (about one in six of its pilots and planes) and is stretched to breaking point, but rallies.

**07** Unable to establish aerial superiority, the Luftwaffe switches to bombing raids on non-military targets and Hitler abandons Operation Sealion. Regarding Great Britain as isolated and powerless, he turns his attention to what he perceives as his main enemy, the Soviet Union.

| 08.07.1940 | 08.07.1940 | 08.13.1940 | 09.19.1940 | 10.31.1940 |
|---|---|---|---|---|
| Admirals of the Kriegsmarine, the German Navy, propose narrowing the invasion area, from between Ramsgate and the Isle of Wight to between Beachy Head and Deal. | Army General Franz Halder "utterly rejects" the revised plan, saying "I might just as well put the troops through a sausage machine." | The Luftwaffe, which has been bombing shipping and other targets since July 10, launches its Eagle Attack offensive against the RAF. | Hitler orders the dispersal of the assembled Sealion invasion armada. | Certain there will now be no invasion, the RAF considers the Battle of Britain ended. |

# THE ASSASSINATION OF TROTSKY

**DATE** **August 20, 1940**
**LOCATION** **Coyoacán, Mexico City, Mexico**
**OBJECTIVE** **To eliminate Stalin's vanquished but still vociferous foe**

**Sixteen years earlier, in 1924, Joseph Stalin had triumphed over Trotsky in the bitter power struggle for leadership of the Soviet Union following Vladimir Lenin's death. In 1929, Trotsky was banished; now he lived half a world away in Mexico. But he remained highly critical, and Stalin neither tolerated criticism nor forgave enemies.**

### A Failed Attack

After exiled sojourns in Turkey, Norway, and France, Trotsky and his partner Natalia Sedova were finally granted visas to Mexico in December 1936, living first at the Kahlo family's La Casa Azul (artists Frida Kahlo and Diego Rivera had campaigned for their asylum). Garden walls were heightened and windows bricked up for improved security. As Sedova later wrote, after the 1936 show trials in which Stalin's rivals "confessed" to plotting his assassination with Trotsky "we had been expecting the assassins with absolute certainty."

On May 23, 1940, they came. The couple was by then living behind high walls of their own in nearby Coyoacán with 13-year-old grandson Esteban and a retinue of bodyguards-cum-secretaries. At 04:00, two dozen men, led by Mexican Communist Party-founder, muralist David Siqueiros, opened fire on the house with Thompson machine guns. (It is believed a member of the retinue was tricked into leaving the gate unlocked.) Other than a bullet graze to Esteban's foot, the family was uninjured.

### A Man of Many Names

Security was tightened. There were no more countryside picnics, turrets were built on the garden walls, and the house could only be entered via an attached garage. But that could not prevent an inside job.

Jaime Ramón Mercader del Río was a Spanish communist recruited by the feared Soviet NKVD secret police during the Spanish Civil War. In Paris, he met American Sylvia Ageloff, a trusted friend of Trotsky. To her, Mercader was Jacques Mornard, a Belgian fellow Trotskyite. When Ageloff went home to the United States, Mercader followed her. Publicly he claimed to be Canadian Frank Jacson and it was under this name she introduced him to Trotsky when the couple moved to Mexico.

### The Fatal Blow

In August 1940, Mercader made his move. Under the pretext of seeking advice on a document, he went into Trotsky's study. He had brought a mountaineering ice axe; the handle had been shortened to fit under his jacket. As Trotsky sat reading the pages, Mercader drove the weapon into his skull.

Although grievously wounded and bleeding heavily, Trotsky remained conscious long enough to order his bodyguards not to kill Mercader but to question him, and not to allow his grandson to witness the scene. He died the following day in hospital.

MEXICO

Gulf of Mexico

Mexico City
Coyoacán

ABOVE: The office in which Trotsky was murdered.
RIGHT: The murdered Trotsky.

## TIMELINE

| 11.07.1879 | 1902 |
| --- | --- |
| Lev Davidovich Bronshtein is born in the Ukraine. | After a prison term and Siberian exile, revolutionary Bronshtein escapes using a false passport in the name "Trotsky," which he adopts. |

## STEP-BY-STEP

**01** First exiled to Almaty, then forced out of Turkey, France, and Norway after Stalin applies pressure to their governments, Trotsky is accepted into Mexico in 1937.

**02** In 1939, Trotsky's grandson Vsevolod (soon to be known as Esteban) comes to live with him. Along with almost all other close family members, the boy's father has been killed on Stalin's orders.

**03** Knowing he is a prime target, Trotsky has tight security. After a failed shooting attack led by David Siqueiros, he rarely leaves his house.

**04** Trotskyite Sylvia Ageloff, whose sister Ruth has served as Trotsky's secretary, is wooed by Jaime Ramón Mercader del Río in his guise as a Belgian.

**05** Having illegally entered Mexico via the US, Mercader is introduced to Trotsky by Ageloff, winning his trust.

**06** On the pretext of asking him to examine some papers, Mercader accompanies Trotsky into his study, where he attacks him. Trotsky survives for another day, but dies from shock and loss of blood.

**07** Both Mercader (his true identity still unknown) and Ageloff are arrested. After four months in hospital for "nervous prostration," she is released. Mercader serves 20 years in jail.

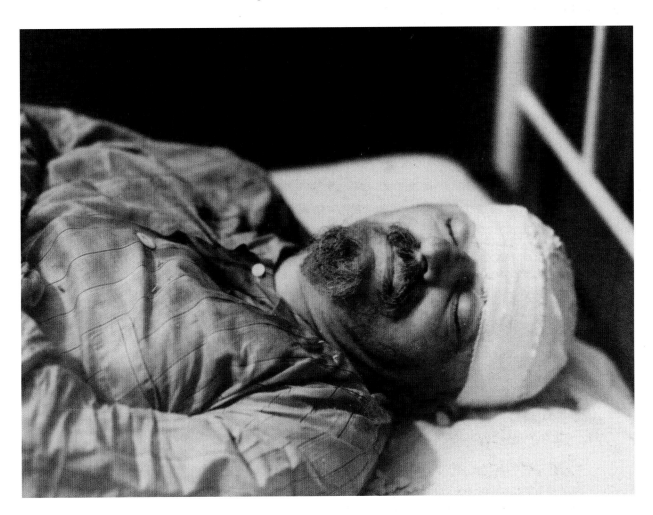

**1917**
Following periods of political exile, Trotsky becomes a key figure in Russia's October Bolshevik Revolution.

**01.1924**
Creator of the Red Army, a leading Bolshevik theorist, and long regarded as Lenin's natural successor, he is out-maneuvered by Stalin and publicly condemned.

**01.1937**
After further periods of exile, Trotsky and second wife Natalia Sedova move to Mexico.

**05.23.1937**
When Siqueiros's assassination attempt fails, Chilean consul general Pablo Neruda oversees his escape to Chile.

**1961**
A year after his release from prison on the Trotsky murder charge, Mercader is given the prestigious Hero of the Soviet Union award in Moscow.

# OPERATION CLAYMORE: THE LOFOTEN ISLANDS RAID

DATE     March 4, 1941
LOCATION Lofoten Islands, Norway
OBJECTIVE To boost British morale by destroying German war supplies

His troops might have been forced from mainland Europe, but Winston Churchill was determined that the British would do more than resist German attacks on Great Britain: they would continue to take the war to the Nazis. To achieve this, they needed a new kind of fighting force. The British Commandos were born.

### Great Britain's Own Storm Troops

Two weeks after the British evacuation from Dunkirk, needing a national morale boost, Prime Minister Winston Churchill proposed what he called "Storm Troops": raiding groups designed to inflict damage on German coastal targets. He wrote: "There ought to be at least twenty thousand Storm Troops or 'Leopards' drawn from existing units, ready to spring at the throat of any small landings or descents."

Just five days later, the first raid was undertaken by British Commandos—their name drawn from the Boer "kommando" fighting units. The following year the Commandos delivered a major morale boost for Britain with a textbook raid on Norwegian territory.

### A Surprise Raid

Like the rest of Norway, the Lofoten Islands, inside the Arctic Circle, were occupied by Germany after 1940. They drew British attention because of their contribution to the Nazi war effort: fishing was the main industry and the fish-processing factories produced glycerine, crucial in munitions manufacture.

A combined naval and army force gathered at Scotland's Scapa Flow for Operation Claymore then struck north. An enemy aerial patrol seemed to spot the flotilla, but to the troops' surprise as they approached the four Lofoten landing spots they found navigation lights blazing: the Germans did not suspect a thing.

### An Invaluable Discovery

By 06:50 the raid had begun. The Allies met almost no resistance from the German troops. By 07:30 locals in "literally hundreds" of tiny local fishing craft set out to work, wrote Captain Caslon. "It quickly became clear to them that our operations were directed against the Germans and that they were not to be molested." Despite the effect it would have on their own livelihoods, the locals cheered on the British, bringing fish and other supplies in gratitude as the raid progressed.

Eighteen factories were destroyed, along with 800,000 gallons (3.6 million Lt) of oil and nine German merchant ships. The Norwegian coastal ferry *Mira* was shot at and sunk, killing up to eight civilians, when it failed to stop as ordered. Then there was the armed German trawler *Krebs*. After an exchange of fire, the trawler was boarded and searched—aboard were two cipher disks, along with a code book. When they departed, just five hours after the raid had begun, the British took with them vital elements of Germany's Enigma code.

ABOVE: A Norwegian quisling under guard on a ship following the raid.

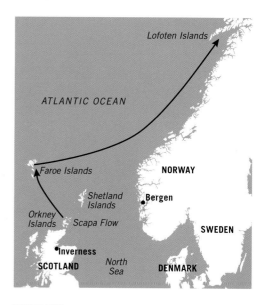

## TIMELINE

**04.09.1940**
German troops invade neutral Norway. Vidkun Quisling, leader of the inconsequential Norwegian National Socialist party declares himself head of the government.

**04.15.1940**
Resistance to Quisling is so fierce the Nazis replace him with an administrative council.

ABOVE: Commandos watching fish oil tanks burn.

BELOW: Vidkun Quisling, a Norwegian army officer whose collaboration with the Germans in their occupation of Norway during World War II established his name as a synonym for "traitor."

## STEP-BY-STEP

**01** The four Allied Commando landing parties disembark at Stamsund, Henningsvær, Svolvær, and Brettesnes.

**02** Although the German occupying force is well armed, they fail to resist; the Allies easily take one facility after another.

**03** Among the German vessels sunk in harbor is *Hamburg*, at the time the world's most advanced fish factory ship.

**04** The Norwegian coastal ferry *Mira* is sunk after failing to stop when ordered to by the Royal Navy. A survivor says the captain had not understood what was happening. As many as eight civilians die.

**05** After attempting to exchange fire with British command ship HMS *Somali*, the armed German trawler *Krebs* is badly hit, killing 14 of the 24 crew. Crucially, *Krebs* had two Enigma cipher disks, and a code book, which were secured by the Commandos.

**06** So easy is the Allied victory, British Lieutenant R.L. Wills finds time to go to Stamsund's telegraph office and send the following message to "A. Hitler, Berlin": "You said in your last speech German troops would meet the British wherever they landed. Where are your troops?"

---

**06.10.1940**

Having been driven further and further north, Norwegian troops capitulate three days after the royal family and government evacuate to London.

**06.1940**

British Prime Minister Winston Churchill orders the creation of specialized Commando battalions to undertake both defensive and offensive operations.

**03.04.1941**

Departing the Lofoten Islands, Allied Commandos take with them 314 local volunteers, 213 German prisoners, and 12 "quislings" (collaborators)—and vital clues to the German secret Enigma code.

**02.01.1942**

Quisling is named "Minister-President" under Reich commissioner Josef Terboven.

**10.24.1945**

Following Norway's liberation, Quisling, who has been found guilty of treason, is executed in Oslo.

# THE GERMAN AIRBORNE INVASION OF CRETE

DATE          May 20–June 1, 1941
LOCATION   Greek island of Crete
OBJECTIVE  To seize this strategically important Mediterranean island

For historian Antony Beevor, the Battle of Crete was the "closest-run battle" of World War II: an unprecedented and since unmatched aerial invasion in which, it seemed, the Allied and Greek resisters had thoroughly defeated the Germans until miscommunication caused a fatal weakness, allowing the invaders to seize victory.

### Pushed South to Crete

In under three weeks in 1941, German and Italian troops drove the Allies from the Greek mainland. Some of the British, Australian, and New Zealanders in the Expeditionary Force were evacuated to Egypt; the others retreated to Crete with Greek army units and militia.

The troops joined the Allied garrison, bringing it to a fighting strength of 30,000. They knew it would not be long before the Germans came. Crete's harbor and airfields made it a strategic stepping-stone for control of the eastern Mediterranean.

### Operation Mercury

The Royal Navy controlled the surrounding sea, so the Germans decided to attack by air. At Eben-Emael a year earlier, the Luftwaffe had shown how effective gliders carrying airborne troops and materiel could be. But that was a small action, and this was a major assault; gliders would be only part of the picture.

At 06:30 on May 20, Operation *Merkur* (Mercury) commenced. German planes dive-bombed Crete's antiaircraft guns, destroying most of them, and strafed and bombed communications and troop positions. Ninety minutes later, gliders descended and 2,000 paratroopers began landing near the three airfields— Maleme, Retimo (Rethymno), and Heraklion—in groups of 200, along with crates of weapons.

### Fighting to the Death

Poor intelligence led the Germans to expect far fewer defenders than they faced. Many Germans were killed by machine-gun fire or hit with mortars before they touched down. A second wave met similar fates; in all, around 2,000 Germans died on the first day. As night fell, the invaders had achieved none of their objectives. But they kept coming, and, by nightfall the next day, troops from Germany's 5th Mountain Division captured Maleme and used a British tank to clear the landing strip, allowing reinforcements, artillery, and supplies to pour in. It was now only a matter of time until Crete fell.

Over the next ten days, the Germans forced the Allies east to Suda Bay. However, the unprecedented ferocity of the civilian resistance shocked the invaders. Men, women, and children fought back with improvised weapons despite brutal reprisals. Many risked death as they hid soldiers who were left behind in the Allied evacuation. Evacuated New Zealand soldier George Weelink said, "I felt ashamed to desert such gallant people."

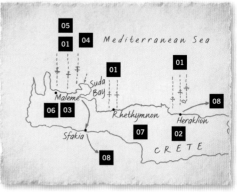

## TIMELINE

| 10.28.1940 | 04.06.1941 |
| --- | --- |
| Italy invades Greece across the Albanian border, starting the Greek-Italian War. It takes just weeks for the Greeks to push them back. | Germany invades Greece and Yugoslavia. |

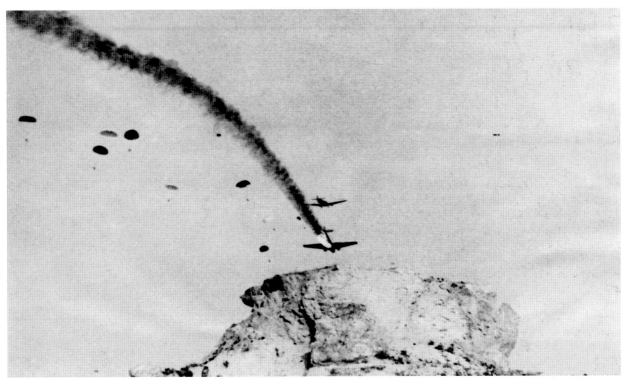

## STEP-BY-STEP

**01** In an unprecedented airborne invasion, German forces enter Crete.

**02** The defenders—Greeks, British, New Zealanders, and Australians—cut down the Germans in huge numbers. The commanders of two of the three German attack groups are killed almost immediately.

**03** Fierce fighting takes place on Hill 107 above Maleme, with the Germans gaining ground.

**04** German aerial patrols sink one British destroyer and damage two cruisers in the island's waters.

**05** Royal Navy ships engage a Crete-bound German convoy, sinking 15 requisitioned vessels with large loss of German life.

**06** Communications are cut between Allied positions, leading to a mistaken withdrawal, German troops seize Maleme. It is the battle's turning point.

**07** Reinforced by a small number of Italian troops, the Germans conquer the island.

**08** Under German fire, the British evacuate two-thirds of surviving Allied troops. Of those left, most are forced to surrender, while others take to the mountains where they hide and fight alongside the Cretans.

**09** Crete remains occupied until the end of the war; resistance to the German occupation is unrelenting for the duration.

TOP: A German Junkers 52 is shot down by British defenses and crashes.

ABOVE: Exhausted New Zealand Engineers awaiting evacuation at Sfakia; photo taken by Lieutenant P.B. Wildey, 7th Field Company.

LEFT: German troops stand by to be airlifted to Crete on the morning of May 20.

---

**04.18.1941**
As the Germans drive the Allies south and approach Athens, Alexandros Koryzis, Greek Prime Minister for less than three months, commits suicide.

**05.20.1941**
With German airborne forces suffering huge casualties, a British victory in the Battle of Crete seems assured.

**05.21.1941**
A tactical error—the overnight withdrawal of a New Zealand battalion from Maleme—gives the Germans the chance to seize the airfield.

**05.23.1941**
The Greek government-in-exile departs Crete on HMS *Decoy*.

**05.28.1941**
The British begin to evacuate, moving 16,000 troops off the island before running out of ships; more than 8,000 are left behind.

# PEARL HARBOR ATTACK

DATE        December 7, 1941
LOCATION    Oahu, Hawaii, US
OBJECTIVE   The surprise immobilization of the US Pacific Fleet

**A quiet Sunday morning turned into one of the most shocking days in American history when Japan, intent on expansion at any cost, daringly—and without warning—attacked the US Fleet based at Pearl Harbor in the American Pacific territory of Hawaii. Thousands of lives were lost, the US fleet was heavily damaged, and the repercussions echoed throughout the twentieth century.**

### First the Battle, then the War

Japan and the United States were not at war when Pearl Harbor, on the island of Oahu, was attacked, but they had been edging toward it for a decade. When Tōjō Hideki became Japanese Prime Minister in October 1941, conflict was inevitable: he saw US forces in the Pacific as a threat to his expansionist plans in Asia.

The Pearl Harbor attack was overseen by Admiral Isoroku Yamamoto, Commander in Chief of the Japanese Combined Fleet, who knew his best chance was a sudden strike on the unsuspecting US Pacific Fleet, based in Hawaii.

### Death from the Sky

At 06:00 on December 7, the first wave of fighters and bombers took off from aircraft carriers 230 miles (370 km) from Oahu. Five two-man midget submarines were also making their way to the harbor. Their targets were the 130 vessels of the US Pacific Fleet, including eight active battleships, as well as Navy and Marine aircraft. At 07:02 two technicians at the US Army's Opana Radar Site, on the island's north coast, detected a mass of approaching aircraft. They reported it, but were told it must be the American B-17 bombers due that day.

At 07:55 the skies over Pearl Harbor filled with almost 200 bombers, fighters, and torpedo planes. In the next 30 minutes the Japanese inflicted enormous damage, including a hit to the USS *Arizona* with a 1,760-pound (800-kg) armor-piercing shell that caused the ammunition magazine to explode, sinking the ship and killing 1,177 crew.

### A Desperate Fight Back

Just a few minutes into the surprise attack, American troops began antiaircraft fire, with limited success. Despite the bombing and strafing at their airfields, Army Air Corps pilots managed to get a few fighters into the air, taking down perhaps a dozen enemy planes.

The lull following the first wave ended at 08:40 when the second wave, around 160 more planes, swept in. By 10:00 it was all over. In just two hours, America had lost 2,388 servicemen and civilians, and 1,178 were wounded; 12 of its ships were sunk or beached and 164 aircraft destroyed. Japan lost 64 men, 103 planes, and the five midget submarines. President Roosevelt, broadcasting to a shocked nation, said that it was "a day that will live in infamy." Four years later the Japanese people would pay a huge price for this act of aggression, which brought the United States into World War II.

## TIMELINE

**09.19.1931**
Defying their own government, Japanese military extremists invade Manchuria, China, igniting a decade of tension with the United States.

**06.25.1940**
Japanese navy warships enter ports in French Indochina (now Vietnam) as Japan demands the right to land its forces.

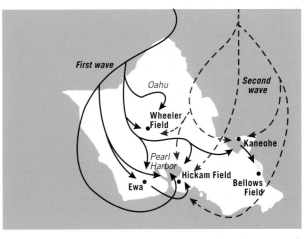

ABOVE: The track of the Japanese carrier strike force.
BELOW: The two separate waves of attacks.

ABOVE: The contorted remains of destroyer USS *Shaw* ablaze in floating drydock at Pearl Harbor following the attack.
LEFT: Battleship USS *Arizona* sinking after being hit.

## STEP-BY-STEP

**01** At 06:40 sailors on the destroyer USS *Ward* detect the conning tower of a Japanese mini-sub entering Pearl Harbor. They sink it, and report the encounter.

**02** Just after 07:00 US radar operators spot a mass of incoming planes. They report the sighting, but are reassured they are friendly.

**03** At 07:55, having reached Pearl Harbor unimpeded, Commander Mitsuo Fuchida sends the coded messages "*To, To, To*" and "*Tora, Tora, Tora*": the attack has begun.

**04** Fifteen minutes later the battleship *Arizona* explodes. It sinks in just nine minutes; only 333 of the 1,510 men aboard survive.

**05** The battleship *Oklahoma* is hit and rolls onto its side, trapping more than 400 crew.

**06** The *California* and *West Virginia* sink, the *Maryland*, *Pennsylvania*, and *Tennessee* are badly damaged, and the *Nevada*, hit as it attempts to escape the harbor, runs aground.

**07** A number of airfields, depots, and barracks on the island are hit, but important oil reserves escape unharmed, as do the Fleet's three aircraft carriers, which are not in port at the time of the attack.

**09.04.1940**
US Secretary of State, Cordell Hull, expresses official concern over Japanese aggression in Indochina.

**09.27.1940**
After Japan joins Germany and Italy in the Axis alliance, the United States stops selling it steel, iron, and oil, but keeps diplomatic talks open.

**11.26.1941**
A Japanese attack fleet of 33 vessels, including six aircraft carriers, sails for Hawaii.

**12.07.1941**
The Pearl Harbor raid occurs. By 10:00, the US Pacific Fleet is in ruins. Over the following days, Japan launches invasions of the Philippines, south China, Malaya, and the Dutch East Indies.

**12.08.1941**
With President Franklin Roosevelt calling December 7 "a date which will live in infamy," the United States declares war on Japan.

# THE HUMAN TORPEDO ATTACK AT ALEXANDRIA

DATE **December 19, 1941**
LOCATION **The port of Alexandria, Egypt**
OBJECTIVE **To destroy vessels of the Royal Navy's Mediterranean Fleet**

**The night of December 18–19 was devastating for the British Mediterranean Fleet owing to two unrelated events. In its early hours, 837 men died when HMS *Neptune* and HMS *Kandahar* sank in an uncharted minefield off Tripoli. Meanwhile, an Italian "frogman" team was mounting an extraordinary, daring attack in the port of Alexandria in Egypt.**

### A Stealth Weapon

Italy's *Siluro a Lenta Corsa* (SLC), or "Slow Moving Torpedoes," had diving planes and ballast tanks with compressed-air release, making them navigable. Their two external "saddles" for scuba divers gave rise to the name "human torpedoes." A submarine would deliver the SLCs to the target port; the divers would take the torpedoes to the targets, detach the 660-pound (300-kg) timer-controlled warheads and secure them, then escape safely before the explosion.

On December 17, Commander in Chief of the Royal Navy's Mediterranean Fleet (based in Alexandria), Admiral Andrew Cunningham, received the first warning message about a decrypted Italian reconnaissance report. The following day he issued an alert: "Attacks on Alexandria by air, boat, or human torpedo may be expected."

ABOVE: The "maiale" (pig) SLC manned torpedo.

### Slipping Through the Net

Despite the alert, three SLCs launched from the Italian submarine *Scirè* at 18:40 that day slid easily into the harbor—because the antisubmarine boom was open for returning British ships. Their targets were Cunningham's flagship battleship, *Queen Elizabeth*, the battleship *Valiant*, and aircraft carrier *Eagle*.

Around 02:30, the crew assigned to attack *Queen Elizabeth* placed their charge, then, blocked by the now closed boom, scuttled their SLC and escaped ashore (they were captured two days later). With *Eagle* out of harbor, its SLC crew targeted the Norwegian oil tanker *Sagona*. (They, too, reached land but were also later captured.) The SLC targeting *Valiant*, which was headed by mission commander Luigi Durand de la Penne, malfunctioned, but de la Penne wrested it into position and set the timer. Surfacing at 03:25, the pair were spotted, seized, and questioned. Refusing to answer, they were detained on board.

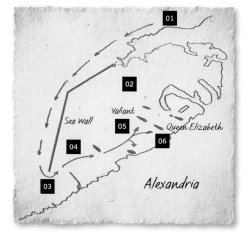

### Disguising the Successful Attack

At 05:47, the *Sagona* mine blew, badly damaging the tanker and HMS *Jervis*, moored alongside for refueling. At 06:00, de la Penne informed *Valiant*'s captain of the imminent explosion; lower decks were cleared in time. Shortly after, it was *Queen Elizabeth*'s turn. Eight men were killed aboard the latter, and both ships were badly damaged, coming to rest on an even keel, on the shallow harbor floor.

During the following weeks, while intense work took place below the waterline, the British went to great lengths to prevent Axis reconnaissance realizing the advantage they now held: gun drills and ceremonial parades took place on the upper decks of *Queen Elizabeth*, and British newspapers ran staged photos of Cunningham broadcasting his Christmas seasonal message from the ship.

## TIMELINE

| 1936 | 08.22.1940 |
| --- | --- |
| Two Italian naval officers successfully test *Siluro a Lenta Corsa* (SLC) navigable torpedoes, which earn the nickname *maiale* (pigs). | A planned SLC attack on Alexandria harbor is thwarted when the British detect and sink the Italian submarine *Iride*. |

RIGHT. Admiral Cunningham "broadcasting the Fleet's Greetings" from HMS *Queen Elizabeth* in a staged propaganda photograph, Christmas 1941. The propaganda photo was in fact taken while the ship was undergoing extensive repairs.

## STEP-BY-STEP

**01** Having left its base in La Spezia, Liguria, 15 days earlier, and picked up SLC crews at Leros in the Aegean Sea, the Italian submarine *Scirè* reaches Alexandria.

**02** The Royal Naval Mediterranean Fleet is a prime target since its job is to safeguard the vital air and shipping base of Malta and Allied supply routes, and to cut off those of the Axis.

**03** The three two-man SLC crews anticipate an arduous task breaking through the antisubmarine netting; they find the boom is open.

**04** Wearing sealed-system breathing apparatuses to prevent telltale bubbles, they head for their respective objectives.

**05** Having activated a timed explosion under HMS *Valiant*, Luigi Durand de la Penne and Emilio Bianchi are captured and locked up below decks.

**06** De la Penne warns *Valiant*'s captain, Charles Morgan, to move his men, but will say no more.

**07** The SLCs badly damage the tanker *Sagona* and take HMS *Queen Elizabeth* and *Valiant* out of the war for nine months and 19 months, respectively.

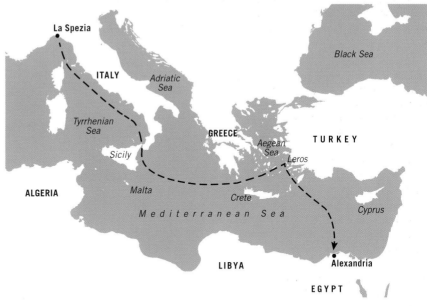

| 09.29.1940 | 12.19.1941 | 12.19.1941 | 08.16.1942 | 06.26.1943 |
|---|---|---|---|---|
| Another planned SLC attack using the submarine *Gondar* is abandoned. | In an enemy minefield, Mediterranean Fleet light cruiser HMS *Neptune* sinks with only one survivor; *Aurora* and *Penelope* are damaged; and *Kandahar* is sunk as it is unsalvageable. | The successful SLC attack in Alexandria swings "the military balance of power in the Mediterranean in favor of the Axis," says British PM Winston Churchill. | HMS *Valiant* returns to service. | HMS *Queen Elizabeth* returns to service. |

# THE AGE OF
# SPECIAL OPERATIONS
## 1941–1945

By June 1940, Axis forces led by Hitler's armies had driven British, French, and Belgian troops out of mainland Europe. Against all odds, more than 330,000 were successfully evacuated from Dunkirk. But as miraculous as this result was, the seemingly inexorable advance of their enemies was a deep blow to the Allies. Rather than crumble, British Prime Minister Winston Churchill vowed to find new ways to fight.

Within weeks he had proposed the creation of specialist raiding groups, which he called Storm Troops, to launch lightning attacks on targets accessible by sea. Less than a month after Dunkirk, his newly organized Special Operations Executive (SOE) Commandos undertook their first operation. Within the year they were making a real impact deeper and deeper into enemy territory, living up to Churchill's aim that they should "set Europe ablaze."

It was the beginning of a new approach to warfare. Operatives were intensively trained in skills, including unarmed combat, explosives, parachuting, maintaining a cover identity, and survival skills, so as to be ready for anything. They had to be self-reliant, resourceful, quick to adapt, and ready to spring into action at a moment's notice.

By 1942, the United States had its own Office of Strategic Services (OSS) operatives trained for missions behind enemy lines. That year British Commandos had great success in the Operation Chariot raid on the supposedly impregnable French port of Saint-Nazaire. But three months later, in an attempt to increase the scope of these raids, an Allied force of more than 6,000 troops including British Commandos, US Rangers, and Canadian soldiers set out to raid the occupied French port of Dieppe only to be cut down in what became a bloodbath.

Special Ops were here to stay, but after Dieppe the Allies utilized their Commandos for smaller, more targeted missions. There were still disasters, including Operation Freshman, the failed glider-borne raid on a Norwegian plant providing a vital ingredient for Germany's nuclear weapons research. But there were great victories, too: in Greece, France, Norway, and Singapore. The Rangers would have one of their most memorable successes in the Philippines, with a bold and skillful raid on a Japanese POW camp at Cabanatuan.

There were also hair-raising secret operations undertaken by troops from regular sections of the armed forces. Notable among these are the Dam Busters bomb attacks and the ill-fated US aerial raid on the oil fields of Ploesti, Romania. The Germans also launched extraordinary airborne operations, both small (the rescue of Mussolini) and large (the invasion of Crete).

In the history of warfare there is a special place for stories of escape. Thanks to the film *The Great Escape,* the doomed mass breakout from Stalag Luft III in 1944 is widely known. The story of the ingenious "wooden horse" escape from the same camp five months earlier is a tale no less gripping. Like so many of these stories, it leaves us in awe of the cool, calm daring of the people involved, who were at their best in the worst of circumstances.

# AUSTRALIAN COMPANIES IN TIMOR

DATE          December 12, 1941–January 10, 1943
LOCATION   West (Dutch) and East (Portuguese) Timor
OBJECTIVE  To continue resisting the Japanese against all odds

Even within Australia, the remarkable courage, ingenuity, and endurance of the yearlong guerrilla war waged in the mountainous jungles of Timor by a heavily outnumbered band of "Aussie Diggers" is largely forgotten. But the tenacity of those few fighters—their very existence unknown for months—boosted Allied morale across the Pacific.

### Handpicked Commandos

In early 1941, 270 Australian soldiers specially chosen for their bush skills, mental strength, and physical toughness began training in secret. This 2nd Independent Company (later renamed 2/2 Commando Squadron) was intended for missions in occupied Europe; Japan's entry into the war changed that.

On December 8, the day after the Pearl Harbor attack, the Company mustered in Darwin with other Australian units to form the 1,400-strong "Sparrow Force." They were to be garrisoned on Timor, a tiny mountainous island in the Malay Archipelago. The west side of the island was held by the Netherlands, an Allied power; the east by Portugal, officially neutral.

### Down, Not Out

Over the following three months, Singapore, New Britain, Ambon, and Java fell to the advancing Japanese. Timor was a clear target, with its Penfui airfield connecting Australia and the US forces in the Philippines. Even with the 1,000 Dutch troops already garrisoned on Timor, the Australians, split between the east and west, lacked the numbers to hold the island. After enemy air raids on Penfui, reinforcements were readied, but the Japanese invaded first.

The Allies fought fiercely for three days until, surrounded, outnumbered, high in casualties, and short of ammunition, the bulk surrendered. Around 100 of the 2/40th Battalion escaped inland, crossing to East Timor where they and a few Dutch soldiers joined the majority of the 2nd Independent Company, who had escaped capture. With the help of *creados*, local Timorese allies, they began waging guerrilla war on the Japanese.

### Ingenious and Indefatigable

For two months this small, unstoppable force was off the radar—Australian military commanders believed them dead or captured. In turn, they thought Australia itself might have fallen. Nonetheless, they fought on, leaving their mountain hideouts to set up ambushes and make hit-and-run attacks, evading aerial patrols and bombings. Their only weapons were Bren and Tommy guns and rifles; their food was crocodile and water buffalo.

Time and again they broke through Japanese lines to scavenge parts for a radio transmitter. What they could not find they made, pouring molten metal into carved bamboo. In mid-April they made contact with Darwin headquarters. Six weeks later, the Royal Australian Navy resupplied them for the first time, and in July reinforcements took their numbers to 700. Against ever-increasing odds they fought on, until finally forced to evacuate in January 1943.

ABOVE: The wireless "Winnie the War Winner," built by the Sparrow Force, being used by (left to right) Signaler Keith Richards, Corporal John Donovan, and Sergeant John Henry Sargent to contact the Australian mainland.

## TIMELINE

| 12.12.1941 | 17.12.1941 |
|---|---|
| Having traveled 516 miles (830 km) from Darwin, the majority of Australia's "Sparrow Force" moves into position around Koepang, in Dutch West Timor. | Despite Portuguese fears that Allied troops will provoke Japan, the 2nd Independent Company and Dutch reinforcements set up in the island's east. |

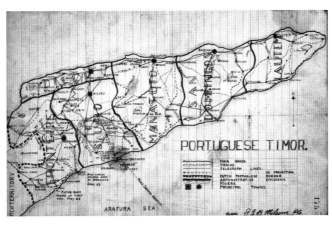

LEFT: Guerrillas in Timor; natives lead a pack train of Timor ponies. BELOW: A sketch map of Timor used by Lieutenant Colonel W. W. Leggatt in his report, written in October 1945, of the actions of Sparrow Force on Timor. Leggatt went into captivity, and was sent to Changi on July 26, 1942.

## STEP-BY-STEP

**01** In the two months they spend in Timor before the Japanese invade, Australian troops forge a strong bond with locals, especially in West Timor.

**02** After the bulk of the Allied force is captured or surrenders, several hundred men from the 2nd Independent Company and 2/40th Battalion escape inland.

**03** Regrouping in the mountainous jungle, they begin a guerrilla campaign against the Japanese, supported by local Timorese known as *creados*.

**04** After two months they have a working radio transmitter. Believing them all dead or imprisoned, Darwin headquarters thinks their initial broadcast is a trick by the Japanese.

**05** On May 27, the Royal Australian Navy commences what becomes a regular resupply run from Darwin to Timor.

**06** In July—fighting a major offensive in Kokoda, New Guinea—Japan steps up its efforts to eliminate resistance in Timor, bringing in reinforcements, and eventually turning the West Timorese against the East.

**07** In September 1943, military documentarian Damien Parer films the guerrillas. His film *Men of Timor* tells the world of their indomitable fighting spirit.

---

**26.01.1942**
The Japanese make air raids on Penfui airfield, returning four days later.

**02.18.1942**
An Australian convoy bringing reinforcements and much-needed ammunition is forced back by Japanese bombers.

**02.19.1942**
Japanese troops invade Timor, meeting stiff resistance despite their greater numbers. They eventually turn the West Timorese against the East.

**04.18.1942**
Using the wireless transmitter they have built and nicknamed "Winnie the War Winner" after Winston Churchill, the Australian Commandos contact Darwin.

**01.10.1943**
The guerrilla remnants of "Sparrow Force" evacuate from Timor; "Z" Lancer Commandos who have been brought in remain another month.

THE AGE OF SPECIAL OPERATIONS

# OPERATION BITING

**DATE** February 27–28, 1942
**LOCATION** Saint-Jouin-Bruneval, Normandy, France
**OBJECTIVE** The seizure of components of German radar for analysis

**Despite things not running entirely to plan, this daring Combined Operations mission to parachute troops into Occupied France in order to capture German technology was accomplished thanks to some quick thinking, improvization, and persistence. The information acquired enabled Great Britain to break through German air defenses.**

## The Battle of the Beams

After the evacuation of the British Expeditionary Force from Dunkirk, much of the weight of the British war effort fell on the Royal Air Force. With each side pinning much on nighttime bombing air raids, understanding how to beat the enemy's radio aerial detection—or radar—system was essential.

German and British scientists commenced "the battle of the beams": a race for radar superiority. The British team, led by Reginald (R.V.) Jones, became concerned the Germans were getting ahead of them. The only way to find out was to seize a German radar device.

## An Airborne Raid

There was just such an installation, code-named "Würzburg," across the English Channel at Saint-Jouin-Bruneval (known in English simply as Bruneval). Experienced army paratroopers would raid it, accompanied by Flight Sergeant Charles Cox, a radar technician who had never parachuted before. They, and the captured radar equipment, would be picked up off nearby beaches by the Royal Navy.

The paratroopers, from the 1st Parachute Brigade, were in five forty-man groups code-named after British admirals: one ("Nelson"), led by Lieutenant Euen Charteris, would secure the beach for the evacuation; "Jellicoe," "Hardy," and "Drake" would seize the villa housing the Würzburg; "Rodney" would provide rearguard protection. Their equipment, including trolleys to move the radar parts, would be airdropped with them. But Charteris's group landed almost 2 miles (3 km) off target, as did some essential equipment, including radios. The radios they were left with did not work properly, limiting messages to those passed between the groups by runners, and they could not radio their evacuation ships.

## Mission Accomplished

The villa group surrounded the building and exchanged fire with a German guard, killing him. Alerted by the noise, more Germans ran over from nearby barracks. While Cox supervised the dismantling of the radar, the other British fought the Germans off suffering one of the two fatalities. The British then wrested three German prisoners and the laden trolleys over barbed wire toward the beach, not realizing, until they were fired on from a pillbox, that Charteris and his men were not yet there.

Charteris's team soon arrived and cleared the machine-gun nest. But there was no sign of the landing craft—and no radio contact. Out of options, the British fired a flare, which brought in the landing craft. With German reinforcements on the cliff tops firing at them, the evacuation was disordered, and six men who failed to reach the beach were left behind with no way of contacting their rescuers. The mission was, however, regarded as an unqualified success, and the information it revealed proved invaluable.

ABOVE: Low-level oblique image of the Würzburg radar installation taken by Squadron Leader A.E. Hill on December 5, 1941, to aid with the location and removal of the radar during the operation.

## TIMELINE

**1936–1939**

Although researched extensively, by many, from the 1920s—including France, Germany, the US, and Japan—Great Britain becomes the first nation to install a radar detection system.

**06.1940**

The Battle of Britain makes it clear that command of the skies over the English Channel is essential for Britain's defense, and that radar superiority is a key strategic advantage.

**ABOVE:** A reconstruction of the raid on Bruneval by war artist Richard Eurich, showing men of the 2nd Parachute Regiment dropping onto the cliff top beside the radar station, with evacuation forces waiting at the water's edge.

**LEFT:** British paratroopers after the Bruneval night raid being taken back to Britain by the Royal Navy.

## STEP-BY-STEP

**01** In late January, 1942, those chosen for the raid train in intense secrecy without knowing what the purpose of their mission is to be.

**02** RAF radar mechanic Flight Sergeant Charles Cox is summoned to the British Air Ministry and is informed that he has been "volunteered" for a dangerous, secret operation. He has to photograph, then dismantle, the German "Würzburg" radar device.

**03** Approaching the French coast at night on February 27, the RAF Whitley bombers—adapted as transport planes and carrying the paratroops—evade heavy antiaircraft fire. All five companies of paratroops are dropped.

**04** The "Nelson" group of Commandos is dropped off target and must make their way back to the beaches through snow and heavy outside Bruneval is quickly secured but, alerted by gunfire, more German troops spill out of the nearby Le Presbytère barracks in the woods 900 feet (275 m) away.

**06** Under fire, the "Würzburg" radar device is dismantled and transported to the beach, but no radio contact with the landing parties can be made. Meanwhile, six British soldiers from the "Nelson" group, now abandoned, split

up and head inland. French villagers risk their lives to help them.

**07** When they have finally been evacuated, the raiders learn the waiting Royal Navy MTBs (motor torpedo boats) were forced into silence to avoid detection from a passing German destroyer patrol.

**08** Six British soldiers who did not make it to the beach are left behind. They are captured by the Germans, despite the help of locals, and become POWs, but all survive the war.

| 11.1941 | 01.08.1942 | 02.27.1942 | Late 1942 | 06.06.1944 |
|---|---|---|---|---|
| Aerial reconnaissance and Enigma decryptions confirm the existence of a German radar installation at Bruneval, near Le Havre, Normandy. | British Combined Operations, under Admiral Lord Louis Mountbatten, inaugurate the plan to raid Bruneval using paratroopers and the Royal Navy. | With conditions—including a full moon, clear skies, and an overnight high tide—finally right, the raid on Bruneval is launched at 22:15. | Analyzing the "Würzburg" device, British scientist R.V. Jones finds it modular and easier to maintain, but less sophisticated than British models, and learns its weaknesses. | The intelligence gathered from the raid opens the way to more effective Allied bombing raids over Europe and, ultimately, Operation Overlord—the D-Day landings. |

# OPERATION CHARIOT: THE SAINT-NAZAIRE RAID

DATE    **March 27–28, 1942**
LOCATION    **Saint-Nazaire, Brittany, German-occupied France**
OBJECTIVE    **The destruction of the only Atlantic dock that could accommodate German battleships**

**In recognition of its sheer audacity, and the courage shown by the sailors and soldiers who ran the enemy gauntlet, the raid code-named Operation Chariot is sometimes called "the greatest raid of all." With cool daring, British forces penetrated the heavily defended German-controlled French port of Saint-Nazaire and destroyed its valuable dock.**

## A Looming Threat

In May 1941, the British had felt the destructive power of the enormous new German battleship *Bismarck* before sinking her. Now her sister ship, *Tirpitz*, had sailed for Norway. The British Admiralty feared it would leave the Baltic and commence raiding operations in the Atlantic.

*Tirpitz's* sheer size made it a threat, but also offered vulnerability. Only one Atlantic port had a dry dock large enough if *Tirpitz* was damaged in battle: Saint-Nazaire in occupied Brittany. If that was out of action, the ship would have to limp all the way back to Germany across the North Sea, dodging Allied ships. This risk would almost certainly keep it in the Baltic.

## An "Impregnable" Target

The German navy, the *Kriegsmarine*, regarded the dock and newly built U-boat pens at Saint-Nazaire as impregnable. Built to resist air attack, they were also 6 miles (9.6 km) inside the Loire River estuary. Although wide, the estuary was navigable only along one central, well-guarded channel. But planners at Great Britain's Combined Operations headquarters had a bold idea: Operation Chariot.

The high spring tide would provide just enough clearance to get shallow-draft vessels over the shoals at the mouth of the Loire. Arriving in disguise by night, a force might get close enough to destroy the dock. The key was onetime US destroyer *Buchanan*, now HMS *Campbeltown*. Specially lightened, it was disguised as a German torpedo boat, its bows packed with 4.8 tons (4.3 tonnes) of depth charges with eight-hour fuses, encased in steel and cement.

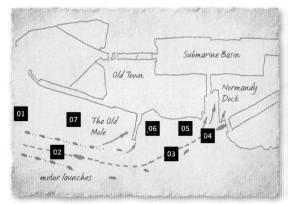

## The Surprise Explosions

With Motor Torpedo Boat 314 leading, and the launches in two columns behind *Campbeltown*, the fleet entered the estuary. Responding to shore challenges using German signals provided by British Intelligence, they claimed to be a returning German convoy. This worked almost until they reached their target when, as sailor Ronald Bannister said, "all hell let loose."

Under intense gunfire and shelling, *Campbeltown* rammed the *caisson* (port gates) and was scuttled. Many launches burned and sank, while others had grenades thrown down onto their crowded decks. Of the 621 men who took part, 169 were killed. More than 200, many badly wounded, were taken prisoner. But they achieved their aim: the Germans were unable to move *Campbeltown* and when it exploded the next day it rendered the dock unusable for the duration of the war. It also killed up to 300 German troops. Two days later, delayed-action torpedoes, which had been planted during the raid, further damaged the area.

## TIMELINE

**10.29.1932**

The biggest ship of its day, the liner *Normandie*, is launched. The enormous dry dock built for it at Saint-Nazaire becomes known by that name.

**02.1941**

Building begins in German-occupied Saint-Nazaire on immense U-boat pens, protected by roofs more than 26-feet (8-m) thick, made of reinforced concrete, steel beams, and granite.

## STEP-BY-STEP

**01** On March 27, 1942, the destroyers *Tynedale* and *Atherstone* remain on patrol outside as the rest of the Allied fleet enters the Loire estuary.

**02** With two of its four funnels removed and the others slanted to disguise it, HMS *Campbeltown* enters the estuary with Commandos lying flat on its deck.

**03** Using German signals, *Campbeltown* proceeds until close to the dock, when suspicious guards spotlight the vessels and start firing.

**04** A German-speaking British officer buys a few minutes by creating confusion insisting his crew are Germans being fired on in error.

**05** Soon, though, intense firing and shelling begins. The wooden Fairmile motor launches burn and sink quickly when hit.

**06** The German onslaught prevents most of the crew of the launches that were to target the mole from reaching it. The other column, targeting the old port entrance, fare only slightly better.

**07** Heading back to sea with survivors from the *Campbeltown*'s Commando demolition teams, Motor Launch 177 is hit and destroyed by fire, with just a handful of men escaping. Despite the losses, the Saint-Nazaire dock is destroyed and five Victoria Crosses and many other honors will be awarded for the raid.

TOP: A house in the Old Town at the harbor showing some of the damage Operation Chariot inflicted.

ABOVE: HMS Campbeltown wedged in the dock gates.

| 02.25.1941 | 05.24.1941 | 01.12.1942 | 03.29.1942 | 11.12.1944 |
|---|---|---|---|---|
| Germany's second Bismarck-class battleship, the huge *Tirpitz*, is commissioned. | The original and namesake of the class, the *Bismarck*, sinks the battle cruiser HMS *Hood* and kills 1,415 men. The shock reverberates throughout Great Britain. | *Tirpitz* leaves Germany bound for Norway, a path often followed by a move into the North Atlantic. | One day after the raid on Saint-Nazaire, the delayed-charge explosives on the *Campbeltown* fire, rendering the ww dock unusable for the rest of the war. | *Tirpitz* is finally destroyed by Allied bombers in Altafjord, near Tromso, Norway. The ship's only action was to bombard Allied shipping at Spitsbergen in September 1943. |

# OPERATION ANTHROPOID:
# THE HEYDRICH ASSASSINATION

DATE        May 27, 1942
LOCATION    Kobylisy, Prague, Reich Protectorate of Bohemia and Moravia
OBJECTIVE   To kill the feared Nazi who was ruling the Czech homelands

**Reinhard Heydrich was considered ruthless even by Nazi standards. Sent by Adolf Hitler to crush Czech resistance, this prime architect of "the Final Solution" to eliminate Europe's Jewish population immediately instituted a regime of fear and reprisal. His death eight months later was the culmination of a remarkable, heroic effort.**

### Choosing a Target
In 1938, Czechoslovakia lost significant territory and a third of its population to Germany, Poland, and Hungary under the Munich Agreement, cosigned by Great Britain. Despite war breaking out, the agreement still stood in mid-1941 when the British recognized the Czech government-in-exile in London.

The Allies put pressure on Czech leaders to galvanize resistance in their homeland, which was now a "Protectorate" of the Third Reich. They responded by planning a high-level assassination—hoping its success would see the Munich Agreement abandoned. Both the murderous new Nazi ruler of the Protectorate, Reinhard Heydrich, and Czech-born Nazi Karl Frank were potential targets—they settled on Heydrich.

### A Frustrating Wait
Operation Anthropoid began on October 2, 1941, with two experienced Czech soldiers chosen for the mission. During paratroop training one was injured and replaced. The new team, warrant officers Josef Gabcik and Jan Kubis, undertook intensive Special Operations Executive (SOE) training in Scotland and England. Overnight on December 28–29 they parachuted into the Protectorate.

Next morning, they found that instead of landing at Pilsen as planned, they were near Prague, 62 miles (100 km) away. Making their way to Pilsen, they contacted resistance members and for the next five months devised various assassination plans, none of which proved workable.

### Eventual Success
In April 1942, Heydrich shifted his base from Prague Castle to a nearby château. This was the opening his assassins needed: his new daily route included a sharply curving road where his open-topped Mercedes had to slow down.

On May 27, with Heydrich in the front beside chauffeur Johannes Klein, Gabcik stepped in front of the car holding a Sten gun. When the gun failed to fire, Kubis pulled out a bomb and threw it at Heydrich. He missed; it exploded near the right front fender. Heydrich ran after Gabcík, gun in hand, before collapsing from a shrapnel wound received in the explosion. Kubis, also hit with shrapnel, outran Klein, who was shot twice by Gabcik as the Czechs escaped, believing they had failed.

That afternoon, surgeons removed material from Heydrich's wound, including metal and horsehair from the car's upholstery. After appearing to recover well, the Nazi died seven days later from an infection caused by the foreign matter. Thousands of Czechs paid for Heydrich's death with their lives, including the assassins, who became national heroes.

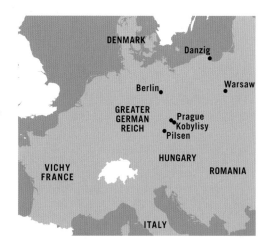

ABOVE: Fire hoses are used to pump water into the church in an effort to force out those taking refuge.

## TIMELINE

| 09.27.1941 | 10.01.1941 |
| --- | --- |
| Notorious Reich security chief Reinhard Heydrich, a close supporter of Hitler, becomes "acting Protector" of Bohemia and Moravia. | Having introduced martial law, Heydrich sentences the Czech prime minister to death and begins purging the intelligentsia. |

ABOVE: Heydrich's car after the attack, showing the tank grenade damage.

BELOW: The bodies of Josef Gabcik and Jan Kubis, on the pavement outside the Karel Boromejsky Church in Prague on June 18, 1942.

## STEP-BY-STEP

**01** In Great Britain, Josef Gabcik and Jan Kubis receive intense SOE training in explosives, infrastructure sabotage, assault combat, and sharpshooting.

**02** After each writes their last will and testament, they are parachuted into the Protectorate.

**03** On a day Heydrich happens to be heading to Berlin to meet with Hitler, the attack is launched.

**04** Gabcik is perfectly positioned to shoot Heydrich, but his Sten gun fails. Heydrich attempts to shoot Gabcik but his pistol also jams.

**05** Kubis throws a tank grenade at the car, causing an explosion whose effects will be fatal, even though Heydrich himself does not initially realize he is hit.

**06** A passing truck takes Heydrich to hospital, where his damaged spleen is removed, foreign matter extracted from the wound, and his collapsed lung, fractured rib, and torn diaphragm are repaired.

**07** Karl Frank immediately declares a state of emergency; reprisals against anyone suspected of assisting the attackers begin.

**08** Heydrich dies seven days after the attack due to complications from wounds the grenade explosion inflicted; Josef Gabcik and Jan Kubis die on June 18, during a prolonged siege of the Karel Boromejsky Church in Prague where they took refuge with other resistance fighters.

---

**05.27.1942**
Hitler orders the Gestapo to "wade in blood" to find those responsible for the attack on Heydrich.

**06.03.1942**
Seemingly recovering, Heydrich is eating a meal in his hospital bed when he lapses into a coma, dying early the next day.

**06.09.1942**
In a vicious act of retaliation, the village of Lidice is destroyed by the Nazis; 173 men are shot; the majority of women and children die in concentration camps.

**06.16.1942**
Plot aider Karel Curda presents himself to the Gestapo, betraying the names of fellow resistance members, leading to thousands of deaths. He is hanged for treason in 1947.

**06.18.1942**
Josef Gabcik and Jan Kubis, and those hiding them in a Prague church, die in an hours-long battle with the SS and Gestapo.

# OPERATION JUBILEE: THE RAID ON DIEPPE

DATE **August 19, 1942**
LOCATION **Dieppe, Normandy, France**
OBJECTIVE **To damage German defensive installations and to gather intelligence**

A tragedy, a fiasco, a terrible loss of life—the raid on Dieppe, code-named Operation Jubilee, has been described as all of these. Bitter feelings about the disastrous operation persist even now, but there is no dispute about the courage of the men who landed on those French beaches.

### A Test Run

Suffering badly on the Eastern Front, Russian leader Joseph Stalin turned to Great Britain and the US: if a Western, or "second," front could be reestablished it would split Germany's resources. The Allies were far from being able to do that. However, British premier Churchill was keen to take his Commando raids to the next level— bigger assaults on German positions close to Britain.

Dieppe was chosen as the first target. The mission's stated aim was to damage enemy installations, including a radar station, and to gather intelligence. But it was also a test run: a real-world assessment of the equipment, the tactics, and the chain of command needed for a major Allied cross-Channel invasion of Europe. Some 5,000 Canadian troops, 1,000 British Commandos, and 50 US Rangers would be delivered to the French coast by a fleet of over 230 vessels, and given aerial cover by 870 Allied planes.

### The Enemy Alerted

First, assault troops were to flank the Germans in a surprise daybreak attack, destroying their artillery. Then the main force would launch a frontal assault, seizing the harbor and town. With these objectives met, they would withdraw before high tide. But almost nothing went to plan.

The landing spots were on six beaches over a 9-mile (14-km) stretch of coastline. Approaching its landing spot at Berneval, to Dieppe's east, the flotilla carrying No. 3 Commando encountered an enemy convoy. The subsequent predawn battle scattered the Commandos' craft. Only 18 men actually landed— too few to neutralize the German artillery as planned, though they did keep its gunners pinned down with sniper fire.

Far worse, though, the battle, clearly visible from the cliff tops, removed all element of surprise. Quickly mobilizing, the Germans were ready to inflict slaughter.

### One Disaster after Another

No. 4 Commando had the only real triumph of the raid, neutralizing the battery of guns on the right flank. Both subsequent flank attacks failed. The South Saskatchewan Regiment landed west of the Scie River, not east as planned. The only crossing was a narrow bridge, and the Germans were waiting. Meanwhile, at Puys, Canadian and Scottish soldiers waded into enemy fire so intense that rescue craft could not approach. All were killed or captured.

Despite this, the main assault party landed and was mown down. Only 27 of the planned 58 tanks made it on to the beach. Those whose tracks were not wrecked by the beach's pebbles were blocked by an antitank wall. Finally the evacuation order was given, but only a fraction of the troops made it safely aboard before the attempt was abandoned, leaving thousands to be taken prisoner.

ABOVE RIGHT: German troops surveying the damage in the wake of the raid.

RIGHT: A destroyed Churchill tank at the raid.

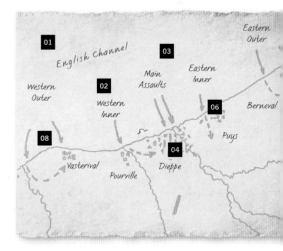

## TIMELINE

**04.25.1942**
Planning begins for an attack on Dieppe, code-named Operation Rutter, in which paratroopers will play a major part.

**05.20.1942**
Canadian and British troops begin two months' training for Rutter on the Isle of Wight.

## STEP-BY-STEP

**01** There are no air raids on Dieppe before Jubilee, in order to maintain an element of surprise.

**02** Of the 6,000-strong landing force, 83 percent are Canadians who have been stationed in Great Britain for two years or more without seeing combat.

**03** At 03:45, approaching their landing spot in the dark, the Allies encounter and engage a German convoy.

**04** Witnessing the battle, the Germans mobilize land, sea, and air forces.

**05** Three of the four Allied flank attacks fail to achieve their objectives.

**06** Landing at Puys late and in sporadic waves, the Royal Regiment of Canada meets intense fire from German positions on the high cliffs. Of the 554 who land, more than 200 die in the brief battle and 289 are taken prisoner.

**07** Believing Jubilee is succeeding, operation command sends more troops to the slaughter.

**08** At 09:30 the order to evacuate is given amid the chaos. By 12:20, landing craft can no longer reach the beaches. The 1,946 men left behind are taken prisoner. More than 1,100 Allied troops have died in the raid.

| 07.07.1942 | 08.19.1942 | 08.19.1942 | 06.06.1944 | 09.01.1944 |
|---|---|---|---|---|
| First delayed by bad weather, the operation is called off after Luftwaffe reconnaissance planes spot the Rutter transport ships. | A revised version of the Dieppe assault plan, code-named Operation Jubilee, is launched at dawn. | By midday, the assault is in disarray and defeated, but much valuable information has been gathered. | The Allies succeed with the huge D-Day aerial and amphibious landings west of Dieppe, enabling them to push the Germans out of France and the rest of Western Europe. | The task of liberating Dieppe is given to the Canadians in honor of their country's previous sacrifice at Dieppe; they receive an ecstatic greeting. |

# OPERATION FRESHMAN: A GLIDER-BORNE RAID ON NORWAY

DATE        November 19, 1942
LOCATION    Rjukan, Telemark, Norway
OBJECTIVE   To sabotage production of heavy water needed for German atomic bombs

**The target was difficult to reach, the training was brief, the equipment faulty, and the escape plan optimistic at best. Even if they had reached their objective, it is unlikely the men sent to Norway on a mission to hinder Germany's nuclear weapons program would have survived, but they never had the chance to find out.**

### Fears of a German A-Bomb

Even before the war, Great Britain and France monitored the Norsk Hydro company's Vemork chemical plant at Rjukan in southeastern Norway. One by-product of its fertilizer production was heavy water, or deuterium oxide—water containing a particular hydrogen isotope, used in making nuclear weapons. In 1942, increasingly concerned about Nazi attempts to build an atomic bomb, Britain's Special Operations Executive (SOE) targeted the plant.

With Vemork perched atop a sheer cliff more than 1,000 feet (305 m) high, SOE decided to mount Britain's first military glider raid. The first stage, code-named Operation Grouse, saw four Norwegian soldiers, all experienced outdoorsmen, parachuted in. They contacted local resistance groups, gathered intelligence on movements at the plant, and placed a homing beacon at a suitable glider landing spot from which the raiders could hike to their objective.

### Problems from the Beginning

A month later—after little training—in Operation Freshman, two Halifax bombers, each towing one of the new Horsa gliders, took off from Scotland's RAF Skitten airfield. The planes had a crew of seven, the gliders had two pilots each, and carried 15 volunteer sappers. Of the 48 men, only seven would return.

Departure was delayed in an unsuccessful attempt to fix the wiring woven into the long hawsers that held the gliders. It should have provided communication with the planes; instead, they were reduced to light signals. A clear, moonlit sky was forecast over the target, but the 400-mile (644-km) journey was marked by thick cloud.

### No Chance of Survival

The first Halifax flew beneath the cloud-cover. Soon after passing into Norway it slammed into a mountain, killing all aboard. The impact also sent the attached glider crashing down. Both pilots and six soldiers died. Two of the survivors hiked to Helleland and sought help. German monitoring made it impossible to launch a rescue mission without alerting them, and the crash survivors were all soon prisoners.

On the other Halifax, the receiver for the homing signal failed to work. Maps were inaccurate, and clouds and snow prevented visual identification. With fuel running low, the plane turned for home. Approaching the coast, it hit heavy turbulence and the iced-up hawser snapped. The glider crashed, killing eight; its survivors, too, were taken prisoner. In accordance with Adolf Hitler's directive, all were executed—something their families did not learn until after the war. Despite this, the failed operation paved the way for a successful one in February 1943.

## TIMELINE

**03.1940**

With war underway, French intelligence agent Lieutenant Jacques Allier spirits out 364 pounds (165 kg) of heavy water from Vemork before the Germans can acquire it.

**12.1940**

Noting Germany's military success with them, the British Air Ministry orders the construction of prototype Horsa gliders to facilitate an airborne attack on Vemork.

## STEP-BY-STEP

**01** Vemork's surrounds are sparsely populated but Oslo is only 60 miles (96 km) away; the possibility of civilian casualties, if tanks of liquid ammonia initially explode, rules out bombing as an action.

**02** While not "a suicide mission," the risks are enormous: if successful, the Operation Freshman raiders are expected to escape by hiking across snowy mountains to Sweden.

**03** With no survivors, it is impossible to know why one of the Halifax bomber "tugs" crashes into a mountain soon after crossing the Norwegian coastline.

**04** Nine of the men in the glider the Halifax was towing survive and are made German prisoners and interrogated.

**05** As the other plane aborts and turns back with its glider, the ice lumps hitting its fuselage are so thick that the radio operator mistakes them for antiaircraft fire.

**06** The iced hawser snaps, crashing the glider, killing three aboard instantly.

**07** Some of the 23 glider survivors are tortured for information; all are executed. The brutal methods include strangulation and being doped with morphine then weighted with rocks and thrown into the sea.

LEFT: The Halifax bomber towed the gliders across the North Sea.

TOP RIGHT: A Royal Air Force Horsa glider, as used in Operation Freshman.

RIGHT: The target: Vemork chemical plant.

---

**09.1941**
First test flights of Horsa gliders are undertaken.

**03.1942**
An SOE agent is sent into Norway to contact Norwegian resistance groups and plan for an attack on the Vemork plant. Operation Grouse formally proceeds in October 1942.

**10.18.1942**
Hitler orders all captured enemy commandos "to be exterminated to the last man"; they are not to be permitted to surrender or be kept as prisoners of war.

**11.19.1942**
The first use of British Horsa gliders is disastrous, with the loss of 41 men, two gliders, and one Halifax bomber in Norway during a failed attempt to attack the heavy water plant at Vemork.

**02.16.1943**
Operation Gunnerside successfully parachutes six Norwegian Commandos into Telemark and completes the mission.

# THE SABOTAGE OF GORGOPOTAMOS VIADUCT

DATE **November 25–26, 1942**
LOCATION **Gorgopotamos River, Phthiotis, Greece**
OBJECTIVE **To cut the Greek rail supply line to Axis troops in North Africa**

Even before Germany invaded Greece in April 1941, the British were working behind the scenes encouraging Greek resistance. After the Allies were driven out of Greece at the end of the following month, a few Special Operations Executive agents remained, among them Christopher "Monty" Woodhouse, who helped pull off a spectacular attack in the Axis-occupied country.

### Cutting a Vital Link

Under German Erwin "Desert Fox" Rommel, the Axis's Afrika Korps had proved surprisingly effective in North Africa. Cutting off the Korps' supplies became a priority.

There were two supply routes, one through Italy and the other a single rail line through Greece that carried up to 48 supply trains per day. Great Britain's Special Operations Executive (SOE) decided the Greek rail link, which connected Salonica (Thessaloniki) with Athens's port, Piraeus, would have to be broken—with no alternative road network, the impact would be major. The codename was Operation Harling.

### Managing the Mountain Guerrillas

Harling focused on the three viaducts in the Brallos mountain pass: Asopos, Papadia, and Gorgopotamos. Three groups of four—a leader, an interpreter, a sapper, and a radio operator—would parachute in, and operation commander Brigadier Eddie Myers, an engineer, would decide which of the bridges to blow. He settled on Gorgopotamos.

The job of recruiting local partisans, or *andartes*, fell to Myers's second in command, Christopher "Monty" Woodhouse, who had spent significant time in Greece and spoke the language fluently. The agents had been briefed about two resistance groups—although it took weeks to locate them—but were not told they were in fierce opposition (ELAS being communist, EDES right-wing), or that, unlike the British government, both opposed restoring the Greek monarchy. Even so, Woodhouse was able to persuade them to work together: the only time this happened.

### Striking by Night

Bringing the explosives down on mules from the cave where they were hidden, the assault force was in position by 23:00 on November 25. A dozen men were half a mile (800 m) down the track in each direction; 40 more attacked each of the enemy garrisons, at the northern and southern ends of the viaduct. The southern garrison was subdued within 30 minutes, but the Italian soldiers at the other end were still fighting back after an hour. Deciding "we must take a risk," Myers signaled to the demolition party to begin work regardless of the fighting.

Around 01:30 the first explosions brought part of the bridge crashing down. The northern garrison was finally beaten and more explosions brought down a further span. At 02:30, with four *andartes* wounded compared to 30 Italian casualties, the order was given to withdraw. The line was unusable for six weeks and the success of the operation inspired thousands of Greeks to join the resistance.

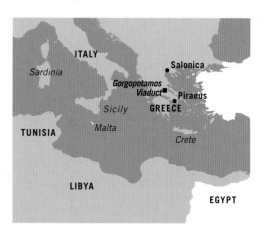

BELOW: Brigadier Eddie Myers.

## TIMELINE

**06.1941**

Hitler launches Operation Barbarossa, his invasion of the USSR, increasingly diverting resources from Africa to the Eastern Front.

**08.13.1942**

Assuming command of the Eighth Army, Great Britain's Field Marshal Bernard Montgomery begins planning the second battle of El Alamein.

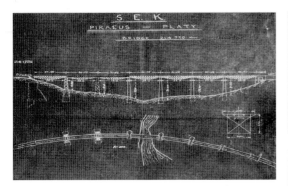

ABOVE: This original blueprint of the viaduct and faded photograph were two of the few items that the agents had with which to plan the raid.

RIGHT: Shortly after the bridge's destruction by Harling Force, this photo was taken by German engineers.

## STEP-BY-STEP

**01** In late August, 1942, SOE are commissioned to disrupt the single Axis-controlled railway supply line running through Greece. The plan is for SOE agents to coordinate a sabotage attack with Greek resistance guerrilla groups.

**02** The 12 SOE specialists assigned to Operation Harling, divided into three groups, comprise one Greek, two New Zealanders, eight Britons, and a 20-year-old half-Scottish, half-Indian sapper Inder Gill, thought to have inspired a character in *The English Patient*.

**03** On September 28, the planned airdrop of the SOE teams into Greece is aborted when

signal fires cannot be spotted. Two days later the airdrop takes place from three planes, but the teams are scattered across the rugged landscape. It takes three weeks for them to regroup, assisted by locals.

**04** Having identified Gorgopotamos viaduct as the best target, the SOE agents set up in a cave above the viaduct, high over a fast-running torrent of snowmelt.

**05** Meanwhile, Major Woodhouse, who learned "to feed on snails, mountain grass, and ground acorns" while working with Greek partisans after the Allied evacuation from Greece, hikes through the mountains

for 17 days, sometimes for 15 hours a day, to find local guerrillas.

**06** Myers develops a detailed plan for the attack. He divides his forces into five groups: two to attack the garrisons at either end of the viaduct, two to provide extra cover up and down the line, and the main sabotage group. Although subduing the Italian guards manning the garrisons takes longer than planned, the operation is a complete success.

**07** Having trekked for a month across to the west coast of Greece, expecting evacuation by submarine, the agents are told they must remain in Greece as the Allied Military Mission.

| 09.30.1942 | 10.11.1942 | 11. 1942 | 11.26.1942 | 12.31.1942 |
|---|---|---|---|---|
| Operation Harling—to destroy Axis supply lines through Greece—is inaugurated as part of a coordinated Allied assault on Axis forces in North Africa. | Victory at El Alamein sees Axis forces in retreat. Increased Allied naval and aerial control of the Mediterranean puts further pressure on Axis supply lines. | Allied forces (Operation Torch) land in French North Africa, opening a second front in the "Desert Campaign." | Working with the partisans, the SOE agents bring down the Gorgopotamos rail viaduct, putting it out of operation for a crucial six weeks. | Now desperately short of supplies and reinforcements, it will be only a matter of weeks before Axis forces in North Africa are neutralized. |

# OPERATION FRANKTON: THE "COCKLESHELL HEROES"

**DATE** December 7–12, 1942
**LOCATION** Gironde estuary and Bordeaux, Gironde, France
**OBJECTIVE** To destroy or damage Germany's blockade-running merchant ships

The British Royal Marines who paddled away from the submarine that delivered them to French waters in the Bay of Biscay on a chilly December night in 1942 knew they had little chance of returning. Their resolute self-sacrifice, in what Lord Louis Mountbatten called this "brilliant little operation," saw them dubbed the "Cockleshell Heroes," a title well earned—if loathed by the man who led them.

## A Difficult Target

While the Royal Navy—under bombardment from the air, mines, and U-boats—attempted to contain them, the Germans regularly broke through the shipping blockade intended to prevent trade with their Axis ally Japan, dispatching radars, fuses, and ball bearings to Asia and receiving in return rubber, opium, tin, and tungsten.

Bordeaux in Occupied France was an important port, with six to ten of Germany's estimated 26 blockade-runners there at any given time. But the Royal Air Force rejected a bombing raid, fearing high civilian casualties, and the Admiralty rejected a conventional seaborne raid because the city was too far up the Gironde, Europe's largest estuary. A new approach was needed.

## Deep Into Enemy Territory

Major Herbert "Blondie" Hasler thought his Royal Marines Boom Patrol Detachment offered the solution. He proposed that a small team paddle 50 miles (80 km) up the Gironde in "Cockle" Mk II collapsible canoes, avoiding detection, to place limpet mines on the docked ships.

Just before 19:20 on December 7, HMS *Tuna* surfaced 9 miles (14.5 km) off the mouth of the Gironde River. Aboard were six canoes (*Catfish*, *Crayfish*, *Conger*, *Cuttlefish*, *Coalfish*, and *Cachalot*), two Marines for each plus a reserve. *Cachalot* was damaged during the launch, but the other five canoes set out up the estuary.

## A High Price Paid

They knew it would be hard fighting the strong tidal current and the twice-daily surge, or race. Trouble struck early, with *Coalfish* capsizing at the estuary mouth. Its crew swam ashore; they would be captured and executed. Next *Conger* capsized, leaving the crew clinging to the upturned hull. *Catfish*, with Hasler, and *Cuttlefish* turned back to rescue them. For an hour, *Conger*'s crew was towed through icy waters by their rescuers as close as they dare get to shore. Attempting to swim the remaining distance, both drowned. Next *Cuttlefish* was swamped. Its crew made it to shore but they too would be captured, interrogated, and executed. At 06:30 the four men in *Catfish* and *Crayfish* dragged their canoes under vegetation on the riverbank, took cover, and rested. They were only halfway to Bordeaux.

After two more exhausting nights they were within reach of the harbor. Finally, on December 11, they set the timed mines on six vessels then escaped downstream, paddling until morning, when they scuttled the boats and set off overland toward neutral Spain. *Crayfish*'s crew were caught and executed. Only *Catfish*'s crew, Hasler and Bill Sparks, helped by the French Resistance, made it home via Spain to learn of their success.

London
Portsmouth
English Channel
Paris
FRANCE
ATLANTIC OCEAN
Bay of Biscay
Bordeaux

ABOVE: The Atlantic Wall, near Bordeaux, France, was designed to keep Allied forces, such as the Cockleshell Heroes, from gaining access to the French mainland.

## TIMELINE

**07.1942**
The Royal Marine Boom Patrol Detachment is formed. Later this would develop into the Commando unit, the Special Boat Squadron (SBS).

**11.03.1942**
Major Hasler's plan for an attack on German blockade-runner merchant shipping at Bordeaux is approved by chief of Combined Operations Admiral Louis Mountbatten and code-named Operation Frankton.

RIGHT: On location for *The Cockleshell Heroes* (1955), Major General Herbert "Blondie" Hasler in conversation with director and star José Ferrer, who plays him. Both Hasler and Sparks served as technical consultants and advisers for the motion picture.

BELOW: The type of canoe used in Operation Frankton; Bill Sparks donated this cockle.

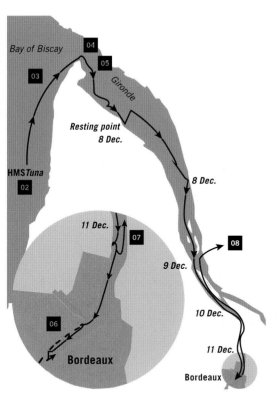

## STEP-BY-STEP

**01** Hasler asks the Marines who respond to his "Volunteers for Hazardous Service" notice: "Do you realise that your expectation of a long life is very remote?" Louis Mountbatten, Chief of Combined Operations, believes Hasler should not go himself; Hasler says it is his duty to the men under his command: "If they go without me and don't return, I shall never be able to face the others again."

**02** On December 7, launching the canoes using one of submarine HMS *Tuna's* guns as an improvised crane, *Cachalot* scrapes against a hatch clamp, receiving an 18-inch (46-cm) tear. Despite its crew's heartfelt pleas, Hasler declares it unseaworthy.

**03** *Coalfish* capsizes. Its crew swims ashore to be arrested, interrogated, and executed.

**04** With the mission barely begun and two boats already lost, *Conger* overturns. *Catfish* and *Cuttlefish* tow its crew toward shore until Hasler says, "I'm sorry, but this is as close to the beach as we dare go. You must swim for it." Corporal George Sheard replies, "It's all right sir, we understand. Thanks for bringing us so far." They drown, probably due to hypothermia.

**05** *Cuttlefish* is swamped by the next tidal race. Its crew is captured and later executed. Meanwhile, *Catfish* and *Crayfish* hide in marshes overnight.

**06** A day later than planned, *Catfish* and *Crayfish* enter the Bordeaux harbor and manage to attach charged limpet mines to six vessels.

**07** After escaping overnight downstream, the crews scuttle their canoes and head overland toward Spain. The crew of *Crayfish* are captured, interrogated, and executed.

**08** After their mission, *Catfish* crew Hasler and Sparks are helped by the French Resistance, reaching home four months later via Spain and Gibraltar.

---

**11.20.1942**
The volunteers selected for the mission complete weeks of intense training on the north Kent coast and in the Solent, Portsmouth.

**11.30.1942**
With six collapsible canoes and their crews aboard, HMS *Tuna* departs Holy Loch, Scotland. Eight days later the Commandos are delivered to the Gironde estuary.

**12.11.1942**
The limpet mines that the two surviving teams have planted on ships in Bordeaux harbor explode, sinking the Dresden, holing the Portland, and damaging Tannenfels and Alabama.

**1943**
British Prime Minister Winston Churchill says that the mission shortened the war by six months. Admiral Louis Mountbatten calls it the Combined Operations' "most courageous and imaginative raid"

**1955**
A fictionalized film version of the operation, *The Cockleshell Heroes*, is released. Throughout his life, Hasler objects to the title phrase.

# OPERATION GUNNERSIDE: THE HEAVY WATER RAID, NORWAY

DATE **February 28, 1943**
LOCATION **Rjukan, Telemark, Norway**
OBJECTIVE **To attempt once again to destroy supplies needed for a Nazi atom bomb**

Three months after its first, disastrous attempt to sabotage production of heavy water in occupied Norway, the British Special Operations Executive (SOE) sent in a second team. This time they were Norwegians. Their endurance and determination were nothing less than astonishing, both during the mission and afterward, as thousands of German soldiers hunted them across the frozen mountains of Scandinavia.

### A Second Attempt

Although Operation Freshman resulted in the loss of British lives, the four-man Norwegian advance team from that operation, code-named Grouse, remained undiscovered. Finally, they received a message from London: combining forces with nearby undercover agent Sergeant Einar Skinnarland and redubbed Team Swallow, they were to assist a second attempt on the plant, Operation Gunnerside.

The leader of the six-man Gunnerside team was its youngest member, experienced skier and outdoorsman Second Lieutenant Joachim Rønneberg, aged 23. After the German invasion of Norway, determined to aid the resistance, he escaped to Great Britain where he received commando training. Called to SOE headquarters after the failure of Operation Freshman, he was told to put together a team to sabotage the Vemork plant, though he was not told why—heavy water that Germany could use in atomic bomb development was produced there.

### Doing the Impossible

The team parachuted in at midnight on February 16. They landed far from their planned drop site on the Hardangervidda plateau; it took a week to meet up with Team Swallow, who confirmed that the Germans had increased security after the Operation Freshman debacle. They made their way over the frozen landscape and, by 20:00 on February 27, were approaching the plant from the other side of a 650-feet (198-m) gorge. The Germans patrolled the 246-feet-long (75-m) suspension bridge that led across to it but did not bother guarding the gorge.

The men voted and, by majority, decided to descend the steep, rugged gorge and ford the icy river. Looking at it years later, Rønneberg said, "You feel it is impossible." Yet they did it, reaching the plant undetected after following the lightly guarded railway line on the other side.

### A Daring Escape

Inside the plant, Rønneberg and a companion started laying the charges. Two others, breaking a window, came to help. They escaped before the charges blew just after midnight: 1,100 pounds (500 kg) of heavy water ran off down the drains and no more could be produced for five months.

While one trained Commando, Knut Haukelid, remained with Team Swallow to encourage local resistance, Rønneberg and the other four escaped on skis, aiming for the Swedish border, 250 miles (400 km) away. Furious German military leaders sent air patrols and up to 3,000 soldiers on the ground to find them. But the Norwegians evaded capture, and two weeks later crossed into neutral Sweden.

TOP: The damaged buildings at the Vemork Hydroelectric Plant.

ABOVE: The Norwegian soldiers and King Haakon VII of Norway at the premiere of the film Kampen om tungtvannet (Operation Swallow: The Battle for Heavy Water) in Oslo, February 5, 1948. Soldiers from left: Knut Haukelid, Joachim Rønneberg, and Jens Anton Poulsson shaking hands with the king and Kasper Idland.

## TIMELINE

**11.19.1942**

Operation Freshman, an Allied glider-borne raid on the Vemork heavy water plant in Telemark, Norway, disastrously fails.

**01.1943**

Piecing together the remains of Operation Freshman, a second raid, using Norwegian personnel and code-named Operation Gunnerside, is planned .

ABOVE: The defenses and frozen terrain surrounding Vemork, with which Team Swallow contended.

## STEP-BY-STEP

**01** Parachuting in, the Norwegian saboteurs wear snowsuits over British uniforms. Over the next two weeks they make contact with the Grouse/Swallow group and approach the Vemork heavy water plant.

**02** On the night of February 27, confronted by a heavily defended suspension bridge, the sabotage team elect to descend and cross an unguarded gorge and freezing river to attack the factory.

**03** At the factory, while the others remain on armed lookout, two pairs of saboteurs, carrying explosives, go in wearing their uniforms—British, to deflect any suspicion from locals.

**04** A contact has been unable to leave a door open as arranged, so Rønneberg and his companion crawl through a cable access tunnel. They subdue a guard and begin to lay charges, as they have practiced.

**05** The other pair, unable to find the tunnel, break a window and join them.

**06** Just before they light the three-minute fuses, the captured guard seeks permission to find his spectacles—the war makes them impossible to replace. They help him do so.

**07** They send the guard, and a sympathetic Norwegian who has stumbled in on the raid, running to safety, and all get out before the explosion. The sound is so dull on a windy night that the Germans do not initially realize what has happened, and all the saboteurs escape. The raid is a success.

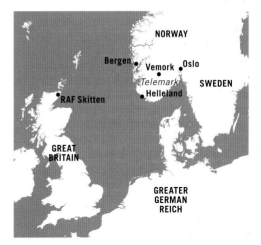

| 01.23.1943 | 02.16.1943 | 11.16.1943 | 12.1943 | 02.20.1944 |
|---|---|---|---|---|
| Unable to locate the drop zone, an RAF plane carrying the Gunnerside saboteurs turns back for England. | This time the six-man team makes the jump, landing 37 miles (60 km) from the Vemork plant. | With heavy water again in production, an American air raid (made without consulting Norwegian resistance) drops more than 700 bombs on Vemork and Rjukan, killing 22 civilians; only 18 bombs hit the plant. | In Germany, now under increasing pressure on the Eastern and the Southern Fronts, the search for war-winning "wonder" weapons becomes a priority—this includes the development of nuclear arms. | Norwegian resistance agents blow up a ferry moving the heavy water equipment and remaining stocks to Germany. Fourteen civilians and four Nazis die in the blast. |

# OPERATION VENGEANCE: THE ASSASSINATION OF YAMAMOTO

DATE        **April 18, 1943**
LOCATION   Airspace above Bougainville Island, Melanesia
OBJECTIVE  The assassination of the Japanese admiral who oversaw the Pearl Harbor attack

**While Japanese Admiral Isoroku Yamamoto did not originate the plans for the surprise attack on US forces at Pearl Harbor, he was their champion and saw the plan become a reality. In 1943, the Americans chanced upon the means to avenge their heavy losses on that "day of infamy."**

### A Message Intercepted

On April 14, 1943, US Naval Intelligence decoded a Japanese message that translated as: "On April 18 CINC Combined Fleet will visit R X Z ..." It was one of thousands the Americans had intercepted, but this one went immediately to Pacific Fleet Commander in Chief Admiral Chester W. Nimitz, Secretary of the Navy Frank Cox, and then on to US President Franklin D. Roosevelt.

The Commander-in-Chief to whom it referred was Admiral Isoroku Yamamoto. To the Americans, Yamamoto was synonymous with the deadly Pearl Harbor attack, and these were details of his movements. With this information the US could attempt to eliminate him. But was that wise?

### "At All Costs Reach and Destroy"

There were two potential drawbacks. First, the Japanese might realize their naval codes had been cracked and change them, putting valuable information out of reach. Second, who would replace Yamamoto: was it a case of "better the devil you know"? To address the latter, Nimitz consulted Chief Intelligence Officer Commander Edwin Layton, who knew Yamamoto prewar when each held diplomatic postings. Layton felt sure no one else in the Japanese navy had Yamamoto's tactical skills. Over all this debate, Roosevelt told Knox to "get Yamamoto."

Nimitz gave the go-ahead for the operation, code-named Vengeance, and Knox sent a top secret message: "SQUADRON 339 P-38 MUST AT ALL COSTS REACH AND DESTROY. PRESIDENT ATTACHES EXTREME IMPORTANCE TO THE MISSION."

### The "Killer Flight"

On April 18, a squadron of 16 Lockheed P-38G Lightnings, fitted with long-range extra fuel "belly tanks" for the 1,000-mile (1,600-km) round trip, left Guadalcanal for Bougainville. To avoid Japanese radar they flew as low as 50 feet (15 m) over the ocean—one pilot counted 47 sharks on the two-hour journey—and took an indirect route designed to deflect code-cracking suspicions.

As they neared the anticipated interception point, the American pilots climbed and began to search the skies. For a moment they were disconcerted by two escorted Mitsubishi "Betty" bombers, rather than one as expected. But as planned, the "killer" flight of four planes, led by Captain Tom Lanphier with First Lieutenant Rex Barber as wingman, attacked the lead "Betty"—Yamamoto's craft—sending it crashing into the dense jungle, while the other flights set upon the remaining planes. The admiral's body was later recovered by the Japanese outside the wrecked plane, but still strapped into its seat. It was a demoralizing loss for his nation.

BELOW: A World War II poster depicting Isoroku Yamamoto.

"I am looking forward to dictating peace to the United States in the White House at Washington"
— *ADMIRAL YAMAMOTO*

What do YOU say, AMERICA?

## TIMELINE

**1919**

Having served in the Russo-Japanese war, young naval officer Isoroku Yamamoto begins a three-year stint at Harvard University.

**1928**

He concludes a three-year posting as a naval attaché to the Japanese diplomatic mission in Washington.

## STEP-BY-STEP

**01** At 07:00, 16 P-38s of the planned 18 take off from Guadalcanal.

**02** They fly low on an indirect route: the cover story will be that Australian coast watchers spotted the Japanese planes and long-range US patrols engaged them.

**03** At 08:00, Admiral Yamamoto and his escort take off from his base at Rabaul, New Britain, on an inspection tour of Japan's Solomon Islands positions.

**04** At 09:34, the US pilots spot the Japanese. They jettison the belly tanks and commence the attack.

**05** Yamamoto's plane is shot down. A postmortem carried out on his recovered body finds machine gun bullets in his jaw and shoulder, indicating he was already dead when it crashed in the dense Bougainville jungle.

**06** A second "Betty" carries Yamamoto's chief of staff Vice Admiral Matome Ugaki; he is one of three survivors when it is shot down into the sea.

**07** One US pilot and his P-38 disappear in unexplained circumstances on the return flight.

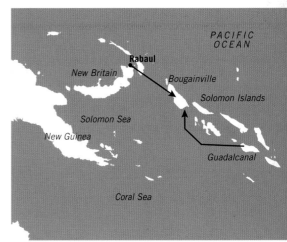

ABOVE: "Miss Virginia" flown by Lt Rex Barber when he shot down Admiral Yamamoto's Betty bomber. Crashed with battle damage on Guadalcanal.

LEFT: A Lockheed P-38 Lightning aircraft as used on the mission.

| 12.07.1941 | 06.07.1942 | 04.18.1942 | 04.18.1943 | 04.19.1943 |
|---|---|---|---|---|
| Despite his personal reservations, once it is clear war with the United States is inevitable, Yamamoto aims for victory, overseeing the Pearl Harbor attack. | US and Japanese fleets, led by Admirals Nimitz and Yamamoto, end the four-day Battle of Midway. It ends in a decisive American victory. | The "Doolittle Raid" becomes the first US aerial attack on Japan, including Tokyo. | In Operation Vengeance, the USAF assassinates Yamamoto. This is assessed by the US as the morale-boosting equivalent of a major naval victory. | Yamamoto is replaced as commander of the Combined Japanese Imperial Fleet by Mineichi Koga. |

# OPERATION CHASTISE: THE "DAM BUSTERS" RAID

DATE    May 16–17, 1943
LOCATION    Ruhr Valley, Germany
OBJECTIVE    To destroy three dams considered key to Germany's war efforts

Military historians still debate the strategic success or otherwise of the "Dam Busters Raid" on Germany, but the incredible skill, courage, and daring of the flight crews who delivered a strange new weapon into the very heart of enemy territory has ensured the raid is one of World War II's most famous operations.

### The Upkeep Breakthrough

The Ruhr Valley's coal mines and steel mills powered German industry, and the water in its dams (protected by anti-torpedo netting) was essential for common use and hydroelectric power. But dam walls are low, often narrow targets; conventional air raids would not work.

The answer was a "bouncing bomb," developed by the inventor Barnes Wallis and code-named Upkeep: a 4.6-ton (4.2-tonne) depth charge triggered to explode 30 feet (9 m) below the surface. Its cylindrical design meant that, given backspin, it would skip across the water's surface to a dam wall and remain in contact as it spun down to the trigger point, ensuring maximum damage.

### Breathtaking Flying Skills

Upkeep could not be just dropped—it required pinpoint precision. What was asked of the crews of the modified Lancaster bombers was hair-raising. Rather than their usual 15,000 feet-plus (4,500 m) bombing height, the huge planes, with 102-foot (31-m) wingspans, had to dodge obstacles in the dark, dropping to just 60 feet (18 m) above the water at 220 mph (354 kph), release their bombs, then pull up sharply. And all this while their bright navigation lights drew enemy fire.

Three dams were targeted for Upkeep's first outing, Operation Chastise: the Möhne, Eder, and Sorpe. Some among the crews were highly experienced, including Wing Commander Guy Gibson, aged only 24; for many others, the raid was their first operational mission.

### Heroism and High Casualties

The 19 Lancasters set out in three waves, flying low all the way. One, brushing the sea, lost its underhanging bomb and flooded, just making it back to base. Two others turned back: one being hit by enemy fire; the other malfunctioning. Five were lost with only one survivor among them: two crashing after hitting power cables; three shot down.

It took five drops to destroy the Möhne dam wall, with another plane and all but two crew lost in the attempt. Two bombs were dropped on Eder, which also collapsed.

Despite two bombs dropped, Sorpe withstood the attack. Two more planes were shot down on the return journey, with no survivors.

In all, 53 of the 133 airmen died and three became prisoners. On the ground, almost 1,294 people drowned when the dams broke, of whom 749 were Ukrainian prisoners of war and hundreds more forced laborers. Within six weeks the dams were repaired, leading some to see the raid as a failure. But factories, mines, and infrastructure had been destroyed and—significantly for 1944's D-Day—up to 10,000 workers had been diverted from coastal defenses.

## TIMELINE

**03.21.1943**
617 Squadron, as it becomes known, is formed. These airmen will be "The Dam Busters."

**04.13.1943**
The first trial drops of inert Upkeep bombs begin off the north Kent coast. Further training runs occur on reservoirs and lakes in Derbyshire and Cumberland.

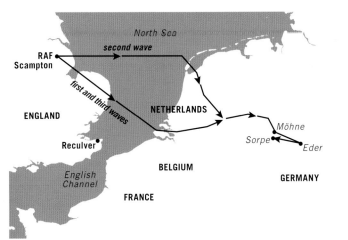

LEFT: No. 617 Squadron practice dropping the "Upkeep" bouncing bomb at Reculver bombing range, Kent.

BELOW: Image of the damaged Möhne Dam following the raid.

## STEP-BY-STEP

**01** Building on existing research, Barnes Wallis from Vickers-Armstrongs develops the bouncing "Upkeep" bomb, despite strong skepticism about this unusual weapon.

**02** A motor spinning it backward at high speed before deployment ensures that when it hits a dam wall, the bomb does not just skip over it.

**03** Using colored goggles to mimic moonlight while it is daytime, 617 Squadron begins a short but intense training period developing the precision bombing that "Upkeep" demands.

**04** Setting out on the mission, they fly under the radar as much as possible, battling stronger than expected winds and, at the Sorpe and Eder dams, mist.

**05** Of the 19 aircraft that set out, ten drop bombs on the three target dams: the Möhne and Eder dams are severely ruptured but Sorpe survives. Another bombs the Bever dam without result.

**06** About 369.6 million tons (335.3 million tonnes) of water pours into the western Ruhr Valley. It kills 1,294 people, destroys 11 factories and badly damages 114, and wipes out 25 rail and road bridges.

ABOVE: The crew boarding their Avro Lancaster A3-G before the raid. Pictured (left to right): Flight Lieutenant R.D. Trevor-Roper DEM; Sergeant J. Pulford; Flight Sergeant G.A. Deering RCAF; Pilot Officer F.M. Spafford DFM RAAF; Flight Lieutenant R.E.G. Hutchinson DFC; Wing Commander Guy Gibson; and Pilot Officer H.T. Taerum RCAF.

---

**05.13.1943**
The last of the specially modified Lancasters, with bomb-bay doors and a gun turret removed to allow for the underhanging bomb and the motor to spin it at 500 rpm when released, is delivered.

**05.16.1943**
With 19 aircraft in three waves, 617 Squadron sets out from Scampton air base, Lincoln. Eight will not return.

**09.19.1944**
Already a decorated hero when awarded a Victoria Cross for his role in Operation Chastise, Guy Gibson, 26, is fatally shot down over the Netherlands.

**08.12.1945**
A protocol added to the Geneva Convention prohibits attacks on dams that may cause "severe" civilian losses.

**1954**
The patriotic and celebratory British film *The Dam Busters* is released. Composer Eric Coates's stirring "Dam Busters March" becomes a staple of British martial and commemorative events.

# OPERATION TIDAL WAVE: BOMBING THE PLOESTI OIL FIELDS

DATE        August 1, 1943
LOCATION    Ploesti (or Ploiesti), Prahova, Romania
OBJECTIVE   To cripple the Axis by attacking a major source of oil

**In 1919, prescient French diplomat Henry Bérenger wrote, "He who owns the oil will own the world." By 1943, with German resources being stretched ever thinner across Europe and North Africa, the Allies knew that a successful attack on Romania's oil fields at Ploesti would be a devastating blow for Hitler.**

### Oil: the Lifeblood of War

The more territory Germany occupied, the wider the gap between its oil supply and demand. With up to half its reserves gone in the failed Russian campaign, lack of fuel was becoming a serious problem. The heavily defended oil fields just outside the Romanian city of Ploesti contributed a third of Germany's total usage.

Operation Tidal Wave identified seven targets in the Ploesti oil fields, to be hit by five groups of United States Air Forces (USAAF) B-24 Liberator bombers. In order to avoid civilian casualties in the city itself, the bombs would be dropped from treetop height.

### "If Nobody Comes Back …"

Romania was too far from England; the planes would depart from Libya. By July, all five bomber groups were in Benghazi. With crews quarantined to maintain secrecy, they began low-flying training, dropping wooden "bombs" on an almost full-scale outline of their (unnamed) targets marked in lime on the desert sand, with telegraph poles substituting for smokestacks.

USAAF mission commander Brigadier General Uzal Ent, estimating 50 percent casualties, requested to be allowed to bomb from above cloud level, but was denied. Even so Ent, who would be on the mission, wrote privately, "If nobody comes back, the results will be worth the cost."

### A Heavy Toll

At 05:00 on August 1, 178 B-24s set out across the Mediterranean, dividing into two formations. By the time they reached Romanian airspace, the leaders were 60 miles (96 km) ahead of the last group: maintaining strict radio silence had prevented them reassembling. The planned single, mass attack could not happen. The lead group, flying low, mistook one road/railroad/river confluence for another that should have led to its target. By the time it swung back, it and the other groups were under attack from both ground and air.

Approaching the refineries, "haystacks" were suddenly revealed as antiaircraft-gun camouflage. Over their targets the American fliers battled the enemy fighters that filled the air, while dodging smokestacks, barrage balloons lowered to trap them, and exploding oil tanks. Despite the chaos, they caused enough damage to knock out 46 percent of Ploesti's output—but only temporarily, the Germans restoring most of it within months.

Only 88 planes made it home, 310 men were killed, 108 taken prisoner in Romania, and 78 interned in Turkey. Never again would the US make a low-level attack against German defenses.

## TIMELINE

**11.23.1940**

Romania abandons its attempt to stay neutral in the War and joins the Axis powers.

**06.12.1942**

Twelve US bombers mount an ambitious attack on the Ploesti oil fields, causing minimal damage. This alerts the Germans to redouble their defenses.

ABOVE: 15th Air Force B-24s leave Ploesti in a state of considerable devastation, amid heavy enemy flak.

LEFT: Columbia Aquila refinery, with bomb craters, after the bombing.

## STEP-BY-STEP

**01** As 178 B-24s take off from airfields around the Benghazi base in Libya, one turns back for an emergency landing but crashes, with only two survivors.

**02** Unknown to the Americans, who are relying on a surprise attack, the Germans track their entire journey.

**03** Over the Mediterranean, a B-24 crashes with no survivors; another, which dives down to check on it, cannot regain altitude and must turn back.

**04** Another 12 planes turn back with mechanical failure.

**05** With the groups now strung out far apart, the lead group of 25 planes mistakenly begins to head toward Bucharest.

**06** In desperation, other pilots and even Ent himself break radio silence to call out "Not here! Not here!" and "Mistake! Mistake!"

**07** Flying at almost 250 mph (400 kph) in close formation, they must turn back toward the target, where the remaining planes are under attack.

**08** Of the 163 bombers that reached their targets, only 88 return to Benghazi, 55 suffering battle damage; of 1,726 men, almost one in five died and 440 more were wounded.

---

**01.12.1943**
At the Allied leaders' Casablanca Conference, the idea of attacking Ploesti once more is discussed. It is estimated that, if successful, the raid could shorten the war by six months.

**07.1943**
Top-secret training begins in Libya for a major USAAF raid on Romania's oil fields.

**08.01.1943**
The USAAF's unusually low-level bombing of Ploesti is fairly successful but very costly.

**10.1944**
Romania is invaded by Soviet troops.

**05.12.1944**
A force of 935 Allied bombers devastate Germany's synthetic fuel factories at Leuna in central Germany. Nazi strategist Albert Speer wrote, "On that day the technological war was decided."

# THE RESCUE OF MUSSOLINI

DATE      September 12, 1943

LOCATION    Gran Sasso, Abruzzo, Italy

OBJECTIVE   To rescue the deposed, captive, former head of state

By 1943, the fascist alliance between Italy's Benito Mussolini and Germany's Adolf Hitler had become increasingly uneasy. Hitler undertook major operations, including the invasion of the USSR, without prior warning, let alone consultation. But an ally was an ally, and when Mussolini was deposed and imprisoned, Hitler mounted a rescue mission.

### A Dictator Fallen from Favor

The Allied invasion of Sicily made it clear even to onetime supporters that Italian dictator Benito Mussolini's reign was doomed. After the Fascist Grand Council dismissed him, he was arrested on the order of King Victor Emmanuel III.

He was held on the island of Ponza and then at the La Maddelena naval base off Sardinia, before the new government, apprehensive about a possible German rescue attempt, moved him to Hotel Campo Imperatore atop the 6,970-foot (2,125-m) Gran Sasso, the highest mountain in Abruzzo in central Italy.

### Germany to the Rescue

The concern was warranted: Hitler had given Luftwaffe General Kurt Student the job of rescuing Mussolini—Operation Eiche (Oak). To assist, Student and Hitler chose Austrian Waffen-SS captain Otto Skorzeny: a choice Student had cause to regret.

With a funicular railway the only access to the peak, the attack had to be airborne. Altitude and terrain made parachutes unviable; gliders would be used. On September 12, as Major Harald Mors and his men secured the funicular base, nine DFS-230 gliders approached the mountain. Reconnaissance photographs proved misleading: the planned landing site behind the hotel turned out to be a steep slope. Instead, they aimed for the boulder-strewn, but flatter, area in front. One glider slammed into the ground, causing some injuries, but the others survived the rough landing.

### A Dangerous Load

Skorzeny had brought Italian General Fernando Soleti with him, and as the armed Germans took up position on the ground, Soleti approached the hotel calling out "Don't shoot!", Skorzeny walking behind him holding a machine gun. The 46 Italian guards followed this instruction and Skorzeny entered unhindered. He clubbed a radio operator starting to transmit news of the raid, then found Mussolini upstairs, and said, "Duce, the Führer sent me to free you."

The plan was for Mussolini to be removed in a single-engine Fieseler Storch plane waiting outside. It was designed to carry just one passenger, but Skorzeny insisted on squeezing in, despite the protestations of pilot Heinrich Gerlach. The plane stuttered over the lip of the plateau and dropped, Gerlach finally wresting it up just 100 feet (30.5 m) off the ground. Back in Germany, with SS chief Heinrich Himmler's assistance, Skorzeny ensured he got the lion's share of credit for the mission, much to the chagrin of Student and Luftwaffe chief Hermann Göring.

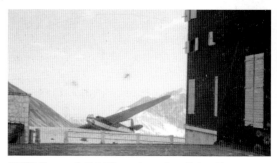

ABOVE: The remote Hotel Campo Imperatore, high on the Gran Sasso.

ABOVE: The DFS-230 gliders were able to land almost on top of their target.

## TIMELINE

**07.09.1943**

The Allies begin a successful invasion of Sicily.

**07.24.1943**

Italy's Fascist Grand Council overwhelmingly votes to dismiss Mussolini.

ABOVE: Mussolini exiting the hotel accompanied by German paratroop commanders.

ABOVE RIGHT: Much against the pilot's will, both Mussolini and Skorzeny board the light Fleseler Storch aircraft that will take them to Practica di Mare airport. There they immediately transfer to a heavier Heinkel and are then flown to Vienna.

## STEP-BY-STEP

**01** New Italian leader Marshal Pietro Baldoglio orders Mussolini to be shot in the event of an attempted escape.

**02** The Nazis charged with rescuing Mussolini learn his location by intercepting a coded message sent by his captors.

**03** The Luftwaffe undertakes reconnaissance over Gran Sasso.

**04** Mission planners believe a parachute drop will fail, so a glider raid is planned.

**05** With planes overhead and reports of German officers nearby, Giuseppe Gueli, overseeing Mussolini's imprisonment, seeks advice from Italian Police Chief Carmine Senise, who advises "prudence," if such a rescue is attempted.

**06** Skorzeny's gliders land outside the hotel on September 12. Italian General Soleti orders the Italian guards not to resist, Gueli agrees. Mussolini is spirited away to Pratica di Mare airport near Rome, then transferred to a Heinkel that delivers him and Skorzeny to Vienna.

**07** Nazi propaganda photographer Toni Schneiders chronicles the raid.

**08** In Germany, those who knew Mussolini are struck by how unwell he seems. SS Colonel Eugen Dollmann says: "I believe Mussolini would have preferred to remain on the Gran Sasso to admire the flight of eagles."

| 07.25.1943 | 09.08.1943 | 09.12.1943 | 09.23.1943 | 04.28.1945 |
|---|---|---|---|---|
| Refusing to accept the decision, Mussolini is arrested and Marshal Pietro Badoglio installed as the new leader. | Badoglio signs an Armistice agreement with the Allies. | Mussolini, ill and dispirited, is freed by German troops and taken to Germany. | He is installed as head of the Nazi puppet state Repubblica Sociale Italiana (Italian Social Republic) at Salò on Lake Garda in Italy. | Attempting to cross into Switzerland disguised as a German soldier, Mussolini is recognized and shot, along with his mistress, Clara Petacci. |

# OPERATION SOURCE: THE MIDGET SUBMARINE ATTACK ON *TIRPITZ*

DATE        September 22, 1943
LOCATION    The Kåfjord (or Kaa Fjord) branch of Altafjord, Tromsø, Norway
OBJECTIVE   To sink or damage the *Tirpitz*, *Scharnhorst*, and *Lützow*.

Although Operation Chariot, 18 months earlier, had kept the huge German battleship *Tirpitz* out of the Atlantic, the threat it posed—especially to Allied convoys bound for the USSR—remained a grave concern for the British. But how was anyone to attack it in its heavily guarded Norwegian base? The new X-Craft provided a possible answer.

### The X-Craft Debut
Among the attack fleet in the huge naval base Germany had created in Norway's Altafjord, beyond the range of British bombers, was the super battleship *Tirpitz*. With battleship *Scharnhorst* and cruiser *Lützow*, it was the target of Great Britain's Operation Source, using the Royal Navy's new X-Craft midget submarines.

These tiny vessels—under 52 feet (15.8 m) long—carried a crew of four and were armed with two external "side cargoes," 1.7 ton (1.5 tonne) explosive charges. The X-Craft had to be maneuvered beneath the target, then the timed charges released.

### Early Troubles
On September 11, 1943, six regular submarines set off for Norway from Scotland, each towing an X-Craft: X-5, X-6, and X-7, which were to attack *Tirpitz*; X-8, which was assigned to *Lützow*; and X-9 and X-10, which were to target to *Scharnhorst*. First X-8's tow broke, then X-7's. Both were reattached, but when X-9's tow parted it was lost with all hands. X-8 experienced further problems when its cargo hatches flooded. The crew evacuated and the craft was scuttled. Finally, the four remaining X-Craft headed to the fjord entrance. But X-10 was plagued with equipment failure, and, despite lengthy repair attempts, had to abort.

### Persistent Daring
Each midget submarine carried a diver trained to cut through underwater barriers but, by closely following returning enemy boats for whom the booms had been opened, X-6 daringly slipped through both the antisubmarine netting and the inner anti-torpedo netting. Then it struck a rock and the periscope caught fire, rendering it "blind." With secrecy no longer possible, X-6 charged the *Tirpitz*, whose crew threw hand grenades and dropped depth charges as the British released one timed charge under the ship, collided with its hull, then released the second. The submarine surfaced and was scuttled, and its crew taken prisoner aboard *Tirpitz*.

X-7 became entangled in torpedo netting entering the harbor but managed to free itself and deploy its charges before becoming entangled again trying to exit. Although it struggled through just before the explosion, it was too badly damaged to escape. Surfacing, it came under fire and only two of the crew, including Lieutenant (Basil) Godfrey Place, got out before it sank. X-5 was lost with all hands after surfacing and being fired on. Nevertheless, the mission was deemed a success, with *Tirpitz* damaged badly enough to keep it out of the war for six months.

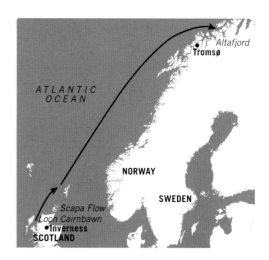

ABOVE: Sub Lieutenant K.C.J. Robinson pictured at the controls of an X-Craft midget submarine in Rothesbay Bay (1944).

RIGHT: An aerial reconnaissance photo of Altafjord, which shows *Tirpitz* at her anchorage where the ship was attacked and damaged by the midget submarines.

FAR RIGHT: The crew of the X-6, which was headed by Lieutenant Donald Cameron RNR.

## TIMELINE

**02.11.1943**
A planned spring attack on *Tirpitz* using the new X-Craft midget submarines is postponed due to equipment failures and lack of training.

**09.11.1943**
Submarines *Thrasher*, *Truculent*, *Stubborn*, *Syrtis*, *Sceptre*, and *Seanymph*, each towing an X-Craft, set out from Loch Cairnbawn, Scotland.

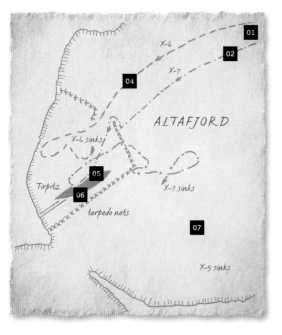

## STEP-BY-STEP

**01** The X-Craft have an operational range over 1,200 miles (1,930 km), but are so cramped that they are towed with passage crews, switching to operational crews near the target.

**02** The rope on a floating mine wraps around the bow of X-7, still under tow. Its commander, Godfrey Place, emerges and frees it with his foot.

**03** Four of the six midget submarines remain, but X-10's numerous technical problems prevent it attacking. As it happens, its target *Scharnhorst* is absent on maneuvers.

**04** Sublieutenant John Lorimer, aboard X-6, sees *Tirpitz*: "My first thought was that she was so pretty, it seemed an awful shame to have to blow her up."

Having set their charges they are forced to surface.

**05** With their timed charges below the ship in which they are now prisoner, the X-6 crew tell the Germans to abort a diving investigation or "in an hour they'll be mashed potato," recalled Lorimer.

**06** The explosions lift *Tirpitz* out of the water, badly damaging its hull, a gun turret, stabilizers, and other equipment.

**07** None of the X-Craft return from Altafjord, and only six of the successful attack crews survived the war as POWs. It was long thought X-5 sank without placing its charges, but recent evidence indicates it may have indeed placed one that remained unexploded until discovered and detonated by the Royal Norwegian Navy in 2011.

---

**09.16.1943**
With towline problems already having affected X-8 and X-7, X-9's tow breaks and it disappears.

**09.22.1943**
Three X-Craft midget submarines enter the harbor at Altafjord and succeed in severely damaging the *Tirpitz*, putting her out of action until April 1944.

**09.15.1944**
Almost a year after Operation Source, an RAF air raid badly damages the repaired *Tirpitz*.

**11.12.1944**
Another air raid finally sinks the *Tirpitz*, killing up to 1,000 crew.

**06.22.1945**
Returned POWs Place and X-6 commander Donald Cameron receive Victoria Crosses from King George VI.

# OPERATIONS JAYWICK AND RIMAU: SABOTAGE RAIDS IN SINGAPORE

DATE        September 26, 1943, and October 1944
LOCATION    Singapore harbor and vicinities
OBJECTIVE   To destroy as much Japanese shipping as possible

Eighteen months after the fall of Singapore to the Japanese in February 1942, Major Ivan Lyon—one of those who had managed to get out—was headed back there, in disguise on a captured Japanese fishing boat with 13 other Commandos. All were aboard for Operation Jaywick, one of Australia's most successful secret raids … albeit one with a tragic sequel.

### Deep Inside Enemy Territory

Seized by British authorities the previous year, the 76-ton (69-tonne) Singapore-based Japanese fishing vessel *Kofuku Maru* was used to rescue 1,100 people before the Japanese occupation. Renamed the *Krait*, it was then put to work by Z Special Unit, Australia's equivalent of Great Britain's Special Operations Executive (SOE). Carrying four British soldiers and ten Australian sailors and soldiers, it departed Western Australia for a raid deep inside enemy territory.

It carried four months' worth of food and water, 50,000 cigarettes for bribes or barter, weapons, and, crucially, four collapsible two-man kayaks—folboats. *Krait* would make for Indonesia's Lingga Archipelago, just south of Singapore. Six men and three folboats would go ashore. They would have to reach Singapore harbor, sneak in, attach time-delayed limpet mines to Japanese ships, escape, and return to the rendezvous point.

### A Complete Success

To deflect suspicion on the heavily patrolled route, the men dyed their hair and skin dark and wore sarongs, posing as local fishermen; they used Japanese-made equipment including sunglasses, and flew a Japanese flag; they dropped nothing, not even matches, overboard; and only one or two were visible on deck at any time.

After a tense, slow journey, the Commandos disembarked on September 18. *Krait* had a suspenseful 12-day wait dodging patrols off Borneo. Meanwhile, the folboat Commandos island-hopped by night and hid by day, reaching their goal on September 26 and successfully planting mines that badly damaged or sank seven vessels, including the tanker *Sinkoku Maru*. They evaded capture, made the rendezvous and, despite some nerve-racking moments, reached Exmouth Gulf in Western Australia unharmed on October 19.

### The Tragic Sequel

Lyon, now a lieutenant colonel, then planned Operation Rimau, in which 23 men (six of them from Jaywick) would again raid Singapore harbor. The first part went as planned: the submarine HMS *Porpoise* transported them to the Rhio Archipelago, where they seized a local junk, *Mustika*, from which they intended to launch 15 one-man Motorised Submersible Canoes (nicknamed "Sleeping Beauties") for the raid, before rendezvousing with the submarine *Tantalus*. The rendezvous never happened, although three Japanese ships were sunk.

After the war it was learned that a police patrol stopped *Mustika* near the harbor. One of the Rimau team opened fire; the operation was blown. They tried to escape but 12 men, including Lyon, were killed, and the rest were captured. One died of malaria, the others were executed just a month before the war ended.

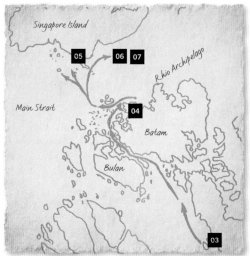

## TIMELINE

**02.15.1942**

The fall of the British colony of Singapore to the Japanese sees hundreds of civilians and 130,000 Allied personnel taken prisoner, among them 15,000 Australians.

**08.13.1944**

Operation Jaywick departs Western Australia to raid Japanese shipping at Singapore.

ABOVE: Onboard *Krait* en route to Singapore (left to right): front row—A.B. Huston, A.B. Marsh, CPL. A.A. Crilly; back row, unidentified, Leading Seaman Cain, Major Lyon, Lt. Carse, Leading Stoker McDowell.

RIGHT: A depiction of Operation Jaywick. Lieutenant Robert "Bob" Page and Able Seaman Arthur "Jo" Jones are shown placing limpet mines on a ship's hull.

BELOW RIGHT: Once a fishing vessel, along with being renamed *Krait*, this watercraft was also ingeniously refitted for its mission.

## STEP-BY-STEP

**01** Carrying the Operation Jaywick task force, *Krait* departs Exmouth Gulf, Western Australia, but has to turn back when a propeller shaft breaks.

**02** The repaired vessel gets under way, but suffers mechanical problems throughout the 4,000-mile (6,430-km), 48-day return journey. Its top speed is 6½ knots.

**03** Disguised as a local fishing boat, *Krait* reaches Panjang Island, where the Commandos and their heavily laden folboats are put ashore.

**04** By September 22 they are within 8 miles (12.8 km) of Singapore harbor.

**05** Driven back by strong currents on their first attempt, they successfully enter the harbor on September 27 and plant the time-delayed mines.

**06** Evading the aerial and maritime forces searching for the saboteurs, the folboats separately reach the rendezvous point, but only one can find *Krait* in the dark.

**07** Although they have resigned themselves to being left in enemy territory, the remaining two crews are picked up when *Krait* returns the following night.

---

**09.26-27.1943**
Mines planted by Operation Jaywick Commandos damage 43,600 tons (39,600 tonnes) of Japanese shipping, boosting the morale of prisoners in Singapore.

**10.10.1944**
Convinced the attack was by local resistance guerrillas, the Japanese launch a wave of arrests, torture, and reprisals against local Chinese, Malays, and POWs.

**09.11.1944**
The Operation Rimau task force departs Western Australia in submarine HMS *Porpoise*.

**09.30.1944**
Having unloaded supplies onto the island of Merapas and the captured *Mustika*, HMS *Porpoise* departs; the pickup rendezvous is set for anytime in the month after November 8.

**11.21.1943**
HMS *Tantalus* arrives at Merapas. There is no sign of the Rimau men. Their fate will only be learned after the war.

# THE "WOODEN HORSE" POW ESCAPE

DATE      **October 29, 1943**

LOCATION   **Sagan (now Zagan), Silesia, Germany (now Poland)**

OBJECTIVE **To break out of a German POW camp and make the "home run" to Great Britain**

**Stalag Luft III was designed to be escape-proof, to thwart the dreams of freedom of its Allied prisoners of war. By early 1943 there had been up to 30 attempts to tunnel out and each one had been foiled. But then one of the men remembered the story of the Trojan horse ...**

### Inspiration Born of Frustration

In mid-1943, Lieutenant Michael Codner and Flight Lieutenant Eric Williams were discussing the multiple failed attempts to tunnel out of the Stalag Luft III camp by Allied air force officers shot down over enemy territory (Codner, an artillery officer, was sent there in error).

The problem was the only readily available cover for digging: barracks 300 feet (90 m) from the perimeter. Sandy soil made such a long tunnel a structural challenge, and the sustained effort required was hard to achieve on limited food rations. Then Codner remembered the siege of Troy and its wooden horse, and adapted that thought to feature a vaulting horse. A radical idea was born.

### Incredible Effort Above and Below

The prisoners' well-organized Escape Committee, which vetted plans and resourced those judged viable, was skeptical, but Codner and Williams secured agreement for the first stage: to build a vaulting horse (ostensibly to keep the POWs fit and occupied), which could conceal tunnel diggers and allow them to remove the soil from the tunnel. Full approval followed and on July 8 a new daily routine began.

The vaulting horse, carried by four men with another hidden inside braced on crossbars, was placed in position 100 feet (30 m) from the perimeter. As other prisoners vaulted overhead for hours, defeating the German seismographs installed to detect digging sounds, Codner and Williams took daily turns to tunnel below, naked and filthy in the stifling, tiny space. Earth removed using bowls or cans went into sacks sewn from cut-off trousers, secured on hooks under the "horse"—12 filled a day. This incriminating evidence was later dispersed beneath the huts. Each time a digger backed out of the tunnel he inserted a trapdoor, replaced the original dirt, then climbed back up inside the "horse."

### Three to Freedom

Meanwhile the supplies they would need to escape Germany were being painstakingly readied: fake identity documents whose "ink" was condensed cooking fat; civilian clothes; an improvised compass. With frustration building among the vaulters (unlike the diggers, their rations were not bolstered), Codner and Williams began working together to quicken the pace and Canadian-born Flight Lieutenant Oliver Philpot joined the digging roster.

On October 29, the three made their escape. Despite numerous close calls, Philpot, posing as a Norwegian quisling, reached safety in Sweden, as did Williams and Codner, traveling together disguised as Frenchmen. The news of their success provided a huge morale boost for the prisoners who remained.

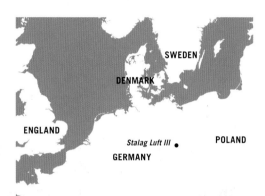

ABOVE: The POWs named their tunnel of escape "Harry," names on the stone slab marking the length of the tunnel commemorate those killed during the escape from Stalag Luft III.

ABOVE RIGHT: The POW camp Stalag Luft III.

## TIMELINE

**04.1942**

The first British prisoners of war arrive at the unfinished Stalag Luft III. Eventually it will hold around 10,500 Allied officers.

**07.08.1943**

Digging the escape tunnel beneath the wooden vaulting horse begins.

## STEP-BY-STEP

**01** Michael Codner and Eric Williams propose a tunnel disguised by a vaulting horse to the Escape Committee of Stalag Luft III's East Compound.

**02** The horse is built, using Red Cross packing cases and wood secreted earlier by prisoners.

**03** Four men carry it and its hidden human cargo to the designated spot each day, using poles slotted through the sides.

**04** Early on, the prisoners "accidentally" tip the empty horse over in sight of the guards, circumventing future suspicion.

**05** With the tunnel barely two feet (0.6 m) wide, and surface airholes too risky, conditions are dreadful.

**06** On the moonless night of October 29, 114 days after starting, the tunnel is almost done.

**07** At 13:00 Codner, Williams, and the supplies needed for the escape are carried out.

Williams seals Codner into the tunnel to finish excavating the final few inches.

**08** The horse is carried away, then back again at 16:15 when another officer seals Williams and Philpot in.

**09** At 18:00 the three emerge, slightly short of their goal but outside the fence, but they nevertheless manage to get away and eventually make it to neutral Sweden.

---

**10.29.1943**
Michael Codner, Eric Williams, and Oliver Philpot escape from the camp.

**03.24.1944**
Seventy-six POWs from the camp's North Compound make "the Great Escape." Just three evade recapture. Contravening the Geneva Convention, 50 are executed.

**1945**
After serving in the Philippines for the rest of the war, Williams writes his first book, the short fictionalized POW story *Goon in the Block*.

**1950**
Williams reworks and expands *Goon in the Block* as *The Wooden Horse* and Philpot publishes his account, *Stolen Journey*.

**03.25.1952**
Codner is ambushed and killed in the Malayan Emergency.

# CLANDESTINE INFORMATION-GATHERING FOR D-DAY

DATE            December 31, 1943–January 1944
LOCATION     The coastline of Normandy, France
OBJECTIVE   Within enemy sight, to gather information for an invasion

**So successful were they in evading detection while carrying out dangerous missions under the enemy's nose, the Commandos of the Combined Operations Pilotage Parties (COPP) received almost no recognition for decades. Yet their work gathering vital data on the beaches of France saved countless lives in the D-Day Normandy landings.**

### Building Invasion Maps

From late 1942, following the raid on Dieppe, the Allies put enormous effort into creating detailed maps and charts of the coastline of northern France. Part of this involved examining thousands of postcards, holiday snapshots, and interviews with prewar tourists familiar with the area. But without reliable, specific information on everything from tidal movements, navigation hazards, and the gradients of beaches to the position of enemy defenses and adjacent roadways, an invasion of the size needed to reclaim Europe from the Germans was unthinkable.

Aerial patrols, undercover agents, and local resistance members all provided crucial details about the occupied land, but the job of providing minute detail on the heavily guarded beaches that might become landing sites went to the navy and army specialists of the COPP—or "Coppists," as they became known.

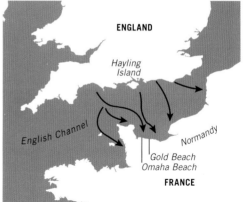

### Nerves of Steel and an Eye for Detail

Two-man Coppist crews had gathered such information in the lead-up to the Allied invasions of Sicily and mainland Italy in the summer and autumn of 1943. However, there they were able to use submarines to get close to shore, paddling the rest of the way in collapsible kayaks, known as folboats. The large submarines could often not get close enough at Normandy, in which case midget submarines or a combination of motor gunboats and smaller shore craft were used to get them to within 600–1,300 feet (180–400 m) of their target beach. From here they swam, wearing bulky rubber suits and carrying all their equipment.

### An Encore Performance

They required nerves of steel and an eye for detail, as exemplified in the mission conducted by Major General Logan Scott-Bowden and Sergeant Bruce Ogden-Smith on New Year's Eve, 1943.

Fighting a heavy current on the wintry, moonless night, Scott-Bowden and Ogden-Smith reached what would become known as Gold Beach, near Ver-sur-Mer, noting measurements using the chinagraph pencil and special white slate they carried. They also took sand and shingle samples for later analysis.

When American planners learned of the pair's success, they asked them to return and survey what would become Omaha Beach and the coast around it. This successful mission took three nights—requiring the pair and their crew to spend four days hiding in an X-Craft midget submarine on the seabed.

## TIMELINE

### 03.1941

Naval officer Lieutenant Commander Nigel Willmott undertakes covert reconnaissance for a planned (later cancelled) invasion of Rhodes, Greece. From this comes the idea for the COPP.

### 08.19.1942

Operation Jubilee, the Allied raid on Dieppe, reveals much about German coastal defenses in Occupied France and also the need for much more detailed intelligence.

ABOVE: Maneuvers of the 29th US Ranger Battalion preparing for Operation Overlord (clockwise from top left): landing exercise on the English coast; a reconnaissance patrol overcoming a barbed wire obstacle; rehearsing an attack on an enemy position.

## STEP-BY-STEP

**01** In order to gather the vital information needed to create highly detailed maps for Operation Overlord (D-Day), COPP crews are assigned to survey the beaches of northern France.

**02** They must dodge enemy patrols in the water and on land, and avoid searchlights when they are working on the shoreline.

**03** The survey of what will become a key British landing site, Gold Beach, is undertaken by Major General Logan Scott-Bowden and Sergeant Bruce Ogden-Smith.

**04** The mission takes place on December 31, a date rumored to have been chosen by Winston Churchill in the belief German defenders would be distracted by celebrations.

**05** The Coppists make detailed measurements and observations and take sand samples—aerial intelligence has raised concerns of underlying peat and clay, which could bog down tanks.

**06** As on all COPP missions it is essential they leave no trace of their presence.

**07** Within days of the planned D-Day landings, all ships' commanders are issued with enormously detailed, top-secret briefing packs concerning routes and target beaches, largely the product of COPP's missions.

---

**09.1942**
Willmott receives permission to begin training a team for covert coastal surveying of potential landing and invasion sites in France.

**1943**
In great secrecy, a COPP depot is set up on Hayling Island, Hampshire, England, with the support of Chief of Combined Operations, Louis Mountbatten.

**01.1944**
Scott-Bowden and Ogden-Smith return to survey what will become the D-Day landing beaches.

**06.04.1944**
The D-Day landings occur. Information gathered by the Royal Military Survey and from COPP's missions proves invaluable.

**9.27.2012**
In an overdue recognition of the secret Commandos of COPP, a memorial to them is unveiled on Hayling Island.

# OPERATION JERICHO: THE RAID ON AMIENS PRISON

DATE **February 18, 1944**
LOCATION **Amiens, Picardy, France**
OBJECTIVE **To breach the walls of a prison holding condemned French Resistance fighters**

**The Resistance movement in Occupied France was very important to the Allies. When a call came to help break out Resistance leaders who were about to be executed by the Gestapo in a French prison, British, Australian, and New Zealand airmen responded with a bold low-level precision raid in broad daylight.**

## A Call for Help

The first step in what would become Operation Jericho was the receipt by British Intelligence of details on the layout and daily schedule of Amiens prison in France, sent by Dominique Ponchardier, courageous head of the local underground Resistance. The intelligence agents did not know what it was for but kept it on file. When a request came to help Resistance members escape from the prison, all became clear.

The winter of 1943–44 was difficult for the French Resistance, with numerous operatives captured; many now held at Amiens had been condemned to death. D-Day approached, for which the Allies needed Resistance help, plus, as the Royal Air Force Museum puts it, "Many an RAF pilot owed his life to the work of the Resistance and here was a chance to return the favour"—by smuggling them out of Occupied France.

## Pinpoint Accuracy

Under the command of Group Captain Charles Pickard, 18 Mosquito bombers would form three waves, the first bombing the prison walls, the second the building itself, and the third attacking only if the first two failed. Twelve Hawker Typhoon fighters would escort them.

The walls were 20 feet (6 m) high and 3 feet (0.9 m) thick, the approach was below treetop height, followed by an immediate sharp climb to clear obstacles. The building sections targeted housed the guards; walls or doors had to be breached to allow prisoners to escape. Pinpoint accuracy was required, though as Acting Air Vice-Marshal Basil Embry assured his men, the prisoners "have told us they would rather be blown up by British bombs than shot by the Nazis."

## Success, Heroism, and Sacrifice

On February 18, the planes took off despite heavy snow. In the blizzard four Mosquitos lost touch and had to turn back, as did four Typhoons. The weather cleared over the English Channel and they regrouped, but another Mosquito turned back with engine trouble just before the attack.

The western perimeter wall was hit first with 11-second delay bombs, then the northern wall. Both were breached. The next wave hit the buildings on the southeast and then the northwest. Scrambled enemy planes engaged the departing planes in a dogfight; four of the RAF raiders were killed and three captured. Of the prisoners, 102 were killed, some by the bomb damage, many by guards' machine guns, but 258 escaped, including 29 political prisoners and 50 Resistance workers, among them allegedly 12 due to be executed the next day. Two-thirds of the escapees would soon be recaptured. Whether or not the raid was truly successful, or indeed necessary, remains an open question.

ENGLAND
Hunsdon Airfield
London
NETHERLANDS
English Channel
BELGIUM
Amiens
Glisy Airfield
FRANCE

ABOVE: Captain Pickard with his pet sheepdog, pictured while resting from operations as Station Commander at Lissett, Yorkshire.

RIGHT (clockwise from top left): 1. The Mosquito bomber uniquely constructed almost entirely of wood. 2. Dust and smoke rising from the prison. 3. A low-level aerial photo of Amiens Prison taken during the raid. 4. The 12-foot-wide breach in the south side of Amiens prison's outer wall, through which the prisoners escaped.

## TIMELINE

**01.1944**
Betrayed to the enemy and being hunted by the Gestapo, Dominique Ponchardier still manages to organize for a British attack on Amiens prison.

**02.1944**
Given the planned D-Day landings to take place in four months' time, it is agreed that the attack should occur, at whatever cost, to support the French Resistance.

## STEP-BY-STEP

**01** Planners set a window of February 10–18 for Operation Jericho; many prisoners are scheduled to face the firing squad on February 19.

**02** At 12:03 on February 18, with the guards at lunch, the raid begins.

**03** With the first two attack waves succeeding as planned, operation commander Group Captain Pickard stands down the third group.

**04** Enemy fighters are scrambled from nearby Glisy airfield, forcing a Mosquito down and killing its navigator.

**05** Pickard's plane is hit by flak; he and his navigator, Broadley, are killed. French villagers rush to help, burning official papers from the plane, hiding its film and camera in a rabbit warren, and taking the bodies to the mayor's house.

**06** Inside the prison some of the Resistance fighters who could have escaped heroically stay to help other prisoners trapped under collapsed walls and floors. Eventually, 102 prisoners die as a result of the attack.

**07** Two Typhoons and their pilots are lost, one while returning in bad weather over the English Channel.

| | | | | |
|---|---|---|---|---|
| **02.17.1944** | **02.18.1944** | **02.18.1944** | **02.19.1944** | **1964** |
| Provisionally scheduled for this day, Operation Jericho is postponed due to bad weather. | Despite a blizzard it is now or never, so the planes depart Hunsdon Airfield, Hertfordshire, England, and proceed with the attack. | The raid is announced as a qualified success: the prison walls are breached, 258 prisoners escape (although 182 are recaptured), and only two Mosquitos and two Typhoons are lost. | The bodies of Charles Pickard and navigator Flight Lieutenant (John) Alan Broadley are buried in Amiens' St. Pierre cemetery (where they remain). | Ponchardier begins a five-year stint as French ambassador to Bolivia, taking a break from his second career as a prolific and best-selling thriller author, under the pen name Antoine Dominique. |

# THE KIDNAPPING OF GENERAL KREIPE

DATE       April 26, 1944
LOCATION    Outside Heraklion, Crete, Occupied Greece
OBJECTIVE   The abduction of the local German commander in Occupied Crete

The phrase "they don't make them like that any more" could have been coined for Patrick ("Paddy") Leigh Fermor. By the age of 20 he had crossed Europe on foot, just for the adventure. Nine years later, as a Special Operations Executive (SOE) operative in Crete, he oversaw a kidnapping that provided one of World War II's most memorable vignettes.

### The Spark of an Idea

In 1943, when his country surrendered to the Allies, Italian General Carta, based on Crete, preferred escape to working with the Germans. SOE officer Patrick Leigh Fermor, helping the resistance on the occupied island, spirited him away to British headquarters in Egypt.

This gave Leigh Fermor a bold idea: if he could get Carta out undetected, perhaps he could kidnap the German commander on Crete and consequently enact the stealthy move with him.

### An Honorable Prisoner

At 09:30 on April 26, 1944, Leigh Fermor, Captain William "Billy" Stanley Moss, and three Cretan resistance *andartes* were waiting near a sharp bend as General Heinrich Kreipe was driven home. Dressed as German corporals, Leigh Fermor and Moss signaled the driver to stop and Leigh Fermor asked in German, "Is this the General's car?" Told it was, he pulled out Kreipe, while Moss knocked the driver unconscious.

In under a minute, Moss was behind the wheel driving off, with Leigh Fermor, wearing the general's hat, beside him, and the flustered general lying on the floor in the back, guarded by the heavily armed Greeks. "You're an honorable prisoner of war," Leigh Fermor told him, "I'm a British major." Having reached the mountains, the others got out while Leigh Fermor drove the car on, abandoned it, and then rejoined them.

### ... the War Had Ceased to Exist

The group undertook a grueling 18-day journey across the island's mountains, handed from one set of local resistance guides to the next. All the while they were being hunted by several thousand German troops. The Germans dropped leaflets that warned they would kill thousands of Cretans in retribution for the kidnapping, and urged informers to come forward.

At dawn one morning, Kreipe murmured to himself, in Latin, the opening lines of Horace's "Ode to Thaliarchus." Knowing the poem, Leigh Fermor completed it.

> The General's eyes swivelled away from the mountain-top to mine ...
> after a long silence, he said: 'Ach so, Herr Major!' It was very strange.
> 'Ja, Herr General.' As though, for a long moment, the war had ceased to
> exist. We had both drunk at the same fountains long before; and things
> were different between us for the rest of our time together.

Finally reaching the coast, they were picked up by a British warship bound for Alexandria. Asked how he had been treated by his captors, Kreipe answered: "Ritterlich" (chivalrously).

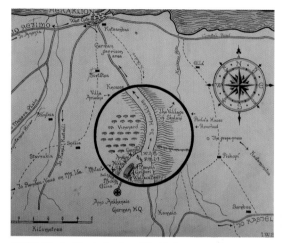

ABOVE: Stanley Moss's drawing of the Kreipe abduction point.

RIGHT: Patrick Leigh Fermor (left) and "Billy" Moss planning the kidnap in a cave on Crete.

## TIMELINE

**05.20.1941**

In the first major airborne assault in history, German paratroops invade Crete, forcing British and Greek forces to withdraw from the island within 11 days.

**03.01.1944**

The "Butcher of Crete," General Friedrich-Wilhelm Müller, is replaced by General Heinrich Kreipe, who has seen action in France and on the Eastern Front.

## STEP-BY-STEP

**01** During spring 1944, SOE agents plan the kidnap of German General Friedrich-Wilhelm Müller, "the Butcher of Crete." When Heinrich Kreipe replaces Müller they alter their target.

**02** As Kreipe travels from his Archanes office to Villa Ariadne (his Heraklion mansion) Leigh Fermor, Moss, and the Cretan operatives strike.

**03** Holding Kreipe hostage they brazen their way through over 20 roadblocks: guards fall back and wave them through when Leigh Fermor calls in German, "General's car!"

**04** Leigh Fermor leaves the car for the Germans to find, with a note pinned to the front seat explaining the kidnap.

**05** Surrounded by *andarte* resistance fighters, Kreipe says, "Please do not put me under the authority of these savages." Leigh Fermor replies, "These people are civilized, you are the ones who are the savages."

**06** While some *andartes* feel Kreipe should be killed for what the Germans have done in Crete, he is consistently treated with courtesy and respect. The group is eventually picked up by a British motor launch from Peristeres beach near Rodakino on May 14.

**07** None of the hundreds of villager guides betrays the agents, despite terrifying German threats; Kreipe is successfully taken from Crete to Egypt, interrogated, then moved to a POW camp in Canada. He is not released until 1947.

ABOVE: Major General Heinrich Kreipe.

| 04.26.1944 | 05.14.1944 | 05.09.1944 | 1950 | 06.14.1976 |
|---|---|---|---|---|
| Adapting a plan to kidnap Müller, SOE operatives and local resistance forces kidnap Kreipe. | Evading a full garrison of German soldiers and aerial patrols, the SOE agents and their hostage rendezvous with a waiting ship near Rodakino. | Having begun to withdraw from parts of the island eight months earlier, the Germans sign an unconditional surrender in Crete, in one of the final acts of the war in Europe. | Moss publishes the memoir *Ill Met by Moonlight: The Abduction of General Kreipe*, which is filmed seven years later (US title *Night Ambush*) and stars Dirk Bogarde. Moss dies aged 44 in 1965. | Heinrich Kreipe dies aged 81. Acclaimed for his travel writing and memoirs, Sir Patrick Leigh Fermor dies aged 96 in June 2011. |

# OPERATION DEADSTICK: AIRBORNE ATTACKS ON NORMANDY BRIDGES

DATE       June 6, 1944
LOCATION   Bénouville and Ranville, Calvados, Normandy, France
OBJECTIVE   To capture, in advance of the D-Day Normandy landings, two key bridges

The image of D-Day that comes most readily to mind is that of thousands of troops pouring off landing craft onto the beaches of Normandy. But, six hours earlier, the first French village had been liberated following an airborne operation that ensured the protection of the eastern flank of the invading Allies.

### "Take Intact the Two Bridges"

Part of the Operation Overlord plan was to seize control of vital infrastructure and minimize enemy defenses in the hours preceding the mass Normandy landings. Thousands of US, Canadian, and British troops would make this airborne overnight attack. The first to land—and the ones that most easily achieved their aim—were from the Oxfordshire and Buckinghamshire Light Infantry, affectionately nicknamed the Ox. & Bucks.

Their mission was to "take intact the two bridges of the Orne River and the channel [canal] of Caen." The bridges were also known by the names of the adjacent villages, Ranville (Orne) and Bénouville (Caen). While the force that followed them would parachute in, Ox. & Bucks. D Company would use Horsa gliders—three headed for each bridge; a total of 180 men. The bridges were strategically important links from the hinterland to the area around the Sword landing beach.

### A Rough but Impressive Landing

Just before 23:00 on June 5, 1944, they took off from Tarrant Rushton Airfield in Dorset, England, under tow by Halifax bombers. At 00:16 on D-Day they executed what Air Chief Marshal Sir Trafford Leigh-Mallory later described as "the greatest flying feat" of World War II: in the dark, five of the six gliders landed precisely positioned in relation to the bridges and to each other.

The positioning was even more impressive considering that a number of the gliders had snagged on wire defenses and crash-landed, briefly knocking out those aboard. All quickly recovered with the exception of the first casualty, Lance Corporal Fred Greenhalgh, who landed unconscious in a pond near the Bénouville/Caen bridge and drowned. To the surprise of the British troops, the noise of the landing did not immediately draw out the German sentries.

### "Ham and Jam"

As the lead troops advanced over the bridge they did, however, encounter sentries. In the firefight that ensued, they lost their second man, Lieutenant Den Brotheridge. Meanwhile, the party's sappers were already under the bridge disabling the charges set there by the Germans.

Using grenades and Sten guns, the British subdued the defenders and took the bridge within 10 minutes; as did the team assigned to the Ranville (Orne River) bridge, with no casualties. On confirmation of this, operation commander Major John Howard ordered the sending of the coded signal "Ham and Jam," indicating both bridges were secured. Ranville then became the first village in France to be liberated.

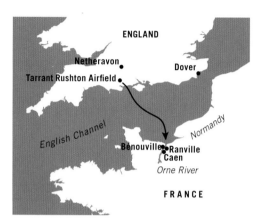

ENGLAND

Netheravon

Dover

Tarrant Rushton Airfield

English Channel

Bénouville   Ranville
Caen

Normandy

Orne River

FRANCE

ABOVE: Two glider pilots from Ox. & Bucks. D Company pictured with Captain Brian Priday, who is holding a Sten gun as used in Operation Deadstick.

## TIMELINE

**03.1944**

At the RAF airfield at Netheravon, Wiltshire, England, six glider crews (uninformed of their true targets) test the viability of the Bénouville/Ranville mission.

**04.1944**

Moving to Dover on the English Channel, where powerful Halifax tow planes are available, they begin extensive training.

ABOVE: Soldiers approaching the Bénouville (Caen) bridge.

BELOW: Horsa gliders used in the bridge capture mission near the Caen Canal bridge at Bénouville on June 8, 1944.

## STEP-BY-STEP

**01** To maintain surprise, the Halifax bombers towing the Horsa gliders are accompanied across the English Channel by extra bombers.

**02** Reaching France, these peel off and bomb a cement factory to the south, deflecting German suspicions.

**03** Despite obstacles that cause them to land with a crash violent enough to break one glider in two, the pilots at Bénouville/Caen end up less than 164 feet (50 m) from their target bridge.

**04** At Ranville/Orne two of the three gliders land very close to the target, the other some miles away.

**05** Even with this reduced attack force, both bridges are captured in minutes.

**06** As directed, they hold the bridges until relieved by the 6th Airborne Division's 7th (Light Infantry) Parachute Battalion, who begin to land about 15 minutes after the bridges have been taken.

**07** The 4,000 6th Division paratroopers are scattered far and wide. Casualties are very high, with many drowning under the weight of their equipment in land defensively flooded by the Germans, and others killed or wounded in action.

| 06.06.1944 | 06.06.1944 | 06.06.1944 | 06.06.1944 | 06.26.1944 |
|---|---|---|---|---|
| The teams set off on the 90-minute flight from Tarrant Rushton in Dorset to Normandy, arriving soon after midnight. | Within minutes of landing, the teams achieve their objectives. | In contrast to the often heavy losses sustained by the ensuing waves of British, Canadian and US airborne troops, the glider bridge assault teams succeed with few casualties. | D-Day: just before dawn, Operation Overlord's massive attacking force arrives on the Normandy beaches. | To honor the liberators, the bridge at Bénouville/Caen is renamed Pegasus Bridge, after the Ox. & Bucks. insignia. The Ranville/Orne bridge will later be renamed Horsa Bridge, after the gliders. |

# OPERATION GAFF: THE ATTEMPTED ASSASSINATION OF ROMMEL

DATE        July 18, 1944
LOCATION    Northern Occupied France
OBJECTIVE   To kidnap or kill German military leader Erwin Rommel

The British had first attempted to assassinate Field Marshal Erwin Rommel back in 1941 (Operation Flipper) when he was still riding high in North Africa. But the raid, based on poor intelligence, was a costly failure, leading to the death or capture of almost all of the Special Air Service (SAS) Commandos. Three years later, with Rommel now in command in France, the organization set out to try again.

## Assassination Targets

In the months leading up to the Allied invasion of Western Europe, Great Britain's Secret Intelligence Service, MI6, was asked by planners to assess the viability of eliminating key enemy figures, among them Field Marshal Erwin Rommel.

The head of MI6, Sir Stewart Menzies, always identified only by his codename, "C," responded on May 11, 1944, with a brief on possible Nazi and Vichy French targets, adding, "We do not believe, however, that their removal will have much, or indeed any effect on the efficient functioning of [the German war machine]." Nonetheless, the SAS was assigned Operation Gaff, a kidnap-or-kill attack on Rommel, now based somewhere in France.

## An Ironic Choice

Rommel, the "Desert Fox" of the North Africa campaign, was an ironic choice, being one of the main voices of reason on the German side. Still a folk hero, his relationship with Adolf Hitler had become strained as he realized his leader was unable to accept the truth that Germany could no longer win the war. Approached by the July 1944 "Valkyrie" plotters, Rommel did not expose their conspiracy (he believed they would simply overthrow Hitler, not kill him).

By May, British Intelligence had learned Rommel was based in the La Rochefoucauld château overlooking the village of La Roche-Guyon. Six SAS Commandos were dispatched on Operation Gaff. Their leader was Captain William Jack Lee, aka Raymond Couraud, French Legionnaire turned gangster-and-smuggler turned Free French fighter, who had been recruited first for the Special Operations Executive and then the SAS.

## A Twist of Fate

Poor weather delayed the planned parachute drop of the Commandos until July 18, when they landed near Orléans. As they soon learned, Rommel's staff car had been strafed by RAF fighter planes the previous day, causing it to roll, badly injuring him. He was not expected to live—in fact, it was initially believed he had already died.

"Lee" and his men aborted their original mission, but set about causing as much havoc for the enemy as possible while making their way through occupied territory to the Allied front in Normandy. Over the following weeks they sabotaged equipment, ambushed road convoys, derailed trains, and attacked German troops. After an assault on the German headquarters at Mantes-la-Jolie, in which they stole documents and escaped after a firefight, they reached the safety of the front lines.

GREAT BRITAIN

Normandy
Mantes-la-Jolie• •La Roche-Guyon
Pontchartrain• •Paris
Orléans•

FRANCE

ABOVE: The funeral procession of Field Marshal Erwin Rommel takes place through the streets of Württemberg.

RIGHT: Erwin Rommel with Adolf Hitler at the opening of Winterhilfswerk, 1942/1943.

BELOW RIGHT: Portrait of Operation Gaff leader, Captain William Jack Lee (Raymond Couraud).

## TIMELINE

**06.06.1944**
D-Day: the beginning of the Allies' successful invasion of Western Europe.

**07.15.1944**
Rommel sends a heartfelt message from the front to try to get Hitler to understand they are losing the war.

## STEP-BY-STEP

**01** The orders for Operation Gaff note the "immense" propaganda value of bringing Rommel alive to Great Britain, but add, "To kill Rommel would obviously be easier than to kidnap him and it is preferable to ensure the former rather than to attempt and fail in the latter."

**02** Though the SAS Commandos do not know it, by the time they parachute into France, Rommel is in hospital, critically injured after his strafed car crashed the previous day.

**03** Learning this, the six-man team abandons its mission and begins making its way on foot to the Allied front line in Normandy.

**04** As they travel, they seize every opportunity to cause disruption by damaging the enemy's equipment and operations.

**05** In an attack on German headquarters at Mantes, they seize military papers.

**06** Given a police-uniform disguise by *gendarmes* in Pontchartrain, Gaff leader Lee (aka Couraud) reaches a US Army position nearby and hands over the papers.

| 07.17.1944 | 07.18.1944 | 07.20.1944 | 10.14.1944 | 10.15.1944 |
|---|---|---|---|---|
| Rommel receives serious head injuries when his strafed staff car crashes and rolls. | The Commandos of Operation Gaff airdrop into France. | The "Valkyrie" plotters' briefcase bomb causes only minor injuries to its target, Hitler, but kills a stenographer and three officers. | With Rommel implicated in the plot, Hitler gives him a choice: a show trial or suicide by cyanide. Rommel commits suicide. | Rommel's official cause of death is injuries from the crash. He is buried with full military honors. |

# THE CABANATUAN POW RESCUE: THE "GREAT RAID"

DATE **January 30, 1945**
LOCATION **Cabanatuan, Nueva Ecija, island of Luzon, Philippines**
OBJECTIVE **To free American and other Allied POWs before they could be executed**

A profound culture clash lay behind Japan's horrendous treatment of prisoners of war (POWs), which saw a death rate among POWs in the Philippines of 40 percent (compared to 1.2 percent in German POW camps). With 500 prisoners—including Bataan Death March survivors—facing imminent death in one such camp, a bold rescue bid was launched.

### An Urgent Rescue Mission

To Japanese soldiers, being taken prisoner was the ultimate dishonor; anyone who allowed himself to be captured deserved little care or respect. In 1942, Japan agreed to abide by the Geneva Convention, but in reality its prisoners of war—British, Dutch, and Australians in Thailand, Burma, and Singapore; Americans and Filipinos in the Philippines—continued to suffer starvation, forced labor, torture, and summary execution.

In October 1944, General MacArthur returned to the Philippines. With American forces pushing north, commandants of Japanese POW camps in their path were ordered to kill their prisoners. On December 14, around 150 US POWs on Palawan were sprayed with gasoline and burned alive. More than 500 prisoners at Cabanatuan, 90 percent American, required urgent rescue before they, too, met a horrific end.

### Deep Behind Enemy Lines

The elite US Army 6th Ranger Battalion and Alamo Scouts sprang into action. As the Scouts gathered intelligence, the Rangers developed a plan. It required local guerrillas and the cooperation of hundreds of villagers because the camp lay 30 miles (48 km) behind enemy lines and was a transit stop for thousands of withdrawing Japanese troops.

Reaching striking range of the camp, across the Pampanga River, and learning a large Japanese force was close, Rangers leader Lieutenant Colonel Mucci agreed to postpone the raid for 24 hours.

### The Journey to Freedom

At 17:00 on January 30, the raiders set out. There would, they knew, be 73 guards on duty and 150 more bivouacking. While two parties of guerrillas blocked the southwest and northeast approaches to the camp and cut phone lines, the Rangers and Scouts would enter the camp front and rear, eliminate the Japanese and free the prisoners. Thirty minutes after the first shot was fired, they had accomplished this for the loss of just two Rangers, one to friendly fire.

But they still had to get the freed men—starving and weakened by dysentery and malaria—safely into US-held territory. Waiting across the river were 25 carts pulled by *carabao* (water buffalo). All along the escape route, villagers were ready with food and water and extra carts. By 03:30 when it reached the most exposed section, a long dogleg highway crossing, the impromptu caravan had 51 carts and took an hour to cross. But by 12:00 it had reached the safety of the 92nd Evacuation Hospital in Guimba—the 511 POWs were free at last.

ABOVE: The Alamo Scouts after the Raid at Cabanautan (left to right): top row—Gil Cox, Wilbert Wismer, Harold Hard, Andy Smith, and Francis Laquier; bottom row—Galen Kittleson, Rufo Vaquilar, Bill Nellist, Tom Rounsaville, and Frank Fox.

## TIMELINE

**12.08.1941**
The day after attacking Pearl Harbor, Japan bombs the Philippines, then a US colony. Two weeks later its army invades.

**03.12.1942**
Unable to stop the Japanese advance, US General Douglas MacArthur is ordered to evacuate. He promises to return.

ABOVE: US Army Rangers and Filipino guerillas cross a creek on their way to the POW camp.

ABOVE LEFT: Prisoners photographed during the Bataan Death March.

## STEP-BY-STEP

**01** On January 30, at 17:00, the raiders leave Pateros, 2 miles (3.2 km) north of the Cabanatuan camp.

**02** In order to prevent barking and roosters giving them away, villagers along the route bind their dogs' mouths and chickens' beaks with bamboo strips.

**03** The Americans crawl a mile (1.6 km) through grass within sight of the guards' towers—75 minutes, "on our bellies heel-to-toe like a long snake," said Scout Galen Kittleson.

**04** At 18:40, a P-61 flies low over the camp, distracting the guards.

**05** There is great tension when the "open fire" signal fails to come from the rear party at 19:30, but at 19:40 the action begins; in under 15 minutes the Americans have control.

**06** Surgeon Captain James Fisher is mortally wounded as fighting winds down. Soon after, Corporal Roy Sweezy succumbs to friendly fire. One POW dies of a heart attack, another remains hidden and is rescued by guerrillas several hours later, but Mucci's men rescue 511.

**07** On the approaches, Joson's Filipino guerrillas are untroubled, but Pajota's guerrillas defeat a Japanese battalion in a fierce two-hour fight at Cabu Creek.

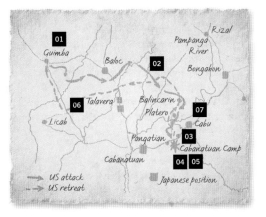

| 04.09.1942 | 05.06.1942 | 10.20.1944 | 01.07.1945 | 01.27.1945 |
|---|---|---|---|---|
| America surrenders the Bataan peninsula; the infamous Bataan Death March, in which 78,000 prisoners were moved 65 miles (105 km) to a POW camp, follows. Untold thousands die in transit. | The remaining US troops in the Philippines surrender unconditionally. | MacArthur returns with the US 6th Army and begins to push the Japanese back. | US Army Intelligence learns about the Palawan POW massacre from escapee Private First Class Eugene Nielsen. | The 6th Army Rangers are given the task of liberating the POWs at Cabanatuan, which they do a mere three days later. |

# OPERATION TOMBOLA: RAIDS BEHIND THE GERMAN LINES IN ITALY

DATE    March 27, 1945
LOCATION  Albinea, Emilia-Romagna, Italy
OBJECTIVE  To disrupt German troops as the Allies advanced in Italy

Although by August 1944 Germany had been pushed out of southern Italy by the Allies, who had reached as far north as Florence, she had not entirely ceded the country of its former Axis partner, the Italians having conceded defeat in September 1943. The "Gothic Line," a fortified frontier from coast to coast across the Apennines, was the last major German line of defense in Italy.

### An "Accidental" Landing

While German forces were in retreat, the fight was not over. Along with Italian partisans, the Allies intended to make things as difficult as possible for the enemy. In early March 1945, the British dropped a Special Air Service (SAS) unit into Emilia-Romagna, behind the "Gothic Line."

The SAS commander was Major Roy Farran, who was instructed not to accompany the team but to run the operation from Florence instead. However, Farran was as wilful as he was courageous. Aboard the US plane as an observer for the drop of the advance party, he "accidentally" fell out—parachute and all—when his Commandos jumped over Mount Cusna.

### Forming the Allied Battalion

Farran and his team were met by Special Operations Executive (SOE) agent Mike Lees, who helped them set up the *Battaglione Alleato* (Allied Battalion) with Italian partisans—many lacking military training—and Russians who had escaped German POW camps. Over the coming weeks, as more SAS Commandos and supplies arrived, Farran put his new group through intensive training.

They then undertook what became the best-known Operation Tombola action, an attack on a German corps headquarters near Albinea. As they made their way to the site Farran received a message instructing him to call off the attack. He decided to ignore it on the grounds that the partisans would lose respect for the SAS and SOE if the operation didn't go ahead.

### A Firefight with Bagpipes

On the misty, moonlit night of March 27, the group—including Commando David Kirkpatrick with his bagpipes—crept up to the compound: Villa Rossi, which housed the commander; Villa Calvi, which housed the staff officers and the operations room; and other assorted billets. Farran split his men into two groups, one for each villa, while Farran and Kirkpatrick remained nearby.

In his memoirs, Farran described how the attack had already started when he ordered Kirkpatrick to play "Highland Laddie," "just to let the enemy know they had more than a mere partisan attack with which to contend." Intense fighting saw Lees and others badly wounded, three Commandos and many Germans killed, and the buildings burned down. Farran and his already exhausted men marched for 22 hours before reaching safety in Cavola. Only US intervention prevented Farran being court-martialed for disobeying orders—twice. The Tombola team went on to conduct more raids into April, before being recalled as the Allies broke through the Gothic Line.

ABOVE: US fighter pilots accept their "escape kits" (cyanide) at an air base in southern Italy, 1945. Although the Germans were facing defeat the fighting continued unabated.

ABOVE: Captain Roy Farran (pictured right) is holding a German Schmeisser sub-machine-gun, during a parade to celebrate the capture of the Termoli port in Italy.

## TIMELINE

| 08.1941 | 01.1942 |
| --- | --- |
| Wounded in both legs and an arm in the Battle of Crete, Army major Roy Farran escapes from a German POW hospital in Athens. | Three months later, Farran is fighting in North Africa. He soon joins the Special Air Service (SAS). |

## STEP-BY-STEP

**01** Major Roy Farran leads Operation Tombola. Later, he will write, "Our job was to cause panic and confusion" behind the lines of the retreating enemy.

**02** Proceeding with the Albinea attack, it takes Farran and his men more than an hour to cover the last few hundred yards up to Villa Rossi, moving quietly enough not to alert the sentries.

**03** As a group attacks both Villa Rossi and Villa Calvi, Farran orders Scottish piper Kirkpatrick to play bagpipes, to the cheers of the British Commandos.

**04** When enemy bullets come "uncomfortably close," Farran pushes Kirkpatrick into a nearby slit trench; he continues to play "from a sitting position" stopping only when a stray bullet damages the pipes.

**05** There is fierce fighting in both villas. When the Germans retreat to the upper floors, the Commandos start fires in the buildings.

**06** Evading the German patrols sent to find them, they march through the mountains for 22 hours to reach Allied lines and safety.

ABOVE RIGHT: Men of the 370th Infantry Regiment near the town of Prato Montignoso in Massa Carrara, Tuscany (Gothic Line) April 9, 1945.

RIGHT: An M10 tank destroyer of the 93rd Anti-tank Regiment passes infantry of the 5th Sherwood Foresters during the advance to the Gothic Line, August 27–28, 1944.

| 07.1943 | 10.1944 | 03.04.1945 | 03.27.1945 | 04.29.1945 |
|---|---|---|---|---|
| Landings in Sicily start the Allied invasion of Italy. Allied troops land on the Italian mainland in September. By then the Italian government has capitulated and declared war on Germany. | The Allied advance in Italy is halted at the "Gothic Line" by German forces that have now occupied Italy. | Farran's advance party arrives in what they refer to as "Tombola Valley" in northern Italy, behind enemy lines. | In an attack on German corps HQ at Albinea, Farran's force kills the German chief of staff and many other officers and men, and destroys maps, documents, and buildings. | German forces in Italy, driven back to the Alps, and now isolated by other Allied forces, agree to an unconditional surrender. |

# THE AGE OF
# COLD WARS
## 1945–1970

Before August 6, 1945, Hiroshima was simply another Japanese city. Now it is forever linked to images of mushroom clouds and the permanent shadows that were all that remained of the people at the center of the atomic explosion that day. US efforts leading up to the deployment of the world's first nuclear weapon were not limited to developing the bomb itself; 11 months before he dropped the bomb, pilot Paul Tibbets had been given the job of assembling and training crews for the mission. Tibbets's desire to honor his mother has ensured that in a strange way she, too, is inextricably linked with Hiroshima. Her name was Enola Gay.

The bombing of Hiroshima and, three days later, Nagasaki brought an end to World War II. Between 65 million and 75 million people had been killed in the war. And yet less than three years after the fighting stopped, the United States, Britain, and France were in a tense face-off with the Soviet Union, their former ally against Hitler. Soviet leader Joseph Stalin had designs on Eastern Europe and was perfectly willing to use force to get his way. In 1948 he cut two million citizens of Berlin off from the outside world. The airlift with which the US and Britain responded was a remarkable, sustained effort that saved a great many lives.

The battle between communism and capitalism that would dominate the world for most of the rest of the century had begun. It would play out in various hot spots. In Asia, these included Korea, where the ideological struggle resulted in the deaths of four million people. The long and deadly fight for control in Indochina was also part of the Cold War. This conflict, which ran for decades, saw 1.5 million troops and civilians lose their lives in Vietnam. It scarred the psyche of the French, who fought hard to hold onto their former colony, and of the Americans and their allies whose adherence to the "domino theory" of communism mired them in an unwinnable war.

Along with the events on a mass scale there were also individuals who became emblematic of the times, including Gary Powers, the U-2 spy-plane pilot shot down over Russia and subjected to a show trial before becoming one of the first people to participate in an iconic Cold War event: the exchange of prisoners on a German bridge.

There were still almost two decades of hostilities between the superpowers left to run in 1970 when the Apollo 13 astronauts faced death in space, but in a sign of how far things had come in just eight years since Powers's capture, the Soviet Union offered NASA any help it could provide. A little warmth had begun to thaw the ice.

# OPERATION CENTERBOARD I: THE *ENOLA GAY* STORY

DATE       August 6, 1945
LOCATION   Hiroshima, Honshu, Japan
OBJECTIVE  The delivery and detonation, during combat, of the world's first atomic weapon

In September 1944, four-and-a-half years after the US government had authorized the secret nuclear weapon research that would become known as the Manhattan Project, bomber pilot Paul Tibbets was given the job of creating and training a special unit to drop atomic bombs on Europe and Japan.

### A Superb Pilot

Lieutenant Colonel Paul Tibbets was chosen above other higher-ranking pilots because of his particular expertise. Lieutenant General Leslie Groves Jr., who ran the Manhattan Project, described him as "a superb pilot of heavy planes."

For the new unit he was heading, Tibbets had his choice of pilots, bombardiers, navigators, and ground crew. They would fly specially modified "Silverplate" B-29 Superfortresses. Secrecy was absolute.

### Dodging the Shockwave

The new 509th Composite Group began work at Wendover Field, Utah. Visiting lead Manhattan Project scientist, J. Robert Oppenheimer, at the Los Alamos research facility, Tibbets learned that the conventional technique of flying straight ahead after dropping the bomb would mean instant destruction. Instead, he had to turn at a tangent to the shockwave: 159 degrees in either direction.

The charges would blow at 1,650 feet (500 m) above the ground to maximize destruction, so Tibbets had no more than 42 seconds to complete the turn: "I went back to Wendover as quick as I could and took the airplane up. I got myself to 25,000ft, and I practised turning, steeper, steeper, steeper and I got it where I could pull it round in 40 seconds. The tail was shaking dramatically and I was afraid of it breaking off, but I didn't quit."

### Operation Centerboard I and II

By the time the bomb was ready, the Allies had triumphed in Europe. With Japan as the sole target, the unit relocated to Tinian Island in the Pacific's Marianas. On August 5, Tibbets got the go-ahead to bomb Hiroshima the following day: Operation Centerboard I. From 15 available planes he chose No. 82 and gave it his mother's name, Enola Gay.

After posing for official photographs, the crew, with Tibbets piloting, departed early the next morning. Three B-29s flew ahead to assess weather at the primary target and the fallbacks, Kokura and Nagasaki. Two more followed *Enola Gay,* one to drop instruments to measure blast effects, another carrying scientific observers. At 08:15 local time (09:15 Tinian time), *Enola Gay* dropped the bomb, nicknamed "Little Boy," precisely as planned. On the ground 140,000 people died from the blast and subsequent acute radiation.

*Enola Gay* flew one more combat mission, three days later, assessing weather over the intended target of the second atomic bomb, Kokura—replaced, in the event, by Nagasaki—in Operation Centerboard II.

ABOVE RIGHT: "Little Boy," the uranium-235 bomb dropped on Hiroshima, received its nickname because it was shorter than the initial design.

FAR RIGHT: Tibbets shortly before take off. He later said, "When I knew we'd be doing that I thought, yes, we're going to kill a lot of people, but by God we're going to save a lot of lives. We won't have to invade."

## TIMELINE

| 02.1940 | 04.12.1945 |
|---|---|
| The US government starts secret nuclear weapon research—it will become known as the Manhattan Project. In June 1942, a $90-million budget is approved. | President Franklin D. Roosevelt dies suddenly; his successor, Harry S. Truman, learns of the project. |

## STEP-BY-STEP

**01** The Japanese cities Hiroshima, Kokura, Niigata, and Nagasaki are shortlisted as possible atomic bomb targets; each has a minimum urban area of 3 miles' diameter (4.8 km) where the effects could be clearly observed. Hiroshima is the only one without an Allied POW camp.

**02** On August 5, Tibbets is told the mission is a go. At 14:00, the "Little Boy" bomb is loaded into his chosen plane. At 16:00, Tibbets has his mother's name—Enola Gay—painted on the plane's exterior.

**03** In the early hours of August 6, seven of Composite Group's modified B-29 bombers take off from Tinian Island, less than 1,500 miles (2,400 km) south of the Japanese Home Islands.

**04** At 06:05 (Tinian time), *Enola Gay* and the observation planes rendezvous over Iwo Jima; after a final weather report at 07:30, Tibbets confirms Hiroshima as the target.

**05** At 08:16 (Tinian time), at a safe distance of 11 miles (17.7 km), the plane is rocked by a 2.5g-force: the explosion's shockwave.

**06** *Enola Gay* and her crew return safely to Tinian. The plane sets off to Japan again four days later as part of the flight to deliver the Nagasaki atomic bomb on August 9.

---

**07.16.1945**
The world's first atomic bomb, "Trinity," is successfully tested in New Mexico. A week later, President Truman provisionally approves use of the weapon.

**08.06.1945**
In the absence of peace terms from Japan, *Enola Gay* delivers and detonates a uranium isotope atomic bomb, "Little Boy," over Hiroshima, Japan.

**08.08.1944**
The Soviet Union declares war on Japan, and begins to invade Manchuria.

**08.09.1945**
Three days after the Hiroshima bombing, the second atomic bomb, "Fat Man," kills 70,000 in secondary target Nagasaki after the crew of *Bockscar* is unable to spot its target at Kokura.

**08.14.1944**
Japan agrees to unconditional surrender terms with the United States.

# THE BERLIN AIRLIFT

DATE    June 27, 1948–May 12, 1949
LOCATION  West Berlin, Postwar Occupied Germany
OBJECTIVE  Providing supplies to the Allied-controlled zone, despite a Soviet blockade

**Just six weeks after the German surrender in World War II, the "Big Three" of the Allies—leaders of the Soviet Union, the United States, and Great Britain—met in Potsdam, Germany. Although they agreed on the division of Germany into four occupation zones, signs of the capitalism versus communism standoff that would dominate world geopolitics for the next 35 years were already apparent.**

### Four Parts of the Whole

At the Potsdam Conference, Joseph Stalin, Harry S. Truman, and Winston Churchill (with his successor, Clement Attlee), agreed to reflect their division of German territory overall with a similar division of the capital, Berlin, deep inside the Soviet zone. Run separately, the zones would each operate as a single economic unit to help Germany's eventual restoration and reunification.

While the Soviets took heavy reparations, dispossessing farmers and putting industry under state control, the Western Allies focused on rebuilding. Conditions were dire for the Germans, with tight food-rationing and labor unrest. Firebrand leaders (many communist) sprang up. It was all frighteningly familiar.

### The Berlin Blockade Begins

To stabilize the economy, at the beginning of 1947 the US and British zones merged into "Bizonia." France initially refused to join, but agreed on the necessity for currency reform: with Reichsmarks almost worthless, the black market dominated, and even cigarettes had become "currency." On June 20, 1948 the new Deutsche Marks—created in great secrecy—were revealed by the Western Allies in Bizonia, the name for the joint British- and US-occupied zones based in Frankfurt-am-Main.

The Soviets, who had a new currency of their own, reacted furiously, boosting troop numbers, imposing electricity cuts on Berlin, and, on June 24, blockading all road and rail access to the city, cutting off two million citizens of the non-Soviet zones from essential supplies.

### A Remarkable Effort

To the US commander in Germany, General Lucius D. Clay, it was "one of the most ruthless efforts in modern times to use mass starvation for political coercion." He warned Truman that if Berlin fell then the rest of Germany would follow, and advocated forcing through with tanks. Truman, approaching an election with record low ratings, had already been criticized for being soft on communism as Soviet control extended through Eastern Europe, and had no wish to spark off World War III.

The answer was an airlift, despite much skepticism about its success. When it began, USAF aircraft in Europe could transport 250 tons (228 tonnes) a day—five percent of the 5,040 tons (4,570 tonnes) Berlin needed to survive. More US and British planes arrived, but not until October was the requirement exceeded. Food (including dehydrated potato and eggs and boneless meat), coal for winter heating, machinery, and more came on planes landing on average every three minutes, day and night. Stalin finally backed down on May 12, 1949, although deliveries continued until September 30, creating a surplus should he try again. No shots had been fired, but the Cold War had begun.

ABOVE: Sacks of coal in Germany waiting to be flown to Berlin as part of the Allied airlift.

## TIMELINE

**03.05.1946**
As relations between Stalin and his wartime allies deteriorate, Winston Churchill says in a speech at Westminster College, Missouri, "an iron curtain has descended across the Continent."

**06.24.1948**
In a move built up to for some time but triggered by the new Deutsche Marks currency introduced by the Western Allies, the Soviet Union cuts off all land access, and power and water supplies, to West Berlin.

ABOVE: A Douglas C-47 during the Berlin airlift. The most famous of the airlift pilots was Colonel Gail S. Halvorsen, nicknamed "the Candy Bomber" after dropping promised sweets to hungry children who had gathered at the Tempelhof airfield fence. He told them to watch for a plane "wiggling its wings."

## STEP-BY-STEP

**01** Arriving in Wiesbaden on "Black Friday," July 28, 1948, to run the airlift, Major General William H. Tunner finds "a real cowboy operation" delivering less than 50 percent of the minimum needs to the beleaguered population of West Berlin.

**02** Systematizing, and boosting plane numbers by adding over 70 C-54 Skymasters and other planes, Tunner raises this to 85 percent in August. One Berliner describes the incessant noise as "music to our ears."

**03** Although West Berlin citizens are often cold and still underfed, only one percent take up the offer of Soviet ration cards.

**04** The three Berlin air corridors—two in, one out—are constantly patrolled by the Soviet air force, whose pilots amuse themselves by buzzing the transports.

**05** Along with the basics, the planes bring newsprint for the free press, millions of seedlings to replace trees chopped for winter

fuel, feed for zoo animals, and Volkswagen cars for the police. They fly out medical patients, children, and goods stamped "Made in Blockaded Berlin."

**06** The 11-month operation delivers more than 2.3 million tons (2 million tonnes) of lifesaving goods.

| 06.27.1948 | 05.12.1949 | 05.24.1949 | 10.07.1949 | 08.31.1961 |
|---|---|---|---|---|
| A joint American-British airlift begins, providing the city's non-Soviet Western zones with supplies, enabling them to withstand the blockade. | The Soviets lift the blockade. | The merged Western Allies' zones form the Federal Republic of Germany—including the western zone exclave of Berlin. | The Soviet-run section of the country becomes the German Democratic Republic. | The Soviets begin construction of the Berlin Wall, constituting a military barrier between the Soviet and Western Allies areas of occupation in Berlin. It is finally demolished 30 years later in 1990. |

# THE BATTLE
# OF IMJIN RIVER

DATE **April 22–25, 1951**
LOCATION **Imjin River, Republic of Korea**
OBJECTIVE **To prevent Chinese forces breaking through the UN line to reach Seoul**

**"Temporary" Soviet and American occupation zones in Korea, either side of the 38th parallel, had hardened by 1948 into two independent countries bristling for war. Five years after the end of World War II, when the North invaded, the United States led a 21-country United Nations' armed support of the South. By April 1951, 4,500 British troops faced 27,000 Chinese on the Imjin River.**

### Outnumbered Six to One
The northern Korean People's Army (KPA) had initially forced the Republic of Korea's army far south. But General Douglas MacArthur took command of UN forces, and within six weeks had pushed north to the Chinese border. He wanted to invade, prompting China to send hundreds of thousands of troops to join the war. The opposing sides forced each other back and forth across the North/South Korea border: Seoul was captured four times.

By spring 1951, the front line was the Imjin River, 27 miles (45 km) north of Seoul—roughly following the border. The three British, and one Belgian, battalions of the 29th Independent Infantry Brigade were to prevent three Chinese divisions breaking through. The British were better armed, trained, and experienced than the Chinese but were outnumbered six to one.

### Wave after Human Wave
During the day of April 22, small parties of Chinese troops ventured across the river, but after dark an entire battalion attacked. The Chinese suffered heavy casualties but just kept coming. During the night, the British were supported by light artillery, but at dawn the gunners came under Chinese fire and pulled back. UN air strikes provided breathing room. The Belgian battalion fought back from its position across the river and withdrew.

That night, Chinese reinforcements attacked in wave after human wave. The 750 men from the Gloucestershire Regiment—"the Glorious Glosters"—were vulnerable, 2 miles (3.2 km) from the Royal Northumberland Fusiliers. Although British and US artillery aided the Glosters, by April 23 they were in trouble, cut off from their own lines and confined to Hill 235.

### Gunned Down So Close to Safety
A daybreak UN relief attempt on April 24 failed, and most of an attempted airdrop of ammunition, water, and radio batteries missed. That night the Chinese attacked again and again. Mid-morning on April 25, the 29th Brigade was ordered to withdraw. Under heavy fire, most did so, but the Glosters were surrounded. They received permission to break out to try to find a way through to safety.

Many were captured. The few who reached their own forces just ahead of the enemy, being mistaken for Chinese, came under fire from UN tanks. Captain Mike Harvey described the nightmarish scene: "[they] opened rapid fire with HMGs and 75mm cannon, and our six leading men fell … [the] Chinese were in pursuit and shooting and bayoneting the men at the tail, mercilessly killing what were now unarmed soldiers." Just 120 of the 750 Glosters made it out.

RIGHT (clockwise from top left): 1. A Gloster pointing to the main supply route through the Imjin River valley as seen from "A" Company's position. The ridge on the left is the route the Chinese used to attack "D" Company in the battle. (Picture taken five weeks after the battle). 2. Men of the Royal Northumberland Fusiliers, who fought to the right of the Gloucestershire Regiment, are shown here moving up to their positions near the Imjin River prior to the attack. 3. Overlooking the Imjin River, a wooden cross marks the grave of Captain R. Reeve Tucker, 1st Gloucester, 29th British Brigade, who died in the battle. 4. The "Freedom Gate Bridge" spanning the Imjin River. It temporarily replaced the structure that was destroyed by the bombs.

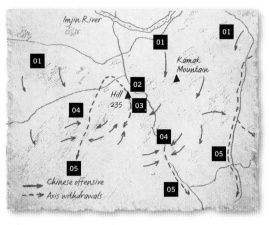

## TIMELINE

| 08.29.1910 | 08.11.1945 |
| --- | --- |
| Japan annexes Korea, turning it into a colony. | General Order No. 1 of Japanese surrender terms requires its troops north of the 38th parallel to surrender to the Soviets and the ones to the south to the Americans. |

## STEP-BY-STEP

**01** April 1951: the 29th Independent Infantry Brigade is strung over a 9-mile (15-km) section of the UN line on the Imjin River; on April 22, the Chinese 63rd Army attacks gaps in the line en masse.

**02** By dawn on the second day of the battle, several Brigade positions have been overrun and the Glosters are pinned down on Hill 235, low on ammunition. Relief efforts fail.

**03** Ordered to hold his ground, at 15:10 on April 24, Gloster Lieutenant Colonel James Carne radios HQ: "What I must make clear to you is that my command is no longer an effective fighting force. If it is required … in spite of this, we shall continue to hold…"

**04** During the last night of the battle, the Chinese attackers are spurred on by trumpets. The Glosters respond with bugle calls.

**05** The following day, the Glosters attempt to reach safety. In all, the Brigade loses 1,091 men—killed, wounded, missing, or captured—630 of them Glosters. Their Chinese opponents are estimated to have suffered some 10,000 casualties, one-third of the 63rd Army. They are among the war's four million military and civilian deaths.

---

**05.10.1948**
The United Nations-supervised elections originally intended as part of Korea's unification only happen in the south; the north refuses the UN access.

**25.06.1950**
The north—now the Democratic People's Republic of Korea (DPRK)—and south—the Republic of Korea (ROK)—plunge into war when the DPRK invades.

**09.15.1950**
General Douglas MacArthur, Supreme Commander of the US-led United Nations force sent to aid the ROK, launches a brilliant counterattack.

**04.11.1951**
Increasingly belligerent when President Truman refuses permission to invade China, MacArthur is stripped of his command due to his insubordination.

**07.27.1953**
Stalin dies in March; two weeks later, the USSR stops supporting North Korea. Finally, in July, a ceasefire agreement is signed; the war has never formally ended.

# THE BATTLE OF DIEN BIEN PHU

DATE       March 13–May 7, 1954
LOCATION   Dien Bien Phu, Tonkin, Vietnam
OBJECTIVE  To force a decisive battle to determine Vietnam's future

**Strategic errors and grievous underestimation of the enemy underpinned France's defeat at Dien Bien Phu—the last gasp in its doomed attempt to regain control of its former Indochina colonial holdings. The harrowing battle left deep scars on the French psyche, and its aftermath brought US troops to Vietnam.**

### "A Hole-in-the-Ground"

Under France's World War II Vichy government, Japan took possession of Indochina. In the postwar power vacuum, Vietnamese communist Ho Chi Minh proclaimed independence. The French initially negotiated with his nationalist Viet Minh movement but, by December 1946, they were at war. Even with US financial aid, France could not prevail. In 1952, its Northern Command evacuated troops from Dien Bien Phu, calling it a "hole-in-the-ground." Yet, in June 1953, the new French commander decided this was the spot to force a major battle.

### The Dien Bien Phu Hedgehog

Appointed in May 1953, General Henri Navarre demurred, saying he had no experience in Indochina. "You will see it with fresh eyes," French Premier René Mayer responded. Navarre promoted General René Cogny to commander for the northern region.

Cogny proposed reestablishing a Dien Bien Phu "mooring point": a lightly defended airbase. However, Navarre decided on a heavily fortified base—a "hedgehog"—supplied by air, to block the Viet Minh supply lines and force the hand of their military leader, General Vo Nguyen Giap. Navarre chose his position on the valley floor. In November, French airdrops began, bringing in an initial force of 10,800, plus ten tanks.

### Utterly Defeated

As French soldiers built the base (giving its eight fortified posts female names), set up mobile field bordellos, and entertained VIPs, Giap's army took up position in the surrounding mountains. Often underfed, Giap's soldiers dragged artillery inch by inch along the rough tracks. On March 13, with Navarre and Cogny based at the Hanoi HQ and tank cavalry officer Colonel Christian de Castries in charge, Giap attacked. The Béatrice artillery base was destroyed almost immediately and its officers killed. A French counterattack failed. By March 15, Giap's artillery had largely disabled the airstrip.

The French suffering had only begun. The weather turned and the valley became a quagmire. Rather than the mobile battle pictured by Navarre, the French were trapped; Giap surrounded them with an outer trench, from which smaller trenches and tunnels snaked inward. His relentless artillery and antiaircraft fire blocked resupplies. The French bunkers filled with the wounded, rations were halved, and amputees were posted on machine guns.

The 56-day ordeal ended on May 7. While casualties for the Viet Minh were around 23,000 compared to France's 6,400 (plus 8,000 captured and 1,600 missing), they were the clear victors; on May 8, a humiliated French government announced its withdrawal from Vietnam.

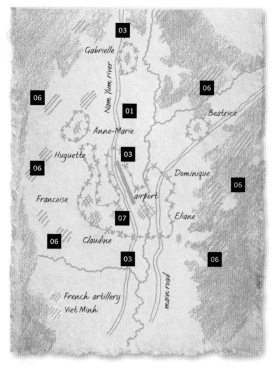

ABOVE: The central French positions at Dien Bien Phu in late March 1954. Some of the fiercest combat of the battle happened at the positions in Eliane.

ABOVE RIGHT: A soldier in a trench during the battle. The French had no idea how outgunned they were until it was too late. To their 32 pieces of artillery, Giap had around 100 howitzers and mortars, and 80 antiaircraft guns.

RIGHT: The French deployed several US-made M24 Chaffee light tanks, as pictured, but these rapidly become bogged down.

## TIMELINE

**11.20.1953**
French troops begin airdropping into Dien Bien Phu.

**12.22.1953**
Only 185 of the 2,100-strong French force, fleeing the province of Lai Chau under Viet Minh attack, reach Dien Bien Phu.

## STEP-BY-STEP

**01** Aiming to emulate the earlier Na San battle success, French commander General Navarre decides to force the Viet Minh into a decisive battle at Dien Bien Phu.

**02** The valley location alarms advisers, who remind him the French held the high ground at Na San.

**03** The Viet Minh cut road access but, with aerial access, the French remain confident.

**04** The terrain is unsuitable for the French tanks; by April 4 only two are operational.

**05** Having taken the airstrip out of action, Viet Minh artillery forces the altitude of airdrops from 2,500 feet to 8,500 feet, greatly affecting accuracy.

**06** Rather than the human wave tactic of Na San, Giap uses tunnels and trenches and his extensive artillery.

**07** French officers succumb to despair: de Castries takes to his bunker early on and artillery commander Colonel Charles Piroth commits suicide by grenade.

**08** Just before they are overrun, Cogny, in Hanoi, tells de Castries: "Listen, old fellow. I realize it's all over, but avoid any form of capitulation. That is forbidden. We must have no white flags."

| 03.13.1954 | 04.26.1954 | 07.21.1954 | 1955 | 07.02.1976 |
|---|---|---|---|---|
| Giap's encircling force attacks. | The battle opponents are keenly aware of the start of the Geneva Conference to decide the future of the region. | In Geneva the Viet Minh agree to a ceasefire along the 17th parallel, pending July 1956 elections to reunify Vietnam; the United States does not. | At the commission of inquiry into the events at Dien Bien Phu, Cogny admits, "my constant pressure on [Navarre] came close to lack of discipline." | After over 20 years of escalating US intervention, the two Vietnams are finally unified, becoming the Socialist Republic of Vietnam. |

# THE MYSTERIOUS DEATH OF "BUSTER" CRABB

DATE    **April 19, 1956**
LOCATION    **Portsmouth Harbor, Hampshire, England**
OBJECTIVE  **To spy on Russian naval ships**

**For decades mystery has surrounded the disappearance of decorated British naval diver and MI6 operative Commander Lionel "Buster" Crabb. Was he killed by the Russians? By MI5 or MI6? Is the headless body buried in his grave really his, or was he spirited back to the Soviet Union after defecting? The truth will probably never emerge.**

### An Unlikely Hero

Lionel "Buster" Crabb was an unlikely diver—a heavy smoker, enthusiastic drinker, and weak swimmer—who became a wartime hero leading the defense against Italian "human torpedo" mine attacks in Gibraltar. He left the Navy in 1948, then rejoined for four years in 1951. After this he remained "attached" to the Royal Naval Volunteer Reserve, but was often short of money.

In October 1955, six Soviet naval ships made a détente visit to Portsmouth. Sydney Knowles, a diver from Crabb's Gibraltar team, claims he accompanied Crabb to spy on the underwater workings of the cruiser *Sverdlov* for MI6 and the CIA.

### The Cover-up Begins

On April 17, 1956, Crabb and a "Mr Smith" (probably Knowles) booked into Portsmouth's Sally Port Hotel. That evening, Crabb asked diving colleague George Franklin to help him—as a favor, nothing official. The next day, three Soviet vessels, including the cruiser *Ordzhonikidze*, brought Communist Party leader Nikita Khrushchev and Premier Nikolai Bulganin for a state visit. Crabb's job was to inspect the cruiser's propeller mechanisms.

Crabb, in scuba gear, and Franklin took a launch out that afternoon. Crabb entered the harbor water but, perhaps after becoming entangled in jetty pilings, aborted the dive. Early the next morning they returned. Crabb dove and resurfaced after 20 minutes with equipment problems. He reentered the water but did not resurface. "Mr Smith" then checked out of the hotel, taking Crabb's baggage: the cover-up had begun.

### Scandal, and a Body at Last

On April 29, the Admiralty reported Crabb missing, presumed dead, after "a test dive at [nearby] Stokes Bay," but journalists had already begun to investigate. On May 4, the Soviets lodged a protest to the Foreign Office about a diver seen near *Ordzhonikidze* in Portsmouth, in violation of an anti-spying agreement for the visit. It became a scandal and on May 14 the British Prime Minister, Sir Anthony Eden, who seems to have been genuinely unaware of the mission, said it had been done "without the authority or the knowledge of Her Majesty's ministers. Appropriate disciplinary steps are being taken." The head of MI6 was duly dismissed.

On June 9, 1957, a corpse without hands, head, and part of the chest was found floating east of Portsmouth. Though the body was wearing precisely what Crabb had been, its size and body hair matched his, the damage was consistent with being so long in the water, and the coroner found that it was him, the discovery fueled conspiracy theories that persist to this day. Maybe, since Crabb neared the *Ordzhonikidze's* propeller, it was simply a ghastly accident.

ABOVE: Crabb's remains being retrieved under police guard.
TOP: The unlikely diver and wartime hero, Buster Crabb.

## TIMELINE

**04.19.1956**

Lionel "Buster" Crabb disappears in Portsmouth Harbor while gathering intelligence for MI6 on a visiting Soviet warship.

**05.06.1956**

The BBC reports that PM Anthony Eden's statements have only heightened speculation that Crabb was on an unauthorized spying mission.

## STEP-BY-STEP

**01** On his third dive in Portsmouth Harbour attempting to spy on Soviet ship *Ordzhonikidze*, Lionel Crabb fails to surface.

**02** His belongings are removed from his hotel by a mysterious companion.

**03** Several days later, four pages of the hotel register are removed, increasing the suspicion that has already started to build.

**04** The Admiralty claims Crabb disappeared on April 29, but it is quickly established he was last seen on April 19.

**05** The scandal grows as the Soviets complain a diver was seen near their ship.

**06** Prime Minister Anthony Eden fuels spying rumors, saying, "It would not be in the public interest to disclose the circumstances in which Commander Crabb is presumed to have met his death."

**07** Revisiting the matter in 2007, highly experienced retired British Lieutenant Commander Rob Poole writes that, given Crabb's health, it seems most likely he "succumbed to oxygen poisoning or possibly carbon dioxide poisoning during his dive … [which] led to unconsciousness and death by drowning." But this does not explain the unfortunate condition of the corpse recovered.

BELOW LEFT: The visiting Soviet vessels.
BELOW RIGHT: Mr D.L. Randall (right) and Mr Ted Gilby (left) found Crabb's body off Pilsey Island in Chichester, Sussex.

| 06.09.1957 | 11.2007 | 11.2007 | 2009 | 2057 |
|---|---|---|---|---|
| A headless and handless corpse in diving gear is discovered floating near Portsmouth. | Former Soviet frogman Eduard Koltsov generates publicity with the claim that he cut Crabb's throat to stop him attaching something to *Ordzhonikidze's* hull. | Crabb's second cousin Lomond Handley tells the media that Koltsov is part of a cover-up and that Crabb was kidnapped and brainwashed by the Soviets. | Publicizing his memoir, Knowles claims Crabb was killed by British Intelligence to stop him defecting to the Soviet Union. | The last of the secret official documents on Crabb are due for release. |

# THE U-2 INCIDENT: GARY POWERS

DATE        May 1, 1960
LOCATION    Airspace above Sverdlovsk Oblast in west-central Russia, then part of the USSR, now Ukraine
OBJECTIVE   To prevent the US conducting overflight surveillance on the USSR

**In 1955, Soviet leader Nikita Khrushchev rejected US President Dwight D. Eisenhower's proposal for open surveillance of each other's nuclear facilities. The first instance of covert Eisenhower-authorized surveillance of the Soviets took place on US Independence Day the following year. And four years after that, on the major Soviet holiday May Day, their spying was exposed.**

### The Arms Race

After Hiroshima, the Soviets hastened their own nuclear weapons research. Each side feared being outstripped, and reliable intelligence was prized. US strategists decided to work toward high-altitude aerial surveillance "overflights." They knew being detected in Soviet airspace might trigger war, but erroneously believed high-altitude flights would elude ground radar. Project Aquatone was born.

Lockheed engineer Clarence "Kelly" Johnson created the U-2 plane (development designation: CL-282), capable of flying at 70,000 feet (21,300 m) and, after much resistance, it was adopted. Pressurized suits developed for its pilots later aided NASA's 1960s spacesuit designs.

### A Fateful Delay

Among the many scientists involved were optical physicist James Baker and physicist and inventor Edwin Land (of Polaroid photography fame). Baker developed a camera to capture high-altitude images in far finer detail than previously possible, and Land convinced Eisenhower that to minimize the risk of provoking war, the surveillance pilots should be employed by the Central Intelligence Agency, not the United States Air Force.

Gary Powers had flown 27 successful U-2 missions, some over the Soviet Union. But a weather delay for his 28th flight proved fateful. A Paris summit between Eisenhower and Khrushchev was scheduled for May 16; to remove any possible provocation, Eisenhower had ordered no overflights after April 30. On May 1, conditions were finally right for the mission slated for three days earlier, and Powers took off from a US base in Pakistan. As the official CIA history puts it, "May Day turned out to be a bad time to overfly the Soviet Union." It was a major holiday, with far lighter air traffic than usual, making the U-2 easier to spot on radar.

### Downed by a Missile

A surface-to-air missile brought down the U-2 and Powers was taken prisoner and interrogated at length by the KGB. While he did not reveal details of the program, the capture of the intact plane and its pilot gave the Soviets proof of what they had suspected all along. Certain the plane would have disintegrated and Powers been killed, the United States first claimed a "weather research plane" had gone astray.

Powers underwent a show trial in Moscow and on August 17 was convicted of espionage and sentenced to ten years: three in prison, then seven of hard labor. However, 21 months after being captured he was released in the superpowers' first prisoner exchange, on the Glienicke Bridge linking East Germany to West Berlin.

ABOVE: Powers received some sharp criticism at home for not destroying his plane's camera and even for not having suicided. Exonerated, he became a news helicopter pilot/reporter, dying with his cameraman in a crash at age 47.

ABOVE RIGHT: The engine of the downed American Lockheed plane piloted by Powers on view in Gorky Park.

BELOW RIGHT Powers's mission survival outfit items.

## TIMELINE

**07.21.1955**
Eisenhower proposes mutual "Open Skies" USA–USSR aerial surveillance; Khrushchev refuses.

**07.04.1956**
On its initial Soviet Union overflight, the U-2 is spotted but cannot be identified. Soviet authorities rightly suspect the US, sending a note of protest.

## STEP-BY-STEP

**01** The U-2 program's most experienced pilot, Gary Powers, takes off from a US airfield near Peshawar, Pakistan, on a weather-delayed Soviet Union overflight.

**02** With little air traffic due to the May Day holiday, Powers's plane is easily tracked by Soviet radar.

**03** Soviet radar operators detect the plane as it nears the Afghan-Russian border and ground all civilian planes in its path.

**04** By the time Powers nears Tashkent, 13 Soviet jets have scrambled to intercept him.

**05** When the jets fail, three V-75 missiles are launched. One accidentally downs a Soviet fighter. Another detonates just behind the U-2, damaging the tail and sending the plane into an inverted spin.

**06** Flung against the canopy and unable to use the ejection seat, Powers hits the canopy release, intending to initiate camera self-destruct before releasing his seat belt and bailing out.

**07** He is, however, sucked straight out. His parachute deploys and he falls safely. Farmers surround him, followed soon after by Soviet officials.

**05.1956**
Gary Powers joins the CIA-run U-2 program as one of its first pilots.

**08.1960**
Less than four months after Powers is captured, the US retrieves its first successful spy-satellite photographs.

**02.10.62**
In a prisoner swap in Berlin, Powers is exchanged for Soviet spy "Rudolf Abel"; at Checkpoint Charlie, the Soviets also release detained student Frederic Pryor.

**02.13.62**
Back in the US, Powers begins an intensive seven-day debriefing.

**02.27.62**
A CIA Board of Inquiry hands down its report, finding Powers did nothing wrong.

# THE SIEGE OF KHE SANH

DATE April 8–July 11, 1968
LOCATION Khe Sanh Combat Base, Quáng Tri Province, Republic of Vietnam
OBJECTIVE To distract and harass American forces at a DMZ combat base

**In a 1954 press conference US President Dwight D. Eisenhower explained "the domino principle" of Indochina: if the region was "lost" to communism, countries including Japan and Australia might follow. Eisenhower's successors adhered to this belief, committing the US to Vietnam for the next two decades.**

### The Growing US Presence

By 1964's end, almost 24,000 US forces were in Vietnam. By December 1967, there were 490,000, supported by allies South Korea, Australia, Thailand, and New Zealand. Their opponents were initially the Viet Cong: communist paramilitary guerrillas. But as the US presence built, so did the involvement of the North Vietnamese—supplied by the Soviet Union and the People's Republic of China.

In 1967, the communist leadership designed a major push to win South Vietnamese "hearts and minds" and inspire an uprising against their unpopular, corrupt government: the Tet Offensive would involve simultaneous attacks on urban centers and military strongholds during the 1968 lunar New Year festival.

### A Second Dien Bien Phu?

The United States had a Marines Corp base at Khe Sanh, in the northwest corner of South Vietnam, just below the demilitarized zone (DMZ), near the Laotian border and the North Vietnamese Ho Chi Minh supply trail. Between October and December, the North Vietnamese commander General Vo Nguyen Giap sent thousands of troops into the area.

US commander General William Westmoreland, convinced Giap was planning a second Dien Bien Phu, rushed reinforcements in by air, road access having been cut months earlier. By mid-January there were 20,000–30,000 North Vietnamese around Khe Sanh, and 6,000 Marines: half in the base itself, half in the surrounding hill positions.

### Constant Bombardment

On January 21, the North Vietnamese attacked, first at Hill 861, then at the base itself. The main ammunition dump went up and the airstrip was damaged, although planes bringing more artillery shells landed safely. The next morning, the nearby village was attacked. Three thousand terrified villagers tried to shelter with the Marines, who refused, fearing sabotage. More than half died. For some weeks the battle raged. Three-hourly American aerial bombing runs did not deter the North Vietnamese. A-4 Skyhawk fighter planes provided cover for the helicopters resupplying the hill positions, while the base received C-130 Hercules airdrops.

The North Vietnamese began pulling out on March 6, although shelling continued and the base's ammunition dump exploded again. By March 30, only a rear guard remained and Marine patrols overran two Viet Cong trench-lines. That day, the 1st Cavalry Division took control in Operation Pegasus, to the disgust of the Marines who denied they were besieged or in need of "rescue." The last shells fell on Khe Sanh on April 8, the day relief troops linked up with the Marines, but the North Vietnamese continued to exert pressure, and only in July, 1968, did the US eventually withdraw, amid much destruction. The final toll has never been fully calculated.

ABOVE: Supplies float down to the Marine defenders of embattled Khe Sanh. Airdrops such as this were almost daily occurences.

ABOVE RIGHT: US troops evacuating amid enemy gun fire. Final estimates of the human cost of the Vietnam war put deaths at two million civilians; 1.1 million North Vietnamese and Viet Cong troops; up to 250,000 South Vietnamese soldiers; 58,000 Americans; 4,000 Koreans, and 900 other Allies.

## TIMELINE

**08.07.1964**
The Gulf of Tonkin Resolution permits President Lyndon B. Johnson to do "whatever necessary" to defend Indochina.

**01.21.1968**
With many in the United States questioning commitment to the war, the North Vietnamese attack US positions at Khe Sanh, possibly to distract US troops from other targets.

## STEP-BY-STEP

**01** Many Marine officers disagree with General Westmoreland's insistence that the US position at Khe Sanh must be held.

**02** The North Vietnamese Army (PAVN) positions 20,000–30,000 troops, many reserves, around the base.

**03** On January 20, the Marines learn, from a claimed communist deserter, that the attack will begin at 00:30 the following day.

**04** It does. Bangalore torpedoes breach Hill 861's defenses, but the Marines regain control just before the main attack on the base begins.

**05** For the first time in the war, the PAVN uses heavy artillery. To avoid the seemingly constant shells, rockets, and mortars, the Marines develop a run-and-duck technique, dubbed the "Khe Sanh Shuffle."

**06** Sharing intense public concern, President Johnson has a Khe Sanh model set up in the White House.

**07** In ten weeks the US drops up to 75,000 tons (68,000 tonnes) of bombs on the PAVN, and debuts the "electronic battlefield" with sensors warning of enemy movements.

**08** Both sides claim Khe Sanh as a victory. But it is the Americans who are eventually forced to withdraw in July 1968, destroying tons of equipment.

---

**01.31.1968**
In the surprise Tet Offensive, the North Vietnamese hit more than 100 major targets, including Saigon and the former capital, Hue.

**03.10.1968**
Already deeply disturbed by Khe Sanh and the Tet Offensive, the US public is shocked when General Westmoreland requests 200,000 more troops.

**03.31.1968**
Johnson announces he is "taking the first step to de-escalate the conflict" in Vietnam.

**01.27.1973**
A ceasefire agreement is signed by all combatants.

**04.30.1973**
The last Americans to die in the conflict do so as North Vietnamese tanks roll into Saigon and the South capitulates.

# RESCUE FROM SPACE: APOLLO 13

DATE　　　April 11–17, 1970
LOCATION　200,000 miles from Earth
OBJECTIVE　To bring three US astronauts home after their spacecraft malfunctioned

Hundreds of millions of people around the world watched breathlessly as Apollo 13's textbook lunar landing mission suddenly went horribly wrong, leaving its three crewmen facing a slow death in outer space. The desperate rescue mission relied equally on scientific ingenuity and the incredible calm courage of the astronauts.

### "We've Had a Problem"

Almost 56 hours into Apollo 13's flight there was a loud bang. A warning light came on. Calmly, John L. "Jack" Swigert said, "I believe we've had a problem here." And the response followed: "This is Houston; say again, please." Commander Jim Lovell came on: "Houston, we've had a problem …" They didn't know it, but one cryogenic oxygen tank had blown up, damaging the other. With its companion cryogenic hydrogen, this oxygen fed fuel cells that generated electricity, breathing oxygen, and water.

An hour later, with just 15 minutes' worth of power left in the command module, *Odyssey*, the crew moved into the adjoining lunar module, *Aquarius*. Designed to house two men for two days, now it became a "lifeboat" for the three until further notice. Houston provided step-by-step instructions as Fred Haise and Lovell powered up *Aquarius*, while Swigert powered down *Odyssey* and transferred critical navigation information.

### A Crucial Repositioning

Apollo had started on a "free-return" course—which would slingshot it around the Moon and back to Earth—then switched to a hybrid trajectory to position it for the Moon landing. Unless they could reverse this, the crew would sail right past Earth to certain death. The only option was a "burn," using *Aquarius*'s Moon-descent engine. To great relief it worked.

*Aquarius*, running just enough power to support life, was too crowded for sleep, and *Odyssey*, at 38° F (3°C), was too cold. If water had only been needed for drinking there would have been an ample supply, but Apollo's mechanisms were water-cooled, so the crew cut back to one-fifth of their normal intake. It was vital to get them home quickly. Two hours after Apollo 13 rounded the Moon, a second burn shaved ten hours off the journey.

### Dealing with Deadly Gas

The buildup of carbon dioxide was a major concern—after a day and a half in the overloaded *Aquarius* it had risen dangerously. *Odyssey*'s canisters, which could remove it, were square and didn't fit *Aquarius*'s round slots. So Houston Mission Control devised a makeshift solution and, using cardboard procedure cards, plastic bags, and tape, Swigert and Lovell began to build it.

There was one more course-correction burn and then the final task: the unprecedented powering up of the cold *Odyssey* for reentry—unshielded *Aquarius* would simply burn up. The heat generated by reentry blacked out radio signals for three tense minutes, but 142 hours and 54 minutes after launch, Apollo 13 and its crew splashed down safely in the Pacific Ocean.

ABOVE: The "mailbox" rig constructed by the crew from duct tape, maps, and sundries on hand, as instructed by Houston. This device was used to purge carbon dioxide from the Lunar Module.

TOP: The crew of Apollo 13 on boarding the USS *Iwo Jima* following splashdown.

## TIMELINE

**05.26.1961**
President John F. Kennedy proposes the Apollo program to the US Congress. Its aim is to put an American on the Moon within nine years—and before the Soviets.

**01.27.1967**
The failure of Apollo 1, when the entire aircrew died as a result of prelaunch fire, is a major setback.

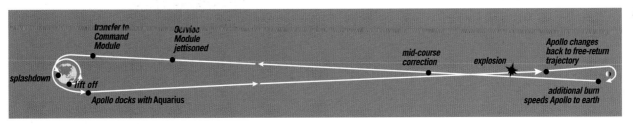

splashdown

transfer to Command Module

Odyssey Module jettisoned

lift off

Apollo docks with Aquarius

mid-course correction

explosion

Apollo changes back to free-return trajectory

additional burn speeds Apollo to earth

## STEP-BY-STEP

**01** Despite minor takeoff glitches, the Apollo 13 mission runs so smoothly that nearly 47 hours in, Houston capsule communicator Joe Kerwin jokes, "We're bored to tears down here."

**02** Nine hours later, an explosion signals a critical oxygen tank failure.

**03** An hour later Houston radios "we are starting to think about the LM [Lunar Module] lifeboat."

**04** The first major success in the rescue is transferring the inertial guidance alignment from *Odyssey* to *Aquarius*, allowing the spacecraft to identify the route home.

**05** Pope Paul VI leads a 10,000-strong congregation praying for the astronauts and, in a sign of how things have improved since the height of the Cold War, Soviet Premier Alexei Kosygin offers any assistance needed.

**06** Approaching the Earth's atmosphere, Lovell (on his fourth Apollo flight) says, "Well, I can't say that this week hasn't been filled with excitement." Houston teasingly replies, "Well, James, if you can't take any better care of the spacecraft than that, we might not give you another one."

ABOVE: While the Apollo 13 crew attempt to bring the damaged spacecraft back to Earth, six astronauts and two flight controllers monitor console activity.

RIGHT: The Apollo 13 Command Module as recovered from the Pacific Ocean on April 17.

**07.20.1969**
The Apollo 11 spaceflight successfully lands an American astronaut crew on the surface of the Moon, inaugurating a four-year burst of US lunar exploration.

**04.11.1970**
Despite problems with the cryogenic oxygen tank, at 14:13 local time, Apollo 13 launches from NASA's Kennedy Space Center, Florida.

**04.13.1970**
Apollo 13's No. 2 cryogenic tank explodes and severely damages the No. 1 tank.

**04.17.1970**
After extraordinary work by its crew and the engineers, scientists, and other specialists supporting them back on Earth, Apollo 13 splashes down in the Pacific, where USS *Iwo Jima* is waiting.

**12.19.1972**
Apollo 17 returns to Earth. It is the last manned US visit to the Moon.

# OPERATION KINGPIN: RAID ON A POW CAMP

DATE       November 20, 1970
LOCATION   Son Tay, North Vietnam
OBJECTIVE  The rescue of over 50 US POWs from a North Vietnamese camp

**From one perspective, the US operation to launch a lightning raid on a North Vietnamese POW camp in Son Tay from a base in Thailand was a great success: an example of how well extensive training and planning can pay off. From another, it was a bizarre failure: the specialist operatives sent in deep behind enemy lines found no one to rescue.**

### A Cry for Help

In early May 1970, US aerial surveillance captured proof of a long-suspected POW compound at Son Tay, 23 miles (37 km) from the North Vietnamese capital Hanoi. The Interagency Prisoner of War Intelligence Committee had been set up three years earlier and by this stage of the war there were around 450 known US POWs in North Vietnam, and almost 1,000 more Americans missing in action.

The committee found that work was being done to increase the camp's size and that it currently held 55 Americans. Photographs seemed to show the letters SAR (Search and Rescue) spelt out in prisoners' laundry at the camp and, in June, the Joint Chiefs of Staff gave approval for planning to begin on a rescue attempt.

### No-holds-barred Training

With huge numbers of North Vietnamese troops within minutes of the camp, any rescue raid would have to be short and sharp. Intensive surveillance and training, code-named "Ivory Coast," now began. The team that would conduct the raid was taken to Eglin Air Force Base in Florida and based in a secure former CIA building. They trained on a full-size mock-up of the camp—although they did not know what it was (many believed they were going to rescue plane hostages).

For three months, first by day then by night, they practiced hitting their marks when the three Sikorsky helicopters landed, and seizing captives. Very unusually, they used live ammunition. At night, a "flare ship" overhead lit the mocked-up compound. Finally, on November 18, with all insignia and uniforms banned, they were flown to Takhli Air Force Base in Thailand. Here they learned their true target and studied a highly detailed miniature made by the CIA.

### Taking No Prisoners

The next morning they flew to Udorn, Thailand, and that night the raid, Operation Kingpin, was mounted. Three specific attack helicopters had target destinations. "Greenleaf" landed in a wrong compound nearby. Meanwhile, "Blueboy" clipped a tree and crashed in the camp compound. "Redwine" landed outside, as planned, and blew a hole in the prison wall but then briefly got into a firefight with the men from "Greenleaf," having mistaken each other for the enemy.

A thorough search revealed no prisoners. Kingpin had been given the go-ahead on October 18. On October 19, the Joint Chiefs of Staff received information the POWs had been moved to another camp, but this was not passed on to the mission planners. A month later, at huge expense, a pointless and potentially very hazardous, but tremendously courageous, raid had been carried out—to no avail.

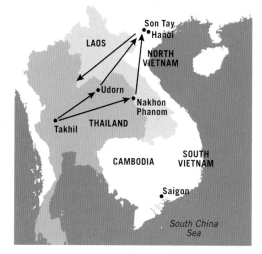

## TIMELINE

**05.1970**
Surveillance photographs reveal a North Vietnamese POW camp at Son Tay, close to Hanoi.

**05.25.1970**
A meeting is convened at the Pentagon under the codename "Polar Circle" to plan a Son Tay rescue raid.

ABOVE: The crash-landing of the lead assault helicopter "Blueboy."

LEFT: A team of 56 members from the US Army Special Forces were flown in to Son Tay in three Sikorskys: one HH-53 "Jolly Green Giant" and two HH-3 "Super Jollies."

ABOVE: Twelve thousand North Vietnamese troops were said to be stationed within 5 miles (8 km) of the targeted prison camp. The camp's proximity to the river was to play an important part in the outcome of the raid.

## STEP-BY-STEP

**01** After intensive training, three US Special Operations assault groups depart from Udorn, Thailand, for a rescue raid on Son Tay POW camp in Vietnam.

**02** The three assault helicopters are escorted by Combat Talon aircraft and pathfinders based at Nakhon Phanom. They are refueled over Laotian air space.

**03** US Naval Task Force 77 launches 57 aircraft to drop diversionary flares, battle simulators, and chaff, to confuse North Vietnamese air defenses and radar.

**04** The "Greenleaf" group mistakenly lands in a guards' base 1,500 feet (450 m) from the camp.

**05** After engaging the North Vietnamese guards, "Greenleaf" takes off and lands again next to the camp, but in the dark briefly engages in "friendly fire" with another assault group.

**06** To their confusion, the raiders find not one POW in the camp.

**07** Twenty-seven minutes after touching down, and 20 seconds ahead of schedule, "Greenleaf" and "Redwine" depart, successfully evading surface-to-air missiles.

**08** The Americans on the raid leave around 150 North Vietnamese soldiers shot dead, but suffer only two minor casualties, one a broken ankle.

**09** They later learn the POWs were moved some weeks beforehand because the camp was flooded when the nearby Song Con River broke its banks. The Viet Cong make the most of the propaganda value of the crashed "Blueboy" helicopter.

**07.13.1970**
Training and planning for the mission is approved, using Eglin Air Force Base, Florida.

**08.08.1970**
"Ivory Coast," as the planning and training is code-named, begins.

**08.19.1970**
The Joint Chiefs of Staff receive information that the Son Tay POWs have been moved. This is not passed on to Operation Kingpin planners or to the White House.

**08.20.1970**
US President Nixon approves the raid, code-named Operation Kingpin.

**10.21.1970**
Kingpin's assault teams return safe, despite the loss of "Blueboy," but empty-handed.

# THE AGE OF
# **TERROR**
# 1972–2012

Many of the events in the Age of Terror still send a shudder through those who were alive to witness them, including the 1972 Summer Olympics in Munich. There was great joy at the start of the Games, held in Germany for the first time since Adolf Hitler controlled the country. But then Palestinian terrorists took members of the Israeli team hostage. Hour after hour, the world watched in shock and disbelief as the standoff dragged on, German authorities unable to gain control of the situation. It unfolded live, right through to the tragic conclusion—the first terrorist event to be broadcast as it happened.

Hijacking was a major fear for international travelers in the 1970s. Four years after the Munich Olympics, Israelis were again targeted, along with other Jewish passengers, when an Air France jet was seized by terrorists and forced to land in Uganda, where the increasingly unhinged dictator Idi Amin was waiting. Israel had been rebuffed when it offered specialist help in Munich, now it was determined to get the hostages out safely. It did so with a daring Commando-led raid that ran almost perfectly.

That was in sharp contrast to the highly complicated plan to rescue Americans who had been seized at their embassy in Iran and held for months. The mission had already been aborted when catastrophe struck—the Commandos got nowhere near the hostages, who had to endure eight more months of captivity.

The Iranians who had seized the US hostages were supporters of the country's new leader, Ayatollah Khomeini. Those who seized hostages in Iran's embassy in London did it as a protest against Khomeini's rule. This was another dramatic siege that took place under television's unblinking eye—the footage of British Commandos from the Special Air Service abseiling in and regaining control in less than 20 minutes made the formerly secretive group famous around the world.

During the 1970s and 80s, Northern Ireland was riven by religion-fueled violence. British Prime Minister Margaret Thatcher earned her "Iron Lady" nickname with her intransigent stand on that matter and many others, including war over remote specks in the South Atlantic Ocean known as the Falkland Islands.

No one cast a larger shadow during this period than Osama bin Laden. In 1988, this immensely rich Saudi Arabian, who had become an Islamic extremist, formed the militant group al-Qaeda. Over the next decade he became more and more outspoken against the West, and the United States in particular, calling for a "holy war" and killing hundreds with attacks on American civilian and military targets. He was known to the Central Intelligence Agency and those keeping abreast of international affairs in this period, but it was al-Qaeda's unprecedented attacks on US soil on September 11, 2001 that made him feared by people throughout the world. It took ten long years, but a team of SEALs finally found him, killing him in a risky but successful raid; a surprisingly quick end for a figure who embodied such long-held dread.

# THE BATTLE OF MIRBAT: THE SAS IN OMAN

DATE      July 19, 1972
LOCATION   Mirbat, Dhofar, Sultanate of Oman
OBJECTIVE  To prevent communist-led Omani rebels seizing the town of Mirbat

**It is still a sore point for many in the British Special Air Service (SAS) that, due to the secrecy of its involvement in fighting the communist rebels who sought to control Oman in the early 1970s, some of its bravest Commandos did not receive the recognition they deserved, prime among them the beloved "Laba."**

## An Arab Uprising

In the 1950s, Oman's repressive Sultan Said bin Taimur called on long-standing supporter Great Britain to quash a rebellion. In exchange, Britain was granted air bases in the Persian Gulf state. After years of suffering, even a 1970 British-sanctioned palace coup to install Said's progressive son, Qaboos bin Said, could not stamp out insurrection. The rebels gained backing from Marxist Yemenis and the Soviet Union.

Qaboos's carrot-and-stick approach would eventually prevail, but to help it along SAS Commandos were secretly sent in.

## Death before Dawn

The small southern harbor town of Mirbat included one fort housing loyalist Dhofar Gendarmerie (DG), another housing local militia, and an SAS British Army Training Team in the mud-brick "BATT House."

On July 19, 1972 Mirbat was the target of a ferocious attack by the communist rebels Omanis called "the Adoo." Before dawn, they slit the throats of DG guards at an outpost 0.6 miles (1 km) from town, but not before one loosed a warning shot, at which the 250 Adoo—armed with rocket-propelled grenades, mortars, a 2.95-inch (75-mm) gun, and AK-47 assault rifles—began firing on Mirbat.

## Courage under Fire

Springing awake, the SAS Commandos ran to the roof, where their 0.3-inch (7.62-mm) general-purpose machine gun, 0.5-inch (12.7-mm) Browning heavy machine gun, and 3.2-inch (82-mm) mortar waited. The DG and militia had only Lee Enfield and Martini-Henry rifles, but a 25-pound (11-kg) field gun with a 3-mile (5-km) range was dug in at the DG-fort's entrance.

Being so outnumbered, the field gun was critical to the defenders, but its Omani gunner was quickly shot down. Huge Fijian-born SAS Sergeant Talaiasi Labalaba ran 1,300 feet (400 m) under heavy fire to reach the gun pit and take over. The enemy came so close Labalaba was sighting down its barrel, not stopping even when an AK-47 round hit him. His countryman Trooper Sekonaia Takavesi and Omani Walid Khamis ran under fire to Labalaba's aid, but both were badly hit. Labalaba kept firing until another, fatal, bullet hit him. Despite his blood loss, Takavesi kept firing his rifle. Amazingly, two more Commandos, Captain Mike Kealy and Tommy Tobin, reached the pit, where Tobin was mortally wounded. Finally, when all seemed lost, Takavesi's ears filled with, as he puts it, "the best sound I ever heard": Omani air force jets, strafing, and bombing the attacking Adoos. They were saved.

ABOVE: The fort at Mirbat: Nine SAS soldiers were pinned down inside the building when 250 rebels launched their assault.
ABOVE RIGHT: The view from the BATT House.

## TIMELINE

**07.23.1970**
Qaboos bin Said unseats his father as Oman's sultan, but rebellion fomented by decades of misery continues.

**1971**
In Operation Jaguar, two SAS squadrons are sent to Oman to suppress dissent both in direct action and by building "Firqat" units of disaffected rebels.

## STEP-BY-STEP

**01** Shortly after dawn on July 19, under heavy insurgent fire, Commando Pete Wignal sends an unencrypted message to HQ in Morse, "… Contact. Under heavy fire …" Very low cloud delays aerial support.

**02** Sergeant Labalaba pounds across from BATT House to the field-gun pit and begins single-handedly firing the three-man gun.

**03** His jaw shattered by an AK-47, he radios, "I've been chinned but I'm OK," and keeps firing.

**04** Sekonaia Takavesi races to the pit to help Labalaba, applies a dressing, then braves the fire again to bring Walid Khamis from the fort.

**05** Khamis is shot, then Takavesi—although he keeps firing his rifle as Labalaba uses the last of the big gun's ammunition. Reaching for a mortar, Labalaba is fatally shot.

**06** Captain Mike Kealy and Tobin reach the pit, where Tobin is mortally wounded. Kealy and Takavesi keep firing at point-blank range. A grenade lands at their feet but does not explode.

**07** Two Omani Strikemaster jets fly under the 150-feet (46-m) cloud cover, strafing and bombing the Adoo.

**08** SAS G Squadron, due to relieve Mirbat the following day, lands behind the enemy in three Bell helicopters, trapping the insurgents in retreat. An estimated 200 Adoos die.

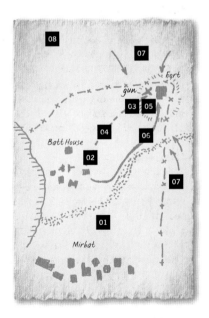

| 07.19.1972 | 10.1972 | 1975 | 11.10.2009 | 05.22.2014 |
|---|---|---|---|---|
| Nine SAS Commandos, and around 45 lightly armed Omanis, defend Mirbat against more than 250 Adoo insurgents. | After weeks critically ill in hospital in England, Commando Thomas Tobin dies of wounds received in Mirbat. | The communist insurgency is finally defeated. | A statue of Talaiasi Labalaba—the man chosen by the SAS as the soldier who epitomizes its spirit—is unveiled at the regimental HQ in Hereford, England. | Sekonaia Takavesi, who survived Mirbat and fought on in the SAS, storming the Iranian embassy in 1980 and more, publishes his memoir, *Brothers in Arms*. |

# THE MUNICH OLYMPICS: BLACK SEPTEMBER

DATE      September 5–6, 1972
LOCATION   Munich, Bavaria, West Germany
OBJECTIVE  To hold Israeli hostages to ransom to secure the release of PLO prisoners

West Germany in 1972 was all but unrecognizable from the country whose 1936 Berlin Summer Olympics had become a Nazi showcase. Determined to demonstrate the extent of the change, organizers of Munich's Games of the XX Olympiad kept security deliberately low-key, a decision that unfortunately opened the way for a terror attack that horrified the world.

### Serenity Shattered

For the first ten days, the Munich Olympics lived up to its organizers' tag: "the Serene Games." Then, at 04:30 on September 5, five men wearing tracksuits and carrying sports bags scaled the 6.5-foot (2-m) fence surrounding the Olympic Village. They were "Black September" terrorists linked to the Palestine Liberation Organization (PLO). Rendezvousing with three colleagues (believed to have entered disguised as workers), they made for the third floor of Connollystrasse 31, home to the Israeli men's team.

Rising to investigate noise in the hallway, hugely built wrestling referee Yossef Gutfreund glimpsed masked men with guns. Yelling a warning, he hurled himself against the door, buying just enough time for two of the delegation to escape and another seven to hide. Wrestling coach Moshe Weinberg knocked one intruder unconscious and stabbed another with a fruit knife. In the melee, another athlete escaped, but Weinberg was shot and killed, as was weightlifter Yossef Romano.

### The Demands Begin

At gunpoint, the terrorists rounded up the remaining nine Israeli athletes and coaches. By 05:10 police had arrived and by 06:00 news outlets began reporting trouble—the media setup for the Olympic coverage meant this became the first terrorist attack televised live. At 07:40 the terrorists demanded the release of 234 imprisoned Palestinians, two in Germany, the rest in Israel, or they would kill their hostages.

They set 09:00 as the deadline, but police negotiators secured extension after extension as they tried to develop a rescue plan. At 17:00, armed German police wearing tracksuits began an intended storming of the building. But authorities allowed media to continue broadcasting live: the terrorists watched the entire poorly planned, and soon abandoned, attempt on TV.

### "They're All Gone"

Now came a new demand: a plane to take the Palestinians and their hostages to Cairo. German authorities pretend to comply, but secretly begin a second, disastrous rescue attempt. From a heliport within the Olympic Village the group was flown at 22:30 to Fürstenfeldbruck Air Base. The Germans somehow counted only five terrorists, so five snipers were waiting—positioned in each other's cross fire, none with night-vision goggles, telescopic lenses, or walkie-talkies.

The terrorists soon realized they had been set up, and an hour later killed all nine hostages. At 03:00, US television's Jim McKay, broadcasting from Munich, broke the news to the world with the words "They're all gone."

TOP: One of the eight Palestinian terrorists stands on a balcony of the Olympic Village after they kidnapped nine members of the Israeli Olympic team and killed two others.

ABOVE: The border patrol helicopter wreck at Fürstenfeldbruck airport near Munich on September 6.

## TIMELINE

**04.26.1966**

Munich beats Detroit, Madrid, and Montreal to become host for the 1972 Summer Olympics.

**08.18.1972**

Germany's Foreign Office alerts Munich to intelligence from its Beirut embassy that Palestinians will stage "an incident" during the Games. No action is taken.

ABOVE: A PLO terrorist at the window of Israeli team accommodation, speaking with members of German negotiating delegation, led by Federal Minister of Interior Hans-Dietrich Genscher (second from left).

LEFT: Armed security forces disguised as athletes take their positions in the Olympic Village attempting a rescue that will be foiled.

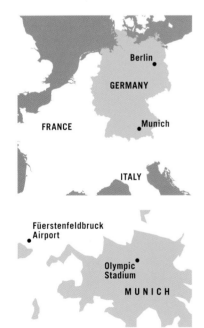

## STEP-BY-STEP

**01** As the hostage standoff develops, Israeli Prime Minister Golda Meir says Israel will never meet the terrorists' demands.

**02** While the hostage drama unfolds, athletics events continue in the stadium.

**03** Having aborted a rescue in the Olympic Village, German authorities move terrorists and hostages to a military air base. Despite providing helicopter transports, they miscount the number of terrorists.

**04** A Lufthansa Boeing 727 sits on the tarmac, fully fueled even though the Germans know the Palestinians have incendiary grenades.

**05** Bavarian police are on the plane. The plan is for them to pretend to be crew; however, just before the helicopters land they decide it is a "suicide mission," leave the plane, and stand in a nearby ditch, unwilling to act without orders.

**06** Even after the terrorists kill one of the police helicopter pilots, the Germans do not storm the field. The terrorists blow up one helicopter and its strapped-in hostages using a grenade and machine-gun the others.

**07** Only then do the German security forces respond.

**08** Eleven members of the Israeli team (six coaches, five athletes) and a German policeman are dead, along with five terrorists; three terrorists are arrested. Two months later, Germany forms a specialist counterterrorism squad, GSG 9. In October, the three imprisoned terrorists are released and flown to Libya in response to the PLO hijack of a Lufthansa passenger plane.

| 09.02.1972 | 09.05.1972 | 09.06.1972 | 09.07.1972 | 2012 |
|---|---|---|---|---|
| Italian weekly *Gente* claims Black September terrorists are planning a "sensational act" during the Games. No action is taken. | The Black September terrorists enter the Olympic Village, taking nine Israelis hostage, and killing two. Less than 24 hours later the hostages would all be dead. | During a memorial service in the Olympic Stadium for the Israelis, Olympics head Avery Brundage controversially announces the Games will continue as planned. | A Foreign Ministry official tells a special German Cabinet meeting that "incriminations" and "self-criticism" about the incident must be avoided. | In the 40th anniversary year of the Munich massacre, London Olympics organizers refuse a request for a minute's silence, despite a 100,000-signature petition. |

# THE ISRAELI RAID ON ENTEBBE

DATE     July 3–4, 1976
LOCATION   Entebbe, Central Uganda
OBJECTIVE The freeing of hostages taken in an Arab-German plane hijacking

Few people outside Africa had heard of Entebbe airport in Uganda until four years after the Munich massacre, when Israeli and other Jewish passengers from a hijacked commercial flight were taken there. For a week, Ugandan dictator Idi Amin reveled in what he saw as a demonstration of his power—then Israel mounted a bold rescue.

### The Uganda–Israel Bond

During most of the 1960s, Israel had a special relationship with the newly independent Uganda, providing economic and military advice and aid. Hundreds of Ugandans studied in Israel and some, including future president Idi Amin, undertook military training there. When he seized power, Israel was the first foreign country Amin visited. But in March 1972, after Israel refused his financial and military demands, Amin expelled all Israelis from Uganda and forged close Arab ties.

### Hijacked!

By 1976, there was a strong Palestine Liberation Organization (PLO) presence in Uganda and it was here Palestinian and German terrorists took the plane they hijacked on June 27: Air France Flight 139 from Tel Aviv to Paris. At the scheduled Athens stop, three men and a woman boarded carrying large packages. Soon after takeoff, revealing their guns, hand grenades, and dynamite, they hijacked the Airbus, with 244 passengers and 12 crew aboard.

They ordered the plane to Benghazi, Libya, for refueling, then flew on to Entebbe, 25 miles (40 km) from Uganda's capital, Kampala. Here they were joined by another three Arab terrorists and were personally greeted by Amin, who put troops at their disposal. The hostages were moved into a disused terminal building and 106 people who had Israeli passports or "seemed" Jewish were kept. The plane's crew elected to stay with them. The others were freed and flown to Paris. The terrorists demanded the release of imprisoned PLO militants—53, in various countries—or they would kill the hostages.

### Flying to the Rescue

The original deadline was July 1 but, making no progress attempting to negotiate via Amin, the Israeli government secured an extension to July 4 and firmed up rescue plans. At midnight local time on July 3, four Israeli Hercules C-130 transports approached Entebbe. In the lead plane was a Mercedes sedan and two Land Rovers—vehicles the Ugandan army used—and 29 Commandos. Following were around 100 paratroopers.

As hoped, the vehicles allowed the Commandos to get within 650 feet (200 m) of the building before being challenged. Opening fire, the Israelis stormed both floors of the terminal, quickly overcoming the terrorists and the Ugandan soldiers, although three hostages were mortally wounded in the gun battle, as was Commando leader Yonatan Netanyahu. Before reinforcements could arrive, the Israelis quickly destroyed 11 Soviet-supplied MiG jets, and loaded the transports, flying the freed hostages to safety via Kenya.

ABOVE: Entebbe airport. The planning of the raid was helped by the fact that an Israeli construction firm built the airport and the blueprints were on hand.

RIGHT: A relieved crowd lifting the squadron leader of the rescue planes upon the Commandos' return to Israel.

BELOW: Israeli soldiers returning from the raid, in the black limousine made to look like Amin's personal vehicle.

## TIMELINE

## STEP-BY-STEP

**01** Having boarded Air France 139 bound for Paris at Athens, two PLO and two German Red Army Faction terrorists force the aircraft to Benghazi, Libya, then on to Entebbe, Uganda.

**02** Neither Egyptian President Anwar Sadat nor the Israeli government can make progress with the Entebbe terrorists; a rescue is planned. It will become known as Operation Thunderbolt.

**03** Detailed information about the terminal layout, number, and position of armed guards is built up by interviewing the released hostages.

**04** At noon on July 3, four Hercules C-130 transport planes leave Sharm el-Sheikh in the Sinai Desert, crossing the Red Sea below radar level; they await the final go-ahead.

**05** After intense discussion, the Israeli government unanimously approves the mission: the message is radioed to the planes.

**06** As the lead plane approaches Entebbe with lights out, the Commandos get in the vehicles and start the engines. Ramp-lowering begins on descent, and as the plane slows they drive out.

**07** Close to the building, they use weapons with silencers to shoot the guards who challenge them. With a squad for every entrance, they then storm the building.

**08** Gunfire kills three hostages. The rest are successfully rescued and flown back to Israel. Later, British hostage Dora Bloch, 74, admitted to hospital in Kampala days earlier, is dragged from her bed and shot by Amin's men in reprisal.

**08.04.1972** Seizing their assets, Amin expels Indian and Pakistani immigrants, calling them "brown Jews."

**09.11.1972** Amin sends his infamous "Hitler telegram" to UN Secretary-General Kurt Waldheim applauding the Munich massacre. World leaders condemn Amin.

**06.27.1976** Amin offers the terrorist hijackers of the Air France airliner safe refuge in Uganda.

**04.13.1979** Fleeing invading Tanzanian forces, Amin escapes Uganda for Libya, then is offered refuge in Saudi Arabia until his death in 2003.

**03.31.2009** Operation Thunderbolt commander Yonatan Netanyahu's younger brother Benjamin becomes Prime Minister of Israel.

# THE ATTEMPTED RESCUE OF US HOSTAGES IN IRAN

DATE April 24, 1980
LOCATION Tehran, Tehran province, Iran
OBJECTIVE To free US hostages held inside the seized US embassy

Planning for a possible military rescue raid on the US embassy in the Iranian capital, Tehran, began on November 4, 1979: the day it was seized by militant students who took the 66 Americans inside hostage. But the raid launched nearly six months later became a disaster that haunted many of those involved.

### Operation Eagle Claw

US President Jimmy Carter was deeply concerned about the hostages, but was determined to try for a diplomatic solution in an attempt to keep the hostages safe and avoid further inflaming tensions in the region.

In March, the Iranians promised they would free the hostages in exchange for various public statements by Carter and an enquiry into the recently deposed Shah's regime. At the eleventh hour they reneged. Carter, who was under pressure from the US public and Congress, authorized Operation Eagle Claw.

### A Plan with Many Parts

Six C-130 Hercules transport planes—three carrying a total of 118 troops, three carrying helicopter fuel—would depart Masirah Island off Oman for a spot in the Iranian desert 200 miles (320 km) southeast of Tehran, code-named Desert One. Eight RH-53D Sikorsky helicopters would fly 600 miles (965 km) from USS *Nimitz* in the Arabian Sea to join them. The troops would transfer to the now refueled helicopters and fly to a hiding spot in the hills 65 miles (105 km) from the city. The next night local sympathizers would drive them to the embassy. They would storm it, free the hostages, be evacuated by helicopter south to Manzariyeh—a town that US Rangers would have secured—and flown from here on C-141 Starlifter transports out of the country. The operation did not even reach stage two, but still eight US troops died.

### Disaster at Desert One

The helicopters were not designed to be flown such long distances at the below-radar heights the plan demanded. Dead reckoning using night-vision goggles, the pilots encountered unexpected heavy dust storms. Two turned back with equipment problems; another limped in to Desert One but could go no further. The operational minimum was six choppers: the mission was aborted.

Two C-130s departed, but in the blinding sand one of the helicopters collided with a fuel transport. Both aircraft exploded. Eight men died and five were injured. Ammunition aboard the aircraft began to explode, peppering the helicopters with shrapnel. Troops were ordered on to the other C-130, which departed leaving the bodies in the blaze. Iranian TV triumphantly broadcast film of the wreckage.

Carter never gave up on the hostages, but their captors only released them on the January 1981 inauguration of his successor, Ronald Reagan, by which time they had spent 444 days in captivity.

ABOVE: "Dragon 2" C-130 crew just before departing for Desert One. Colonel Charles Beckwith commanded the mission's Delta Force. During the preparations he was asked by a member of the Joint Chiefs of Staff about the chances of success. He replied, "Sir, the probability of success is zero and the risks are high."

## TIMELINE

**08.1953**

A CIA-backed coup ousts Iran's elected prime minister in favor of Mohammad Reza Shah Pahlavi, a pro-Western absolutist dictator.

**01.16.1979**

A popular uprising overthrows the Shah. Religious leader Ayatollah Ruhollah Khomeini, exiled during the Shah's reign, returns to lead the country. A wave of anti-Western passion engulfs Iran.

## STEP-BY-STEP

**01** The day before the rescue mission, on a flight out of Tehran, a CIA agent happens to sit next to a Pakistani cook released from the US embassy compound, gleaning details of where precisely hostages are being held.

**02** After five months' planning and training, Operation Eagle Claw is launched.

**03** A C-130 with the advance party lands at Desert One.

**04** The chosen site is adjacent to a road. In quick succession, a bus, a small fuel truck, and a pickup truck happen along. Signaling them to stop has no effect, so the Americans open fire.

**05** The bus, with 44 passengers, pulls up; the fuel truck explodes; its driver jumps out and escapes in the pickup.

**06** The other planes arrive, but no helicopters. Radio silence is maintained.

**07** After severe dust storms and equipment failure, only six helicopters arrive, an hour late. One is unusable; although only three helicopters were strictly needed, the mission is aborted.

**08** Refueling before departure, two aircraft fatally collide and explode, killing five airmen and three Marines.

**09** Amid the conflagration, it is judged too dangerous to undertake the contingency destruction of the remaining helicopters, so they are left behind, a major propaganda coup for the Iranians.

RIGHT (from top): 1. Three RH-53D Sea Stallion helicopters lined up on the flight deck of the nuclear-powered aircraft carrier USS *Nimitz* in preparation for the mission.
2. The wreckage of an American helicopter after the aborted attempt to rescue hostages from Tehran. The helicopter collided with a refueling plane, killing eight servicemen.
3. Evacuees from the US Embassy in Tehran, Iran, are briefed upon their arrival at the air base terminal.

| 02.14.1979 | 11.04.1979 | 11.17.1979 | 04.25.1980 | 01.20.1980 |
|---|---|---|---|---|
| Militant students seize the US embassy in Tehran; the Iranian government quickly restores US control. | Angered by the US allowing the Shah in, students again seize the embassy, taking 66 hostages; in a surprise move, Khomeini supports their actions. | Khomeini releases 13 of the hostages. | The day after the rescue mission fails, the hostages are split up and moved to hidden locations. In July, one more hostage is released for medical reasons. | Two minutes into Ronald Reagan's presidency, the remaining hostages are released. |

# THE IRANIAN EMBASSY SIEGE, LONDON

DATE        April 30–May 5, 1980
LOCATION   London, UK
OBJECTIVE  To free the hostages taken by an Iranian splinter group

**Despite its members' heroism, Great Britain's Special Air Service (SAS) was a secret group largely unknown to the public. Then terrorists seized hostages in an embassy in the heart of London. After six days, SAS Commandos were sent in. The next 17 minutes brought lasting fame to the regiment and its motto, "Who Dares Wins."**

## An Embassy Under Siege

It began with Oan Ali Mohammed entering the five-story Iranian embassy in London, passing Trevor Lock, the Diplomatic Protection Group police officer assigned to the embassy, who had ducked in out of the rain for a coffee. Lock saw Oan pull a machine pistol from his bag. With no time to draw his .38 revolver, Lock rushed the gunman, pushing him over backward. Oan fired, shattering a window above the door, bringing five more heavily armed terrorists running in. At gunpoint, they made hostages of Lock and the 25 others in the building: 17 staff and eight visitors.

## Stalling for Time

Oan, who spoke English, said they represented the DRFLA—the Democratic Revolutionary Front for the Liberation of Arabistan (the Iranian province of Khuzestan). Opposed to Ayatollah Khomeini, who had taken power in Iran 15 months earlier, they demanded Khuzestan independence and the release of 91 prisoners, or they would blow up the building and its occupants.

Police negotiators soon arrived and began working around the clock, trying to achieve a peaceful resolution while international media reported live and police cordoned off crowds, including pro- and anti-Khomeini demonstrators. With the British government adamantly opposed to deals, the negotiators stalled for time. At first Oan, code-named Salim, apologized for "all the trouble" and released some hostages, but as days passed he became agitated.

## Who Dares Wins

SAS anti-terrorist Commandos had been preparing for Operation Nimrod for days, planning a range of scenarios and rehearsing. By Monday, the terrorists were extremely tense. Embassy press attaché Abbas Lavasani had clashed with them from the beginning, incensed at their insults toward Khomeini, and did so again that morning. They had been threating to shoot someone for days, and now they did so, throwing Lavasani's body out onto the steps.

At this, the use of SAS force to end the siege was authorized. In six teams they stormed in: through a roof skylight, which would be blown up to confuse the terrorists; through the rear ground floor; abseiling from the rear roof to the first- and second-story balconies and—as seen around the world—via the front first-story balconies, after blowing in the windows. Another hostage died in the cross fire, all the others were rescued; all but one of the terrorists were killed. It was all over in 17 minutes, creating an indelible image of SAS daring and prowess.

ABOVE: The SAS scramble into position outside the Iranian Embassy during the siege.

RIGHT: One hostage, BBC sound engineer Sim Harris, escapes from the Iranian Embassy across a first-floor balcony under instructions from a masked SAS trooper just after the rescue attack was launched.

## TIMELINE

**04.30.1980**

UK police officer Trevor Lock manages to hit the emergency button on his police radio as Iranian terrorists seize the embassy he is guarding.

**05.01.1980**

The terrorists release their first hostage, a female employee.

## STEP-BY-STEP

**01** According to SAS Commando Pete Winner, smoke screen generators were ready, but Prime Minister Margaret Thatcher wanted clear TV footage of the rescue raid, to deter other terrorists.

**02** A Commando abseiling down the rear swings too far, smashing a window. Not all the teams are yet in position, but the terrorists are alerted so the operation commander radios "Go! Go! Go!"

**03** Windows on the first two stories have reinforced glass; explosives must be used.

**04** A support Commando's abseiling harness becomes jammed. He is burned by curtains set on fire by stun grenades before his colleagues cut him loose.

**05** To prevent Oan firing on one Commando outside, Lock tackles him, grappling until two more Commandos enter; they shout "Trevor, move away!", and shoot Oan.

**06** Manhandling the panicked hostages down the stairs to safety, a Commando realizes one is really a terrorist, holding a grenade. At the bottom of the stairs they shoot him. The pin remains in the grenade.

**07** The hostages are handcuffed face down in the garden; there is one too many—the only surviving terrorist is quickly unmasked.

---

**05.02.1980**
They release a male BBC journalist who claims illness. He briefs the police on their weapons and setup.

**05.04.1980**
They release a Pakistani tourist and a pregnant embassy secretary.

**05.04.1980**
Finally, they release a Syrian journalist, leaving 20 hostages.

**05.05.1980**
They blindfold Abbas Lavasani, who has repeatedly remonstrated with them, tie him to a banister, and fatally shoot him.

**05.05.1980**
Following this, the SAS Commandos enter, subduing the terrorists, and freeing the hostages. The building catches fire and is gutted. It remains empty and unrestored for years.

# THE PEBBLE ISLAND RAID

**DATE**      May 14–15, 1982
**LOCATION**   Pebble Island, Falkland Islands, South Atlantic Ocean
**OBJECTIVE** To neutralize the threat to an upcoming amphibious British landing

**Although they had superior weapons, training, and experience, the British troops sailing toward an invasion of the Falkland Islands were vulnerable to air attack from their Argentinian opponents. The Pucarás ground-attack aircraft on Pebble Island were of particular concern, so a team of SAS Commandos was sent in.**

### War in a Windswept Outpost
To the British, the island group off the southern tip of South America is known as the Falklands; to Argentinians they are the Islas Malvinas. To outsiders it seems an unlikely trigger for international conflict: the two main islands and 200 smaller ones have a total population under 3,000, with just one town plus a few small settlements. The main industry is sheep farming and the rugged, windswept islands have an average annual temperature of 42 °F (5 °C).

In 1833, Great Britain claimed it as a territory; Argentina disputed this for a century and a half. Then, in April 1982, the Argentine military junta—needing a distraction from domestic unrest—broke off the seemingly interminable UN-overseen negotiations and invaded. Great Britain responded forcefully.

### Gathering Intelligence
By the end of April, more than 10,000 Argentinian troops were on the islands, most barely trained conscripts, lacking equipment, shelter, and food. Advance British units had already engaged the Argentinians on land and sea, and a fleet carrying a 28,000-strong invasion force was nearing. In preparation for its landing, units were sent to neutralize Argentinian defenses, in particular a forward air base under construction on Pebble Island.

On the night of May 11, eight SAS Commandos, complete with canoes, were landed on Keppel Island adjacent to Pebble Island. They "yomped" (as a march in full gear was known) overland, and set up an observation point. For 24 hours they kept watch over activity on Pebble Island, then canoed across to it under cover of darkness, dug in above the airstrip, and observed equipment and troop movements.

### All According to Plan
At midnight on May 14, 49 additional Commandos landed on Pebble Island. In squads, they set up mortars and machine guns covering the approach to the airfield from the tiny settlement where the bulk of the Argentine troops were. At their signal, the destroyer HMS *Glamorgan* began raining shells on the airfield's fuel and ammunition dumps. Then teams went to work on the 11 aircraft and the radar station, destroying them with plastic explosive grenades and rockets.

As their withdrawal began, the Argentinians mounted some resistance, but this petered out after the British shot the officer who seemed to be leading. Two Commandos were slightly wounded, but otherwise the raid was a textbook success.

## TIMELINE

**04.02.1982**
Argentina invades the Falkland Islands. The 85 Royal Marines garrisoned there surrender. War is never formally declared.

**04.03.1982**
Argentina ignores a UN Security Council order to withdraw troops and resume negotiations.

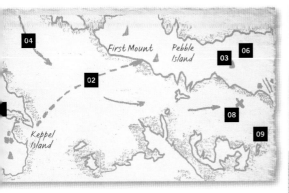

## STEP-BY-STEP

**01** Sea King helicopters from the UK Task Force flagship aircraft carrier HMS *Hermes* drop an advance SAS team on Keppel Island on May 11.

**02** They cross the island on foot. After 24 hours' observing Pebble Island, they canoe across overnight on May 13–14.

**03** From the high ground of First Mount they observe the airstrip and the settlement, where the 25 island locals and up to 150 Argentinians are based.

**04** The ships in the raid task group—*Hermes*, destroyer *Glamorgan*, and frigate *Broadsword*— approach, as a South Atlantic gale builds.

**05** To minimize helicopter flight time in the wind, *Hermes* comes within 40 miles (64 km) of the island. *Glamorgan* closes to seven miles (11 km)—adequate shelling range.

**06** The 49 Commandos helicoptered in overnight on May 14–15 include a specialist artillery spotter to direct *Glamorgan*'s fire to ammunition and fuel dumps.

**07** Teams systematically destroy the radar and 11 aircraft, including six Pucará ground-attack planes. Explosives are placed in the same spot in each plane to prevent leaving enough parts to allow a rebuild.

**08** Having neutralized the threat for the invasion to come, the Commandos depart.

ABOVE: The cruiser HMS *Glamorgan*.

TOP: The flight deck of HMS *Hermes* with eight British Aerospace Sea Harriers, and four RAF Harrier GR3s of No. 1 Squadron RAF, along with a Sea King helicopter of No. 820 Squadron, Fleet Air Arm.

| 04.05.1982 | 04.25.1982 | 05.02.1982 | 05.21.1982 | 06.14.1982 |
|---|---|---|---|---|
| A British Task Force of more than 100 ships, carrying a 28,000-strong invasion force, sets out for the Falklands. | British advance forces recapture South Georgia, another South Atlantic territory seized by Argentina. | Despite being outside the British-declared Total Exclusion Zone around the islands, the Argentinian cruiser General Belgrano is sunk, killing over 320. | After key tactical raids, including Pebble Island on May 14–15, mass British troop landings begin. | Argentina's forces surrender. During the 74-day conflict, 255 British and more than 640 Argentinian troops died, as did three islanders. |

# THE SABOTAGE OF THE
## *RAINBOW WARRIOR*

DATE    July 10, 1985
LOCATION    Waitemata Harbour, Auckland, North Island, New Zealand
OBJECTIVE    To prevent environmentalists protesting against French nuclear tests

**The explosion that ripped through the flagship vessel of environmental activist organization Greenpeace at a New Zealand mooring, with its crew aboard, was quickly identified as deliberate sabotage. This was the act of a foreign government; not a "rogue state" but the home of *Liberté*, *Egalité*, *Fraternité*.**

### Pacific Peace
By 1985, France had a two-decade history of nuclear tests in the South Pacific, centering on Mururoa Atoll in French Polynesia. The international environmental organization Greenpeace had almost as long a history protesting against them, having first sailed to the test site in 1972.

Greenpeace's British-registered flagship, *Rainbow Warrior*, had spent three days moored in the harbor of New Zealand's largest city, Auckland, preparing to lead a flotilla in a "Pacific Peace Voyage" to Mururoa to protest about the next round of French testing (by now held underground). The visit was also a marketing opportunity, and the 130-foot (40-m) refitted trawler had been open to the public. After the sightseers had gone, members of the flotilla gathered aboard to make plans and discuss how they might handle the kind of aggression that French authorities had previously shown protesters.

### Explosions in the Night
At 23:00, the visitors departed, leaving 11 crew aboard. Four, including engineer Hanne Sorenson, headed to their cabins, though Sorenson changed her mind and headed out for a walk before bed. Seven others, including Portuguese photographer Fernando Pereira, stayed up talking.

Just before midnight the ship went dark. The sound of breaking glass was followed by a dull explosive thud—some thought they had been hit by a tug. Pereira raced down to his cabin to get his expensive camera gear, then a second explosion went off, sinking the ship, and drowning Pereira.

### French Suspects
Police divers soon discovered two plastic-explosive limpet mines had been placed on the hull, one near the propeller, the other near the engine. By the following day they were hunting French suspects, following tip-offs about a couple who had hired a campervan; a man who had behaved oddly at the ship's open day; and four men on the yacht *Ouvéa*.

On July 24, Alain Mafart and Dominique Prieur, posing as Swiss honeymooners, "the Turenges," were arrested. Initial passport offences charges were upgraded to arson and murder, at first under their aliases; then their identities as French secret agents were revealed. Even after this, the French government denied its involvement—to international disbelief. Finally, on September 22, Prime Minister Laurent Fabius acknowledged it had been state-sanctioned terrorism, saying, "Agents of the DGSE [Direction Générale de la Sécurité Extérieure] sank this boat. They acted on orders." The operation had been code-named "Satanique." French Defense Minister Charles Hernu was forced to resign.

ABOVE: Dominique Prieur returning home after her imprisonment for her involvement in sinking the Greenpeace vessel.

*PACIFIC OCEAN*

Nouméa

Mururoa Atoll
Hao Atoll

Norfolk Island

**AUSTRALIA**    **Auckland**

**NEW ZEALAND**

## TIMELINE

| 04.23.1985 | 06.22.1985 |
|---|---|
| French agent Christine Cabon reaches Auckland to infiltrate the Greenpeace office. | Yacht *Ouvéa* arrives from New Caledonia carrying three French combat divers, a doctor, and supplies including explosives. |

ABOVE: The *Rainbow Warrior* sinking in Auckland harbor.

## STEP-BY-STEP

**01** On July 10, members of a Waitemata boating club find the behavior of a scuba diver in the harbor unusual enough to note the registration of the campervan in which he departs.

**02** After the initial explosion on the moored *Rainbow Warrior* a few hours later, its crew makes for safety. Fernando Pereira intends to bring his cameras with him.

**03** The second explosion sinks the ship, killing Pereira. Hanne Sorenson is initially mistakenly believed to have been another casualty.

**04** Tracing the van's registration, police arrest two agents posing as Swiss newlyweds. They wil be the only French agents to face justice for the attack.

**05** Another public tip-off leads police to a car whose occupants were observed meeting the "newlyweds"; this in turn leads to the yacht *Ouvéa*.

**06** The Australian government, presumably under pressure from France, but citing legal technicalities, refuse New Zealand police requests to detain *Ouvéa*'s crew on Norfolk Island.

**07** *Ouvéa* sets sail, purportedly for Nouméa, but never arrives. New Zealand police believe it was scuttled and the agents picked up by a waiting French submarine.

---

**07.07.1985**
In the last of staggered arrivals, the 11th known French agent reaches Auckland the same day as *Rainbow Warrior*. Three days later, *Rainbow Warrior* is mined and sunk.

**07.12.1985**
Following public tip-offs, New Zealand police question "Swiss honeymooners" when they return a rented campervan.

**16.07.1985**
Police fly to Norfolk Island to interview *Ouvéa*'s crew but lack evidence to hold them. However, bilge scrapings later test positive for explosives.

**07.26.1985**
Two days after the "Turenges" (Alain Mafart and Dominique Prieur) are charged with murder and arson, a warrant is issued for *Ouvéa*'s crew, whereabouts now unknown.

**11.22.1985**
Having pleaded guilty to manslaughter, the unmasked Mafart and Prieur are sentenced to ten years' jail; they serve a fraction of this after a deal with the French government.

# THE LOUGHGALL AMBUSH

DATE        May 8, 1987
LOCATION    Loughgall, County Armagh, Northern Ireland
OBJECTIVE   The prevention of further armed actions by known IRA members

**All the recurring elements characterizing the sectarian violence that scarred generations in Northern Ireland were to be found in the Loughgall ambush: deadly IRA terrorism, overwhelming and unhesitating British firepower, and the killing and maiming of civilians whose homeland's villages and towns had been turned into deadly battlegrounds.**

### A Wanted Man

Jim "the Executioner" Lynagh had been acquitted of one murder, but British security forces in Northern Ireland suspected him of at least two dozen others. He was a member of the Provisional Irish Republican Army, sometimes known as "the Provos," the militant wing of the group opposing the British presence in Northern Ireland, and a strident critic of efforts to reach a peaceful solution to the Irish "Troubles." Lynagh had been near the top of wanted lists for six years by the time he set out to bomb the police station in a tiny village in County Armagh in 1987.

### A Bomb-laden Excavator

Over the two previous years, the IRA had launched a number of deadly attacks on Northern Ireland police stations, including using mortars to kill nine officers in Newry, and using a mechanical excavator with a bomb in its front scoop to destroy a station in The Birches. British intelligence learned that another attack was being planned, this time in Loughgall. They set up an ambush.

Approaching the Loughgall police station at 19:15 on May 8 in an excavator and a Toyota van, Lynagh's group had no idea that 24 Special Air Service (SAS) Commandos armed with machine guns and semiautomatics lay in wait, three inside, the others hidden outside.

### The Deadly Firefight

The van pulled up and a man wearing blue workers' coveralls and a balaclava got out and began firing an assault rifle at the station. The SAS Commandos inside began firing back. At least four more men got out of the van and began firing. With the Commandos outside now also firing upon them, the attackers drove the excavator through the station's wire fence, an oil drum containing plastic explosives in its raised front scoop. The bomb exploded, collapsing the front of the building, as the firefight continued.

To avoid tipping off the IRA, the road had not been blocked off. Just as the mayhem began, a blue coverall-clad civilian, Anthony Hughes, and his brother, Oliver, started to drive into "the kill zone," then tried to reverse out. The Commandos, mistaking the brothers for terrorists, fired on the car. Anthony was killed; Oliver survived with grievous injuries, having been shot 14 times. All eight IRA attackers were also killed, in the largest single incident loss for the organization during the modern "Troubles."

## TIMELINE

## STEP-BY-STEP

**01** British intelligence services learn of an upcoming IRA attack.

**02** They know the location—Loughgall Police Station—and the date (May 8), but not the time.

**03** On May 7, three volunteer Special Branch officers in the guise of local police occupy the station, with three heavily armed SAS Commandos.

**04** The following day, undercover operatives and 21 SAS Commandos patrol Loughgall's lanes.

**05** In the early evening, they spot a blue van traveling close behind an excavator, both stolen. They recognize the tactic from the earlier attack at The Birches and radio HQ.

**06** After a reconnaissance drive-by, the IRA turn the vehicles back to the station. They open fire on the building.

**07** The Commandos open fire in response. The armed excavator crashes through the security fence to the building.

**08** The bomb explodes as the firefight continues. The Commandos kill all eight of Lynagh's men, including Lynagh, without challenging them.

**09** An innocent passing driver, Anthony Hughes, is also killed by the SAS, and his brother, Oliver, badly injured.

ABOVE: At the scene of the damaged police station on May 9, 1987. Most of the IRA gunmen killed were in the van pictured at the time of their death.

RIGHT: The eight-man IRA unit killed by the counterterrorist units following the bomb: (clockwise from top left) Declan Arthurs, 21; Seamus Donnelly, 21; Antony Gormley, 25; Eugene Kelly, 25; Patrick Kelly, 25; James Lynagh, 32; Patrick McKerney, 32; and Gerard O'Callaghan, 29.

| 1969 | 1969–1998 | 05.08.1987 | 04.10.1998 | 05.04.2001 |
|---|---|---|---|---|
| The Londonderry march is seen as the beginning of "the Troubles"—Protestant and Catholic paramilitary groups spring up and clashes occur regularly. | The violence perpetrated by the Provisional IRA, seeking the reunification of an independent Ireland, and Protestant "Loyalist" groups in the North, sees growth in extreme acts of terrorism. | Weapons are taken from the IRA dead at Loughgall. Forensic analysis links them to more than thirty other attacks. | The "Good Friday Agreement" signifies a potential end to 30 years of sectarian and political violence in Northern Ireland and on mainland Britain. | The European Court of Human Rights orders the British government to pay £10,000 to five victims' families because authorities did not effectively investigate the deaths. |

# BRAVO TWO ZERO: IRAQ

DATE        January 22–27, 1991
LOCATION    Al-Anbar Governorate, Iraq
OBJECTIVE   To identify mobile Scud missile launch sites and destroy their communications

It is surely the most publicized secret mission in military history. Eight men went into the Iraqi desert on a crucial mission; only five returned. Three of them published accounts of what happened, with conflicting details and interpretations of events. Intensive reporting by other, independent sources has helped build a clear view of this failed but daring operation.

### Hunting the Scud Launchers

Allied Gulf War commander General Norman Schwarzkopf opposed using British Special Air Service (SAS) Commandos in Iraq in the First Gulf War, preferring aerial firepower and citing the drain on resources if the SAS required rescue. Then Iraq fired Scud missiles on Israel, potentially inflaming a wider conflict.

Scuds were poor weapons but, if they were not neutralized, Israel would counterattack. Static launch sites could be easily bombed; the problem was the mobile Scud launchers, largely hidden from aerial reconnaissance. Schwarzkopf agreed to British commander General Sir Peter de la Billière's proposal to use SAS teams to hunt them. He was reassured that if the Commandos struck trouble they would handle it themselves.

### Calling into the Void

On January 22, an eight-man team identified by its radio call sign, Bravo Two Zero, landed in northwestern Iraq. The other SAS teams operating there took modified Land Rovers, but Bravo's leader, "Andy McNab," decided not to, despite the regimental sergeant major's entreaties.

At dawn, realizing they had been dropped near an enemy position in an area with virtually no cover, they radioed for help. But the wrong frequency had been supplied; they got no answer. The next day, a goatherd stumbled upon them. Compromised, they used the supposedly fail-safe satellite emergency communication system. Again, no response. Then, they say, they encountered an Iraqi army unit in an armored personnel carrier and other vehicles. Surviving the ensuing firefight, they sent a tactical beacon distress call. Again, no response.

### Death, Capture, and Torture

With communications cut, the procedure was to reach a rendezvous point, where a helicopter would meet them. It never arrived. They set out for the Syrian border 100 miles (160 km) away. In the freezing darkness they became separated into two groups, one of three men ("Chris Ryan," "Mal," and Vince Phillips) and the other of five. Resting by day, they began walking again on the snowy night of January 25. Phillips fell behind and died of hypothermia. "Mal" was captured by Iraqi troops, while "Ryan" continued the epic trek to Syria, becoming the only one to escape.

The other group hijacked a taxi and almost made it to the border. But a checkpoint confrontation erupted into a firefight in which Robert Consiglio was shot and killed. Steven Lane died of hypothermia trying to cross the Euphrates River. The remaining three, "McNab," Lance Corporal "Dinger Pring," and the shot "Mike Coburn" were captured and, with "Mal," interrogated under torture. They were freed on March 4, after the brief war ended.

ABOVE: The mobile Scud missiles lacked precision but were easily hidden from aerial attacks.

RIGHT: Desert sandstorms regularly blow across Al-Anbar Province in Iraq making aerial missions virtually impossible.

## TIMELINE

**08.1990**
Iraq invades Kuwait, provoking an "Allied" response. The war is over by March 1991.

**1992**
General Sir Peter de le Billière, "godfather of the modern SAS," publishes his first autobiography *Storm Command*, incorporating changes requested by the Ministry of Defence (MoD).

## STEP-BY-STEP

**01** The eight-man Bravo Two Zero team parachute into the Iraqi desert late on Tuesday, January 22. They begin observation tactics.

**02** Discovered by a local goatherd on Thursday, they send a satellite message: "Compromised, request immediate extraction."

**03** They get no response, although a subsequent documentary reports that the SAS "Gulf-daily" log for January 24 records the request for extraction.

**04** With no help forthcoming, they strike out across the freezing desert by night.

**05** They inadvertently separate into two groups. In one group, the Commando Vince Phillips dies of hypothermia. "Mal" is captured. "Ryan" evades capture in the desert.

**06** In the other group, there is disagreement: some, including "Coburn," want to trek cross-country to avoid detection but "McNab," the leader, disagrees, believing they need a car.

**07** They seize a taxi, driving it toward the Syrian border. Stopped at a roadblock, they try to shoot their way out; one Commando, Consiglio, is killed. Another, Steven Lane, dies of hypothermia. The rest are captured.

**08** Rescue helicopters set out late on Saturday January 27, but do not find the men.

**09** The mission ends with three dead and four captured—all later released. Only "Ryan" escapes to Syria, cross-country.

SYRIA

Al-Anbar

IRAQ

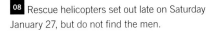

**1993**
"Andy McNab" (a pseudonym in keeping with SAS secrecy; real name since revealed as Steven Mitchell) publishes *Bravo Two Zero.*

**1995**
"Chris Ryan" (Colin Armstrong) publishes *The One That Got Away.*

**1996**
The UK Defence Council reveals a new contract imposing a lifetime gag on serving and future SAS members, preventing them writing or talking about their service.

**2002**
Historian, explorer, and Arab specialist Michael Asher publishes *The Real Bravo Two Zero*, having found no record of a firefight. In 2003, the Second Iraq War breaks out.

**2004**
After a five-year legal struggle with the MoD, "Mike Coburn" publishes *Soldier Five: The Real Truth about the Bravo Two Zero Mission.*

# BLACK HAWK DOWN

DATE        October 3–4, 1993
LOCATION    Mogadishu, Benadir, Somalia
OBJECTIVE   To capture the Somali warlord Mohamed Farrah Aidid and his key lieutenants

**US troops were welcomed when they entered Somalia in 1992 to assist United Nations' humanitarian relief, named Operation Restore Hope, but they soon found themselves in conflict with warlord Mohamed Farrah Aidid. In October 1993, a planned 90-minute mission to arrest Aidid and his close lieutenants became a horrific 17-hour ordeal in a city-turned-war-zone.**

### The First Black Hawk Down

At 15:30 on October 3, a 115-strong US air-and-ground force under US command left its Mogadishu base to arrest members of Mohamed Farrah Aidid's Somalia National Alliance (SNA), meeting at the nearby Olympic Hotel. Quickly reaching the site, Rangers fast-roped down from Little Bird and Black Hawk helicopters and secured the area, under fire. As Delta Special Forces operatives brought 24 SNA members (but not Aidid) out of the building to the waiting convoy, Black Hawk "Super 6-1," circling overhead, was hit by a rocket-propelled grenade (RPG). It crashed in an alley three blocks away.

The two pilots died on impact, wreckage trapping one. A Little Bird managed to evacuate two of the wounded; other crash survivors took up defensive positions as armed Somalis flooded in. A six-man Ranger team arrived on foot, then a 15-man Combat Search and Rescue team in a Black Hawk—as they roped down, their helicopter was hit, forcing it to return to base.

### Besieged by Murderous Mobs

Two more Black Hawks were hit; one crashed less than one mile (1.6 km) away. Co-pilot Mike Durrant was badly beaten and seized by a Somali mob who brutally killed the others aboard and the two snipers guarding them. Then they shocked the world by dragging the bodies through the streets.

At the first crash site, the besieged US troops took shelter in nearby buildings, trying to keep the mob there off the downed helicopter. As evening fell, water and ammunition were dropped in from a Black Hawk, which withdrew after being hit.

### An Agonizing Rescue

The drive from base to hotel had taken just nine minutes, but the streets were now a battleground; the convoy spent hours under constant fire ramming barricades of burning tires, unsuccessfully trying to reach the first crash site. Suffering mass casualties and two trucks down, it was ordered back to base. Two other rescue parties were also forced back.

Finally, at 01:55, a relief column including Pakistani and Malaysian troops in armored personnel carriers, supported by gunships overhead, reached the besieged soldiers. By 05:40 they had freed the trapped pilot's body and headed out, but the vehicles were so full of wounded and dead that more than two dozen troops were left to run alongside, under fire. They finally reached safety at 06:30. Eighteen Americans and two Malaysians were killed in the battle, and 88 soldiers wounded. The Red Cross estimated 1,000 Somalis died.

SOMALIA

• Mogadishu

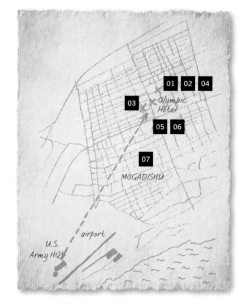

## TIMELINE

**01.1991**
Despotic Somali leader Mohamed Siad Barre is overthrown; subsequent clan violence brings the country to its knees.

**04.24.1992**
The UN authorizes humanitarian relief operations in Somalia.

## STEP-BY-STEP

**01** After a successful raid on the Olympic Hotel, a Black Hawk "Super 6-1" helicopter is hit by an RPG, sending it into a crash that kills both pilots.

**02** A Little Bird helicopter reaches the crash site, rotors almost brushing the walls. Its two pilots rescue two casualties while returning fire from the gathering mob.

**03** Armed Somalis attack US troops at the crash site, the hotel, on the city's streets, and in the air.

**04** Rangers, a CSAR team, and then, on foot, the remaining assault and blocking forces from the hotel, arrive at the first crash site. Around 90 US troops take shelter in an unrelenting firefight.

**05** A second Black Hawk is brought down. Snipers Gary Gordon and Randall Shughart are providing aerial cover. With ground forces unable to get through, they repeatedly ask to be dropped to the crash site.

**06** They give up their own lives but save pilot Michael Durant.

**07** Ten hours after the crash, the relief column reaches the first crash site. It takes hours more to free the pilot's body, but the Ranger code is no man left behind, dead or alive.

**ABOVE RIGHT: A US Marine Corps helicopter surveying a residential area in Mogadishu for any hostilities as part of Operation Restore Hope.**

**RIGHT: The wreckage of a jeep burning after it was destroyed by a remote-controlled bomb on October 3, 1993.**

| 12.08.1992 | 06.05.1993 | 06.17.1993 | 07.12.1993 | 09.25.1993 |
|---|---|---|---|---|
| The US steps up its involvement, deploying troops to Somalia in Operation Restore Hope. | The Somalia National Alliance (SNA) forces ambush UN Pakistani soldiers, killing 24 and wounding 44. | Somalia's UN envoy issues an arrest warrant for SNA head Mohamed Farrah Aidid. | US helicopter gunships attack an Aidid compound. A mob nearby kills four Western journalists and displays their bodies. | The SNA brings down a US Black Hawk with an RPG, killing three soldiers. |

# THE 9/11 ATTACKS

DATE      September 11, 2001
LOCATION  New York, Washington, and Pennsylvania, United States
OBJECTIVE To cause maximum fear, death, and destruction

**No one who saw the 9/11 terror attacks unfold will ever forget them. Even for people watching TV on the other side of the world, the horror was visceral. Death and destruction on this scale was unprecedented, and it was covered live as it happened, in locations familiar to millions around the globe.**

### The Work of al-Qaeda

The world had known previous large-scale terror acts—on a single day in 1990, for instance, Tamil militants killed more than 770 unarmed Sri Lankan police—but none were as public or devastating as the 9/11 attacks.

They were the work of radical self-proclaimed Islamist group al-Qaeda, led by Osama bin Laden. The mastermind was Khalid Sheikh Mohammed, uncle to Ramzi Yousef, who planned the unsuccessful 1993 bombing of the New York World Trade Center (WTC) with, as the FBI learned, the intention of causing its twin towers to collapse.

### Planes as Weapons

For their weapons, the 19 suicide terrorists chose commercial passenger planes. In groups they boarded flights at four different airports, taking box cutters and other concealed weapons through security checks. Eight were randomly chosen for extra screening and two were flagged as suspicious by a gate agent, but all were cleared to proceed.

Twenty minutes after takeoff, two of the flight attendants on American Airlines Flight 11 from Boston to Los Angeles contacted the airline to report two flight crew had been stabbed. "I think we're getting hijacked," said Betty Ong. Twenty-seven minutes later the plane flew into floors 93 to 99 of the WTC's North Tower, killing all aboard and hundreds in the building. The Fire Department of New York and the city's police department (NYPD) started dispatching help within seconds. Seventeen minutes later, at 09:03, United Airlines 175 smashed into the South Tower between floors 77 and 85, also killing all aboard and hundreds in the WTC.

### More Deadly Crashes

At 09:12, two people aboard American Airlines Flight 77 from Virginia to Los Angeles called loved ones saying their plane had been hijacked. At 09:36, US Vice President Dick Cheney was taken by Secret Service agents to a bunker under the White House (President George W. Bush was in Florida), and one minute later Flight 77 smashed into the nearby Pentagon, killing all aboard and 125 people in the building.

Just as WTC's South Tower was collapsing, killing 600 workers and rescue personnel, passengers from United's Flight 93—now 20 minutes from Washington—called their loved ones and learned their hijackers were terrorists. It is believed the passengers decided to try to seize the plane back; to prevent this, the hijackers crashed into a Pennsylvania field killing all aboard. Twenty-five minutes later, the North Tower collapsed, killing another 1,400 people. In all, it is believed 2,977 were killed in the attacks.

BELOW: Both of the World Trade Center's towers collapsed after being hit by the hijacked commercial passenger planes.

## TIMELINE

**04.19.1995**

American anti-government extremists blow up a building in Oklahoma City, killing 168 and injuring hundreds in the worst terrorist attack on American soil until 2001.

**03.20.1993**

US and UK commitment to the Second Iraq War provokes widespread criticism, especially in the Islamic world.

## STEP-BY-STEP

**01** Between 05:45 and 07:15, terrorists board commercial flights in Portland, Maine; Boston, Massachusetts; Newark, New Jersey; and Dulles, Virginia. Information provided by flight attendants on Flight 11, including the hijackers' seat numbers, is invaluable in the subsequent investigation.

**02** Trying to make a cabin announcement, Flight 11 hijacker Mohamed Atta inadvertently calls air traffic control, saying, "We have some planes …"

**03** Hearing this, an air traffic controller alerts the military wing of the airspace protection unit, the Northeast Air Defense Sector (NEADS), which dispatches jets to find and tail Flight 11.

**04** Evacuation of the WTC North Tower begins as soon as it is hit. WTC South Tower occupants are initially told to remain, then four minutes later, at 08:59, its evacuation begins.

**05** An estimated 10,000–14,000 people are leaving the WTC buildings when the second plane hits. As they evacuate, hundreds of emergency workers enter the buildings.

**06** As well as those killed in the Pentagon attack, 106 are severely injured by fire.

**07** At 17:20, WTC Building 7 collapses.

**08** The following afternoon, the final WTC survivor is rescued.

RIGHT: Emergency personnel outside one of the World Trade Center's towers.
BELOW RIGHT: One of the towers mid-destruction.
BELOW: Emergency crews respond to the destruction caused to the Pentagon by the jetliner that crashed into its southwest corner.

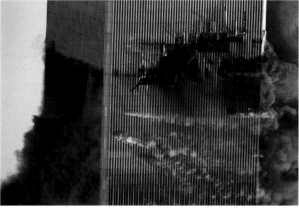

| **09.11.2001** | **09.20.2001** | **10.07.2001** | **03.01.2003** | **2006** |
|---|---|---|---|---|
| Al-Qaeda terror attacks in the US kill almost 3,000 people. | US President George W. Bush says, "Any nation that continues to harbor or support terrorism will be regarded by the United States as a hostile regime," launching the "War on Terror." | Bush launches "Operation Enduring Freedom," more commonly known as the Afghanistan War. | Confessed 9/11s mastermind, Khalid Sheikh Mohammed, is captured in Pakistan; he also claims responsibility for the 2002 murder of US journalist Daniel Pearl. | Khalid Sheikh Mohammed is moved to Guantanamo Bay, where he remains in 2014, awaiting trial. |

# THE KAMCHATKA SUBMARINE RESCUE

DATE      **August 4–7, 2005**
LOCATION  **Bering Sea, off the Kamchatka Peninsula, Russian Federation**
OBJECTIVE **Freeing seven Russian submariners trapped deep in the ocean**

**The post-Soviet decline of Russia's navy continued unchecked in the years after the *Kursk* disaster in 2000, but the next time its submariners became trapped the response was very different. Eager to avoid another public relations disaster, it sought help from anyone who could provide it. British and American teams raced to get there in time.**

### Avoiding a Second *Kursk*

In August 2000, explosions aboard sent the Russian nuclear submarine *Kursk* 355 feet (108 m) down to the Barents Sea floor. At least 23 of the 118 crew survived the explosions, tapping out signals to the rescuers they expected. Officials repeatedly intimated that release was imminent but, in reality, Russia lacked rescue capability, and refused international offers of help, allowing the survivors to slowly die on the sea floor. In 2003, another Russian submarine was lost in the Barents Sea.

By the time the Priz-class submarine *AS-28* was lowered from support ship *Georgy Kozmin* on Thursday, August 4, 2005, attitudes had shifted. *AS-28* was a 44-feet (13.4-m) deepwater rescue vessel, designed for a crew of four plus up to 20 rescued submariners. Within two hours of its launch it was in trouble, tangled on something 620 feet (190 m) below the surface. By Friday, its own efforts having failed, Russia sent out an international rescue call.

### Cold, Dark, and Trapped

Fully stocked with oxygen, food, and drinking water, the *AS-28* could theoretically stay submerged for five days. But it was far from fully stocked. When they sent their distress signal, the seven crew had just 7.4 pints (3.5 L) of water, two packets of crackers, and only 72 hours' worth of oxygen.

They wrote letters to their loved ones, put on thermal suits, and switched to minimum power use. To preserve heat they lay in a row, the outer two men moving into the middle every two hours. They allowed themselves a cracker and a sip of water every eight hours.

### Scorpio to the Rescue

On the surface, Russian officials gave out strangely mixed messages: the submarine's propeller was trapped on a fishing net; no, it was a military antenna cable; it had gone down on a training mission; no, it was attempting cable maintenance. Regardless, British and US rescue teams were on their way.

The British were first on scene, reaching Petropavlovsk, Kamchatka, on the evening of Saturday, August 6. Doggedly overcoming challenges posed by outdated Russian equipment and local bureaucracy, they finally reached the site with their Scorpio Remotely Operated Vehicle (ROV) and made contact with AS-28 at noon on Sunday, 67 hours after it had become trapped. Persisting through yet more equipment challenges, they had all seven of the submariners safely out by 16:30—just in time.

**ABOVE: The Scorpio Remotely Operated Vehicle is loaded into a C-5A Galaxy aircraft at San Diego, California, as part of the mission to rescue the trapped sailors.**

## TIMELINE

**08.12.2000**

Underwater monitoring picks up two explosions aboard Russian nuclear submarine *Kursk*, which sinks to the Barents Sea floor.

**08.13.2000**

*Kursk* survivors are heard knocking on the hull. Russia refuses British and US offers of help. Soon, no more knocking is heard.

## STEP-BY-STEP

**01** *AS-28* becomes entangled. The second rescue submarine that should have been on its support ship cannot help—it is ashore for repairs.

**02** Russian surface attempts to hook *AS-28* and drag it free fail.

**03** US and British teams set out, the Britons arriving first after an 11-hour flight. Local plane-unloading machinery is inadequate but a specially equipped USAF C-5 Galaxy has arrived from Yokota, Japan.

**04** The ship waiting at the port is so decrepit they decide, for safety, they must find scrap steel and weld on a platform for the Scorpio's crane. The captain upholds regulations, decreeing only one of the four welders may work at a time.

**05** After a six-hour voyage, the international force reaches *AS-28*. Operators on the surface guide the Scorpio as it cuts through each of four entanglements. The submarine moves slightly, damaging the Scorpio's claw.

**06** The Scorpio is brought to the surface, repaired, and redeployed, cutting the final obstruction. Rescuers signal *AS-28* to blow the ballast tanks. Finally it rises.

**07** The submariners are free.

**ABOVE LEFT:** Russian sailors evacuate *AS-28* after surfacing in the Bering Sea.
**LEFT:** The control center for the US Navy's Deep Submergence Unit Scorpio is loaded onto a Russian ship..

| 08.16.2000 | 10.09.2001 | 08.30.2003 | 08.04.2005 | 08.05.2005 |
|---|---|---|---|---|
| Russia formally requests help from Great Britain and Norway, but by August 21 the Russian navy announces all 118 *Kursk* crew are dead. | The remains of the *Kursk* and its crew are finally brought to the surface. | Russian defense officials blame carelessness for the sinking of the *K-159* nuclear submarine in the Barents Sea, killing nine. | Ironically, a newly developed Russian rescue submarine *AS-28* runs into trouble soon after launching in the Bering Sea. | Russia calls for international help to rescue trapped submariners on *AS-28* off remote Kamchatka. Great Britain and the US immediately respond. |

# THE RESCUE OF AUSTRALIAN MINERS

DATE      April 25–May 9, 2006
LOCATION      Beaconsfield, Tasmania, Australia
OBJECTIVE      The extrication of two miners from a tiny cage deep underground

At 21:23 on Tuesday, April 25, 2006, 17 men were working a public holiday night shift in the Beaconsfield Gold Mine in northeastern Tasmania when a 2.3 seismic event occurred, causing a heavy rockfall. Fourteen sheltered in the mine until the danger passed, then reached the safety of the surface, but three could not be found.

### Trapped Deep Underground

Larry Knight, Todd Russell, and Brant Webb were 3,035 feet (925 m) down, using a machine called a telehandler (in essence, a cross between a crane and a forklift) to install retaining mesh for a newly built bund wall. Knight was driving the telehandler, with Russell and Webb standing in an open metal cage at its front, attaching cable to the wall.

Knight had left the machine to get more mesh when two rockfalls hit. An 880-ton (800-tonne) rockfall crushed the telehandler, but encased the 3.9 x 4.2 foot (1.2 x 1.3 m) metal cage that kept Russell and Webb alive. Unbeknownst to them, a 132-ton (120-tonne) fall killed Knight. Another, smaller one, blocked the access drive.

### "Hello?"

By 16.45 on Wednesday, a camera-equipped, remote-control earthmover was clearing the rockfall blocking the drive. At 07:23 on Thursday, searchers found Knight's body in the next rockfall. On Friday, tunneling began through the largest fall. Meanwhile, the trapped pair collected seeping water from the rocks in their helmets and eked out a single muesli bar between them.

At 17:40 on Sunday, five days after the collapse, the underground manager and foreman approached the blocked area and, hoping against hope, called out, "Hello?" Two "hellos!" came back. Rescuers estimated it would take at least 48 hours to drill a hole large enough to get them out.

### Out—Safe

In fact, it took a week, because of the instability of the rock and its denseness: five times harder than concrete. On Monday a 3.5-inch (90-mm) hole was drilled through, and water, liquid food, "space blankets," and glow-sticks were passed along a pipe to the men. Fear of further collapse saw the drilling attempt abandoned; a specialized "raisebore" machine to pulverize the rock was located. A camera was sent through the pipe; seeing the images, rescuers ruled out overhead and side tunnels as too dangerous. They would tunnel upward, then briefly across.

At 04:27 on the 14th day, they finally broke through. Both men were freed within half an hour. Although both had some bone damage, they walked out of the mine at 06:00, receiving huge cheers as they symbolically moved their ID tags from the red "In U/Ground" side of the shift board to green "Out–Safe."

ABOVE: Tasmanian miner Todd Russell hugs his son Liam, 5, after being rescued the Beaconsfield gold mine, early 09 May 2006, in Beaconsfield, Australia.

## TIMELINE

| 06.27.2003 | 04.18.2005 |
|---|---|
| A memo from Beaconsfield Gold Mine Underground Manager Pat Ball notes increased seismic activity, which will "eventually" lead to rockfalls. | A consultant engineer employed by the mine advises management that seismic activity is a definite "cause for alarm." |

## STEP-BY-STEP

**01** Protected by the steel cage they were working in, miners Todd Russell and Brant Webb survive under a large rockfall. Larry Knight is killed.

**02** Five days later, after discovering the men, rescuers get a small microphone into position. With typical Australian bluntness, Russell's first words are: "It's ****ing cold and cramped in here. Get us out!"

**03** The miner's colleagues voluntarily work 12-hour shifts in a desperate effort to release them.

**04** On the eighth day, drilling is abandoned for fear of triggering another collapse.

**05** Instead, a large, low-vibration raisebore machine is brought in. It pulverizes the rock to powder as it goes. Chemicals are used to make the rock surface more brittle.

**06** To keep it true on its path tunneling horizontally under the rockfall, the raisebore must be fixed to a base; eight truckloads of concrete are needed to create this.

**07** The last section is the riskiest in terms of another rockfall. It is tackled with hand drills, jackhammers, and low-impact explosives until finally the two trapped men are free.

3,035 feet (925 m)

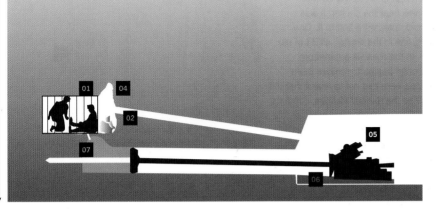

**ABOVE:** Todd Russell (left) and Brant Webb (right) wave as they emerge from the Beaconsfield mine after 14 days trapped underground.

**ABOVE LEFT:** Rescuers go to work to save the two trapped Australian miners.

**05.25.2005**
The consultant notes that "larger events are getting more frequent and worrying."

**04.25.2006**
A seismic event causes the mine to collapse, trapping three men.

**05.09.2006**
Brant Webb and Todd Russell are freed two weeks after being trapped by a collapse in the mine that killed Larry Knight.

**02.26.2009**
The coroner investigating the circumstances of Knight's death finds the seismic activity was not an act of nature, but was caused by mining.

**2012**
Having reopened in 2007, the mine ceases operations.

# THE RESCUE OF CHILEAN MINERS

**DATE**    August 5–October 13, 2010
**LOCATION**    Mina San José (San José Mine), near Copiapó, Atacama, Chile
**OBJECTIVE**    The odds-defying rescue of 33 men trapped deep beneath the Earth's surface

On August 5, 2010, a massive rock collapse destroyed a 300-feet (100-m) deep section of the San José gold and copper mine in Chile's remote Atacama Desert. No one yet knew it, but below the collapsed section 33 miners were alive. The intense 69-day effort to save them, covered by worldwide media, was unprecedented, as was the outcome.

### First Attempts Foiled

Soon after the collapse, with the earth still shifting and groaning, a search party descended the spiral access ramp that corkscrewed 2,360 feet (720 m) down the mine. At 1,300 feet (400 m) they stopped: 772,000 tons (700,000 tonnes) of rock had blocked access to everything below.

The mine's special operations emergency squad fared no better. Chile's government called in expertise from its own mining company. As miners' relatives, colleagues, and media gathered on the surface, the experts tried for days to stabilize the mine enough to push through from the ramp, before being forced to change tactics.

### Los 33

Given the miners' limited food and air, hope for any survivors of the collapse was almost gone. A refuge shelter 2,300 feet (700 m) down offered one faint chance. Nine drilling rigs began trying to cut six-inch (15-cm) shafts to it. The combination of rock density and high-speed drilling made the required accuracy almost impossible. But on day 17, a drill broke into a tunnel near the shelter. It was turned off, and lowered. When it was pulled up two notes were tied to it. One said: "*Estamos bien en el refugio los 33*" (We are fine in the shelter, all 33 of us).

The news brought euphoria, as did contact with the men via a miniature camera and telephone cable. Then the real challenge began: to remove them safely, and to keep them alive; those on the surface were told not to reveal that this may take three months. Three of the shafts became the miners' lifelines, conduits for the provision-packed hollow pipes dubbed *palomas* (carrier pigeons).

### The Ordeal Ends

The first of what would be three separate attempts to drill a narrow pilot hole leading to the men, then widen it to fit an adult-sized cage—the "Fénix" (Phoenix) capsule—in order to extricate them one by one, began on day 26. On day 43 the pilot hole reached them, but it would be 25 long days before the rescue could begin.

After the hole was widened, the top section was reinforced with welded tubing and a winch-and-pulley installed and tested. At 23:18 on day 68, the capsule began its descent; 53 minutes later the first miner, Florencio Avalos, reached the surface. At 21:56 on day 69 the final trapped miner, shift leader Luis Urzúa, whose careful planning kept the men alive, emerged, to jubilation.

ABOVE: Diagram of the "Fénix" (Phoenix) class rescue capsule. 1. Television monitor. 2. Stabilization wheels. 3. Winch. 4. Hollow rescue capsule.

## TIMELINE

**08.05.2010**

A mine collapse traps 33 men deep underground. As well as a small shelter, they have access to 0.5 mile (800 m) of clear adjoining tunnels.

**08.07.2010**

Two days after the first collapse, a second wipes out sections of the mine's interconnecting ventilation shafts. Only two weeks later do anxious rescuers learn that the trapped miners are still alive.

ABOVE: Manuel González, the first rescuer, prepares to descend into the San José Mine.
RIGHT: The drilling tower of the so-called special drill "Schramm T-130" in action during rescue operations.

SOUTH AMERICA

PACIFIC OCEAN

● Mina San José

Santiago ●

CHILE

ATLANTIC OCEAN

## STEP-BY-STEP

**01** In the mine shelter, Luis Urzúa rations two days' emergency supplies: little more than a spoonful of tuna and a sip of increasingly rancid milk every second day.

**02** The rescuers receive two notes written by Mario Gómez, one for his wife, the other saying *los 33* have survived.

**03** Communications and a supply system are established. NASA advises on diet; too speedy a reintroduction to solid food could be fatal.

**04** Drilling requires plentiful water; the Atacama Desert is one of the driest places on Earth. Water tankers roll in.

**05** Medicines counter bacterial, fungal, and viral conditions that the men are at risk of contracting.

**06** With the first attempt to drill a rescue shaft (Plan A) estimated to take three months, a more powerful drill starts (Plan B). It cuts through 879 feet (268 m) in just three days, but then fails.

**07** A huge oil-platform drill (Plan C) joins the effort, but the first and second drills are repaired at last. It is the second (Plan B) that finally breaks through, allowing a single-person capsule pulley to be installed, which begins to bring the trapped miners to the surface.

| 08.31.2010 | 09.05.2010 | 09.19.2010 | 09.24.2010 | 10.13.2010 |
|---|---|---|---|---|
| The first drill (Plan A) begins work on a vital pilot hole. | A faster and larger drill (Plan B) fails. | As the damaged but repaired Plan B drill begins widening the rescue shaft, the massive Plan C drill begins. | Day 50: a new record for survival trapped underground. On day 68 a rescue capsule begins to lift the miners one by one to the surface. | The last miner is brought to the surface safely. |

# TARGET: OSAMA BIN LADEN

DATE      May 2, 2011
LOCATION  Abbottabad, Hazara, Pakistan
OBJECTIVE To kill or capture the man responsible for deadly terror attacks

In 1996, the CIA set up a unit code-named "Alec Station" to hunt Islamic militant Osama bin Laden, who had called for a "holy war" against the United States. After al-Qaeda's 9/11 attacks, the agency threw itself at the hunt, but it would be a decade before they had—almost certainly—found him.

### Degrees of Certainty

The CIA went into overdrive, but year after year passed with analysts intercepting calls and e-mails, and studying satellite images, television broadcasts (of videos, often from caves in what was thought to be Afghanistan), and interrogation records. By early 2011, they believed bin Laden was holed up with his family in a compound in Abbottabad, close to the Pakistani capital, Islamabad.

On April 28, US President Barack Obama and his most senior advisers considered a raid on the compound, which the CIA was now "60% to 80% sure" housed bin Laden. Secretary of State, Hillary Clinton, and CIA Director, Leon Panetta, argued for it; Vice President, Joe Biden, against. Obama slept on it— Pakistan was an uneasy US ally; this raid would violate its sovereignty. The next morning he authorized the mission: Operation Neptune's Spear.

### The Stealth Mission

On the moonless night of May 1, two stealth Black Hawk helicopters took off from Jalalabad, in US-occupied Afghanistan, carrying 23 Navy SEALs, a CIA interpreter, and combat dog, Cairo. Fifteen minutes into the 90-minute flight to Abbottabad they crossed into Pakistan where they flew "nap of the earth": low-level, just above the jagged terrain.

A second, backup team of SEALs in two large Chinook helicopters flew to Swat, 50 miles (80 km) from Abbottabad, while an extra Chinook waited just inside the Afghan border. In the White House Situation Room, Obama and senior advisers watched grainy video from a drone above the compound and listened to the audio feed.

### "We got him."

Trying to hover over the compound to allow the SEALs to fast-rope down, the first helicopter began to crash. The pilot protected his team by putting it down nose-first, but the element of surprise was gone. Three SEALs ran to a stand-alone building where they killed bin Laden's courier, Abu Ahmed al-Kuwaiti. Their colleagues opened the compound gate letting in the second helicopter's SEALs. Inside the main building the Commandos killed al-Kuwaiti's brother and his wife, and bin Laden's son Khaled, 23, before reaching bin Laden and his youngest wife, Amal, 28, on the top floor.

The feared terrorist stood behind Amal, hands on her shoulders. Shot in the calf, she fell, leaving a clear target. Bin Laden was killed before he could reach for his nearby weapons. As the SEALs radioed this news to Jalalabad, Obama said quietly, "We got him. We got him."

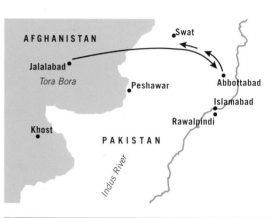

ABOVE: A US Army Chinook helicopter offloads Coalition Forces soldiers at a landing zone in the Tora Bora region in Afghanistan during Operation Torii. Torii forces consisted of over 400 members from the US Military, Royal Canadian Army, and Afghanistan Military Forces, whose mission is to gather intelligence, exploit, and deny entrance to four underground sites, while looking for Osama bin Laden.

## TIMELINE

**1957**
Osama bin Laden is born in Saudi Arabia, one of 50 children of a self-made billionaire. He enjoys many visits to Western countries as a youth.

**1988**
Bin Laden forms jihadist militant group al-Qaeda ("the Base"). Exploiting modern technology, and encouraging suicide strategies, his movement emerges from the Russia/Afghan war.

ABOVE: US President Barack Obama and Vice President Joe Biden, along with members of the national security team—in the White House's Situation Room on May 1, 2011—receive an update on Operation Neptune's Spear, via live feed from drones operating over the bin Laden complex.

LEFT: Osama bin Laden's compound in Abbottabad being demolished, February 26, 2012.

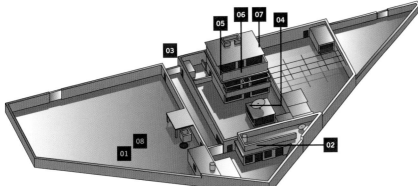

## STEP-BY-STEP

**01** When the first helicopter crash-lands in bin Laden's compound, the backup Chinooks set off for Abbottabad.

**02** In a guesthouse, the SEALs kill bin Laden's trusted courier Abu Ahmed al-Kuwaiti.

**03** The dog Cairo and translator "Ahmed" remain outside the compound, sending away curious locals.

**04** At the entrance to the main house, al-Kuwaiti's brother Abrar steps out with an AK-47. He and his wife are shot and killed.

**05** It is completely dark in the house, but the Commandos have night-vision scopes. They clear ground floor rooms one by one, continually expecting booby traps. Women and children are grouped together.

**06** Blasting apart a metal gate, they climb to the upper floors. Khaled bin Laden emerges with an AK-47 but cannot see the intruders. The SEALs' point man whispers, "Khaled, come here …" in Arabic. Stepping out, Khaled is shot and killed. The SEALs then approach the final bedroom.

**07** Bin Laden almost seems to accept that he is, finally, cornered. He offers some resistance, but is shot dead.

**08** The SEALs then blow up the crashed helicopter, gather computers, mobile phones, and USB drives, and depart, with bin Laden's body, in the remaining Black Hawk and a Chinook. In all, they spent 38 minutes in the compound.

**09** After positive identification, bin Laden's body is buried at sea and his compound is later destroyed to prevent any attempts at a shrine for the master terrorist.

| 1994 | 08.07.1998 | 09.11.2001 | 12.2001 | 05.02.2011 |
|---|---|---|---|---|
| Following his admiration for the February 1993 attempted bombing of New York's World Trade Center, Saudi Arabia revokes bin Laden's citizenship and freezes his extensive assets. | Bin Laden declares "holy war" on the US: al-Qaeda bombings of American embassies in Kenya and Tanzania kill 224. Two years later, al-Qaeda suicide bombers attack, killing 17 sailors on the USS *Cole*. | Bin Laden claims al-Qaeda is responsible for the most audacious terrorist attacks ever: crashing hijacked passenger aircraft into the WTC twin towers, and the Pentagon, Washington, DC. | Three months after the 9/11 attacks, bin Laden evades US forces in Afghanistan's Tora Bora caves. | After almost a decade of chasing him, US forces eventually track down bin Laden in Pakistan. |

# THE "IMPOSSIBLE ODDS" RESCUE, SOMALIA

DATE      January 25, 2012
LOCATION  Hiimo Gaabo, Galmudug, Somalia
OBJECTIVE To free American and Danish aid workers held for ransom in Somalia

Aid workers Jessica Buchanan and Poul Hagen Thisted suffered 93 days of captivity at the hands of Somali kidnappers before they were rescued in a flawlessly executed mission conducted by members of US Navy Sea, Air, and Land (SEALs) Team 6, which had leapt into the headlines after killing Osama bin Laden in 2011.

### The Green Line

By 2011, American Jessica Buchanan, age 32, had worked in Africa for seven years: first in Kenya, then in Somalia with the aid organization Danish Refugee Council (DRC), teaching locals how to avoid land mines. She and her husband of two years, Erik Landemalm (another DRC employee), lived in Hargeisa in the relatively safe north of the country.

That October, despite misgivings, Buchanan and Danish colleague Poul Hagen Thisted, 60, flew 480 miles (770 km) southeast to Galkayo to conduct staff training. The city's North and South sections straddled "the Green Line": the North controlled by the government; the South by hard-line Islamists.

### Sold Out and Kidnapped

A three-vehicle convoy took Buchanan and Thisted to DRC's South Galkayo compound. They ran their training session to a backdrop of gunfire in the streets, then climbed into the convoy for the 20-minute drive to North Galkayo. But the security manager paid to ensure their safety had sold them out to "land pirates"; they were seized at gunpoint and driven into the desert.

In a country where the average annual income is $US600, the kidnappers told the pair they were demanding $45 million ransom. Using Buchanan's cell phone, they called Landemalm, but DRC's emergency protocols, instituted immediately on the kidnapping, meant all Buchanan's key contact numbers diverted to the negotiator waiting in its Nairobi office.

### "We're Here to Take You Home"

Weeks, then months, passed. The ransom demand eventually dropped to $10 million, and the kidnappers moved the captives dozens of times, always camping out, often in freezing conditions. However, their use of mobile phones allowed monitors to use GPS technology to constantly track their movements. Buchanan and Thisted ate only a small can of tuna and campfire bread daily. After three months, Buchanan developed a urinary tract infection, telling the negotiator she was so ill she feared she might die. Intelligence advisers confirmed to US President Barack Obama that if the infection reached her kidneys it could be fatal within weeks. He authorized a rescue mission, despite very high risk, in very hostile territory.

On the dark night of January 25, 12 Navy SEALs parachuted close to the pirates' camp, then hiked in. The kidnappers, armed with AK-47s, returned their fire. Buchanan thought it was a rival gang until a SEAL said, "Jessica, we're with the American military. We're here to take you home, and you're safe." The nine pirates were killed and the aid workers were taken out in a waiting helicopter. Thisted would later say it was his lucky break to be captured with an American.

ABOVE: The captors produce a "Proof of Life" video as part of their ransom demands.

ABOVE RIGHT: Al-Shabab militants are active throughout Somalia and Eastern Africa and are in constant clashes with Western forces; Inset: the two captives, Jessica Buchanan (top) and Poul Hagen Thisted (below).

## TIMELINE

| 10.24.2011 | 10.25.2011 |
| --- | --- |
| From a guesthouse in North Galkayo, Jessica Buchanan text-messages her husband: "If I get kidnapped on this trip, will you come and get me?" | Buchanan and coworker Poul Hagen Thisted are kidnapped by Somali "land pirates." |

## STEP-BY-STEP

**01** A dozen black-masked Navy SEALs parachute from a C-130 Hercules two miles (3.2 km) from the kidnappers' latest camp.

**02** The new-moon darkness gives cover as they approach silently.

**03** Six of the nine heavily armed pirates are sleeping within arm's reach of their hostages, but are stupefied by narcotic khat leaves.

**04** While some SEALs guard the hostages with their own lives, others dispatch the pirates in a quick firefight.

**05** One SEAL carries the ill Buchanan in his arms as they run to the prearranged helicopter pickup spot.

**06** They administer medication then, uncertain if other hostiles are nearby, form human shields around the hostages.

**07** When a SEAL asks if she left anything in the camp, a dazed Buchanan tells him about a small pouch containing a ring made by her late mother; he goes back and retrieves it.

**08** Two helicopters land. With the hostages safe in one, their rescuers depart in the other.

ABOVE: US President Barack Obama (with first lady Michelle) telephones John Buchanan to give the news that his daughter Jessica was rescued by US Special Operations Forces in Somalia on January 25, 2012.

| 11.21.2011 | 11.23.2011 | 01.21.2012 | 01.23.2012 | 01.25.2012 |
|---|---|---|---|---|
| US counter-terrorism adviser John O. Brennan meets Denmark's justice minister to discuss the situation. | US President Barack Obama meets with Brennan and other advisers to consider options. | With Buchanan seriously ill and the kidnappers refusing a $1.5 million ransom, US security officials finalize rescue plans. | They confirm the details and present the plan to Obama, who gives the go-ahead. | US Navy SEALs rescue the hostages. |

# INDEX

# INDEX

# INDEX

# INDEX

# INDEX

# INDEX

# INDEX

# INDEX

## PICTURE CREDITS

(Abbreviations t=top, b=bottom, l=left, r=right)

### ALAMY

**2:** World History Archive; **10–11:** 19th era; **13:** (t) ClassicStock; **15:** (tl) North Wind Picture Archives; (tr) Ivy Close Images; **16–7:** (c) Image Asset Management Ltd.; **18:** (cr) Lanmas; **19:** (t) Nathan Benn; **20:** (tr) Ivy Close Images; **23:** (t) Heritage Image Partnership Ltd; **25:** (r) North Wind Picture Archives; **27:** North Wind Picture Archives; **28:** (tr) Lebrecht Music and Arts Photo Library; **30–1:** (c) Image Asset Management Ltd.; **31:** (r) North Wind Picture Archives; **33:** (t) Picade LLC; **37:** (t) Image Asset Management Ltd.; **38:** (cr) Angelo Hornak; **39:** (c) Interfoto; **40–1:** (t) Alan Novelli; **42:** (tr) Hilary Morgan; **45:** (t) Lordprice Collection; **46:** (r) Interfoto; **47:** (t) The Print Collector; **49:** (tl) Prisma Archivo; (b) Hilary Morgan; **51:** (t) Stock Montage, Inc.; **53:** (t) North Wind Picture Archives; **54:** (tr) North Wind Picture Archives; **57:** (t) Timewatch Images; **60:** (br) Niday Picture Library; **63:** (t) Niday Picture Library; **64:** (tr) The Print Collector; **65:** (t) The Print Collector; **69:** (tr) M.Brodie; **70–1:** PAINTING; **72:** (r) Image Asset Management Ltd.; **76:** (cr) Image Asset Management Ltd.; **77:** (t) Classic Image; **81:** (c) Image Asset Management Ltd.; **83:** (tr) The Art Archive; **85:** (t) Royal Geographical Society; **90–1:** (c) Photos 12; **91:** (tr) akg-images; **93:** (t) Marc Hill; **94:** (cr) Chronicle; **95:** (b) Lebrecht Music and Arts Photo Library; **98:** (t) Niday Picture Library; **99:** (t) The Protected Art Archive; **102–3:** (c) The Print Collector; **103:** (t) dpa picture alliance; **108–9:** Chronicle; **109:** (tr) Chronicle; **115:** (t) DIZ Muenchen GmbH, Sueddeutsche Zeitung Photo; **113:** (t) Interfoto; **116:** (tl) Mary Evans Picture Library; (tr) DIZ Muenchen GmbH, Sueddeutsche Zeitung Photo; **122:** (tr) Lordprice Collection; **124:** (r) Peter M. Wilson; **125:** (c) Pictorial Press Ltd; **129:** (t) DIZ Muenchen GmbH, Sueddeutsche Zeitung Photo;

**134–5:** Interfoto; **138–9:** Trinity Mirror / Mirrorpix; **141:** (t) Interfoto; **145:** (t) DIZ Muenchen GmbH, Sueddeutsche Zeitung Photo; (br) Interfoto; **147:** (tr) War Archive; (br) Norimages; **151:** (tr) Pictorial Press Ltd; **156–7:** Trinity Mirror / Mirrorpix; **159:** (t) GL Archive; **166:** (cr) Craig Stennett; **168–9:** Interfoto; **169:** (tr) and (bl) Interfoto; **174:** (br) Pictorial Press Ltd; **175:** (t) Marka; **177:** (t) Interfoto; **185:** (tr) GL Archive; **186–7:** (t) PF-(aircraft); **186:** (br) Trinity Mirror, Mirrorpix; **191:** (t) Keystone Pictures USA; (b); **195:** (tr) and (br) RIA Novosti; **206:** (tr) epa european pressphoto agency b.v.; (br) dpa picture alliance; **207:** (tl) and (tr) dpa picture alliance; **224:** (br) PCN Photography; **225:** (t) Richard Levine; (br) PCN Photography; **231:** (tr) dpa picture alliance archive; **233:** (tl) epa european pressphoto agency b.v.

### ART ARCHIVE

**20–21:** (c) British Library; **22:** (r) Victoria and Albert Museum London/ DeA Picture Library; **24:** (cr) Museo Ciudad Mexico/ Gianni Dagli Orti; **26:** (r) Biblioteca Nazionale Marciana Venice/ Gianni Dagli Orti; **29:** (tr) Eileen Tweedy; **32:** (tr) National Maritime Museum London/ Eileen Tweedy; **44:** (tr); **47:** (b); **50:** (r) British Library; **52:** (r) Superstock; **56:** (tr) National Army Museum London/ National Army Museum; **62:** (tr) National Army Museum London/ National Army Museum; **74–5:** National Army Museum London / National Army Museum; **75:** (tr) Gordon Boys' School (Woking)/ Eileen Tweedy; **80:** (cr); **82–3:** DeA Picture Library; **84:** (tr) Culver Pictures; **100:** (tr) DeA Picture Library; (br) Nicholas J. Saunders; **104:** (tr) Culver Pictures; **105:** (tl) and (tr) Culver Pictures; **114:** (cr) Private Collection; **123:** (t).

### AUSTRALIAN WAR MUSEUM

**136:** (tr) Damien Peter Parer; **137:** (tl) Damien Peter Parer; **165:** (tl) P00986.001; (tr) ART27649; (br) 067338.

### CORBIS

**209:** (b) David Rubinger; **211:** (cr) Bettmann; **213:** (t) Hulton-Deutsch Collection; **216:** (tr) Thierry Orban/ Sygma.

### GERMAN FEDERAL ARCHIVES:

**92:** (tr) Bundesarchiv; **120:** (br) Bundesarchiv; **121:** (t) Bild 146-1971-011-31; **141:** (br) Bild 101II-MW-3722-03; **143:** (t) Bild 146-1972-039-44; (bl) Bild 146-1972-039-14; **149:** (tl) Bundesarchiv; (tr) Bundesarchiv; (bl) Bundesarchiv; **160:** (cr) Bild 101I-567-1503A-05; (br) Bild 101I-567-1503A-02; **161:** (tl) Bild 183-J15420; (tr) Bild 101I-567-1503C-03.

### GETTY IMAGES

**167:** (t) Hulton Archive / Stringer; **197:** (t) Agence France Presse; **217:** (t) Stringer; **223:** (b) AFP/ Stinger; **228:** Getty Images (br); **229:** (l) AFP/Getty Images; (r) AFP/ Getty Images; **235:** (t) AFP/Getty Images

### IMPERIAL WAR MUSEUM

**93:** (cl) Art.IWM ART 2745; **101:** (t) Lawrence T.E., Q 59193; **111:** (t) Q 20636 ;(bl) Q114301; **119:** (t) HU 5206; **126:** (tr) N 417; **127:** (t) N 399; **132:** (tr) MAR 564; **133:** (t) A 7968; **138:** (br) D 12870; **139:** (tr) Art. IWM ART LD 3475; **148:** HU 66773; **151:** (tl) MAR 583; **156:** (tr) IWM FLM 2343; **157:** (br) CH 18005; **163:** (bl) A 19625; (br) A 19635; **170:** (br) CH 10251; **171:** (br) C 4740; **175:** (br) B 5233; **180:** (br) E 26182. **188:** (l) BF 10277; (r) BF 10119; **215:** (t) FKD 453; (b) MH 27570.

### LIBRARY OF CONGRESS

(RN = Reproduction number; CN = Call number)

**34–5:** RN: LC-USZ62-117176, LC-USZ6-2164, CN: Illus. in E179.D48 [General Collections]; **55:** RN: LC-DIG-ppmsca-23076, CN: DRWG/US – Munger, no. 1 (B size) (Cabinet A) [P&P] Unprocessed in PR 13 CN 2001:064; **58–9:** John D. Morris & Co., RN: LC-USZ62-50639, CN: LOT 4416-D (1863); **67:** (t) RN: LC-DIG-ppmsca-33072; **68:** (tr) RN: LC-USZ62-76814, CN: LOT 8351, no. 15; (br) RN: LC-USZ62-76819,

# PICTURE CREDITS

CN: LOT 4168, no. 49; LOT 8351, no. 13; **88–9:** RN: LC-DIG-ggbain-22366, CN: LC-B2- 3932-4; **97:** (t) RN: LC-DIG-ggbain-21247, CN: LC-B2- 3784-6; **107:** (bl) LC-DIG-ggbain-35198, CN: LC-B2- 5871-14; **180:** (tr) LC-DIG-ppmsca-09549 .

## TOPFOTO

**192:** (br); **193:** (bl) and (br).

## U.S. National Archives and Records Administration

(NAI = National Archives Identifier; LI = Local Identifier)

**96:** (tr) Berryman Political Cartoon Collection, Record Group 46, NAI: 6011165, LI: A-076; **113:** (br) CW-004; **130–1:** Record Group 21, NAI: 296001; **179:** (tl) Record Group 127, NAI: 532548, LI: 127-N-114541; **181:** (tr) Record Group 111, NAI: 531277, LI: 111-SC-205289; **184:** (tl) Record Group 77, NAI: 519394, LI: 77-BT-15; **189:** (bl) Record Group 111, NAI: 531427, LI: 111-SC-410709; **211:** (br) Record Group 330, NAI: 6377351, LI: 330-CFD-DF-ST-84-08125.

## WIKIMEDIA COMMONS

**12:** (cr) Travelling Runes; **14:** (tr) Panigia. mouuu2; **36:** (r) The National Archives (United Kingdom), SP14/216; **41:** (bl) Engraving from Ormerod, G. (2nd edition, ed. T. Helsby), *History of the County Palatine and City of Chester*, 1882; **48:** (br) *Portrait of Flora MacDonald*, Allan Ramsay; **69:** (tl) Survey of India; **90:** (t) Published as a postcard in Europe, Private Collection – Wartenberg Trust; **102:** (tr) postcard, J Revyn, 213 Chaussée de Louvain, Bruxelles; **106:** (tr) sourced from *Red Dusk and the Morrow* (http://archive.org/stream), 1922; **116:** (tr) Narodowe Archiwum Cyfrowe, Sygnatura: 2-12179; **118:** (br) Imperial War Museum (public domain); **121:** (t) Bild 146-1974-061-017, German Federal Archives; **204:** (cr); **210:** (cl) U.S. Air Force; **223:** (t) U.S. Air Force; **225:** (bl) TSGT CEDRIC H. RUDISILL, USAF; **152:** (br) Leif Ørnelund; **155:** (c) U.S. Air Force; **158:** (tr) U.S. Air Force; **162:** (c) Imperial War Museum (public domain); **171:** (tl); **178:** (cr) U.S.

Army; **181:** (br) Imperial War Museum (public domain); **182–3:** (t) U.S. Air Force; **191:** (br) Starry, Donn *A Mounted Combat in Vietnam*; (www.history.army.mil/books/ Vietnam/mounted/chapter1.htm#p1); **192:** (tr) Imperial War Museum (public domain); **194:** (cr) Russian International News Agency (RIA Novosti) (rian.ru); **199:** (br) NASA; **201–2:** (t) http://www.sontayraider. com/SontayRaiderPreparationforinsertion. htm; **201:** (cl); (tr) U.S. Air Force (http:// www.hurlburt.af.mil); **182–3:** http://www. nationalmuseum.af.mil/.

## OTHER VARIOUS SOURCES

**6:** (bl) Public Domain; **8:** (br) Department of Defense (US); **41:** (r) www.chestertourist. com; **43:** (r) National Portrait Gallery, London; **60–1:** NARA; **72:** (tr) http://www. britishbattles.com; **73:** (t): http://www. britishbattles.com; **78:** (tr) flat-brokefilms (flat-brokefilms.co.uk); (br) Reproduced with the kind permission of Clifford & Josie Parker of The Captain's House; **79:** (t) flat-brokefilms (flat-brokefilms.co.uk) ; (bl) Reproduced with the kind permission of Clifford & Josie Parker of The Captain's House; **86:** (tr) Somme Heritage Centre; (br) Somme Heritage Centre; **87:** (t) Norman; **98:** (br) njcu.org **105:** (br) City of StPete (www.stpete.org), Flickr; **110:** (tr) http://navsource.narod.ru/ (accessed 21/06/2014); **116:** (br) http://ww2today. com/8-november-1939-hitler-escapes-assassination (accessed 21/06/2014); **120:** **127:** (bl) Riksarkivet (National Archives of Norway); **129:** (br) DA-10739-F, Wildey, Peter Benjamin, Alexander Turnbull Library; **142:** (b) Holocaust Research Project **146:** (br) Public Domain; Office for Emergency Management. Office of War Information; **154:** (c) Domestic Operations Branch. Bureau of Special Services; **172:** (tr) copyright The Estate of William Stanley Moss—reproduced by permission, Drawing held at the Historical Museum of Crete; **173:** (t) copyright The Estate of William Stanley Moss—reproduced by permission; **189:** (br) defenseimagery.mil, Walker, 111-SC-371720; **196:** dcfenseimagery. mil, Walker, DF-SN-82-00885; **198:** (tr) US Navy; (br) http://spaceflight.nasa. gov (accessed 19/06/2014); **202–3:** U.S Department of Defense, http://www. defense.gov; **204:** (t) brianharringtonspear

Flickr; **208:** (tr) US Army Africa, Flickr; (br) Ministry of Defense Photo Archive; **211:** (tr) U.S. Navy; **212:** (cr) militaryarmament. tumblr.com/; **218–219:** aap newswire; **220:** (tr) Public Domain; (br) Public Domain **221:** (t) U.S. Navy, http://www.navy.mil; **227:** (tl) and (bl) U.S. Navy, http://www.navy. mil; **231:** (tl) Gobierno de Chile, Flickr; **232:** (cr) Expert Infantry; Flickr; **233:** (tr) White House, Flickr; **234:** (r) Public Domain; **235:** (br) White House, Flickr.

## COVER IMAGES

(from top to bottom)

Warner Bros. Entertainment Inc; Ministry of Defence (UK); The Art Archive / DeA Picture Library / G. Nimatallah; Ministry of Defence (UK).

## CAPTIONS FOR OPENERS

**10–11:** Fireships attacking Spanish Armada. **34–5:** A wood engraving (1876) by Richard Miller Devens depicting the capture and burning of Washington. **58–9:** James E. Kelly's drawing shows General Meade's Council of War convened on the night preceding the commencement of the battle of Gettysburg. **88–9:** Shells being sorted at Black Tom. **134–5:** Destroyed "Churchill" tanks of the 14th Canadian Army Tank Regiment during the raid on Dieppe. **182–3:** During the Berlin Airlift, U.S. Navy Douglas R4D and U.S. Air Force C-47 aircraft unload at Tempelhof Airport. **202–3:** A U.S. Navy visit as part of counter-piracy operations off the coast of Somalia.

## MAPS AND DIAGRAMS

All map and diagram artwork created by James Mills-Hicks.

*Every effort has been made to trace copyright holders and gain permission for use of the images within this book. We would be grateful for any information concerning copyright.*

## Author

Hazel Flynn is a writer and editor with a fascination for human stories, including those woven into history's great moments. *Missions Impossible* is the fourth book she has authored or co-authored. Previous titles include *Lani's Story* (HarperCollins) and *Hazel's Journey* (Pan Macmillan) about former Australian "first lady" Hazel Hawke, which was shortlisted for a national Human Rights Award.

She is a former publisher and commissioning editor of non-fiction at Random House and Murdoch Books, where she originated and developed many best-selling and critically lauded books. She is also a highly experienced journalist, whose roles have included Contributing Editor for *Reader's Digest* magazine international editions and Senior Editor for *Who Weekly* magazine, and a former radio producer and broadcaster. Hazel is based in Australia.

## Consultant Editors

Andrew  and Ailsa Heritage together conceived, commissioned, and edited a range of historical titles for Times Books, London, including several editions of *The Times Atlas of World History; Past Worlds: The Times Atlas of Archaeology; The Times Atlas of The Bible; The Times Atlas of the Crusades; The Times Atlas of the Second World War; and The Times Atlas of World Exploration.*

For 15 years Andrew was publisher for Cartography, History and Popular Culture at Dorling Kindersley, overseeing titles including the *DK Atlas of World History; Timelines of World History; World War I; World War II; The Story of the West; Coming Free; Destination America;* and *Battle.* Meanwhile, Ailsa worked as consultant cartographic editor on *The Cambridge Atlas of Warfare; The Penguin Atlas of the Third Reich; The Atlas of World Religion* and *The Atlas of World Art for OUP,* and numerous collegiate textbooks on world history for Pearson.